Henry Wallace, Harry Truman, and the Cold War

Also by Richard J. Walton

The United States and the Far East

Canada and the U.S.A.

Cold War and Counterrevolution:
   The Foreign Policy of John F. Kennedy

Congress and American Foreign Policy:
   The Presidential-Congressional Struggle

The United States and Latin America

Beyond Diplomacy

America and the Cold War

The Remnants of Power:
   The Tragic Last Years of Adlai Stevenson

Richard J. Walton

Henry Wallace, Harry Truman, and the Cold War

The Viking Press

NEW YORK

Library of Congress Cataloging in Publication Data
Walton, Richard J
Henry Wallace, Harry Truman, and the Cold War.
Bibliography: p.
Includes index.
1. Presidents—United States—Election—1948.
2. United States—Foreign relations—1945-1953.
3. Wallace, Henry Agard, 1888-1945.
4. Truman, Harry S., Pres. U.S., 1884-1972. I. Title.
E815.W34   329'.023'730918   76-17540   ISBN 0-670-36859-8

Printed in the United States of America
Set in VIP Palatino

Acknowledgments
Houghton Mifflin Company: From *The Price of Vision: The Diary of Henry A. Wallace,
1942-1946*, John Morton Blum. Copyright © 1973 by the Estate of Henry A. Wallace
and John Morton Blum. Reprinted by permission of the publisher Houghton Mifflin
Company, Boston.

William Morrow and Company, Inc.: From *Harry S. Truman* by Margaret Truman. Copyright © 1972 Margaret Truman Daniel.

The New Leader: Excerpts from a January 1947 editorial, Henry Wallace's reply, and ex-
cerpts from Donald Harrington, May 6, 1948. Reprinted with permission from *The New
Leader*, January 1947 and May 1948. Copyright © The American Labor Conference on
International Affairs, Inc.

The New York Times: From Anne O'Hare McCormick's column of July 26, 1948.© 1948
by The New York Times Company. Reprinted by permission.

W.W. Norton & Co., Inc.: From *Eleanor and Franklin* by Joseph P. Lash. Copyright ©
1961 by Joseph P. Lash.

The Philadelphia Inquirer: Excerpts from a July 23, 1948 editorial and a July 27, 1948
editorial.

The Progressive: From "Progressives and the Presidency" by Rexford Guy Tugwell. Copyright © 1949, The Progressive, Inc. Reprinted by permission from *The Progressive*, 408
West Gorham Street, Madison, Wisconsin 53703.

Harry S. Truman Memorial Library: From *Memoirs* by Harry S. Truman.

The University of Iowa: Excerpts from The Henry Wallace Papers.

For Mary

Foreword

Although I concentrate largely on matters of foreign policy in this book, I am conscious that I am dealing with only one aspect of Henry A. Wallace the Presidential candidate. Henry Wallace was ahead, well ahead, of his time in other respects as well.

At a time when women were usually relegated in political campaigns to stamping envelopes and other such "women's work," the Progressive Party gave women important substantive jobs and campaigned for broader women's rights. Wallace came out strongly for the eighteen-year-old vote long before either of the major parties. Wallace advocated sweeping economic reforms that have yet to be made, although the recent failures of the American economic system may well force such changes. The Progressive Party adopted the principle of one-man, one-vote long before the historic Supreme Court ruling to that effect. And it adopted related party reforms, giving political access to a wider spectrum of society, a quarter of a century before the Democratic Party did. Most important, Henry Wallace mounted the most vigorous attack on political Jim Crowism in American history. In his campaign swings across the South, he was the first to refuse to appear before segregated audiences and refused to stay in hotels that did not welcome black staff members, usually putting up in the homes of black supporters.

A number of times in the pages to follow I invite readers to examine the platform of the Progressive Party on this or that specific point. Such an invitation is offered now on the above points (see Appendix). The sophisticated reader might wonder why anyone should waste time reading a party platform, because, traditionally, platforms are ritual documents ignored by the candidates as soon as the convention ends. But this platform did embody the principles of the Progressive Party, and it was on this platform that Henry Wallace campaigned.

Acknowledgments

The basic work on the Henry Wallace campaign of 1948 is Curtis D. Macdougall's *Gideon's Army*. For sheer volume of information and as a narrative account it will never be surpassed. If it were not that I had something different in mind, I would have abandoned my own project after a first reading of this encyclopedic study. Professor Macdougall's work is more than a rare achievement in scholarship. It is a manifestation of courage and perseverance as well. His book was researched and written in that American dark age whose most notorious figure was Senator Joseph R. McCarthy. Although there can be no doubt as to the indispensability of Macdougall's book, it took him a decade to find a publisher. Even then, it was necessary to publish the book in three volumes, with each volume coming out as the publisher and Macdougall raised sufficient money to print it.

There is a further debt owed Professor Macdougall. In the course of his research he amassed a vast amount of primary material that he later turned over to the Wallace Collection at the University of Iowa, where, as the Progressive Party Papers, it is open to anyone with a serious interest.

My deepest personal gratitude must go to the late C. B. Baldwin, Wallace's campaign manager and friend, and to his wife, Lillian, also a leading figure in the Progressive Party. Both answered my many questions fully, frankly, and cheerfully, neither of them embittered by living as a sort of outcast during what would have been their most productive years. "Beanie," as everyone called him, was in his prime when the Progressive Party folded but he was never again able to find work commensurate with his ability, despite his long years of achievement at the upper levels of the New Deal and the CIO. But the Baldwins were both convinced, despite the price they paid, that they had done the right thing.

The Baldwins not only made available to me the enormous quantity of Progressive Party material they have preserved for history but they guided me through it so I could find what I was looking for. For students of that crucial and tumultuous period this material is a treasure.

There are others I must thank. Ralph Shikes, publicity director for Wallace, shared with me his memories of the campaign. He, too, suffered during the McCarthy years but he, like the Baldwins, remained committed to progressive causes. So also was Palmer Webber, leader of the Wallace campaign in the South, who gave me generously of his time. And Carey McWilliams, recently retired as editor of *The Nation*, on numerous occasions took time to share with me his unique knowledge of the American Left, an experience as fascinating as it was helpful.

Earl Rogers of the University of Iowa Library was unfailingly helpful and constantly astonished me not only with his grasp of the huge Wallace Collection but of Wallace materials elsewhere. Dr. Josephine Harper, reference archivist, and Katherine Thompson were of great assistance at the Wisconsin State Historical Society in Madison, repository of the valuable papers of the Americans for Democratic Action. Most helpful, too, were Dr. Philip Lagerquist, chief archivist, and Dennis Bilger of the Harry S. Truman Library.

And there was Mary.

These people made this book possible.

PUBLISHERS' NOTE

The Progressive Party platform, which was to be included in this volume as an Appendix, unfortunately had to be deleted due to lack of space. We regret that we were unable to adjust Mr. Walton's references to it in his text and notes.

THE PUBLISHER'S NOTE

The Proofreader was uncertain about this objection which
was to be inserted in this volume as an
Appendix, unfortunately had to be deleted
due to lack of space. We regret this; we
were anxious to state that Watson's note
were to fit the text and notes

Contents

. . . The wisdom of our actions in the first three years of peace will determine the course of world history for half a century. . . .

—HENRY A. WALLACE, 1941

1

Wallace and Roosevelt

The election of 1948 is remembered chiefly for the astonishing triumph of President Harry S. Truman, who, according to the political pundits and the public-opinion polls, was not supposed to have a chance against his Republican opponent, Thomas E. Dewey. But this election had a far deeper significance than the upset victory of a scrappy politician over a dull one. The campaign that preceded it was the last time that the basic assumptions of American foreign policy were questioned until the mid-1960s. Not until five Presidential elections later did American voters begin to re-examine the anticommunism that had been the motivating force of American foreign policy since the death of Franklin D. Roosevelt in April 1945.

Most of the protesters of the mid-1960s were too young to remember that in the 1948 election the anticommunism which was so fully accepted by Truman and Dewey had been challenged by a third Presidential candidate, Henry A. Wallace. It was a forceful challenge, and brave, for by 1948 the clouds of that Dark Age later known as McCarthyism had already begun to lower over the land. To challenge American foreign policy in that twilight hour was to challenge not only a policy, not only a President, but the notion that only a strong and resolute America stood between Freedom and the Communist hordes.

Perhaps it is not pride that goeth before a fall but self-righteousness, a self-righteousness swollen by the knowledge that never in human history had one nation so dominated the world. To a succession of Presidents and to most Americans, led to their beliefs by these Presidents and their attendants in politics, the press, and academe, America had not only the capacity to reshape the world but the right, even the obligation.

Henry Wallace and his supporters saw it differently. They believed that if the United States continued Harry Truman's "get-tough" policy with the Soviet Union, disaster would result. They argued that the United States should make every effort to achieve peaceful coexistence with Russia. They were convinced, as Wallace expressed it during the campaign, "that there are no differences between the Soviet Union and the United States which cannot be reconciled without sacrificing a single American principle or a single American life."[1]* Wallace and his supporters were reviled for this conviction. Yet what they were advocating in 1948 became the very policy of détente practiced by Richard M. Nixon a quarter of a century later, a policy that he believed, justly, was the crowning achievement of his years in office and that he hoped would establish sufficient political credit with the American people to spare him political punishment for Watergate.

Henry Wallace and his dwindling band of supporters were Red-baited[2] in 1948 for advocating détente and Wallace, after a vigorous, imaginative, and adequately financed campaign, could attract only slightly more than a million votes.[3] Twenty-four years later, Richard Nixon, one of the great Red-baiters of the late 1940s and 1950s, made peace with the Communist world his central plank and ran up one of the great landslides in political history. One of the sad features of this story is that among Wallace's most severe critics were some of those who became early or, more often, late opponents of the Vietnam war. It is hardly fanciful to suggest that if Wallace had been heeded, or simply if free debate on foreign policy had not been silenced, the Korean war might have remained solely a civil war and perhaps the American involvement in Indochina would have ceased rather than grown. But so vehement was the response to

* The numbers refer to the Notes beginning on page 357.

Wallace's criticism of our foreign policy that no basic foreign-policy debate occurred again for a decade and a half.

Anyone wishing to comprehend how the United States ended up in the horrors of Indochina should examine this Wallace campaign, for it was the last time serious questions were asked until those first stirrings of the antiwar movement in the early 1960s. But by then it was too late. Such was the momentum of the American intervention begun in the Truman years that it smashed forward into the next decade, taking a ghastly toll, until, in 1975, it finally staggered to a halt, victim of its own folly.

This book is concerned with the 1948 election and the events leading up to it that caused Henry Wallace to run. There was never a chance he could win and he knew it, although he would not have been human had he not dreamed, when for a few months those huge crowds turned out for him, that maybe a miracle was possible. This book is not a detailed, day-by-day account of the Wallace campaign. Curtis Macdougall, with his *Gideon's Army*,[4] has rendered such an effort superfluous. Rather, this book deals with the substance of Wallace's criticisms and proposals. Perhaps more important, it considers the response to the Wallace campaign by the Truman administration, by the press, and by anti-Wallace liberals.[5]

To many younger readers, Henry Wallace is a rather shadowy figure dimly remembered from historical accounts of the New Deal, but if his challenge to American foreign policy had been better known to the antiwar protesters of the 1960s, he might have become the patron saint of the Movement, for he was a "dove" and a "peacenik" long before those terms were coined. Or, to put it another way, he was a "revisionist" even as the history of the first Cold War years was unfolding.

Henry Wallace was the pre-eminent figure of the early 1940s, after only President Roosevelt himself. He was uni-

versally regarded as Roosevelt's heir to the New Deal wing
of the Democratic Party. He was Vice President during most
of World War II; he served at FDR's insistence over the protests of the party bosses, and had, for a time, more direct
executive responsibility than any Vice President before or
since. FDR chose him as Vice President after he had been
for eight eventful years secretary of agriculture, by general
agreement the most effective in American history. As Bruce
Catton, who worked under Wallace at the Department of
Agriculture, suggested, "he may well have been the most
efficient Cabinet member in the Roosevelt administration.
He kept himself very closely informed about what was
going on in his department and knew precisely how to deal
with various problems as they came up. He was indeed a
first-rate administrator, as a director of men and in handling a large government department."[6]

Before Roosevelt nominated him to be secretary of agriculture, a post his father had held under Harding and Coolidge, Wallace had been editor of *Wallace's Farmer*, perhaps
the most widely respected farm journal in the United States.
He was also a pioneer in agricultural economics and did
work of the first importance as a plant geneticist. A student
of George Washington Carver, his work on the development of hybrid corn was of major and lasting consequence
to the bounty of American agriculture. His concept of the
"Ever Normal Granary," a modernization of the Biblical
concept of establishing food banks to see the world through
lean times, is even more pertinent now than when he first
suggested it. Even then it had a great influence on what became the United Nations Food and Agriculture Organization. And at a later time when he was accused of Communist leanings, Wallace was delighted to point out that he
was the only Presidential candidate who had been a successful businessman. His Pioneer Hi-Bred Corn Co. was a
multimillion dollar concern. Wallace was also the author of
a number of books, ranging widely across his many interests. A particular interest was the application of religious

ethics, a social gospel, to political, economic, and social problems. He believed, some critics have said naïvely, that capitalism could evolve into a more humane system. Whatever his faults, and they will be discussed, it would be difficult for any fair-minded person not to see him as a serious man of unusual achievement as politician, scientist, economist, businessman, social thinker, and author.

Henry Wallace's views toward the world in general and the Soviet Union in particular were consistent from the 1920s until 1948, when he committed political suicide by running against Harry Truman. Regarding the world as a whole, he was an out-and-out internationalist, serving for a time as president of the Non-Partisan League of Nations Association. He called for a reduction of tariff barriers as a way to encourage world trade and when the world-wide Depression of the 1930s came, he argued that high tariff walls were largely to blame.

Regarding the Soviet Union, Wallace's views were always mixed. He did not hesitate to praise or criticize in the 1920s, 1930s, or 1940s—although after his split with Truman in September 1946, his criticisms of Russia were usually overlooked. At first he had little sympathy with the new Communist government, predicting in the fall of 1917 that Lenin's government would not last. But by the 1920s, with the Communists still firmly in control, Wallace began to modify his views somewhat, expressing a cautious admiration for Russia. He was distressed by the greedy capitalism of the West in the booming 1920s and by the fact that the Western nations were practicing imperialism to help their economies. He saw Russia, in 1924, as "building a new industrial system out of the wreck that the world war left."[7]

After World War I, as after World War II, there was a "Red Scare" in the United States. Wallace had no sympathy with it then or later. He suggested that the United States should aid Russia with its sophisticated technology—a development that began in the early 1920s, quickly died, and has just begun to resume in recent years—and even thought that this country might rejuvenate its revolutionary and frontier traditions through its contact with the Russian experiment. This latter seems a rather romantic notion now, but it must be remembered that Wallace was entertaining such ideas in the early days of the Communist government, before the brutal grip of Stalinism became known to the world.

However, even in those early days Wallace had reservations. One, his distaste for Bolshevik atheism, is hardly surprising, given his deep dedication to Christianity. Another was based on what might be termed his agricultural nationalism. He cautioned that the success of the Soviet state would mean that Russia would no longer be a potential market for American farm surpluses, and he advocated programs to control domestic farm production. On this score he was, of course, dead wrong. More than a half century after the Revolution, even after the Soviet Union had become one of the two most powerful nations on earth, the Russians needed to purchase huge quantities of foodstuffs from the United States. But the world was much different then, and Wallace was far from the only one wrong about world markets for American farm products.

By 1933, when President Roosevelt was considering whether or not the United States should extend diplomatic recognition to the Soviet government, Wallace was still of two minds. Because of his revulsion against Stalin's murderous treatment of the Kulaks, because of his concern about American farm markets abroad, and because of a fear that Russia would eventually attempt to disrupt capitalism, Wallace opposed recognition. On the other hand, his conviction of the need for national economic planning—basic to the Soviet system—caused him to term Lenin a prophet of a new world order. Not until Henry Wallace became Vice President were his views on the Soviet Union of major consequence.

Although Wallace, like his father, had long been a Republican, he was an independent one. Given his independence and the state of the economy, it is not surprising that in 1936 he became a Democrat and vigorously attacked the Republican Presidential nominee, hapless Alf Landon. By 1938 Paul Appleby, Wallace's closest aide at agriculture, was trying to line up support for Wallace at the 1940 convention, hoping that if FDR decided not to try to break the two-term tradition, Wallace would get the nomination. Still, when war broke out in Europe a year later, Wallace quickly and enthusiastically supported a third term for Roosevelt. When the convention opened in Chicago in July 1940, Roosevelt had not yet made known his choice for the Vice Presidency, and there were a number of contenders. When word began to spread that Wallace was the man, something close to open rebellion split the Democratic ranks. The conservative southerners and the big city bosses did not want Wallace, the former because they thought him too liberal, the latter because they suspected him as a renegade Republican. When the situation threatened to get out of hand, Eleanor Roosevelt was rushed out to Chicago to quiet them down. While she did so, Harry Hopkins, Roosevelt's alter ego, was passing the word that FDR might not run unless Wallace were nominated on his ticket.[8] This had the expected disciplinary effect: not only did Roosevelt have an extraordinary grip on his party, one perhaps unequaled in our history, but the polls made it plain that he was the only Democrat who could win.

Roosevelt's reasons for picking Wallace were simple. He thought him the best man for the job, especially with a major war looming over the horizon. As he told his labor secretary, Frances Perkins, Wallace "would be a good man if something happened to the President. He is no isolationist. He knows what we are up against in this war that is rapidly engulfing the world."[9] Judge Samuel Rosenman, FDR's intimate and speech-writer, said that Roosevelt thought Wallace was a man "in whose hands the program of the New Deal—both domestic and foreign—would be safe."[10] And Mrs. Roosevelt believed that her husband "felt that Wallace at that time could be trusted to carry out our politics in foreign affairs if by any means he, Wallace, found himself hurled into the Presidency."[11]

These reasons may have persuaded some delegates, but almost certainly political reality was the determining factor. Without Roosevelt the Democrats could not win. Not only had the New Deal failed to end unemployment, but Roosevelt had not been able to make the Democratic Party truly cohesive. It was still a coalition of warring tribes with only Roosevelt's political magic holding it together. And Roosevelt seemed to be serious about not running unless he got Wallace. Rosenman wrote that FDR had a letter drafted in which he formally declined the nomination, and regarded the nomination of the liberal Wallace as vital to the party's future. The letter said, ". . . until the Democratic Party makes clear its overwhelming stand in favor of liberalism and shakes off all the shackles of conservatism and reaction it will not continue its march to victory. . . . It would be best not to straddle ideals. It would be best to have the fight out."[12] It would be well to keep these words in mind when considering, a couple of chapters hence, the abortive and irresolute attempt by some Democratic liberals to deprive Harry Truman of the 1948 nomination because they believed that Truman had strayed far from Roosevelt's liberal path.

So Wallace got the Vice Presidential nomination. While this delighted two important wings of the Democratic Party, the liberals and labor, it angered the southerners and the big city bosses. As we shall see, they got their innings four years later.

Henry Wallace became Vice President in January 1941, but it was not until the United States entered the war in December of that year that he received major executive responsibility. Just ten days after Pearl Harbor Roosevelt created the Board of Economic Warfare and named Wallace to head it.[13] Never before, nor since, has a Vice President had so much direct executive authority. There is no way to exaggerate the importance of the BEW to the war effort, for it was fundamental in the mustering of America's extraordinary economic strength, so essential to the Allied victory. The BEW was divided into three sections: the Office of Imports, which was responsible for procuring strategic materials for use in American factories and to preclude their purchase by the Axis powers; the Office of Exports, which used its licensing authority to prevent strategic materials from getting to the enemy; and the Office of Warfare Analysis, which determined the economically important targets for strategic bombing. The vigorous prosecution of BEW's work in all these areas by Wallace and Milo Perkins, the executive director, who was an old friend and associate, soon got them into political hot water. FDR, as many writers have noted, seemed to glory in administrative untidiness, and his subordinates in almost every field inevitably got into fierce battles, with each claiming that the other was getting in the way and hampering the war effort. Wallace soon had two conservative, and redoubtable, foes: Secretary of State Cordell Hull and Secretary of Commerce Jesse Jones. Hull claimed that the BEW was encroaching on state's domain (is there anyone so fierce as a bureaucrat whose empire is invaded?), while Jones accused Wallace of being a reckless spendthrift.

But the deeper reason for the clash may have been philosophic. Wallace and Perkins attempted to use the BEW to further their liberal goals of social reform. They believed that well-paid, well-fed, and healthy workers would be more productive, especially in Latin America, where many of the vital commodities were purchased. Thus, the BEW wrote provisions into its procurement contracts that the Latin American governments or private contractors "furnish adequate shelter, water, safety appliances, etc.," for its workers, consult "as to whether the wage scale is such as to maximize production," and cooperate "in a plan to improve conditions of health and sanitation"—with the United States paying half the costs of such plans.

To Hull and Jones and southern senators who were their chief political bulwarks, this was nothing less than socialism. Their idea of the postwar world was a scattering of little capitalistic republics, similar to and subservient to the United States. And if these countries wanted American aid after the war, they would have to play ball now. Wallace did not think that way. "He sought postwar trade with any nation, whatever its system of government or pattern of property ownership. And, during the war, he wanted American credits, trade and contracts to turn the calendar toward the century of the common man. He lost."[14]

Hull never hid how he felt about Wallace's running of the BEW, but his comments, however pungent, were kept within the administration. Not so with Jones, a crusty Texan financier, who let the Senate and press know exactly how he felt. Wallace, unfortunately, replied in kind. Roosevelt often sympathized with Wallace, occasionally took his part, but eventually became disgusted with the public fireworks and in effect said, "the hell with both of you." He manipulated his tables of organization and in June 1943 both Wallace and Jones found themselves on the sidelines.[15] But their battling days were not over, and a couple of years later they went several more tough rounds, with Wallace narrowly winning a split decision.

Although Wallace now had much less executive responsibility, he still had another important job and went at it enthusiastically. FDR was entirely preoccupied with winning the war; the commander in chief pushed aside the liberal leader. That role fell to Wallace, who seized it eagerly. Throughout the war years he spoke frequently about the need to return to liberalism after the war and about his concept of the postwar world. His most famous wartime speech, delivered on May 8, 1942—originally entitled "The Price of Free World Victory," but soon known as "The Century of the Common Man"—was one of the most widely quoted and disputed speeches of the war. It was also one of the most widely distributed. At first it was little noticed, but then the liberal New York newspaper *PM* published it twice, and A. N. Spanel, who for decades has made a practice of purchasing advertising space to publicize his views on current issues, placed it in *The Washington Post* and *Women's Wear Daily*. These appearances generated thousands of requests for copies. Then some twenty thousand copies were sold within a few weeks, when L. B. Fisher issued it as a pamphlet. At the same time, various federal agencies were distributing hundreds of thousands of copies.[16]

The speech rang with references to Christ, Christianity, the Bible, the Old Testament; it was very much the product of Protestant liberalism. Indeed, it often reads like the pulpit sermon of a fiery and visionary Protestant preacher— perhaps not a bad description of one aspect of Wallace's character. Although much of it was devoted to the need to strain to the utmost to defeat the Nazis (hence its original title), much of it was devoted to Wallace's vision of the postwar world. But it is well to remember that Wallace delivered it just six months after the United States entered the war, when the news from the fronts was not good, and that the speech was cleared by FDR. One can assume therefore that, at the very least, Roosevelt was willing to have such idealistic, and upsetting, words floated as a trial balloon.

. . . Everywhere the common people are on the march.

When the freedom-loving people march—when the farmers have an opportunity to buy land at reasonable prices and to sell the produce of their land through their own organizations, when workers have the opportunity to form unions and bargain through them collectively, and when the children of all the people have an opportunity to attend schools which teach them truths of the real world in which they live—when these opportunities are open to everyone, then the world moves straight ahead. . . .

The march of freedom of the past 150 years has been a long-drawn-out people's revolution. In this great revolution of the people, there were the American Revolution of 1775, the French Revolution of 1792, the Latin American revolutions of the Bolivarian era, the German Revolution of 1848, and the Russian Revolution of 1917. Each spoke for the common man in terms of blood on the battlefield. Some went to excess. But the significant thing is that the people groped their way to the light. More of them learned to think and work together.

The people's revolution aims at peace and not at violence; but if the rights of the common man are attacked, it unleashes the ferocity of a she-bear who has lost a cub. . . .

The people, in their millennial and revolutionary march toward manifesting here on earth the dignity that is in every human soul, hold as their credo the Four Freedoms enunciated by President Roosevelt in his message to Congress on January 6, 1941. These four freedoms are the very core of the revolution for which the United Nations have taken their stand. We who live in the United States may think there is nothing very revolutionary about freedom of religion, freedom of expression, and freedom from the fear of secret police. But when we begin to think about the significance of freedom from want for the average man, then we know that the revolution of the past 150 years has not been completed, either here in the United States or in any other nation in the world. We know that this revolution cannot stop until freedom from want has actually been attained. . . .

We failed in our job after World War I. We did not know how to go about building an enduring world-wide peace. We did not have the nerve to follow through and prevent Germany from rearming. We did not insist that she "learn war no more." We did not build a peace treaty on the fundamental doctrine of the people's revolution. We did not strive wholeheartedly to create a world where there could be freedom from want for all the peoples. But by our very errors we learned much, and after this war we shall be in a position to utilize our knowledge in building a world which is economically, politically, and, I hope, spiritually sound.

Modern science, which is a by-product and an essential part of the people's revolution, has made it technologically possible to see that all of the people of the world get enough to eat. Half in fun and half seriously, I said the other day to Madame Litvinov: "The object of this war is to make sure that everybody in the world has the privilege of drinking a quart of milk a day." She replied: "Yes, even half a pint." The peace must mean a better standard of living for the common man, not merely in the United States and England, but also in India, Russia, China, and Latin America—not merely in the United Nations, but also in Germany and Italy and Japan.

Some have spoken of the "American Century." I say that the century on which we are entering—the century which will come out of this war—can be and must be the century of the common man. Everywhere the common man must learn to build his own industries with his own hands in a practical fashion. Everywhere the common man must learn to increase his productivity so that he and his children can eventually pay to the world community all that they have received. No nation will have the God-given right to exploit other nations. Older nations will have the privilege to help younger nations get started on the path to industrialization, but there must be neither military nor economic imperialism. The methods of the nineteenth century will not work in the people's century which is now about to begin. India, China, and Latin America have a tremendous stake in the people's century. As their masses learn to read and write, and as they become productive mechanics, their standard of living will double and treble. Modern science, when devoted wholeheartedly to the general welfare, has in it potentialities of which we do not yet dream. . . .

Cartels in the peace to come must be subjected to international control for the common man, as well as being under adequate control by the respective home governments. . . . With international monopoly under control, it will be possible for inventions to serve all the people instead of only the few.

Yes, and when the time of peace comes, the citizens will again have a duty, the supreme duty of sacrificing the lesser interest for the greater interest of the general welfare. Those who write the peace must think of the whole world. There can be no privileged peoples. We ourselves in the United States are no more a master race than the Nazis. And we can not perpetuate economic warfare without planting the seeds of military warfare.[17]

This has been a long extract, but no summation or para-phrase would serve to give the flavor and the substance of Henry Wallace. To many in 1942, perhaps to some now, these words seem radical, possibly indicating the lean to-ward socialism or communism of which he was later accused. But if he was unsound in this speech, exactly where? He specifically rejected the American Century, that term of Henry Luce, publisher of *Time, Life,* and *Fortune,* who saw America as a sort of latter-day Britain presiding wisely over the world and remaking it in the American image. But the history of the past three decades, when that clearly was the program followed by all American Presidents, reveals the folly of Luce's concept.

One can only speculate how the world might be now if the thousands of billions of American funds devoted to the anti-Communist crusade, or even a fraction of them, had been devoted to the kind of peaceful development Wallace wanted. As to any indication of Wallace's so-called social-ism or communism, would it not be difficult to deny that in the *ideals* of democracy, socialism, and communism there is much that is common? It is in the practice of these systems in which the failures, often terrible failures, lie. Wallace specifically called for freedom of religion, of expression, and from "the fear of secret police"—hardly a call for commu-nism Soviet style. On the other hand, it is difficult to deny that various Communist nations have made genuine con-tributions to the welfare of their people. And while democ-racy American style has brought freedom and material well-being to many Americans, is it possible to deny that many of our countrymen even now have not received a full mea-sure of economic and social justice?

Wallace continued to speak in a similar vein throughout the war years. On November 8, 1942, at a rally of the Congress of American-Soviet Friendship at Madison Square Garden in New York, he said, "It is no accident that Ameri-cans and Russians like each other when they get ac-quainted. Both peoples were molded by the vast sweep of a rich continent. Both peoples know that their future is greater than their past. Both hate sham." And he noted that Tocqueville had observed that the United States and Russia "seem to tend toward the same end although they start from different points." Wallace then reiterated the central point that is still valid today: "The new democracy, the democracy of the common man, includes not only the Bill of Rights but also economic democracy, ethnic democracy, educational democracy, and democracy in the treatment of the sexes."[18]

On March 8, 1943, at a religious conference, Wallace went into greater detail about the need for Soviet-American cooperation: "We shall decide some time in 1943 or 1944 whether to plant the seeds for World War No. III. That war will be probable if we fail to demonstrate that we can furnish full employment after this war comes to an end and fascist interests motivated largely by anti-Russian bias get control of our government. Unless the Western democracies and Russia come to a satisfactory understanding before the war ends, I very much fear that World War No. III will be inevitable. . . ."[19]

And a year later, on April 9, 1944, *The New York Times* carried an article by Wallace called "The Dangers of American Fascism," in which he sounded the same theme: "Fascism in the postwar era will inevitably push steadily for Anglo-Saxon imperialism and eventually for war with Russia. Already American fascists are talking and writing about this conflict and using it as an excuse for their internal hatred and intolerance toward certain races, creeds, and classes."

By mid-1944 the big question was the election in the fall. Would Roosevelt run for a fourth term? With the war still on, there seemed little doubt that he would. But would Wallace again be his running mate? By now it was obvious to Roosevelt's intimates that he was sick and exhausted. While it is doubtful that the extent of his physical deterioration was understood by any but the very inner circle, and perhaps not even by them or FDR himself, it was clear that the choice of a Vice-Presidential candidate was crucial. Wallace wanted it and, according to those close to him then, expected it, believing he was still Roosevelt's first choice. The only choice that mattered.

Wallace, however, did not go to great lengths to secure the renomination. His distaste for the maneuvers and manipulations of politics was legendary, and his closest associates were often driven to distraction by his refusal to play the game: many have told stories of Wallace falling sound asleep when political matters were being discussed. This distaste for politics was at once a great virtue and a great failing. It is possible, but not necessarily so, that a single-minded drive for the nomination would have succeeded. But that was not Wallace's style—and he was not about to change—even when the ultimate political prize was at stake. One can wish that Wallace had made an exception, for this was no little matter, not a mere question of one politician or another becoming Vice President and then President. What was at stake was the entire course of world history.

In any case, Wallace did not have the opportunity to go to great lengths. Just two months before the convention, in mid-May, Roosevelt asked him to leave on a mission to Soviet Asia and China. He was to be gone until July 10, a week before the convention. There might well have been some purpose in his visiting China to try to spur on Chiang Kai-shek who was, as usual, dragging his feet in the war against the Japanese, continuing to husband his strength for the postwar struggle with Mao Tse-tung's Communists. But why did Wallace have to spend nearly a month trudging around Siberia? So well known is the Russian use of Siberia as a place of exile for its undesirables that the term has passed into American usage. Not a few of Wallace's supporters believed that Roosevelt was sending Wallace to political Siberia, removing him from the action at the most crucial time. Whatever Wallace may have thought, he was always loyal to Roosevelt and off he went, leaving his political fortunes in the hands of supporters.

On the evidence of his diary, Wallace had a marvelous time, trekking through muddy farms and inspecting factories and hospitals in Siberia. When he reached China, he noted:

> I like the Gimo [the common and irreverent American abbreviation of Generalissimo] but fear his lack of vision will doom him to Kerensky's fate. I was very sad after the second conversation. . . .[20]
>
> I like him but I do not give him one chance in five to save himself. . . .[21]
>
> I am beginning to think they would almost prefer to lose the war rather than to see the old China upset in any way. . . . Everyone agrees that the enlisted man and the Chinese junior officers are splendid material. I was greatly impressed with them myself. But the damned smiling grafters above? They stand for mediocrity forever continued.[22]

While Wallace was gone, the politicking continued at a furious pace. Everything depended on Roosevelt. With the Vice President away, his political enemies, the same people who had opposed his nomination in 1940, did everything they could to convince FDR that Wallace was not strong within the party and would be a fatal handicap in the election. There have been innumerable accounts of the 1944 convention and the events leading up to it, but no one knows exactly what influenced Roosevelt's decision. To liberals, in those intense weeks before the convention, he often said he favored Wallace.[23] Particularly fascinating are Wallace's diary accounts of what happened prior to that time, especially in the meetings with Roosevelt, when FDR implied he was for Wallace and would work for his renomination but never flatly said so.[24] FDR, of course, was no stranger to political duplicity. Or—what is quite possible— he liked Wallace too much to come right out and tell him he would be dropped; although, given Wallace's loyalty, he would have accepted the decision—he told the President so—and all the frantic dealing, and double-dealing, would have been avoided.[25]

In any case, Roosevelt, perhaps reluctantly, decided that Wallace had to go. Possibly he did not like the way Wallace had handled the Board of Economic Warfare fracas with Jesse Jones. Perhaps he did not think Wallace was sufficiently skilled a politician to hold the Democratic Party together. Certainly, an active Vice President, with the President's support, could have gathered more supporters and disarmed more critics than Wallace did during his four years. He did not even try. Perhaps FDR believed that Wallace would be a handicap in the election against Thomas Dewey and Senator John W. Bricker of Ohio, who were nominated by the Republicans shortly before Wallace returned to Washington. Or maybe Roosevelt was too old and sick and tired to withstand the anti-Wallace pressure.

Whatever the reasons, on the day Wallace returned to Washington, he met with Secretary of Interior Harold Ickes and Judge Sam Rosenman, at the President's instructions. They tried to get Wallace to withdraw but he told them that he did not want to talk politics and that, in any case, he was seeing the President himself that afternoon.[26] Roosevelt in turn tried obliquely to get Wallace to withdraw, saying he did not want him to have to face public rejection. This, of course, was nonsense. Wallace would not be rejected by the party if Roosevelt wanted him. Besides, Wallace was clearly the most popular Democrat after Roosevelt himself. At a later meeting he showed the President a poll that indicated that 65 per cent of the Democrats preferred him to only 2 per cent for Truman. And he told Roosevelt that he had many more pledged delegates than any other candidate.

At their last meeting, according to Wallace, "As I shook hands with him he drew me close and turned on his full smile and a very hearty handclasp, saying 'While I cannot put it just that way in public, I hope it will be the same old team.' "[27] But the most Roosevelt did publicly for Henry Wallace was to write a letter to Senator Samuel D. Jackson of

Indiana, who was scheduled to be permanent chairman of the convention. Jackson read the document to the convention on its second day. After some introductory remarks the President had written, "The easiest way of putting it is this: I have been associated with Henry Wallace during this past four years as Vice President, for eight years earlier while he was Secretary of Agriculture, and well before that. I like him and I respect him and he is my personal friend. For these reasons I personally would vote for his renomination if I were a delegate to the convention."

Some might see that as a rather lukewarm endorsement, but whatever positive effect it might have had was quickly undercut by the next and final paragraph: "At the same time I do not wish to appear in any way as dictating to the convention. Obviously the convention must do the deciding. And it should—and I am sure it will—give great consideration to the pros and cons of its choice."[28]

This was an invitation to pick someone else. And party chairman Robert E. Hannegan of Missouri had someone in mind. He was busy circulating mimeographed copies of a letter he had convinced Roosevelt to write: "Dear Bob, You have written me about Harry Truman and Bill Douglas. I should, of course, be very glad to run with either of them and believe that either one of them would bring real strength to the ticket."[29]

That same afternoon Henry Wallace seconded the Presidential nomination of Franklin Roosevelt. Wallace knew he was fighting for his political life, that he needed every delegate he could get. But he did not trim his views. This passage, with delegate reaction indicated, is from the *Official Proceedings* of the convention: "The future belongs to those who go down the line unswervingly for the liberal principles of both political democracy and economic democracy regardless of race, color or religion (applause and cheers). The poll tax must go (applause and cheers; boos). Equal educational opportunities must come (applause and cheers). The future must bring equal wages for equal work regardless of sex or race (applause and cheers)."[30]

That evening Roosevelt's acceptance speech was broad-cast to the delegates. As it drew to an end, some Truman signs began to appear among the crowd. And then a Wallace parade, with signs and banners, and cheers, cheers that rocked the stadium. It was plain, for a moment at least, that the convention wanted Wallace. Senator Claude Pepper, chairman of the Florida delegation and an articulate liberal and Wallace supporter, concluded that it was then or never. Although he knew the Vice-Presidential nomination was not scheduled until the next day, he tried to get the chairman's attention and move that the nomination be held right then. This is what Pepper wrote to Curtis Macdougall:

. . . I began to wave my banner and to shout for recognition from the chairman. However, struggle as I might I could not get his recognition. I was confident, however, that he had seen me and no doubt divined what I had in mind.

Finally I pushed my way up the middle aisle to the gate leading to the platform. Fortunately this was manned by an old friend of mine who readily let me on the stairway leading to the platform. When I got near the top of the stairway the chairman suddenly recognized someone standing near him who made a motion that the convention should then adjourn. The chairman quickly put the question and although the noes obviously overwhelmed the ayes the chair declared the ayes to have it and the convention ad-journed. This action was followed by loud booing from a consider-able part of the audience.[31]

That was Wallace's last chance. The next day he got to within about a hundred of the 589 votes needed—con-siderably more than Truman and a scattering of "favorite sons." But then the political bosses' efforts began to pay off, and soon Truman had the nomination. Eleanor Roosevelt tried to console Wallace. "I had hoped by some miracle you could win out, but it looks to me as though the bosses had functioned pretty smoothly. I am told that Senator Truman

is a good man, and I hope so for the sake of the country."
Later, as we shall see, she was to criticize both men severely, opposing Wallace's bid for the Presidency and giving only the most routine support to Truman's. But at this
time she was all for Wallace. She had done "her utmost" to
keep her husband "from dropping Wallace as his running
mate even though she had to agree with him that Wallace
was not a good politician. 'I wrote a column on Wallace but
Franklin says I must hold it till after the convention. I wish I
were free.' "[32] And Wallace had another powerful friend
who also later turned against him, Philip Murray, head of
the Congress of Industrial Organizations (CIO).

Obviously, Wallace had needed only one supporter: FDR.
This is the way he saw it: ". . . there is no doubt in my
mind as to his intentions when I returned from Alaska on
July 10. (He wanted to ditch me as noiselessly as possible.)
And then he apparently changed momentarily when my
presentation clearly indicated that he had been lied to by
his advisers."[33]

An insight into Roosevelt's Byzantine handling of the
nomination for Vice President was given Wallace by Senator Alben W. Barkley of Kentucky when they had lunch a
couple of weeks after the convention. Wallace wrote in his
diary for August 1, 1944:

> . . . It seems that the President's letter to Jackson on my behalf
> and the President's letter to Hannegan on behalf of Truman and
> Douglas were typed and signed the same day and both within 24
> or 36 hours of the time the President had told me with such deep
> feeling, "I can't say it publicly but I hope it will be the same old
> team. . . ."

Barkley says if the convention had not been dictated to by the
President, I would have gotten the nomination. Barkley says he
himself got into the race only when the word was passed around
that the President did not want me. Barkley declared that he himself would have been glad to support me if the President had kept
hands off.[34]

Wallace nonetheless believed that it was his duty to work hard for Roosevelt's election. When he said this to Barkley, "Alben could not help coming back to the theme, however, of 'It makes you awfully depressed when you know a fellow will do things like that. He may be a smart politician but how can he go in two different directions at the same time?' "[35] Barkley was hardly alone in believing Wallace had been double-crossed. The press was filled with similar assessments. The 1944 convention demonstrated what was demonstrated in the conventions of 1968 and 1972: that the struggle for the body and soul of the Democratic Party is never-ending.

Wallace did work hard for Roosevelt, campaigning all over the country. And as Vice President he occasionally saw FDR, frequently recording in his diary his concern over the President's health. On August 16 he dictated: "It is curious how many people think the President is completely washed up physically."[36] On November 10, three days after the election, Roosevelt presided over a Cabinet meeting. This is part of what Wallace dictated: "When the President showed great emotion regarding J.J., I became conscious for the first time that he had aged very greatly. At the train I thought he looked remarkably well. He has lots of vitality left in his system and is out to get J.J. Just the same, I would judge from the character and quality of his remarks that his intellect but not his prejudices will now begin to fade pretty rapidly. He will have to take awfully good care of himself to last out the four years in a state of competent leadership."[37]

On December 20 Wallace had a private meeting with FDR and afterward dictated these remarks: "It was obvious to me that the President's mind roams as far afield as ever, that he still talks endlessly about everything under the sun but that he is losing considerable of his old power of focus. His mind isn't very clear anymore. His hand trembles a great deal more than it used to. . . ."[38]

But Wallace, of course, had concerns other than the President's health. He continued to speak out on foreign policy and other issues of liberal concern. Roosevelt told him in a private meeting that "I was four or six years ahead of my time, that what I stood for would inevitably come."[39] In a pamphlet, *Our Job in the Pacific*, Wallace called for "the emancipation of . . . colonial subjects" in India, Burma, Malaya, Indochina, the Dutch East Indies, and so on.[40] This terribly upset the British, but in this Wallace was in total agreement with FDR, who often spoke of the need for the European powers to end colonialism and marked this as a specific goal of his postwar policy.

Just after the election, Eleanor Roosevelt told Wallace she would like to see him. This is Wallace's account of the meeting:

When I saw Mrs. Roosevelt, she told me that the liberals looked on me as the outstanding symbol of liberalism in the United States. She said that she was going out to the CIO convention on November 20 and she wanted to know whether I would head up a greatly broadened PAC. [The National Citizens Political Action Committee had been established by the CIO and other liberal leaders to rally support for Roosevelt in the 1944 election. C. B. "Beanie" Baldwin, one of Wallace's top aides in the Agriculture Department as head of the Farm Security Administration, was the day-to-day head of PAC. He later became Wallace's campaign manager.] She felt that Sidney Hillman was not suitable for heading up such a broad liberal organization. She said furthermore that even though I had a position in the government, she thought I could go in on such an organization. She said she knew that I could not answer offhand such a matter. Later in the day I called her up and told her the first thing that occurred to me was that whatever was done should have the complete and enthusiastic blessing of Sidney Hillman. Second, I told her that I felt the only way any liberalism could express itself on a national basis was through the Democratic Party and I felt it would be damaging to the Democratic Party and to the liberalism boys if I should take the position she suggested. In brief, I turned down the proposition flatly but nicely. I can't help wondering, however, to what extent her husband is up to his usual maneuvering tricks.[41]

Henry Wallace also went to the national CIO convention in Chicago that November as principal speaker and after the Vice President addressed the delegates, CIO President Philip Murray said:

Henry Wallace, to the workers of the U.S.A. symbolizes the aspirations of the common man. We love him because he is one of us, a common man.

The principles which he has enunciated here this morning are the ones to which the CIO adheres. So to you, Vice President Wallace, we do extend our heart-felt appreciation for the crusading work which you have undertaken as a leader of men and we shall join with you and the multitudes in advancing the cause, the cause of our country, the cause of its people.

So, Henry, come over here; I am going to place on the lapel of your coat a "distinguished service medal."[42]

The following month, December, Wallace spoke at a testimonial dinner for Marshall Field, the liberal department-store magnate and newspaper publisher. Wallace asserted, "The people are on the march all over the world and there is nothing the reactionary forces in the United States can do to stop it—but we can, if we are sympathetic, channel those revolutionary forces for the constructive welfare of the whole world."[43]

In view of the disclosures in early 1975 about J. Edgar Hoover, long time director of the Federal Bureau of Investigation, an item from the Wallace diary of December 19, 1944, is interesting indeed. Wallace said, "I got it on very good authority yesterday that Edgar Hoover continually has Drew Pearson [a widely syndicated newspaper columnist] shadowed. Hoover specializes on building up a file against the various public figures and especially against the columnists. . . . Hoover is apparently on his way toward becoming a kind of an American Himmler."[44] One can flirt with the delicious notion that if Wallace had succeeded Roosevelt, he might have had the nerve to fire Hoover. Evidently, every President since wanted to fire Hoover for his interference in politics, his arrogance, and his highhandedness. But those FBI files he controlled, with information about the sexual, drinking, and other personal habits of prominent persons, were presumably Hoover's insurance policy.

Inasmuch as Henry Wallace's later split with Harry Truman was based on his contention that Truman was departing significantly from Roosevelt's policy, two entries in Wallace's diary about Cabinet meetings in late December 1944 and early January are most interesting. Referring to the situation in Greece, where civil war had broken out soon after the Germans had withdrawn—the British were supporting the royalists, who were opposed by a growing force of insurgents, some Communists and some not—Roosevelt told his Cabinet that "he thought the best solution was to give both sides in Greece all the rifles and ammunition they wanted and then everybody pull out and let them fight it out."[45] A couple of weeks later he made a similar statement.[46]

Roosevelt was speaking casually, but clearly his disposition was not to take sides, to let the nature of the Greek balance of forces take its course. In later years, however, Truman decided to intervene on the side of the royalists. This decision, which became known as the Truman Doctrine, was a pivotal one in American and world history. We will see, a couple of chapters hence, what Wallace thought of that decision.

During these last weeks of the third Roosevelt term, Wallace's future was being decided. He discussed this difficult subject with Secretary of the Treasury Henry Morgenthau, Jr.:

Morgenthau is very eager for me to be in the Cabinet. He said folks had been talking about my being either Secretary of Labor or Secretary of Commerce. I told him I hoped the President would not ask me to be Secretary of Labor: that I didn't want the post; that I would do everything I could to avoid being Secretary of Labor. I told him I wanted to be Secretary of Commerce. He asked if the

President knew that and I said yes, that I had told the President that on August 29 and had sent him a wire recently. . . . He said he was going to be seeing Mrs. Roosevelt. He asked if Mrs. Roosevelt knew what I wanted. I said no, I hadn't told her. He said Mrs. Roosevelt was very, very strong for me. When he told me this I couldn't help but think that this would make me weaker with the President because I have the feeling that at the present time he fights everything she is for. I didn't care to say this to Henry Morgenthau, however. Morgenthau said he was exceedingly anxious for me to be in the Cabinet because he felt otherwise the forces of reaction were in serious danger of taking over the President. He thought Ickes, he, and I could work together.[47]

The August 29 meeting that Wallace was referring to is an important one, which sheds light on the second Henry Wallace–Jesse Jones confrontation, whose fireworks enlivened, if not brightened, the early weeks of the fourth Roosevelt administration. This is what the Wallace diary recorded about that earlier meeting: "The President said he thought the election was going to be very close but in case we won, one of the first things we would do would be to sit down and make a list of the folks we were going to get rid of, said the first one on the list would be Jesus H. Jones. I said, 'Well, if you are going to get rid of Jones, why not let me have Secretary of Commerce with RFC [Reconstruction Finance Corporation] and FEA thrown in? There would be poetic justice in that.' The President said, 'Yes, that's right.' "

There is every reason to believe that Wallace was genuinely interested in the job at the Commerce Department. A full-employment economy—he later wrote a book called *Sixty Million Jobs*—he saw as a first domestic priority after the war, and he believed that greatly expanded international trade was essential to world peace. Both those goals could best be sought at the Commerce Department. Roosevelt's reasons are not quite so clear, but then his often were not. He was grateful for the extraordinary support Wallace was giving the Democratic ticket even though he had been dumped from it. And quite possibly he wanted to get rid of Jones because he believed that the Texan had worked against his third and fourth nominations; in other words quite possibly FDR was more interested in getting Jones out than Wallace in. This is what some of those close to Roosevelt believe.[48] But whatever the reasons, Roosevelt did not handle the matter skillfully or tactfully. Some cite the mishandling as an indication of his declining health. This is the extraordinary letter he wrote:

Dear Jesse:

This is a very difficult letter to write—first, because of our long friendship and splendid relations during all these years and also because of your splendid services to the government and the excellent way in which you have carried out the many difficult tasks during these years.

Henry Wallace deserves almost any service which he believes he can satisfactorily perform. I told him this at the end of the campaign, in which he displayed the utmost devotion to our cause, traveling almost incessantly and working for the success of the ticket himself, he gave of his utmost toward the victory which ensued.

He has told me that he thought he could do the greatest amount of good in the Department of Commerce for which he is fully suited. And I feel, therefore, that the Vice President should have this post in the new administration.

It is for this reason only that I am asking you to relinquish this present post for Henry and I want to tell you that it is in no way a lack of appreciation for all that you have done and that I hope you will continue to be part of the government.

During the next few days I hope you will think about a new post—there are several ambassadorships which are vacant or about to be vacated. I make this suggestion among many other posts, and I hope you will have a chance, if you think well of it, to speak to Ed Stettinius.

Finally, let me tell you that you have my full confidence and that

I am very proud of all that you have done during these past few
years.

> With my warm regards,
> Always sincerely,
> FRANKLIN D. ROOSEVELT [49]

A politician did not have to be as shrewd as Jesse Jones was
to recognize that he was being unceremoniously bounced.
If Roosevelt had genuinely wanted to keep him, he would
have made two or three attractive offers or, better yet,
would have called Jones in and explained, with that formidable charm of his, why he felt Wallace had to have the
job. The tactless letter also dismayed Wallace's friends, for it
gave the impression that the idea of dumping Jones was
Wallace's alone. Since Jones's devoted friends among the
conservative senators were already anything but friendly to
Wallace, a political brawl was certain to erupt.

And erupt it did, with the redoubtable Jones setting it
off. On Inauguration Day, when Jones received Roosevelt's
letter, he composed a reply in which he minced no words.
And Jones released both letters to the press. His reply still
sizzles:

Dear Mr. President:

I have your letter of today, asking that I relinquish my post as
Secretary of Commerce which carries with it the vast financial and
war production agencies within the Reconstruction Finance Corporation and its subsidiaries so that you can give it to Henry
Wallace as a reward for his support of you in the campaign.

You state that Henry thinks he could do the greatest amount of
good in the Department of Commerce and that you consider him
fully suited for the post. With all due respect, Mr. President, while
I must accede to your decision, I cannot agree with either of you.[50]

As FDR sailed off in late January 1945 for his historic
meeting at Yalta, Wallace and his supporters had to contend
with a distinctly unpromising political situation. Jones let

loose another salvo four days later, questioning Wallace's competence to direct agencies that annually loaned $30 to $40 billion in credit to American corporations. Such an enormous investment in war plants and material "should not be made the subject of careless experimentation. . . . Certainly the RFC should not be placed under the supervision of any man willing to jeopardize the country's future with untried ideas and idealistic schemes."[51]

Jones's words fell on sympathetic ears. As Wallace said before the Senate Commerce Committee holding hearings on his nomination, "You know and I know that it is not a question of my 'lack of experience.' Rather, it is a case of not liking the experience I have."[52] Wallace did not make many converts, for a couple of days later the committee not only voted 14–5 to separate the lending powers from the Commerce Department but entirely rejected Wallace's nomination by the same vote. In those inauspicious circumstances his name went to the full Senate for a vote.

Wallace, however, had his defenders in the liberal wing of the Democratic Party. Among them was James Loeb, Jr., executive secretary of the Union for Democratic Action, which later became the Americans for Democratic Action (ADA). His statement is noteworthy, perhaps even amusing, given his bitter opposition to Wallace just a couple of years later. Loeb said, "The 14 members of the Senate committee who voted against Wallace stand condemned before the American electorate for having betrayed the people's will. The fight is not for Henry Wallace the man but for the ideals for which he stands."[53] The Senate stripped the lending agencies from the Commerce Department by a vote of 74–12 on February 2, and the House did so by an even more overwhelming 399–2 on February 17. Clearly, Wallace was not popular in a Congress that was no longer the New Deal body of a decade before. Nonetheless, his appointment limped through the Senate on March 1, 1945, by a 56–32 vote.

At Yalta, meanwhile, FDR was kept fully informed. His

wife wrote, "Of course Jones has behaved horribly & your letter when published was hard on Wallace. I know you wrote it hoping to make Jones feel better but I guess he's the kind of dog you should have ousted the day after election & given him the reasons. He would not have published that letter! . . . People like Oscar Ewing are telling newspapermen that 'Henry is a nice guy, but he shouldn't have RFC.' So tomorrow I'm going to call Mr. Hannegan & ask what he and the Com. are doing to back Wallace."[54]

And Eleanor Roosevelt kept after her husband, even at long distance: "Your message came through to Barkley but we wish you had added a little word for Wallace. We assume you take it for granted we know you believe Wallace will help you to do the job, but a little reassurance would be helpful!" But FDR did not seem terribly interested and at one point a friend of Mrs. Roosevelt asked her if FDR really wanted Wallace.[55] In fairness to the President it must be noted that he was engaged at Yalta in matters of the greatest moment, was far from the scene, and was in very bad health.

Yet if Wallace was unpopular in Congress and was not getting much help from Roosevelt, he was still regarded by the liberal wing of the Democratic Party as the President's rightful heir, even if he were no longer FDR's Vice President. On January 29, 1945, the Union for Democratic Action sponsored a testimonial dinner in New York for Wallace. The date—little more than a week after Wallace had been succeeded by Harry S. Truman—clearly meant that as far as Democratic liberals were concerned, he was still their man. Among the speakers were Walter Reuther, then a vice president of the United Auto Workers; Henry J. Kaiser, the liberals' favorite capitalist; James G. Patton, president of the National Farmers Union; and Eleanor Roosevelt, reading a message from her husband. It was a blue-chip gathering of what might be termed Establishment liberals.

At this time, as he was for nearly two more years, Wallace was opposed to a third party. But the very fact that he mentioned one was an indication of many liberals' concern about the direction the Democratic Party was taking. He said, ". . . I still hope and pray for a united progressive Democratic Party. The strategy of the enemy is to break the Democratic Party in two. They want to push you and me into the futility of a third party. I think we can win within the framework of the Democratic Party. I hope that we are not now in for a political realignment like that which substituted a Republican Party for the Whig Party nearly a century ago. There will be far less trouble in this country if the progressives can find full and free expression in the Democratic Party."[56]

These were the early stirrings of ideological conflict that even now is yet to be resolved. Perhaps, unless the party realignment that Wallace spoke of takes place, the conflict will never be resolved, with the Democratic Party, depending upon circumstances, held together by the centripetal force of common interests, largely economic, or strained almost to the point of dissolution by the centrifugal forces of philosophic difference.

On April 12 Roosevelt died. With him died many things: the New Deal, which had languished during the war and which, it was expected, he would revive; his foreign policy, far from explicit, to which both Harry Truman and Henry Wallace laid claim; and, of course, his Democratic Party, much larger than the Republican Party, but much less cohesive.

As far as millions of mourning Americans were concerned, Henry A. Wallace was Roosevelt's legitimate heir. His office at the Department of Commerce was flooded with messages, many of them grieving, in which the writers turned to him for consolation.[57] People wrote to him in their homely way about their problems and hopes. He had become a surrogate for FDR, who, for millions, had been a father figure, almost a god. And he was swamped with invitations to speak. He had long been a sought-after speaker, but now these invitations multiplied. Among those who felt this way was Hubert H. Humphrey, a young public-relations man who had just announced that he would run for mayor of Minneapolis. On the day of Roosevelt's death Humphrey wrote to Wallace about political matters, saying, among other things, that "I want to keep reminding you that Minnesota is expecting you to be our Presidential candidate in 1948. As I have said to you on previous occasions, I will do everything within my power to help mobilize the progressive forces in this great midwest area behind you and your program." Appended to the letter was this handwritten postscript:

5:05 P.M.

I've just heard of the death of our great President. May God bless this nation and world.

I scarcely know what to say. It is as if one of my own family had passed away.

If ever we needed men of courage—stout-hearted men, it is now. I simply can't conceal my emotions. How I wish you were at the helm. I know Mr. Truman will rise to the heights of statesmanship so all important in this hour. But, we need you as you have never been needed before.[58]

2

Wallace Splits with Truman

Henry Wallace was Roosevelt's heir but Harry Truman was his successor. It was an awkward situation for both men, but there is every reason to believe that each wanted it to work out. Each was devoted to the country and each regarded himself as a loyal follower of FDR. But that makes them sound closer than in fact they were, and they soon developed irreconcilable differences as to what foreign policy would best serve the nation. And being loyal to FDR was not as simple as following a compass needle pointing north. Roosevelt was a political magnet, to be sure, but he was not quite so constant as the North Pole. To one man he stood in one place, to another somewhere else. Citing Roosevelt's words, private or public, as justification for a course of action was really a creative exercise. Like Holy Writ or, perhaps more suitably, like the Constitution, Roosevelt could be, and was, cited to justify almost any political action. So the potential for a split was there from the beginning.

At first, however, it seemed that it might indeed work out. Personal feelings, whatever they may have been, aside, there were good practical reasons for Truman to keep Wallace in the Cabinet. On one level, Truman could value Wallace's service as secretary of commerce, based on his success as secretary of agriculture. Perhaps more important, he needed Wallace's political support, for Wallace was much the bigger political figure of the two. In those first uncertain months, an ordinary man, standing in the place so recently filled by a giant, hardly wanted to offend another who, in the minds of millions, was the rightful heir. As for Wallace, it seems plain that he wanted to serve the new President loyally, as he had for so long the old. And Wallace, too, had his political reasons. He wanted to ride herd on the new President so that he would not stray too far from the progressive path. And assuming normal political ambition—which no one ever doubted Wallace had in full measure—he knew that loyal service was his best course, for party politicians favor loyalty above all else.

Was Wallace bitter that a relatively unknown newcomer was sitting in the White House? Did he feel cheated that he was not there? He would not have been human had he not turned such thoughts over in his mind, especially when, just after Roosevelt's death, Mrs. Roosevelt wrote to him in these terms: "Though I hope to see you today and perhaps to talk with you more about my hopes for America and the future, I do want you to know that I feel that you are peculiarly fitted to carry on the ideals which were close to my husband's heart and which I know you understand. . . ."[1] Indeed, in October 1943 she had told Mr. and Mrs. Wallace at a private dinner in the White House that if FDR decided not to run for a fourth term in 1944, "she and the President would be for me as the logical one to carry out the policies of the President."[2]

Some of Wallace's critics have written or said that his split with Truman was motivated by bitterness and the desire for revenge, but if that was the case, he certainly hid it well. In the months after Truman took office Wallace wrote many letters praising Truman's good start, soliciting support for the new President, and urging supporters not to work in his behalf for the 1948 nomination. The day after Roosevelt's death Wallace, in reply to a telegram from Anita McCormick Blaine, the multimillion dollar heiress of Cyrus Hall McCormick, inventor of the reaper (she was later a generous supporter of the Progressive party), wrote, "President Truman is getting off to an unusually fine start and you may count on me to do my utmost to help him."[3]

And to Vincent Swan of Buffalo he wrote on April 19, 1945, "I know that you have spent your money unselfishly and have given generously of your time in your efforts to aid me. Nevertheless, I believe that the work you are doing in my behalf is harmful. All of us should be devoting our time and energies to winning the war and securing lasting peace and full employment after the war. One of the best ways to realize these objectives is to elect a Congress in 1946 which will work with the President. I strongly urge you, therefore, to immediately discontinue you efforts in behalf of 'Wallace in '48' and ask that you concentrate upon a progressive Congress in 1946."[4]

These letters continued past the first hopeful flush in the days immediately after Truman took office. In a letter dated February 27, 1946, nearly a year later, Wallace wrote to Powell W. Glidewell, Sr., of Reidsville, North Carolina: ". . . I am happy to know that you and I agree that the country will best be served if the Democratic Party is always the progressive, forward-looking party. I believe that it is my duty to work in the Cabinet. While I am grateful to you, I must tell you that I am not in any sense a candidate for either President or Vice President in 1948."[5]

And four months later Wallace wrote to Horace S. Kircher of Philadelphia, "I shall continue to do everything I can not only for the election of a progressive Democratic Congress in 1946—but also for the best interests of all the people right on through to 1948 and thereafter. And I know that you will do your part in the challenging task before us. But I am sincerely of the opinion that what effectiveness I have in this work would be impeded if there were any advancement of my personal interests. Therefore, I have made it a policy not to lend my encouragement to any person or organization seeking to advance my name in connection with the Democratic presidential nomination in 1948."[6]

These letters do not sound like those of a man driven by ambition or bitterness. Indeed, his correspondence makes Henry Wallace seem like an attractive man.[7] Although there is ample testimony from his associates that he was shy and ill at ease in small groups of strangers, his letters were often warm and friendly, and he wrote many gracious little personal notes, more than one would expect of so busy a man. This interest in people must have somehow communicated itself, for he received many personal letters. Often they contained poems. Some one once said that the raw material of history—letters, diaries, and so forth—is more interesting than history itself. In Wallace's case, his letters and diaries demonstrate not only the wide range of his interests in such matters as agriculture, science, economics, labor, atomic energy, and, of course, politics, but the depth of his knowledge and his genuine humanity.[8]

As secretary of commerce, Henry Wallace of necessity devoted most of his time and energy to reorganizing an oldline department which, he believed, badly needed revitalization. Although foreign trade was certainly within his departmental scope, foreign affairs as such was not. Yet it was a constant preoccupation, for he soon began to feel that Truman was dangerously departing from Roosevelt's conviction that the peace of the world depended on getting along with the Russians. Each believed he was following FDR's path, and each had no trouble finding documentation for his belief: Truman, Roosevelt's statements about his disappointments with Russian behavior and the need to be firm; Wallace, statements that it was possible to get along with Russia. And because he had been Vice President and was, as he knew, the head of the liberal wing of the Democratic Party, Wallace had no hesitation, however much it may have irritated Truman, in speaking his mind on foreign affairs. The first meeting between the two men that appears in the Wallace diaries (April 27, 1945) records two conclusions about Truman that reappear constantly in later entries. Wallace says, "Truman was exceedingly eager to agree with everything I said. He also seemed eager to make decisions of every kind with the greatest promptness. Everything he said was decisive. It almost seemed as though he was eager to decide in advance of thinking."[9]

That Wallace noticed Truman's decisiveness is hardly surprising, for his reputation to this day is largely based on that quality, admirable in most eyes. But the decisiveness seemed to Wallace to be contradicted by what he saw as Truman's eagerness to please. At this time, of course, Truman had been in office but two weeks and it is entirely reasonable that he should want as a matter of courtesy to be friendly with the man who might well have become President. But Wallace was to make this same observation repeatedly. As to the decisiveness, on which Truman prided himself, it may have been more apparent than real—the way Truman saw himself, the way he thought a President should act. But even if Truman were genuinely decisive, should he not in such crucial times have considered his decisions more carefully, more thoughtfully? He was proud of his ability to make a momentous decision and then go to bed for an undisturbed night's sleep, but might not the nation be better served by presidents who are kept awake by the magnitude of the decisions they must make and have made?

This is not to suggest that Truman was not a serious man. But the times, even more after the war than during it, were as complex as any that had ever faced an American President. For the first time in its history the United States was *the* dominant power in the world, and it was a new world, totally different, not for Truman alone but for every world leader. The great empires that had ruled Asia, the Middle East, and Africa were at the point of collapse. The losing nations—Germany, Japan, and Italy—were in ruins, but so were the victors—Britain, France, and Russia. With the crumbling of the great empires the inherent drive for self-government and social change manifested itself in nationalism.

Perhaps it was inevitable, given this country's lifelong sense of manifest destiny, that America should survey a prostrate world and decide, with the very best of intentions, that it should be remade in the American image to the extent possible. And given America's strength and everyone else's weakness, it may also have been inevitable that that extent seemed very great indeed. Some believe that this impulse was at heart economic, the natural outthrust of American capitalism. That was certainly a factor, a major factor, but my own conviction is that it was more a drive buried in the American psyche, a belief that America was the best the world had produced or ever could. It was not only an opportunity but an obligation to Americanize the world. And the sole threat, the sole possible competition, was communism, Russian communism, which had to be opposed wherever it presented itself. Truman knew it was a great task but believed it could be done. So did Eisenhower and Kennedy and Johnson. So, for decades, did Nixon.

Hubris it was, and so monumental that only a decade of bloody frustration in Indochina ended it, one can hope, for once and for all. This hubris took the shape of globalism, a new imperialism, a Pax Americana. Harry Truman and his chief advisers, even such intelligent men as James Byrnes, George Marshall, and Dean Acheson, did not understand the nature of this new world. It was a world ripe for revolution, and the United States, so proud of its birth in revolution, did not understand.

The Truman administration almost immediately confused the perfectly normal competition between two great powers, the United States and Russia, and the world-wide desire for national self-determination. In a blunder of tragic proportion the United States concluded that to oppose Russian communism along its European and Asian frontiers it was necessary to oppose revolution everywhere. It would be fatuous to suggest that Wallace predicted the exact shape of the tragedy to come, for he did not. But he did say, time and time and time again, that if the Truman administration continued on the course that it began in 1945, disaster would result.

The Cold War was not a one-sided enterprise, and it is not my intention to suggest that it was; nor do I intend to

suggest that the United States did not have a legitimate concern for the people behind what became known as the Iron
Curtain. But one can feel distress, even loathing for what
the Russians did in Eastern Europe in the years after the
war and still recognize the hypocrisy in much of America's
concern. If one is concerned about the lack of freedom in
Eastern Europe, should one not feel the same way about the
people in Greece, in Iran? Repression seemed to be abomin-
able in Communist countries, acceptable in anti-Communist countries.

What I do suggest is that given America's enormous
strength when World War II ended, given Russia's terrible
devastation (some 20 or 25 million lives lost) and its need to
devote itself to reconstruction, and given Russia's fear and
suspicion of the West (remember the Western military intervention in Russia at the end of World War I) the major
responsibility for a peaceful world rested with the United
States. A United States strong and prosperous, with the
atomic bomb in its arsenal, should have taken steps to reas-
sure Russia. With that incontestable strength it should have
had the patience to persevere in that reassurance even when
Russia, as she sometimes did, acted badly. And while Russia did sometimes behave badly, even unforgivably, it was
never in those first postwar years a military threat to the
West requiring a militaristic policy by the United States. So
grievous were Russia's wartime wounds, so powerful was
the United States, that such a threat simply did not exist.
That fact was as plain in Washington as it was in Moscow—
or should have been.

As soon as the European war ended, and months before
the end of the war in the Pacific, the United States abruptly
ended Lend-Lease aid to Russia. Even earlier, on April 23,
Truman had met Soviet Foreign Minister V. M. Molotov,
who was in the United States for the founding meeting of
the United Nations, and scolded him for Russian intentions
as to Poland. At the UN meeting in San Francisco, the

United States was antagonizing Russia. One of the members of the U.S. delegation was Adlai Stevenson, and on May 3 he met with Henry Wallace, who noted:

. . . At the conclusion, just before he was leaving, Adlai Stevenson told me personally how much disturbed he was about the conference at San Francisco. He said the Russians were right with regard to Argentina [which had been sympathetic to Germany during the war] and that many people in the State Department realized this to be the case. It happened, however, that Nelson Rockefeller placed the unity of the hemisphere above the unity of the world and that he felt it was more important to bring in Argentina than to work out a satisfactory world formula. This may not be stating it quite fairly to Nelson Rockefeller. The only conclusion I could reach, however, from Stevenson's statement was that we had definitely entered an era of power politics with the United States on one side and Russia on the other. As Stevenson put it, Russia will look at the United States and say, "There is the United States with twenty American republics plus Liberia plus the Philippines, representing a total of twenty-three votes in the Assembly. Add in the other Latin nations and the British Commonwealth and where does it leave Russia?" Stevenson said that under such circumstances the Russians necessarily would tend to play their own game, not trusting the world organization. They would see themselves outvoted again and again in the Assembly. I must confess that Stevenson's analysis of San Francisco made me feel very much depressed concerning a constructive outcome on behalf of world peace. It begins to look like he is right in suggesting that we are entering an era of power politics rather than world organization. Of course the superficial appearances may indicate to the contrary.[10]

The following day Wallace attended a Cabinet meeting and then recorded this entry in his diary:

Truman's decisiveness is admirable. The only question is as to whether he had enough information behind the decisiveness to enable his decisions to stand up. Thus far I would say the evidence would indicate a net plus on small things and even on medium-sized things. The query is as to whether his decisions in the international field have been wise. On the whole it seems to me that his attitudes have been such as to increase the liability of disagreement with Russia. In this connection the June 24, 1941, *New York Times* story may furnish the key to his fundamental slant. According to this story Truman said two days after Russia was invaded by Germany, "If we see that Germany is winning we ought to help Russia, and if Russia is winning we ought to help Germany. And that way let them kill as many as possible, although I don't want to see Hitler victorious under any circumstances. Neither of them think anything of their pledged word."

The fear I have is that his instinctive attitude toward Russia may prevent Russia from coming into the war at the right time against Japan. Russia, in view of the attitude we are now taking, may reach the conclusion that it is desirable to see as many Americans and Japanese killed as possible.[11]

Toward the end of that month, May, Truman received the former governor and senator of Minnesota Elmer A. Benson, acting chairman of the National Citizens Political Action Committee, and C. B. Baldwin, its executive director. They raised the question of U.S. policy toward Russia. Truman banged his fist on the desk and spoke to this effect: "We have got to get tough with the Russians. They don't know how to behave. They're like bulls in a china shop. They're only twenty-five years old. We're over one hundred years old and the British are centuries older. We've got to teach them how to behave."

When Benson responded that if there were to be peace, it would be necessary to get along with the Soviet Union, Truman replied, "That is right." But Benson and Baldwin understood that for Truman the "get tough" part of the policy was the more significant, and as they were leaving the White House, one turned to the other—they could not remember which—and suggested that it might be necessary to form a third party to carry out Roosevelt's policies.[12]

This kind of meeting occurred time and again. On the one hand, Truman would say that he wanted peace with the

Russians, that he wanted to get along with them, but then he would balance that by saying it was necessary to get tough with them. There is nothing particularly strange about this. The Russians were, and are, difficult to understand, and Truman, like many Americans, had contradictory views toward them and was uncertain of their intentions, as they, no doubt, were uncertain of his. There is no reason to disbelieve the sincerity of his assertions that he wanted to get along with the Russians. It is just that he, like the Presidents that succeeded him, genuinely believed that the Russians would behave only if we were tough.

This was an exceedingly difficult time for Truman and his advisers. There were matters of the gravest importance at issue between the United States and the Soviet Union. Washington and Moscow were locked in stubborn disputes over the future of Eastern Europe—particularly Poland, where Stalin's view of a "democratic" government appeared to be a betrayal of his solemn commitments to Roosevelt and Truman. The two nations wrangled over the postwar government of Japan, economic aid to a devastated Europe (especially Eastern Europe and Russia), the shape of the United Nations, control of atomic weapons, the future of China, reparations, and, perhaps most important, the future of Germany, which was central to the future of Europe. Any one of them would have strained relations, especially when the two countries were committed to vastly different political and economic systems that made mutual suspicion inevitable. With all these controversies erupting at once and with the armies of the two suspicious nations eyeing each other warily across thousands of miles of occupied territory, extreme difficulty was inescapable.

That Truman wanted to serve the American national interest in each of these serious matters was normal and appropriate. He was obligated to do no less. This in itself did not lead to the disastrous course in American foreign policy. What did lead to disaster was the psychology, the psychosis even, that Truman and his administration brought to these matters. They soon came to perceive these matters not as exceedingly difficult specific problems with a difficult negotiator, but as constituting in the aggregate a challenge to American resolve. Compromise was perceived in Washington as a sign of weakness versus a foe that understood strength and strength only. This is not to suggest that the way to approach Stalin was as a spineless supplicant. But Truman and his successors came to believe that Washington's terms for settlement were the only fair ones and that these terms could be achieved only by the relentless application of economic and political force backed plainly by military might. When compromise is seen as surrender, when an adversary is perceived as a mortal foe and not as merely a nation seeking to serve its national interests, when Stalin was perceived not only as a deadly tyrant but as a Hitler bent on world conquest, a militaristic approach to the Soviet Union was inevitable. But Stalin and his successors refused to be intimidated into good behavior, and their response in kind only heightened the tensions that had caused so much misery to so many peoples of the world. Looking at it selfishly, as Americans, we can see that this perception of the Communist world, that it understood only force, established in the early Truman years, and continued for two decades thereafter by his successors, has brought terrible consequences to the United States: death and injury in two wars, violent internal dissension, and a staggering waste of material, moral, intellectual, and psychic resources.

Wallace had a far different perception of the Soviet Union. He believed that, as difficult as the Russians were to deal with, they genuinely wanted settlements that would not require the sacrifice of vital national interests by either side. In short, what in recent years has been called détente. Thus, given his attitude and his job, it was only natural that Henry Wallace favored postwar trade with Russia, and in the first months after the war he was far from alone. The September 1945 *Fortune* ran a poll in which more than 90 per cent of the businessmen answering believed it was in the long-term interest of the United States to promote trade with Russia, and placed Russia second only to Latin America as the area in which they expected to increase business. Professor Selig Perlman wrote that trade with Russia would serve a diplomatic purpose: "We have no sword big enough to brandish over Russia, but we can deeply influence her foreign policy, her plan for Western Europe, and for certain portions of Asia, by the inducement of assisting her in her economic restoration and expansion. Our economic necessity might thus become the foundation of our diplomatic opportunity." And an American official after conferring with Stalin said that he "made no secret of his feeling that trade with the United States would provide a basis for political cooperation with the West."[13]

On May 10, 1945, Wallace attended a dinner at Stuart Symington's home, along with some men from the National Planning Association who were preparing a meeting of that group at which they intended to announce plans for expanding the American economy. Wallace noted:

. . . I told them that none of their plans were any good unless we could be sure of peace between the United States and Russia; that at present it looked like the United States was getting ready to embark on an era of power politics and imperialism in international affairs.

Senator [Wayne] Morse [from Oregon, then still a Republican] spoke up very vigorously to say that in the cloakrooms on the Hill there was an immense amount of anti-Russian talk. [A GE executive] said that General Electric had already sold to the Russians equipment to take care of nine units of the Dneprostroi dam. In the first dam General Electric had equipped five of the units and the Russian government had equipped four. General Electric apparently feels very proud it has been called on to do the whole job this time.

I suggested it might be a good thing if the top men from General Electric, Westinghouse, United States Steel, J. P. Morgan, etc., would go to Russia and come back with orders and also with a plan regarding the imports we would be willing to accept from

Russia. I said a tangible action of this sort would mean more than a thousand speeches.[14]

But Truman and his top advisers saw little advantage to the United States in such trade. It was not encouraged and before long was actively discouraged.

As obvious as the advantages of Russian trade were to Wallace and others, just as obvious were the reasons it was not encouraged. On May 6, 1945, Wallace attended a picnic at the home of Edward B. Burling, a partner in what was probably Washington's best-known law firm, Covington, Burling, Rublee and Acheson. People "spoke in horrified tones of Russia. . . . More and more it begins to look like the psychology is favorable toward our getting into war with Russia. This must not be. It seems incredible that our people should drift toward this whirlpool which will inevitably end in world communism."[15] And on May 18, after a Cabinet meeting, Wallace spoke with Truman and asked him not to "accept the representations made to him by the State Department [about Russia] without looking at them twice. He [Truman] said he had no confidence in the State Department whatsoever and that he was going to get new leadership as soon as possible." Truman soon thereafter named James Byrnes to succeed Edward Stettinius, who, by general agreement, was not up to the job.

Later in that same conversation, Truman remarked to Wallace that Russia had not lived up to its Yalta promises regarding Poland, but that

all of his wires to Stalin had been couched in the most friendly language. He also said that Russia would not let us send people in to Rumania, Bulgaria, Austria, Hungary, and Berlin. I couldn't quite understand this because it is my understanding that we already have people in some of these places or soon will have.

The President said the Russians were like people from across the tracks whose manners were very bad. He said, however, that his one objective was to be sure to get the Russians into the Japanese war so as to save the lives of 100,000 American boys. Apparently,

Lend-Lease is still being continued to Russia via Vladivostok or Magodan. . . .

Joe [Joseph F.] Guffey [Democratic senator from Pennsylvania] came in to say that Averell Harriman had been meeting with the senators at lunch and that he had made a very favorable impression. Harriman among other things made it clear that Russia would not fight. Apparently, the tough doctrine that Harriman has sold to the President is based on Harriman's belief that the Russians will not fight. . . .[16]

It should not have taken Harriman to convince Truman that the Russians would not fight. After the terrible beating they had taken from the Nazis—perhaps the most terrible in the history of war—they were in no position to fight. Beyond that, the Russians would not have been human if they did not have an almost irresistible yearning for peace. There is another observation that must be made. The history of the Cold War abounds in ironies. At the time that it most mattered, when the pattern of anti-Communist crusade was being established, Averell Harriman advocated a tough policy toward Russia. Twenty years later, after not opposing the Vietnam war when it was being started by the Kennedy administration in which he was a high and influential official, he became something of a hero to the antiwar movement by opposing the Vietnam war when its failure was manifest.

Harriman and Wallace frequently clashed. This entry from the Wallace diary of May 12, 1945, explains why:

. . . At the luncheon, Don Nelson [a top wartime aide to FDR and Truman] spent all this time talking about Russia. He said the way we were going we would certainly have war with Russia, and there was absolutely no need of it. He said he knew exactly how the trouble arose. It appears he put the responsibility chiefly on Averell Harriman. He said that Averell last August began with his policy of getting tough with Russia. Don said that Averell really knew nothing about Russia, that he didn't know the Russians, that Russia could get along all right without us, and that our methods of dealing with Russia were just no good—they were not factual. He also said there was a faction in the Army that was looking toward war with Russia. He said this also was utterly foolish—that the Russian Army was better than our Army because the Russian soldiers would put up with more hardship; that they were more flexible and more ingenious. Don also spoke about Ed Stettinius going along with Averell Harriman. . . .

Nelson really felt very strongly with regard to both Stettinius and Harriman—feeling that while they were both exceedingly pleasant people and well-meaning people, yet their ignorance was such as to make them very dangerous to the peace of the world at the present time. He felt that unwittingly they had taken a stand at San Francisco which was leading us toward a conflict with Russia.

He said he hoped to see the President early next week, and that he had a memorandum worked out which he would leave with the President, concerning the kind of trade we might have with Russia. He thinks that President Truman might have the same interest in this which Roosevelt had had, and it might be possible with Truman to prevent Harriman from blocking things. . . .[17]

On May 16 Wallace met with Anna Boettiger, Roosevelt's daughter. She said she had just been with Truman. ". . . She said that Truman said that all his advisers had urged him to be hard with the Russians. I said to Anna Boettiger, 'How does the President feel this has worked out?' Anna Boettiger said the President now feels that it was a mistake. This means to me that Don Nelson had a very deep effect on President Truman. . . . Anna Boettiger feels that one of the great contributions by her father was holding relationships with Russia on a constructive and stable basis. It was obvious she feels the new President has not done well on this front."[18]

The next evening Wallace attended a Russian reception. He reported that there were almost no high-ranking Americans. The "whole atmosphere" reminded him "somewhat of that which existed back in 1940, when Russia was so unpopular in the United States." He spoke with Madame Gromyko, who "expressed to me the most vigorous opinion

that everything depended on me to maintain friendly relationships between Russia and the United States. I told her I
would do everything I could." But Wallace was not President or Vice President or secretary of state. He was secretary of commerce and almost without exception Truman's
foreign-policy advisers were hard-liners.

But while Wallace's fears about Truman continued to
grow, it was not a steady growth. There were times when
he was encouraged, when it appeared to him that Truman
was making genuine and effective efforts to get along with
the Russians. One such time was when Truman, at the urging of Harriman and Charles E. Bohlen, sent Harry Hopkins, Roosevelt's closest and most trusted adviser, to Moscow to talk with Stalin. On May 29, while Hopkins,
Harriman, and Bohlen were still in Moscow, Wallace met
with Truman: "Truman said that by sending Harry Hopkins
to Moscow he had straightened out a fundamental misconcep-
tion of Stalin and that Stalin was going to come along all
right now. . . . It was obvious . . . that Truman now feels
much more kindly toward the Russians than he did before.
Apparently, Harry Hopkins has been really helpful in Moscow. . . .

"Truman said he realized that our relationship with Russia had to be solved before we could go ahead with satisfactory planning of domestic affairs. He also mentioned that he
had refused several times to meet with Churchill because he
felt he ought to meet with Stalin first."[19]

While most of his time was spent at his new job, Wallace
continued to stress, in every forum available to him, the
necessity for good relations between the United States and
Russia. It is interesting to note that he feared that prominent among those trying to "stir up trouble" with Russia
was the Roman Catholic Church of the United States. This
was not a case of a Protestant being prejudiced against
Catholics, but a serious concern. And, although a detailed
discussion of this issue is beyond our scope here, the
Church was indeed active in anti-Communist causes, some-

times to a degree that alarmed some Catholics.

Wallace frequently heard from Catholic clergymen who took issue with his approach to the Soviet Union and often he replied to them. On June 13 he wrote to a Jesuit priest, the Reverend Edgar R. Smothers of St. Joseph's Mercy Hospital, Ann Arbor, Michigan:

I am quite well aware of the fact that many Socialists as well as many Communists are materialistic. This especially applies to Karl Marx and his materialistic dialectic. I don't happen to believe in those principles myself but that doesn't mean I can look with equanimity when those who talk about the materialism of the Russians try to stir up war with Russia. I repeat again, so far as the function of government is concerned, I don't see anything so irreconcilable in our aims and purposes as to justify the continuous effort to stir up misunderstanding between our nation and the Russian nation that has been going on.[20]

Two weeks later he wrote to another Catholic priest, the Reverend Bertrand Weaver of St. Gabriel's Monastery, Boston:

I appreciate the reasonable tone of your letter of June 7 and will agree with you that the Russian system as presently practiced lacks many of the freedoms that mean so much to us. However, it must be said that the Russians today have more of the political freedoms than they have ever had. Undoubtedly, they still have a long way to go but they are moving in the right direction.

From what I saw of the people in Soviet Asia I would not call them slaves. Therefore, I disagree with your inference that it is necessary to fight Russia because "the world cannot exist half slave and half free." I shall continue to denounce those who, either directly or indirectly, are endeavoring to promote a war between the United States and England on the one side and Russia on the other. I am sure that neither the people of the United States nor of Poland nor of China want a third world war.[21]

By mid-1945 Democratic liberals were beginning to get restive. Truman was, of course, in an impossible position.

To most liberals, no one could fill Roosevelt's shoes and only Wallace could come close. Truman was hardly their man, and as he began to replace Roosevelt people in the administration with his own, usually more conservative than their predecessors, they grumbled. Within three months Truman replaced Attorney General Francis Biddle, Secretary of Agriculture Claude Wickard, Secretary of Labor Frances Perkins, and Secretary of the Treasury Henry Morgenthau. Wallace and Harold Ickes were the last members of the New Deal Cabinet left, and Wallace felt lonely. Late in July he wrote to Frances Perkins, "Without you in the Cabinet, things don't seem quite right. You and Henry Morgenthau had been such old-time friends of the President [Wallace, like most New Dealers, still thought of the dead Roosevelt as the President] that it seems now as though the Roosevelt flavor has completely gone out of the Cabinet. . . ."[22]

Many of these liberal Democrats looked to Wallace for direction. He learned from Eleanor Roosevelt that "Jim Loeb and the other liberals of New York want her to find out from me any instructions which I have for them. They are . . . waiting for me to give the word. . . ."[23] But Wallace had not changed his mind since he had declined Mrs. Roosevelt's suggestion a few months before that he publicly become leader of the Democratic liberals. Clearly such a move would have jeopardized his relations with Truman, and he was convinced he could be a more effective force for liberalism within the Cabinet.

By autumn more and more Truman policies were bothering Wallace and the liberals. First, Truman was the object of widespread criticism because he was not doing enough to get desperately needed food to Europe, where hundreds of thousands of people faced starvation. He asked Congress for much too little money for the United Nations Relief and Rehabilitation Administration and then did little to support the request. Roosevelt had always made it plain that after the war he was going to exert pressure on the European imperialists to set their colonial peoples free. Now, to the contrary, Japanese troops were instructed not to turn Indochina over to Ho Chi Minh's nationalists, and the French in Indochina and the Dutch in Indonesia used American arms against nationalist rebels. The State Department's response to these actions was to ask that U.S. markings be removed from the weapons.

But Wallace's main objection that fall concerned Truman's policy regarding atomic weapons and Russia. Before discussing that, however, it is important to establish that Wallace was not a pacifist and that he was a supporter, as he had been before World War II, of military preparedness. At a Cabinet meeting on August 31 the President had read a draft statement about military policy and asked for comment. There was general agreement that it was fine. Wallace noted, "I then went on to suggest that a real military program for the country must of necessity be based on science, both in increased scientific personnel and also more laboratory equipment. Second, I said if the world situation was as serious as [Under] Secretary [of War Robert P.] Patterson had indicated, it would be desirable to have the Secretaries of War and Navy cooperate very closely with the Public Works Administrator to bring about a decentralization of our industry and population. Third, I indicated the desirability of having some standing committees which could throw us into mobilization more rapidly. . . ."[24]

One wonders how Secretary Patterson had described the world situation and how Wallace reconciled this with his view of the world, but just as Truman must have occasionally had doubts about the hard-line approach to the Soviet Union so too must Wallace have sometimes entertained doubts as to his different approach.

Wallace, however, had no doubts about atomic weapons and the Soviet Union. Before going into the controversy that developed, it is necessary to refer, all too briefly, to another controversy, one that has continued to this day, about the use of the atomic bombs against Japan. An entire literature has developed on this question and any extended discussion could consume most of the space I prefer to devote to other matters. Basically, the debate revolved around two questions: why did Truman use the A-bomb and should he have used it? On the grounds of irrelevancy to the purposes of this study, I will put aside two important aspects of this continuing debate: should such an inhumane weapon have been used under any circumstances and was there a racial aspect to dropping it on Japan? Some have argued that there was no military necessity to use atomic bombs, that Japan was at the point of capitulation, that the punishment she had already received together with the entry of Russia into the war against her would have been enough to force her capitulation. The argument continues that the bombs were dropped in an attempt to end the Pacific war before Russia could enter it, as it had pledged to do about three months after the end of the war in Europe, and to warn the Russians they had better behave. There is evidence for this argument, but at the same time it is difficult to dismiss the assertion that Truman and his advisers were genuinely convinced that the atomic bomb would save thousands of American lives by making the invasion of Japan unnecessary. My own conclusion is that Truman had two goals in mind: ending the war quickly and warning the Russians that the United States possessed, and would use if necessary, a weapon more terrible than had ever existed.

Almost immediately the Truman administration began formulating an atomic-weapons policy, and the task was turned over to Henry L. Stimson, the seventy-eight-year-old Republican secretary of war, who within weeks would be ending a lifetime of service to the nation with the preparation of a memorandum that is one of the most important documents in the history of the United States. That is the kind of sweeping statement which any student of history should be suspicious of, but since Truman's decision not to share atomic information with Russia was a pivotal one, as important as, perhaps even more important than, the decision to establish the Truman Doctrine, such a characterization is not exaggerated. But the reader can judge for himself.

Actually, there were two memoranda, a short covering one and a longer one setting forth his proposals. He submitted them to President Truman on September 12. This is what Stimson wrote in the covering memorandum:

. . . I am not unmindful of the fact that when in Potsdam I talked with you about the question whether we could be safe in sharing the atomic bomb with Russia while she was still a police state and before she put into effect provisions assuring personal rights of liberty to the individual citizen.

I still recognize the difficulty and am still convinced of the ultimate importance of a change in Russian attitude toward individual liberty, but I have come to the conclusion that it would not be possible to use our possession of the atomic bomb as a direct lever to produce the change. I have become convinced that any demand by us for an internal change in Russia as a condition of sharing in the atomic weapon would be so resented that it would make the objective we have in view less probable.

I believe that the change in attitude towards the individual in Russia will come slowly and gradually and I am satisfied that we should not delay our approach to Russia in the matter of the atomic bomb until that process has been completed. . . .[25]

. . . In many quarters [the atomic bomb] has been interpreted as a substantial offset to the growth of Russian influence on the continent. We can be certain that the Soviet government has sensed this tendency and the temptation will be strong for the Soviet political and military leaders to acquire this weapon in the shortest possible time. Britain in effect already has the status of partner with us in the development of this weapon. Accordingly, unless the Soviets are voluntarily invited into the partnership upon a basis of cooperation and trust, we are going to maintain the Anglo-Saxon bloc over against the Soviet in the possession of this weapon. Such a condition will almost certainly stimulate feverish activity on the part of the Soviet toward the development of this bomb in what will in effect be a secret armament race of a rather desperate character. There is evidence to indicate that such activity may have already commenced. . . .

Whether Russia gets control of the necessary secrets of production in a minimum of say four years or a maximum of twenty years is not nearly as important to the world and civilization as to make sure that when they do get it they are willing and cooperative partners among the peace-loving nations of the world. It is true that if we approach them now, as I would propose, we may be gambling on their good faith and risk their getting into production of bombs a little sooner than they would otherwise.

To put the matter concisely, I consider the problem of our satisfactory relations with Russia as not merely connected with but as virtually dominated by the problem of the atomic bomb. Except for the problem of the control of that bomb, those relations, while vitally important, might not be immediately pressing. The establishment of relations of mutual confidence between her and us could afford to await the slow progress of time. But with the discovery of the bomb, they became immediately emergent. Those relations may be perhaps irretrievably embittered by the way in which we approach the solution of the bomb with Russia. For if we fail to approach them now and merely continue to negotiate with them, having this weapon rather ostentatiously on our hip, their suspicions and their distrust of our purposes and motives will increase. It will inspire them to greater efforts in an all-out effort to solve the problem. If the solution is achieved in that spirit, it is much less likely that we will ever get the kind of covenant we may desperately need in the future. This risk is, I believe, greater than the other, inasmuch as our objective must be to get the best kind of international bargain we can—one that has some chance of being kept and saving civilization not for five or for twenty years, but forever.

The chief lesson I have learned in a long life is that the only way you can make a man trustworthy is to trust him; and the surest way to make him untrustworthy is to distrust him and show your distrust. . . .

Since the crux of the problem is Russia, any contemplated action leading to the control of this weapon should be primarily directed to Russia. It is my judgment that the Soviet would be more apt to respond sincerely to a direct and forthright approach made by the United States on this subject than would be the case if the approach were made as a part of a general international scheme, or if the approach were made after a succession of express or implied threats or near threats in our peace negotiations. . . .[26]

The matter came before the Cabinet on September 21. Stimson opened this crucial Cabinet meeting, the last he was to attend, with a comprehensive statement in which he said "all of the scientists with whom the War Department worked were convinced that there was no possible way of holding the scientific secret of the atomic bomb and that, therefore, they felt there should be a free interchange of scientific information between different members of the United Nations." Later Stimson said that he "recognized that any interchange of scientific information with the other United Nations would bring into the foreground the problem of Russia. He then entered into a long defense of Russia, saying that throughout our history Russia had been our friend—that we have nothing that Russia wanted and that Russia had nothing that we wanted. He said our relationship with Russia during recent months had been improving. President Truman agreed to this."[27]

Others at the Cabinet meeting went one way or the other or took no definite stand, but Wallace came out entirely for Stimson (as did Dean Acheson and, representing Harold Ickes, Abe Fortas). He elicited from President Truman the clarification that what was being discussed was not factory technique or "know-how" for the manufacture of atomic weapons but solely the basic scientific information involved. This distinction is important because somehow the Cabinet discussion was leaked, and the press reported that Wallace favored giving atomic bombs to Russia. At first Wallace believed that Mathew J. Connelly, Truman's appointments secretary, had done the leaking, but some years later it became apparent that James Forrestal, secretary of the navy, a bitter opponent of sharing atomic information with the Russians, was the source.

Wallace was probably the only one at the meeting with any substantial scientific knowledge. Not only had he gained world renown as a plant geneticist but he had long had an avid interest in science generally. Wallace warned that there was no way to keep the atomic information secret for very long. He expanded on his views three days later in response to a request by the President that each Cabinet member comment, in writing, to Stimson's proposals. In this letter Wallace not only reflected his own views but conveyed those of such eminent atomic scientists as Leo Szilard and Nobel laureates Enrico Fermi and James Franck. Szilard and Fermi, of course, were two of the scientists most instrumental in getting Roosevelt to begin the atomic program. Wallace had hurried to Chicago after the Cabinet meeting to consult the scientists:

. . . At the present time . . . there are no substantial scientific secrets that would serve as obstacles to the production of atomic bombs by other nations. Of this I am assured by the most competent scientists who know the facts. . . .

With respect to future scientific developments I am confident that both the United States and the world will gain by the free interchange of scientific information. In fact, there is danger that in attempting to maintain secrecy about these scientific developments we will, in the long run, as a prominent scientist recently put it, be indulging "in the erroneous hope of being safe behind a scientific Maginot Line."

The nature of science and the present state of knowledge in other countries are such that there is no possible way of preventing other nations from repeating what we have done or surpassing it within five or six years. If the United States, England, and Canada act the part of the dog in the manger on this matter, the other nations will come to hate and fear all Anglo-Saxons without our having gained anything thereby. The world will be divided into two camps with the non-Anglo-Saxon world eventually superior in population, resources, and scientific knowledge.

We have no reason to fear loss of our present leadership through the free interchange of scientific information. On the other hand, we have every reason to avoid a shortsighted and unsound attitude which will invoke the hostility of the rest of the world.

In my opinion, the quicker we share our scientific knowledge (not industrial and engineering information) the greater will be the chance that we can achieve genuine and durable world cooperation. Such action would be interpreted as a generous gesture on

our part and lay the foundation for sound international agreements
that would assure the control and development of atomic energy
for peaceful use rather than destruction. . . .

I should like to stress that the present situation is a dangerous
one and calls for early action.

The danger will increase and our position and that of international security will further deteriorate if we continue to follow our
present course of maintaining useless secrecy and at the same time
building up a stockpile of atomic bombs.[28]

On October 11 Wallace testified on science legislation before three Senate subcommittees, one of the Military Affairs
Committee and two of the Commerce Committee. In all
three he "unqualifiedly" endorsed federal support for scientific research, and added:

it is absolutely essential that Government support of such activity
impose no restraints on the freedom of the individual investigator
to pursue the truth where it may lead him and throw no cloak of
secrecy over him that would prevent the free and reciprocal interchange of scientific information (not industrial know-how of
military value) on a sound international basis. . . . [Also,] Unless
we take the lead in working with other nations to restore the international exchange of information which has always characterized
scientific endeavor, we shall be encouraging a policy of secrecy
and the concentration of research energy on the destructive aspects
of science.[29]

Wallace continued to meet with atomic scientists and at
one such meeting, on October 17, J. Robert Oppenheimer
told him that he very much wanted to see him.[30] Oppenheimer was the director of laboratory at Los Alamos,
New Mexico, where the atomic bomb had been perfected. It
was Oppenheimer, who was later, in one of the most ap-
palling instances of injustice of the McCarthyite period,
termed a security risk, hounded in public, and deprived of
his security clearances.[31] They arranged to meet at 8:00 a.m.
two days later and talk while Wallace walked to work.

. . . Oppenheimer told me that last spring before the first atomic exhibition took place, the scientists were enormously concerned about a possible eventual war with Russia. . . '. He says Stimson had a most statesmanlike view of the whole matter and that the last thing he did before departing as Secretary of War was to write down this view. In this statement he fully considers the peril of the threat of the bomb to Russian-American relations. Apparently Stimson advocated turning over to Russia as well as to other nations the industrial know-how as well as the scientific information. I told Oppenheimer that this phase of the matter never appeared in Cabinet meeting.[32]

From this it appears clear that Truman had not distributed to his Cabinet members, at least not to Wallace, the Stimson memos, and that Stimson in his Cabinet presentation had not gone as far as he had in the memos. How much significance should be read into that is hard to say. But Wallace's written comment to Truman had been based solely on the oral presentation. Although the Stimson memo is not explicit in suggesting turning over technological as well as scientific information, it certainly can be read that way. In any case, Stimson recommended a direct approach to Russia that involved more than merely a scientific exchange.

To get back to the Oppenheimer conversation, Wallace's diary entry goes on to say:

I never saw a man in such an extremely nervous state as Oppenheimer. He seemed to feel that the destruction of the entire human race was imminent. . . . He has been in charge of the scientists in New Mexico and says that the heart has completely gone out of them there; that all they think about now are the social and economic implications of the bomb, and that they are no longer doing anything worthwhile on the scientific level. He wanted to know if I thought it would do any good for him to see the President. I said yes. . . . He says that . . . Secretary [James F.] Byrnes has felt that we could use the bomb as a pistol to get what we wanted in international diplomacy. Oppenheimer believes that

that method will not work. He says the Russians are a proud people and have good physicists and abundant resources. They may have to lower their standard of living to do it but they will put everything they have got into getting plenty of atomic bombs as soon as possible. He thinks the mishandling of the situation at Potsdam has prepared the way for the eventual slaughter of tens of millions or perhaps hundreds of millions of innocent people.

The guilt consciousness of the atomic bomb scientists is one of the most astounding things I have ever seen.

It was about this time that the Truman administration was deciding to reject Stimson's bold advice. Related to that crucial decision was another: to ask Congress for universal military training. Wallace along with other Cabinet members attended the joint session of Congress, where Truman made this request, and noted later, "As I listened to the President . . . I couldn't help thinking about the effect the message would have on Russia. It was almost like the prelude to the declaration of World War III. . . . Somehow it frightened me."

After the President's address, Truman and Wallace and some others were invited by Leslie L. Biffle, secretary of the Senate, to have lunch in his dining room. Wallace records that "Jimmie Byrnes and [Michigan Senator Arthur H.] Vandenberg were talking about the Polish question. Vandenberg was very savage against the Russians. . . ."[33] Vandenberg was the Republican leader on foreign policy and had enormous influence on the establishment of Truman's bipartisan "containment" policy against Russia.

In mid-November Truman met in Washington with Prime Minister Clement Attlee of Britain and Prime Minister Mackenzie King of Canada, and they agreed on a declaration concerning the peacetime application of atomic energy. The declaration became in essence the Baruch Plan that was submitted to the United Nations and rejected by Russia in mid-1946. Truman had decided to do exactly what Stimson had advised against, for in his memo Stimson had said, "I emphasize perhaps beyond all other considerations the importance of taking this action with Russia as a proposal of the United States—backed by Great Britain—but peculiarly the proposal of the United States. Action of any international group of nations, including many small nations who have not demonstrated their potential power or responsibility in this war would not, in my opinion, be taken seriously by the Soviets."[34]

On November 16, the day after the declaration was announced, Truman indicated during a Cabinet meeting, according to Wallace's diary, that he thought he, Attlee, and King had done a pretty good job. Wallace was not quite so enthusiastic, and immediately raised the objection Stimson had raised in advance: " . . . I noted that the international commission was to be set up under the United Nations Organization to prepare recommendations for submission to the Organization. I said I assumed this meant that this action was to be taken by the Assembly of the United Nations and this meant that the small nations would be in on it in a big way. I said no doubt this problem had been fully considered but it seemed to me that the small nations, as they considered the commission and its recommendations, would conceivably create considerable confusion."

What Wallace did not note here was that the Assembly was completely dominated by the United States, its Allies, and its Latin American client states, and that in the Assembly the greatly outvoted Soviet Union would have no veto. Wallace went on to consider a sentence of Section 8 that said, "The work of the commission should proceed by separate stages, the successful completion of each one of which would develop the necessary confidence of the world before the next stage was undertaken."

. . . I said this sentence suggested that Russia would have to pass the first grade in moral aptitude before she would be allowed to enter the second grade in moral aptitude. I said I thought there was a fifty-fifty chance that Russia might accept. The President

said that this step-by-step procedure is one which we have found
is best in dealing with the Russians. I did not say so in Cabinet
meeting but I suspect the Russian agreement to come along will
depend on just how far along her scientists are. If they have made
a really great advance they may not care to accept England, the
United States, and Canada as their teachers in international moral-
ity.[35]

It was not surprising that the Soviet Union rejected the
American approach. Their reasons have been concisely
summarized by the historian William G. Carleton:

. . . Under the Baruch Plan, the United States would retain its
stockpiles during the whole period of transition while other countries would be bound by international agreement to do nothing to
secure atomic secrets for themselves. Agents of the Atomic Authority would inspect Soviet territory, and the Soviet Union was
extremely skittish about international inspection on its territory. If
accused of violations, the Soviet Union, shorn of the veto, would
be tried before an international body in which it would be in a
distinct minority. Because of its minority position and its Communist system, the Soviet Union feared it might not be awarded its
share of atomic plants, or might not be able to buy from the Authority its share of denatured fissionable materials; and thus the
Soviet Union would be fatally handicapped in the development of
economic production. If atomic energy became vital in industrial
production, the Soviet Union might be staking its whole economic
future on the decisions of an international body dominated by
unfriendly nations. The very peculiarity of its system impelled the
Soviet Union to reject the plan, which was about as fair and fool-
proof as could be devised under the circumstances.[36]

Russia did what the United States would have done
under the same conditions. It was not about to leave decisions crucially affecting its national security to an international organization completely dominated by an unfriendly
nation. In response, the Soviet Union called for the immediate destruction and outlawing of atomic weapons. It wanted
atomic control to be placed under the Security Council,

where it had a veto. And Russia pushed for general disarmament that would include both conventional and nuclear weapons.

The United States, however, insisted then, as it continued to do, upon effective inspection within the Soviet Union. It also insisted that general disarmament must be preceded by a general settlement of the difficult postwar political issues. Thus, the old chicken-and-egg question: Is disarmament possible before a political solution or is a political solution possible without disarmament? Perhaps such a conundrum is not beyond the ingenuity of man to solve but the United States and the Soviet Union have yet to solve it. Perhaps they have never really tried.

The situation at the end of the war was hardly exotic. The nation with a uniquely powerful weapon did not want to surrender that advantage without getting something substantial for it. The nation without the weapon did not want to negotiate with that weapon held over its head. Stalemate. It could be broken only by a bold action by one side or the other. There were risks on either side, but it is possible that the United States suffered the greater failure of nerve—as it did later in 1963, when it was to settle for only a partial not a total outlawing of nuclear testing. For Russia, the risk included being at the mercy of a nation whose friendship was far from certain. But if the United States had destroyed its stock of atomic weapons, it would still have been incontestably stronger, because Russia was just beginning to rebuild from the terrible devastation of the war, while the United States, relatively untouched, was much stronger at the end of the conflict than it had been at the beginning. Furthermore, even though many American political leaders refused to believe it, American scientists said that the Soviet Union would, if there were no agreement, be able to develop the atomic bomb itself within a few years. That the American scientists were correct in this prediction was borne out by the fact that it took Russia only four years to develop its own bomb and begin a nuclear race that continues to this day. Thus, the Truman administration held on to a short-term advantage at the cost of causing a bitter and long-lasting animosity.

Maybe it was not a failure of nerve. Perhaps the Truman administration made the calculated decision to carry "this weapon rather ostentatiously on our hip" in order to get whatever political concessions it could for as long as the United States was thus uniquely armed. One cannot say with confidence what would have happened if Truman had chosen to follow Stimson's course, but history records what did happen because he failed to. Russia simply refused to be bluffed by the bomb. As far as one can tell without access to Moscow's thinking, Russia went ahead as if the bomb did not exist.

It is not groundless speculation to conjecture that things might have been very different. The international tensions that eventually led the United States to Korea and Indochina might never have developed to that tragic extent. The nuclear testing that polluted the atmosphere for a decade and a half might have been avoided. And billions upon billions wasted by both countries could have been used in ways that could have enriched both nations and the world. There is no way to overstate the magnitude of the opportunity that was missed. Maybe things would not have turned out much differently, even if Truman had been more conciliatory; but he should have taken the chance. Surely, things could not have turned out worse than they did.

The improved relations Stimson had mentioned in his last Cabinet meeting were adversely affected by Truman's decision not to take Stimson's advice about the bomb. But Wallace was still hoping for an improvement, for in his private meetings with Truman the President seemed to agree with him. This is from the diary of October 15: ". . . He [Truman] said Stalin was a fine man who wanted to do the right thing. I said that apparently the purpose of Britain was to promote an unbreachable break between us and Russia. The President said he agreed. I said Britain's game in international affairs has always been intrigue. The President said he agreed. I say Britain may have plenty of excuses for playing the game the way she does; it may fit into her geographical position, but we must not play her game. The President said he agreed. . . . He returned to the fact that Stalin is an honest man who is easy to get along with— who arrives at sound decisions. . . ."[37]

Later that day Wallace had a conversation with Marquis Childs, the syndicated liberal columnist: "He asked what my relations were with the President and I said they had been most friendly; that the President had cooperated with me in everything I had wanted. Childs rejoined, 'Well, that is one of the difficulties with the President; he does that way with everyone . . .' "

It was difficult for Wallace to determine whether Truman genuinely agreed with him or whether he agreed with whomever he happened to be speaking to at the time or whether he was using Roosevelt's slippery technique of allowing visitors to believe he agreed with them even if he did not.

The same thing happened when Wallace spoke to the President on October 26:

. . . I pointed out at some little length the dangers of playing a one-sided game on the side of the British; and that it was advisable to make the Russians a loan proportionate to their needs comparable to the loan made to the British.

I pointed out that the Russian attitude in the Balkan States was not so greatly different from our attitude with regard to Mexico and Cuba. . . .

I said that Russia, with her more or less illiterate neighbors, untrained in democratic processes, would inevitably take, in terms of her situation, steps somewhat corresponding to those which we have always taken with regard to our more or less illiterate neighbors with poorly established democratic processes. Truman replied that, yes, Russia was always talking about a cordon sanitaire. He talked as though he completely agreed with me and as though the thing he most wanted in the world was an understanding with Russia which would make impossible a third world war. . . .[38]

Yet while Truman was talking like that to Wallace, his administration had already decided not to give Russia the $6 billion reconstruction loan she had asked for, and, rather then tell Russia that, Washington simply did not say anything.[39] Since V. M. Molotov had told Ambassador Harriman how important his government regarded such a loan, its refusal, for that is what the lack of a response amounted to, was bound to aggravate relations.

This loan was among a number of things discussed by A. B. Gromov, first secretary of the Soviet embassy, at a luncheon with Wallace and Edwin S. Smith, director of the National Council of American-Soviet Friendship.

. . . Gromov did most of the talking. It was obvious from what Gromov said that the Russians are deeply hurt by the various actions of the United States relative to the atomic bomb, Great Britain, Argentina, and Eastern Europe. He can't understand why we are getting ready to loan so much money to Great Britain and are not prepared to loan much to Russia. He was very critical of Jimmie Byrnes. I told him Jimmie Byrnes had defended Russia against Senator Vandenberg and he found that hard to believe. He wanted to known why Jimmie Byrnes played England's game so exclusively. I told him it was traditional for Southerners to be friendly to England because England had been friendly to the South at the time of the Civil War. He was very critical of our letting Argentina into the San Francisco Conference. He cannot understand why we let Argentina get away with all kinds of anti-democratic programs while at the same time we insist on democracy in the Balkan States. . . .[40]

In November 1945 the situation in China came up before the Cabinet from time to time. The discussions gave Wallace the impression that Truman and Byrnes were not very well informed.[41] On November 27 Wallace was at a Cabinet luncheon when Truman walked in with a roll of yellow tele-type paper in his hand, saying, "See what a son-of-a-bitch did to me." The President then read the story of how Patrick J. Hurley, his representative in Chungking to the Chiang Kai-shek government, had just resigned and, at the National Press Club, had accused the administration, the State Department and its Foreign Service officers of having no China policy and of being soft on the Chinese Commu-nists. This was the first in a rising crescendo of attacks on loyal, intelligent Foreign Service officers who outraged American supporters of Chiang by their accurate, hard-hit-ting reports about the corrupt and incompetent Nationalist government. Over a period of time a number of these Foreign Service officers, among the best in the State Depart-ment, were harassed out of government service, some of them alleged to be, on the basis of no evidence whatsoever, security risks. Not only were these fine and capable men subjected to the rankest injustice but the nation gave up their service when it could least afford the loss. One of the reasons that the United States later plunged into the morass of Asia was that these skilled observers had been driven out of government service by anti-Communist hysteria, and most of those remaining were afraid to report anything that might not conform to the reigning anti-Communist dogma, fearing that they would then be open to charges of disloy-alty, to disgrace, or to being fired with little hope of em-ployment elsewhere.

After discussing the Hurley statement, which Wallace thought "a marvel of political demagoguery," the President turned to the situation in China, saying "that both England and Russia wanted a weak and divided China. He said we were the only big nation that wanted a united democratic China [by which he meant united under Chiang Kai-shek]. The President said that unless we took a strong stand in China, Russia would take the place of Japan in the Far East. I thought to myself, This (the President's attitude) means World War Number III. . . . The various statements seemed to be as utterly contradictory as Hurley's own actions of the past month." Wallace also records that "the President and Jimmie Byrnes were getting ready to get hold of Marshall to talk him into going out to China. It was also suggested that he stop off in Moscow on the way. Marshall is very strongly anti-Russian, and if he takes the job, this may produce a rather unusual situation."[42]

The next day, November 28, Wallace spent a few minutes with the President. According to his diary, Wallace warned Truman not to let the United States take sides in the ancient British-Russian rivalry, "but that at the present time it appeared we were playing the British game and a fascistic game. I told him that the British actions in Greece had been pretty bad." Wallace also told Truman that he did not think that Jimmie [Byrnes] "really understood just what was going on. He said he agreed with me entirely; that he didn't realize I had watched the situation so closely as to catch what he was up against. He said the grand thing about the Hurley resignation was that it was going to give him a chance to get into the State Department to straighten it out."[43].

What is one to make of Truman's appearing to agree with Wallace? Perhaps some light is shed on this by the observations of two astute, well-informed government officials that Wallace spoke to later that day. After a luncheon Wallace gave a lift to Harry Dexter White, assistant secretary of the treasury, who said he had to see him:

. . . The point he wanted to make was that everybody recognized that the administration was very rapidly going to pieces on both the domestic and the foreign front. He thought I ought to come out in the very near future and make a very forthright speech in order to dissociate myself as nearly as possible from the impending wreck. . . . I told White that the situation was so critical now that I thought I should do what I could to help the President and that I found the President had expressed himself as willing to be helped. White broke out rather impatiently, saying, "Yes, that is the trouble, the President always uses good words but never does anything, or if he does act he acts weakly or on the wrong side."

White was also worried about sending Marshall to China, noting that not only was he anti-Russian but that the Russians knew he was. Later Wallace met with one of the State Department's top experts on China, John Carter Vincent, who brought him up to date on the situation there. "As nearly as I can discover, he is absolutely sound in his views. . . . He welcomes the Marshall appointment but is deeply concerned about the underlying trend both in the direction of helping British imperialism and with regard to the State Department itself. I cheered him up by saying that I thought the President was definitely susceptible of education. He made the same point as Harry White to the effect that the President oftentimes seems to use the right words but not to do anything effective."[44]

It is important to note that both Harry Dexter White and John Carter Vincent, like Wallace himself, were later accused of being pro-Communist. Even though such accusations were still some time off, the atmosphere that produced them was beginning to take shape. On the day that Wallace swore in Dr. Edward Condon, the distinguished scientist, as director of the Bureau of National Standards, he learned from Senator Brien McMahon, the Connecticut Democrat who was pre-eminent in atomic-energy matters, that "the FBI and the War Department claimed Condon was a 'pink.' I told McMahon that if Condon was a 'pink' then he, McMahon, was a 'pink' and so was I. I might also have said, although I didn't, that if Condon is a 'pink' the FBI and certain segments of the Army are Nazis."[45] To depart from the consensus, to dissent was already risky business.

Before leaving the discussion of China, we must take note of an observation by Henry Wallace: "The dangerous thing . . . is the suggestion that Truman is going the whole way with the Generalissimo [Chiang Kai-shek]. This means unless the Generalissimo shows a more enlightened attitude than he did to me in June of 1944, there will sooner or later be revolution in China and the United States will lose influence there and Russia will gain."[46]

More than fifteen years before President Eisenhower in his farewell statement warned the nation about the "military-industrial complex," Wallace and Harold Ickes were concerned about such a combination.

I exchanged telephone views with Harold Ickes and we both have the idea that a certain small group of scientists which works pretty closely with a certain small group of industrialists, who in turn work very closely with the War Department, are trying to control the atomic energy thing in their own way. [Boris] Pregel [a friend and sometimes adviser was an expert on radiation who loaned Columbia University the uranium for the first experiments in the development of atomic energy] says the only way the atomic energy thing can be made safe for the world is to develop the peacetime potentialities as rapidly as possible. After noting the way in which the Army has spread rumors about Pregel, Szilard, and Condon, I am inclined to think [it] will knife anybody who, directly or indirectly, fights the legislation which they are pushing. The war psychology has gotten into their blood and the ends justify the means. I am expecting them to circulate the most absurd stories.[47]

On November 9 Wallace wrote an important letter to Truman advocating that the Atomic Energy Commission, the establishment of which was before Congress, be democratized and demilitarized. He recommended that there be *"much more* emphasis" (his italics) on atomic energy for peaceful purposes than for national defense. And, he said, "it would be much more in keeping with American democratic principles and traditions to provide that neither the administrator nor the deputy be an active member of the armed forces." Wallace also warned that "the continuation of wartime security regulations, such as those imposed in the development of the atomic bomb, into peacetime re-

search activities would greatly retard scientific progress and
would probably drive many of our most talented scientists
into other fields."[48] But as the AEC developed during the
Truman years and later, it became a part of the Cold War
apparatus and virtually indistinguishable from the Defense
Department.

In December Wallace told the President he was "seriously
disturbed" by the fact that the atomic bombs and material
for their construction were under the control of General
Leslie Groves and urged that these things be put under the
control of a man appointed by Truman. Groves tended to
run the atomic-bomb program the way J. Edgar Hoover ran
the FBI, as if he did not have to answer to higher authority.

. . . I told him General Groves was a Roosevelt hater and a Mrs.
Roosevelt scorner. (Condon had told me that Groves in 1943 at Los
Alamos had called Roosevelt a son-of-a-bitch and had told two off-
color stories about Mrs. Roosevelt.) I told the President that Groves
felt that Roosevelt had made some blunders with regard to the international handling of atomic energy and that he, General Groves,
would straighten the matter out on his own. . . .

I told the President the point I was making was merely that there
was always a certain group in the Army who had their own ideas
as to what constituted national security and that if the situation either on the national or the international front got bad you couldn't
tell what they would do, especially if they had something like the
atomic bombs at their disposal. . . .[49]

Wallace returned to this concern the next day, December
14, at a Cabinet meeting when a question about the number
of atomic bombs came up. Secretary of War Patterson said
he did not want to know how many atomic bombs there
were.

. . . The President at this moment chimed in to say that he
didn't really want to know. I promptly intervened to say with the
greatest earnestness, "Mr. President, you *should* [his emphasis]
know; also the Secretary of War should know, and the Secretary of

the Navy." I . . . returned to the original theme and hammered with all the energy I could to the effect that the President himself must have this information. The President retreated in some confusion and said he guessed he should know and then covered up by saying, "I do know in a general way." Jim Forrestal agreed with me, saying that while he, himself, did not want the information he felt definitely the President should have it; that it was a necessary protection for him in case any investigation ever were made. I thought it was utterly incredible that Patterson and the President should be willing to trust full information and responsibility on this to a man like Groves and his underlings without knowing what was going on themselves.[50]

It was also incredible that the President and the secretaries of war and navy professed not to want to know how many atomic bombs there were. Incredible, and totally contrary to the American principle that the military should be subordinate to civilian authorities. And dangerous, for Groves was an arrogant, high-handed man, who, beyond that, challenged the loyalty of those who disagreed with him and later caused the most extreme difficulties for some of the scientists, including Dr. Oppenheimer, who had worked in the Manhattan Project under Groves.

That may have been the trouble with Harry Truman, if Wallace's analysis is correct, that he was surrounded by Cold Warriors. Wallace's diary for December 11, 1945, has these words: "It is more and more evident that the President arrives at his decisions on the spur of the moment on the basis of partial evidence. He does *so* like to agree with whoever is with him at the moment [his italics]."[51] And in the field of foreign affairs, those most often with him were what a later age would term hawks: Byrnes, Acheson, Patterson, Forrestal, Harriman, *et al.* Wallace, of course, was not a hawk but the Commerce Department had only a limited role in foreign affairs; and neither was Ickes, but the Interior Department had virtually no role in foreign affairs. Some critics of America's Cold War policies have, as noted earlier, written of the administration's desire for an American *imperium* for economic reasons, as a function of American capitalism. While this was certainly a factor, my own view is that the explanation must be sought more in the national psyche than on Wall Street, a latter-day Manifest Destiny somehow mixed in with a fateful confusion of Stalin with Hitler. These men around Truman saw Munichs everywhere. They recognized that Russia was not a military threat and would not be for some time to come, but they wanted to put Russia in its place now, for once and for all, to end the threat before it began.

These last weeks in 1945 and the first weeks of 1946 were when Truman set the course that successive administrations followed for more than two decades. Pivotal was the now-famous Truman memorandum of January 5, 1946. Even Byrnes was not tough enough for Truman, who scolded Byrnes for conceding too much to Russia at the recently ended Moscow conference and for proceeding too independently. [Allied foreign ministers had met to discuss the entire range of postwar problems. A number of times Stalin met personally with Byrnes and other foreign ministers.] Then he told Byrnes that the United States must confront Russia not only in Iran and Turkey but in Rumania and Bulgaria, and all along the Danube. ". . . we should maintain complete control of Japan and the Pacific. We should rehabilitate China and create a strong central government there. We should do the same for Korea. . . .

"Then we should insist on the return of our ships from Russia and force a settlement of the Lend-Lease debt of Russia."

Earlier in the memo Truman used such language as this: "Unless Russia is faced with an iron fist and strong language another war is in the making." And he ended with these words: "I'm tired of babying the Soviets."[52]

Wallace knew the direction U.S. policy was taking but he did not give up trying to change it. Late in December President Truman had asked his Cabinet members to make suggestions for his January State of the Union address. One can be sure that Truman wanted Wallace to suggest topics and language dealing with matters within the jurisdiction of the Commerce Department. Nonetheless, Wallace in his response suggested language dealing with world affairs, such as this passage.

Harmonious relations must of necessity be maintained among the three nations most particularly responsible for stability during the transition—the Union of Socialist Soviet Republics, the British Commonwealth, and the United States of America. Each of these itself is proof that unity and harmony are possible among diverse social groups and political entities. Workable relations must and will be constructed or maintained among these great world powers as the essential basis for stability among all peoples of the earth. Differences of language, tradition, political institutions, and social customs tend perhaps to make this task more difficult as between the Russians and ourselves; but, on the other hand, similarities of social objectives and the complete absence of direct conflicts in national interest make it easier. The Russians and the Americans deeply desire to maintain good mutual relations and these two peoples have the will and the wit to do just this.[53]

You will not notice any such language in Truman's subsequent address. But what you will notice in this passage is a lack of anything specifically favorable about Great Britain. There is no doubt that Wallace had deep suspicions about the British. Perhaps he was an instinctive anticolonialist. Perhaps it was his upbringing in the Middle West, where there was a long tradition of anti-British feeling. Or perhaps it was his observations of Britain's postwar behavior. There are many references in his diary to what he considers poor behavior by the British.

Then on December 29 Wallace recorded an extraordinary perception about the people who were trying to foment war with the Soviet Union:

. . . I began to speculate about the forces that are interested in trying to bring about such a war. In addition to a small group in the

Catholic hierarchy there is also a small group among the English Tories and a small group in the American Army . . . a small group among the American big-business hierarchy, a substantial group among the Chinese Nationalists, the London Poles, and in general the more wealthy people who live in the countries close to Russia. Also there is a small group in the Navy (note for example Admiral [Harold S.] Stark's statement in the Pearl Harbor hearings with regard to communism being a greater danger than Naziism); also there should be included in this group a very strong element in the Republican Party. All of these people feel that it is only by the United States whipping Russia that they have a chance to maintain their present position. Against this group is found the peace-loving people everywhere. Unfortunately, the love of peace is a general sentiment and doesn't bind people together in the same way as hatred binds together those who are intent on producing war between specific countries. The bulk of the Catholics, the bulk of the British, and the bulk of the common people everywhere do not want a third world war. These various groups that want a third world war in order to lick Russia are not at the present time working together but as time goes on they will tend more and more to coalesce. This is the great danger of the future.[54]

Wallace was, of course, invited to the best dinner parties in Washington, and there he regularly encountered others in the top echelons of government, those who knew what was going on and those who made it go on. At almost all of these dinner parties, most of the guests, although not all, were for taking a hard line with the Soviet Union. One of the most famous hosts in Washington—then and for decades later—was the columnist Joseph Alsop. He and Wallace seemed to like each other, although their foreign-policy views were worlds apart. At one Alsop dinner a tough policy was being advocated by the columnist and one of his guests, William Gaud, recently appointed executive assistant to Secretary of War Patterson. These parties were evidently a bit racier than one thinks of Washington parties, for at one point, according to Wallace's diary for January 2, 1946, Gaud said the United States ought to "kick the Russians in the balls," and when Ben Cohen seemed to be agreeing with Wallace and Supreme Court Justice Hugo Black that a more conciliatory line might be taken, Alsop called the idea "a barrel of horse-shit." More important, though, was Alsop's view on how the armed forces viewed the need to "encircle" Russia:

. . . Alsop, apparently getting his information from Gaud, says that the Army is insisting on complete encirclement of Russia, with air bases in Iceland, Greenland, the Aleutians, and Okinawa. The Navy is standing for much the same thing. Alsop says frankly that if he were Russia, seeing this going on, he would declare war on the United States at once. Joe says that the United States free-enterprise system is no good to meet the competition it will have to meet in the future; that we will have to have a more centralized form of government. In other words, Joe believes in totalitarianism for the United States to meet the totalitarianism of Russia. He is, to use his own words, "disturbed as hell."[55]

While Wallace was sticking to Washington, liberals around the country, distressed at the direction the Truman administration was taking both in domestic and foreign affairs, were beginning to establish various organizations. We've already mentioned the National Citizens Political Action Committee (NC/PAC) headed by Beanie Baldwin and Elmer Benson, and the Union for Democratic Action (UDA), the predecessor of the Americans for Democratic Action, for which James Loeb, Jr., was the driving force, with the eminent theologian-philosopher Reinhold Niebuhr as the leading light. Another group, one that along with NC/PAC became part of the Progressive Citizens of America and later, the Progressive Party, was the Independent Citizens' Committee of the Arts, Sciences and Professions (ICC/ASP). This extraordinary group enlisted many of the most famous people of the time. Chairman was Jo Davidson, the sculptor whose bust of FDR is familiar from the Roosevelt dime. Treasurer was Fredric March, and on the board of directors were William Rose Benet, Van Wyck Brooks, Louis Calhern,

Marc Connelly, Norman Corwin, Albert Einstein, Moss Hart, Lillian Hellman, Paul Robeson, and the astronomer Harlow Shapley. Among the initiating sponsors were Franklin P. Adams, Mary McLeod Bethune, James Cagney, Eddie Cantor, Aaron Copland, Russel Crouse, Bette Davis, Agnes De Mille, Olin Downes, Howard Fast, Edna Ferber, Ben Grauer, Oscar Hammerstein, Miriam Hopkins, Langston Hughes, Fritz Mahler, Thomas Mann, Yehudi Menuhin, Fritz Reiner, Edward G. Robinson, Artur Schnabel, M. Lincoln Schuster, Mark Van Doren, Max Weber, Orson Welles, and William Zorach.[56] And that is only a brief sampling. Many of them became members of the Progressive Party and stuck with Wallace to the end. Others dropped out because of genuine differences of opinion, and still others were frightened off by the Red-baiting.

In 1946 NC/PAC and ICC/ASP sponsored a series of fund-raising dinners at which, variously, Henry Wallace and other prominent New Dealers were featured speakers. One such meeting, on January 31, 1946, drew more than a thousand persons to the Hotel Commodore in New York. The principal speaker was Democratic Senator Claude Pepper of Florida, who was, until Wallace left the Cabinet, the leading public critic of American foreign policy. In his speech he attacked the "sinister and reactionary forces" which, he said, were blocking FDR's plans for peace in the postwar world. And he criticized the press for what he termed almost daily attacks on Soviet Russia.[57]

A few days later, on February 9, Stalin delivered a famous speech that marked an escalation of the Cold War. He declared that the forces of capitalism and imperialism that had caused World War II still held sway outside the Soviet Union and that therefore he saw no chance of establishing a peaceful international order. Thus Stalin felt it necessary to call for increased efforts for national defense, even at the expense of consumer goods. This speech greatly alarmed the Truman administration, and illustrates splendidly the series of actions and reactions that characterized the Cold War, with first one side taking an action that alarmed the other, causing the other to react in a way that alarmed the first, setting off still another chain of action-reaction, which set off another, until it became difficult to determine where the unhappy cycle began. But Henry Wallace had his idea of where the cycle began, and he discussed it in his diary of February 12: ". . . I thought [Stalin's speech] was accounted for in some measure by the fact that it was obvious to Stalin that our military was getting ready for war with Russia; that they were setting up bases all the way from Greenland, Iceland, northern Canada, and Alaska to Okinawa, with Russia in mind. . . . Stalin obviously knew what these bases meant and also knew the attitude of many of our people through the press. We were challenging him and his speech was taking up the challenge."[58]

Wallace returned to the subject in his diary for the next day, after he had been speaking with General H. H. "Hap" Arnold of the Army Air Corps.

. . . Arnold also came down strong for the Army being in the transport service in a big way in order to be ready for the next war. I asked him who he was going to fight. He didn't answer this question but later suggested how important it was to have a continuous line flying all the time between Greenland and Alaska. Undoubtedly such a line would be directed specifically against Russia and would be so interpreted. Obviously there is no commercial traffic between Greenland and Alaska. Apparently the Army feels that there are going to be raids from Moscow via the North Pole. I hadn't realized before what a direct threat our air bases at Fairbanks and Greenland are to Russian security. I read over Stalin's speech last night and was impressed at the vigor with which he was taking up the various challenges which we have been making all the way from the President on down.[59]

If Stalin's speech alarmed Washington, Winston Churchill's famous speech at Fulton, Missouri, on March 5, alarmed Russia and those Americans who opposed Truman's hard-line policy toward Moscow. The night of the

Churchill speech, given with Truman sitting on the platform in apparent approval, Mr. and Mrs. Wallace were at Dean Acheson's for dinner. Among the other guests were Richard Casey, Australian minister to the United States and Mrs. Casey, Mr. and Mrs. Charles Bohlen, and Mr. and Mrs. Walter Lippmann. Although the Wallaces did not yet know the content of the speech, the others apparently did. Churchill had not only delivered his Iron Curtain line and termed the Communists "a growing challenge and peril to Christian civilization" but called for a "fraternal association of the English-speaking peoples." Not only Stalin some time later but many British and Americans immediately took that to mean a military alliance aimed at Russia. Churchill also cautioned against making known the secrets of the atomic bomb.

According to Wallace's diary, "Mrs. Acheson spoke in lyrical terms" about the speech while Mr. and Mrs. Casey "became glowing in their comments." After learning the gist of Churchill's speech, Wallace "promptly interjected that the United States was not going to enter a military alliance with England against Russia; . . . I said instead of talking about military alliances it was high time to talk about an effective method of disarmament. I said it would destroy the United Nations to have two of the chief members of the United Nations ganging up against a third member. . . ." After another outburst by Casey, Wallace recorded that "suddenly everyone became very polite and the matter did not come up again until after dinner. . . ."

When it did,

. . . I advocated a program that we have an agreement on disarmament and that the United States and Britain then proceed to show the backward peoples of the world that their system would give them a higher standard of living than the Russian system. I said that what Russia feared was encirclement by the United States and England; that she saw us busily setting up military and naval bases whose only object could be to attack Russia.

Bohlen made fun of this idea and said that it was not the United States which was on the offensive; that it was Russia. I said it was very unfortunate that Churchill had made the kind of speech he was reported to have made, because he was the one who back in 1919 was calling the Bolsheviks such names and doing everything he could to assemble an Allied force to destroy the Bolsheviks. I said I didn't see how these warlike words of Churchill now could have any more real influence on the Russians than his warlike attitude toward the Bolsheviks had in 1919. I said the American people were not willing to send American boys anywhere to fight now; that certainly the Russians did not want to fight anybody now; that in all probability the situation would finally work out on a basis that would cause the Russians completely and utterly to distrust us; that it would cause the Russians to engage in a race with us in the making of atomic bombs; that while they might be a long way behind us at the present time they would have enough bombs to destroy us fifteen years hence; that with the Russians completely distrusting us because of the way we had handled them they would not scruple fifteen years hence to drop bombs on us without warning; that they would have no hesitation in continuing their fifth-column activities in all the nations of the world; that they could use these fifth columnists effectively to destroy our form of government. . . .[60]

A week later Wallace discussed Churchill's speech with Truman. Truman said he had not seen the speech in advance and that Churchill had put him on the spot. However, it was reported in the press then and confirmed later that Truman had gone over the speech before Churchill delivered it. "I said that the peace of the world hinged on the United States and not on a military alliance between Britain and the United States. He agreed." Wallace went on to say that even if Russia were wrong on every stand it was nonetheless the proper policy of the United States to serve as a go-between between Britain and Russia and not as Britain's defender. "Truman declared up and down that the United States was not going to enter into an alliance with England." Then Wallace told the President that "the British Empire was going to have so much trouble that it would very probably be beyond our strength to bolster the empire up, and that therefore we ought to devote our attention to bringing about a just relationship between Britain and Russia in their conflicting spheres of influence." Walter Lippmann agreed and in his first column after the Acheson dinner opposed an Anglo-American alliance that would attempt to preserve the *status quo* in the British Empire.

Wallace then spoke favorably of the new ambassador to Russia, General W. Bedell Smith, who was succeeding Harriman, who had resigned. He suggested that the embassy in Moscow get a new staff that "would be more sympathetic in their dealings with the Russian government."[61]

An incident concerning Bedell Smith demonstrates that Truman was becoming impatient with Wallace's suggestions about foreign policy. No doubt Truman was hearing the dinner-party talk about how Wallace was, in effect, criticizing the administration's foreign policy, and, of course, he heard Wallace's earnest lectures in their private meetings. Wallace now—believing that Smith was "going to be a much better man in Russia than Harriman. He will talk very frankly with the Russians but at the start, at any rate, he won't have that concealed hatred for the Russians which animates Harriman. . . . He is going to make quite a little change in the embassy personnel"[62]—made a proposal for "a new approach" to the Russians. In a letter to Truman on March 15, he said he hoped that General Smith would

succeed in breaking the present diplomatic deadlock in U.S.-Soviet relations. . . .

I am deeply convinced that General Bedell Smith's task would be made easier and his success more lasting if we could also at the same time discuss with the Russians in a friendly way their long-range economic problems and the future of our cooperation in matters of trade. We know that much of the recent Soviet behavior which has caused us concern has been the result of their dire economic needs and of their disturbed sense of security. The events of the past few months have thrown the Soviets back to their pre-1939 fears of "capitalist encirclement" and to their erroneous belief

that the Western world, including the USA, is invariably and
unanimously hostile. . . .

Truman replied with a little note, thanking Wallace for
his letter and saying that "I have seen General Smith and
discussed conditions with him. I believe he is going to Russia with the right attitude in mind. I have great hopes of his
getting our relations on a better plane. He impresses me as
being a capable person."[63]

In the meantime Wallace had met with Smith, which was
entirely normal, since foreign trade was a legitimate concern of the Commerce Department, and showed him the letter to Truman; he then wrote a note to the President saying
that Smith wanted to take a copy with him to Moscow.[64] On
March 21 Wallace sent Truman another note: ". . . On con-
sulting with General Smith this morning I find that you did
not pass on to him the letter which I sent you and which he
thought would be helpful. I wondered if this was an over-
sight or if you felt it would be unwise for him to have this
letter. If you feel it would be unwise for him to have the letter I should like to know it so that I can get over to our Office of International Trade exactly what your attitude is with
respect to promoting the maximum of foreign trade with
Russia. We don't want to get out of line with over-all policy. . . ."[65]

There was a bit of bureaucratic maneuvering here. Truman had told Wallace he would give the letter to Smith.
Smith told Wallace he wanted the letter but told the President he wanted the original if Truman would initial it to indicate his approval. As Truman wrote in his *Memoirs*, "I ignored this letter of Wallace's. I had expressed my policy to
Bedell Smith and had suggested the approach he should
take to the Kremlin. I could see little to be gained from the
Wallace proposal." Truman simply was not interested in expanding Soviet-American trade or trying new approaches.
Nor was he terribly keen on Wallace's devotion to foreign
affairs. "He began to devote much of his energy to the

problems of our relations with Russia and to spend much time away from his duties as Secretary of Commerce."[66]

During these same few days Wallace was concerned with the message Harriman had brought home from Russia. On March 13 Harriman addressed the Business Advisory Council, one of the most influential business groups in the country:

. . . It was a strictly anti-Russian speech. Harriman made it clear that he was in accord with Winston Churchill and that we should be tough with the Russians, even though by so doing we were running the risk of war. He said the communists in every country in the world were simply stooges for Stalin and that they were out to overthrow our form of government. It was mostly old, old stuff of the kind we have heard for the last twenty-five years. . . . The BAC found it very impressive and were in enthusiastic accord with Harriman. They will now go out over the country and spread the word that we are going to get tough with Russia even though it means war. Harriman made the point, however, that he was sure Stalin did not want war, and that he was going to do everything he could to expand territorially without war. Harriman thinks we are in the same position relative to Russia in 1946 that we were relative to Germany in 1933; that the important thing is to stop Russia before she expands any further.

There, again, was the Hitler-Stalin analogy, which seemed to be imbedded in the consciousness, perhaps the subconsciousness, of American policy-makers for two decades and more.

Wallace reported that there was an enthusiastic response to the speech by Paul G. Hoffman, president of Studebaker, a Republican who was later appointed by Truman as the first administrator of the Marshall Plan.[67] Hoffman said the talk ought to be given in every town in the country, that Harriman should go on a speaking tour. Harriman replied that if he said all over the country what he had said there, "all the commies in the CIO would be after him."

There was considerable discussion then on how important it was to fight any organization that had any commies in it. It was obvious to me as I listened to Harriman and those in the discussion afterward, that these businessmen don't have the slightest idea of what is going on in the world or what is going to happen. It was also obvious to me that Harriman in spite of the fact that he has been in Russia for several years, never really found out what the score was. He is a nice fellow whom I like personally but I don't think he understands either Russia or the world situation. He and his kind if they have their way will bring on a war which will result in the United States eventually becoming a dictatorship either to the left or the right.[68]

Wallace's worry about this spreading national concern over communism was reflected again in a diary entry for the day after the Harriman speech. Sidney Hillman had asked him to speak before the American Labor Party convention. The ALP was a left-wing party in New York state, whose membership was growing, while that of both the Democratic and Republican parties was shrinking. But Harold Young, his friend and personal assistant, "was very much disturbed about my speaking . . . because there are a number of commies attached to the American Labor Party. Hillman denies that these commies have any significance. . . . The word 'communist' is used so loosely nowadays that no one can say what the truth is. Anyone who is further left than you are and whom you don't like is a commie. Of course the reverse of it is that anyone who is further to the right than you and whom you don't like is a fascist."[69]

These must have been perplexing days for Wallace. On the one hand, the Truman administration was plainly taking a tougher and tougher line with the Soviet Union. On the other, there was interest within the administration in having Henry Wallace go to Moscow to talk with Stalin. Bedell Smith told him he should "come over to Moscow at the right time because he thinks that I can help ease over some particularly difficult situation. I said I would like very much to do that but I thought it was important for us both to think it over very, very carefully before we made a move in this direction." Then when Wallace mentioned Smith's proposal to Truman the following day and said that he thought they should be cautious about any such trip, the "President said he thought it might be a good idea if I went to Russia. When he said this I backed off a little further from it.

"It seems curious that all of a sudden a great many people, including Jimmie Roosevelt, seem to have reached the conclusion that I could do a lot of good by going to Russia."[70]

Not only was Truman apparently sympathetic toward Wallace's going to Moscow but he approved of a Wallace speech that was a direct and unmistakable reply to the speech Harriman had made a few days before. According to Wallace, "He read every page of it carefully and agreed with it all." Given its substance that was quite remarkable. Wallace spoke on March 19 at a Russian Relief dinner honoring Harriman. He did not mince any words. He told of the American debt for the Russian contribution to victory, spoke of their fear of capitalist encirclement, and termed any thought of war between Russia and the U.S.A. as "monstrous and preposterous." Not content with that, he termed Stalin's speech of the month before as a challenge to "a race in furnishing the needs of the common people without war or business crisis." He then pleaded for mutual understanding by the Russians and Americans and ended up with a criticism of Churchill: "The common people of the world will not tolerate a recrudescence of imperialism even under enlightened Anglo-Saxon atomic bomb auspices. If the English-speaking people have any destiny at all, it is to serve the world not to dominate it."[71]

It is not surprising, therefore, that a few days later when Joseph Alsop came in to see him he was "very much disturbed" about the speech.

. . . He claimed my foreign policy was diametrically opposed to that of the President and Jimmie Byrnes. I said to him that the President had read every sentence of my speech in my presence and had said that it was only common sense. Joe was completely floored and said that Truman was a much smaller man than he had thought; that apparently he doesn't realize that Jimmie Byrnes and I are going in completely opposite directions. He said to me, "I think you are in a completely indefensible position in the Cabinet." I said to him, "So you are going to try to write columns to get me out." He said, "No, Henry, I am your true friend." He said, "I agree completely with you on your domestic policy but I think your foreign attitude is altogether wrong." I replied, "I think yours is altogether wrong and that it leads inevitably to war." He came back with the statement that I and the liberals who were going along with me were acting just exactly like [Neville] Chamberlain and Sir John Simon acted in 1938. I said to him, "So you think that Stalin today is equivalent to Hitler and Russia is equivalent to Germany. . . .

Joe was on the verge of hysterics and I couldn't help feeling sorry for him. He thinks the whole world is going to be ruined because we don't get sufficiently tough with Russia. I think it is going to be ruined because of our trying to put Russia in an impossible position by ganging up with Britain against her. I am sure that Joe and the hard-boiled element in the State Department are wrong and Joe is sure that I and the liberals are wrong.[72]

On April 12, 1946, the first anniversary of Roosevelt's death, a memorial rally was held and it attracted the biggest names of the New Deal. Mrs. Roosevelt was there as was every member of the Cabinet at the time of FDR's death except President Truman and Harold Ickes. Henry Morgenthau, Jr., was the chairman and introduced the featured speaker, Henry Wallace, as "the one who more than anyone else is carrying on the spirit of the late President." Wallace was greeted with loud applause and cries of "Wallace in '48."[73] Wallace was still not interested in making a try for the Presidency and for the next year or so consistently discouraged any talk of that sort. But his old friend and colleague Beanie Baldwin was still convinced that a third party might well be inevitable. The NC/PAC rally for Roosevelt, although not a fund-raiser, was so successful that an enthusiastic Nathan Strauss, owner of a radio station, pledged $10,000 to the organization on the spot.

This and earlier successful fund-raising events allowed Baldwin and his staff to plan a so-called School of Political Action Techniques. Held June 26–29 in Washington, the "school" offered thirty-nine courses in five categories: political strategy, political organizations and administration, political groups, political research, and public relations. Students from all over the country, limited to five hundred, heard experts in various fields talk on these subjects, as well as Postmaster General Robert Hannegan, the Democrat national chairman, and Senator Wayne Morse, Republican of Oregon, each assert that his party was the proper vehicle for liberals. Wallace was induced from his office to join the group on the spur of the moment, and he told the students that while the Democratic party needed a "rebirth" it was still "ten times more likely to serve a progressive cause than the Republican party." He conceded, however, that after twelve years in power his party had lost some of its zeal and needed a little "chastening."

Baldwin thought the school was excellent but wanted to send the students back home with a strong message: what was it to be? He recognized that he was part of a small minority that wanted to work immediately toward establishing a third party. But he decided to be bold in his closing address and told the five hundred activists that there was a chance that they might be the advance guard of a new political party. Baldwin told them that there was little likelihood that the Republican would ever be a liberal party. Wallace was right in saying that the Democrats could still be liberal, but he had not told them how it was possible to overcome the "unholy coalition of forces between the two parties."

If the Democrats "continue on the road to reaction as in the past eighteen months," then "there will be a third party whether Mr. Truman likes it, or whether Mr. Hannegan likes it, or whether Henry Wallace likes it. . . . Through the organization of progressive groups throughout the country you are building a machine: a people's machine which can be used to make the Democratic the more progressive party, perhaps to help slightly in the direction of the Republican Party; but if leadership is not responsive to the needs of the people, the same machinery can be used for a third party."

The next day, according to Curtis Macdougall, Wallace met Baldwin, grinned, and said, "Maybe you're right."[74] Even though Wallace was still thinking in terms of liberalizing the Democratic Party and influencing Truman to modify his policies against the Soviet Union, the progressives like Beanie Baldwin were already preparing the political ground for the Progressive party. Meanwhile, Wallace, continuing along his chosen course, replied to a letter from the Right Reverend Frank W. Sterrett, Bishop of Bethlehem, Pennsylvania, that he had gone "all out" for a loan to Britain in numerous speeches and before the Senate:

. . . The thing which disturbs me about Britain is the easy assumption of racial superiority on the part of those who usually manage British affairs. I have talked to Churchill about this and know his attitude. I felt it was necessary to make a very strong statement to counteract the very unfortunate impression created by Churchill's Fulton, Missouri, speech.

I think it is important for the United States to play up the UNO as a force for world peace but to avoid entering into an alliance with either England or Russia. I think it is a serious mistake to give Russia the impression that we are ganging up with England against her. Of course it would be equally serious to give England the impression that we are ganging up with Russia against her. Frankly, however, I see considerable danger of the one and no danger whatsoever of the other. That is why I spoke as I did.[75]

Yet critical as Wallace was publicly, and to a much greater degree privately, of the administration's foreign policy, he continued loyal to the Democratic Party. On June 14, speaking in St. Louis under the joint auspices of the Liberal Voters League and NC/PAC, he dismissed talk of a third party, since it would be "impossible for a third party to get on the ballot in enough states to make anything approaching an effective challenge. . . . As far as 1948 is concerned, a third-party effort would insure beyond all doubt the election of a reactionary Republican—give him the name of [John] Bricker or whatever name you want." It was time, he said, "for third-party advocates to stop kidding themselves. . . . I say, in all sincerity, that the progressive forces of this country have no basis today for disillusionment in the Democratic Party as an instrument of national progress."[76]

Such a statement must have tested his party loyalty painfully, for just the previous month President Truman, in a rage over the decision of two railroad unions to strike the government-seized railroads, went before Congress and asked for emergency executive powers to draft the strikers into the Army. Liberals were horrified and liberal newspaper columnists trotted out references to Hitler and Mussolini. (One can only wonder what Wallace would have thought of his President if he had known of the handwritten speech to Congress that Truman fortunately allowed his speech-writers to tone down somewhat. Even such an admirer as the historian Alonzo Hamby called the draft "incredible." In it Truman accused the labor movement of communism and a lack of patriotism: "Come along with me and eliminate the Lewises, the Whitneys, the Johnsons, the Communist Bridges and the Russian Senators and Representatives and really make this a government of by and for the people." As Hamby writes, it is hardly possible that Truman really intended to say these things publicly, but even with a generous discounting for anger and frustration, it does seem to indicate his true feelings toward labor and about Communists.[77] At the time it seemed that this futile draft-the-strikers appeal would destroy the labor support essential for a Democratic victory in 1948, but later the labor leaders decided that they needed Truman as much as Truman needed them and, with few exceptions, they fell into line.

Perhaps the final split between Truman and Wallace was always inevitable, even if each, for his own reasons, wanted to avoid it. That their views on the approach to the Soviet Union were irreconcilable becomes obvious when you read Wallace's famous letter of July 23, 1946, to President Truman. It is a remarkable document and the present-day reader must remember that it was not written with the hindsight of thirty years we now possess but written in the very early days of what came to be called the Cold War. Furthermore, it was directed against the already considerable momentum of American foreign policy. We have learned in recent decades how seldom, to our serious and lasting detriment, Presidential advisers have had the independence of mind to oppose the conventional wisdom of the time and, if they oppose it, the courage to inform the President of their opposition and persist in it.

Although the entire document merits reading, it was twelve single-spaced pages long, substantial extracts will have to suffice:

. . . I think that at the moment the [American] people feel that the outlook for the elimination of war is dark, that other nations are wilfully obstructing American efforts to achieve a permanent peace.

How do American actions since V-J Day appear to other nations? I mean by actions the concrete things like $13 billion for the War and Navy Departments, the Bikini tests of the atomic bomb and continued production of bombs, the plan to arm Latin America with our weapons, production of B-29s and planned production of B-36s, and the effort to secure air bases spread over half the globe from which the other half of the globe can be bombed. I cannot but feel that these actions must make it look to the rest of the

world as if we were only paying lip service to peace at the conference table.

These facts rather make it appear either (1) that we are preparing
ourselves to win the war which we regard as inevitable or (2) that
we are trying to build up a predominance of force to intimidate the
rest of mankind. How would it look to us if Russia had the atomic
bomb and we did not, if Russia had 10,000-mile bombers and air
bases within a thousand miles of our coast lines and we did not?

Wallace then discussed the American proposal for international control of atomic energy, a plan that he believed
had a "fatal defect":

Is it any wonder that the the Russians did not show any great enthusiasm for our plan? Would we have been enthusiastic if the
Russians had a monopoly of atomic energy and offered to share
the information with us at some indefinite time in the future at
their discretion if we agreed now not to try to make a bomb and
give them information on our secret resources of uranium and
thorium? I think we would react as the Russians appear to have
done. We would have put up a counter-proposal for the record,
but our real effort would go into trying to make a bomb so that our
bargaining position would be equalized. That is the essence of the
Russian position. . . .

The factors causing Americans to distrust Russia were
also discussed by Wallace:

Our basic distrust of the Russians, which has been greatly inten-
sified in recent months by the playing up of conflict in the press,
stems from differences in political and economic organization. For
the first time in our history defeatists among us have raised the
fear of another system as a successful rival to democracy and free
enterprise in other countries and perhaps even our own. I am convinced that we can meet that challenge as we have in the past by
demonstrating that economic abundance can be achieved without
sacrificing personal, political, and religious liberties. We cannot
meet it as Hitler tried to by an anti-Comintern alliance.

It is perhaps too easy to forget that despite the deep-seated differences in our cultures and intensive anti-Russian propaganda of some twenty-five years' standing, the American people reversed their attitudes during the crisis of war. Today, under the pressure of seemingly insoluble international problems and continuing deadlocks, the tide of American public opinion is again turning against Russia. In this reaction lies one of the dangers to which this letter is addressed.

This is, I believe, the only passage in the letter where Wallace can be seriously faulted. He was right as far as he went but he was not entirely fair to the administration and to the public. There was a genuine concern in the United States about the fate of the peoples of Eastern Europe, about their lack of the civil liberties so precious to Americans. And it is true that the Soviet Union had legitimate fears that caused it to want a band of subservient nations separating it from its former, and perhaps future, invaders to the west. Also it is true that Americans did not see the similarity between the sphere of influence Russia was beginning to construct and the sphere of influence that the United States had long taken for granted in Latin America. But that these things were true does not negate Americans' genuine concern about Eastern Europe. Apart from the justice of recognizing such a concern, it would have been better politics to have taken note of this concern. It he had, there was a chance, albeit a slight one, that Truman might have been more sympathetic.

Wallace was on firmer ground when he turned to the factors that caused the Soviet Union to distrust the West:

. . . The first is Russian history, which we must take into account because it is the setting in which Russians see all actions and policies of the rest of the world. Russian history for over a thousand years has been a succession of attempts, often unsuccessful, to resist invasion and conquest—by the Mongols, the Turks, the Swedes, the Germans, and the Poles. [For some reason Wallace omitted Napoleon and the French.] The scant thirty years of the existence of the Soviet Government has in Russian eyes been a continuation of their historical struggle for national existence. The first four years of the new regime, from 1917 through 1921, were spent in resisting attempts at destruction by the Japanese, British, and French, with some American assistance, and by the several White Russian armies encouraged and financed by the Western powers. Then, in 1941, the Soviet State was almost conquered by the Germans after a period during which the Western European powers had apparently acquiesced in the rearming of Germany in the belief that the Nazis would seek to expand eastward rather than westward. The Russians, therefore, obviously see themselves as fighting for their existence in a hostile world.

Second, it follows that to the Russians all of the defense and security measures of the Western powers seem to have an aggressive intent. Our actions to expand our military security system—such steps as extending the Monroe Doctrine to include the arming of the Western Hemisphere nations, our present monopoly of the atomic bomb, our interest in outlying bases and our general support of the British Empire—appear to them as going far beyond the requirements of defense. I think we might feel the same if the United States were the only capitalistic country in the world, and the principal socialistic countries were creating a level of armed strength far exceeding anything in their previous history. From the Russian point of view, also, the granting of a loan to Britain and the lack of tangible results on their request to borrow for rehabilitation purposes may be regarded as another evidence of strengthening of an anti-Soviet bloc.

Finally, our resistance to her attempts to obtain warm water ports and her own security system in the form of "friendly" neighboring states seems, from the Russian point of view, to clinch the case. After twenty-five years of isolation and after having achieved the status of a major power, Russia believes that she is entitled to recognition of her new status. Our interest in establishing democracy in Eastern Europe, where democracy has by and large never existed, seems to her an attempt to re-establish the encirclement of unfriendly neighbors which was created after the last war and which might serve as a springboard of still another effort to destroy her.

Wallace then discussed what the United States might do to reduce the Russian distrust of the Western world:

We should ascertain from a fresh point of view what Russia believes to be essential to her own security as a prerequisite to the writing of the peace and to cooperation in the construction of a world order. We should be prepared to judge her requirements against the background of what we ourselves and the British have insisted upon as essential to our respective security. We should be prepared, even at the expense of risking epithets of appeasement, to agree to reasonable Russian guarantees of security. The progress made during June and July on the Italian and other treaties indicates that we can hope to arrive at understanding and agreement on this aspect of the problem. . . .

We should make an effort to counteract the irrational fear of Russia which is being systematically built up in the American people by certain individuals and publications. The slogan that communism and capitalism, regimentation and democracy, cannot continue to exist in the same world is, from a historical point of view, pure propaganda. Several religious doctrines, all claiming to be the only true gospel and salvation, have existed side by side with a reasonable degree of tolerance for centuries. This country was for the first half of its national life a democratic island in a world dominated by absolutist governments.

We should not act as if we too felt that we were threatened in today's world. We are by far the most powerful nation in the world, the only Allied nation which came out of the war without devastation and much stronger than before the war. Any talk on our part about the need for strengthening our defenses further is bound to appear hypocritical to other nations.

This appeal for coexistence and détente was written in a year when Richard Nixon was about to enter American history as a congressional candidate whose campaign consisted almost entirely in exploiting America's rising fear of communism. And these paragraphs were an appeal for an end to "McCarthyism" written in the same year that the man who gave it its name was entering American history as a successful candidate for the Senate.

After a long and detailed discussion of possible economic relations between the United States and Russia, Henry Wallace came to this conclusion:

. . . It will be fruitless to continue to seek solutions for the many specific problems that face us in the making of the peace and in the establishment of an enduring international order without first achieving an atmosphere of mutual trust and confidence. The task admittedly is not an easy one. There is no question, as the Secretary of State has indicated, that negotiations with the Russians are difficult because of cultural differences, their traditional isolationism, and their insistence on a visible *quid pro quo* in all agreements. But the task is not an insuperable one if we take into account that to other nations our foreign policy consists not only of the principles that we advocate but of the actions we take. . . . Even our own security, in the sense that we have known it in the past, cannot be preserved by military means in a world armed with atomic weapons. The only type of security which can be maintained by our own military force is the type described by a military man before the Senate Atomic Energy Committee—a security against invasion after all our cities and perhaps 40 million of our city population have been destroyed by atomic weapons. That is the best that "security" on the basis of armaments has to offer us. It is not the kind of security that our people and the people of the other United Nations are striving for.[78]

There are several things that must be said about this extraordinary letter. First, it should dismiss for once and for all the claim often made by Wallace's critics during the 1948 campaign, that he was parroting words put in his mouth by Communists and Communist sympathizers. His public statements before and during the campaign were totally consistent with the views expressed in this letter, which he wrote when still a member of the Truman administration, subject to all the pressures to conform that exist in every American administration. Most of his colleagues at the top echelons were Cold Warriors and his dinner companions were such as Dean Acheson, Joseph Alsop, Chip Bohlen, *et al.* He was not in a nest of Communists when he wrote this letter.

Second, and this is more important, there is little evidence that his views were given much serious consideration. Later, when the letter was made public, the press seldom discussed the substance of his views but concentrated on the politics of his statements. It seems in the nature of the American press, with few exceptions, to care more about the politics than the substance of political debate, but that is hardly an excuse for government officials. I do not know how much thoughtful consideration was given to Wallace's letter by Truman and his advisers, but in his *Memoirs*, Truman dismisses it in four paragraphs, only one of which discusses the substance:

Altogether, Wallace could see every reason why the Soviets would or should distrust us and no reason why our policy might bear fruit. His conclusion, therefore, was that we should change our policy in order to "allay any reasonable Russian grounds for fear, suspicion and distrust." But he had no specific proposals how this might be accomplished without surrendering to them on every count.[79]

During his last couple of months in the Truman administration, Wallace's doubts continued to grow. On July 24 his diary entry recorded:

The President spoke very vigorously in one part of the meeting about the necessity of cutting down on the budget, saying that he had already pruned it about $3 billion. He said the place to cut was in the askings of the Army and Navy. This agreed completely with conversations I had had with him earlier. But within half an hour he was saying that after the last war we had cut our Navy too much; that we had to be careful not to cut our Army and Navy; that if we had not cut our Army and Navy after the last war there would not have been World War II. I was utterly amazed that he could go two different directions within the hour. It reminded me of Tuesday when within the hour he spoke about being patient with Russia to me and then at the Cabinet luncheon agreed completely with Jimmie Byrnes in a number of cracks he took against Russia. I suspect there has never been a President who could move in two different directions with less time intervening than Truman. He feels completely sincere and earnest at all times and is not disturbed in the slightest by the different directions in which his mind can go almost simultaneously. I say this realizing that he has always agreed with me on everything.[80]

Wallace's doubts included not only Truman's intellect but the substance of the decisions Truman was making or moving toward. At a Cabinet meeting on July 26 Secretary of the Navy Forrestal reported that "we had our Marines strung out very thinly all over China along the railroads; that in many places there were only five to fifteen Marines; that the Chinese Communists could clean them out at any time and that it was a perilous situation and something ought to be done about it. Forrestal then said he didn't think we should get out of China."

After Forrestal complained about the number of Russian propagandists in China, it occurred to Wallace that the United States might make the same mistake with China that it had made with Russia, try to turn back the clock: ". . . All this indicates to me rather clearly that the United States is going to make the same mistake with China that we made with Russia after the last war. China eventually will be very much more progressive than the present Kuomintang crowd and these progressives will feel that they have earned their place in the sun as a result of help from Russia and in spite of the opposition of the United States. It will not make for the maximum of trade and good will in China."[81]

In one of Wallace's last diary entries before the final blowup with Harry Truman he was quite disturbed:

Stuart Symington [new assistant secretary of war for air] reported on his trip around the world. He said that all military folks, with the exception of General [Lucius DuB.] Clay [U.S. military commander in Berlin], preached the doctrine of war with Russia. Clay was the only one who thought we could learn to get along with the Russians. . . . [General Mark W.] Clark's attitude is much more hard-boiled than that of Clay. . . .

Symington said that in talking with Bedell Smith and with Clay he reached the conclusion that Russia definitely did not want war; that she couldn't possibly be ready for war in less than ten years and it would probably take fifteen; that she certainly couldn't be pressed into war until she had the atomic bomb. Symington said, however, that one thing the Russians should realize is that we can be pushed so far and no further. It all indicates to me that the American military is spoiling for a fight. They don't realize that the Russian slant may be very similar to our own. In other words, the Russians can be pushed only so far and no further. And so we shall both go on being tough and building up armaments and making sure that the next war and the next depression will be bigger and worse than the last one. Three cheers for the military! They are so helpful to humanity. . . .[82]

During the spring and summer of 1946 there was a great deal of political ferment. Truman's request for congressional authorization to draft striking railroad workers—which was soon sidetracked in the Senate—had outraged union leaders. The Brotherhood of Railway Trainmen, the Transport Workers, the United Automobile Workers, the Textile Workers, the International Fur and Leather Workers, the International Ladies Garment Workers, the United Packinghouse Workers, the Teamsters, and other unions angrily attacked Truman and there were more frequent mutterings of the need for a third party. The National Farmers Union announced on July 11, 1946, that it had "lost confidence" in Truman, and Harold Ickes, who had become executive chairman of the Independent Citizens Committee/Arts, Sciences and Professions, remarked that although he opposed a third party, it might become necessary even if it were not practical. All during this time Beanie Baldwin was strengthening and broadening the National Citizens Political Action Committee. And Wallace himself, as was customary for a Cabinet member, made frequent political speeches, appearing in California, New York, Massachusetts, Missouri, and Pennsylvania. What is interesting, however, is that while a number of the speeches were under Democratic Party auspices, more than half were be-

fore NC/PAC and other independent groups. To the disgust
of some conservative Democrats, who not infrequently boy-
cotted his appearances, Wallace, while still loyal to Truman,
was maintaining his independence.[83]

During much of August Wallace was on vacation at his
newly purchased farm in South Salem, New York (about
fifty miles from New York City, along the Connecticut border), which was to be his permanent home for the rest of
his life. Then on August 29 he went to Mexico, where he attended the opening session of the Mexican Congress, talked
with President Avila Camacho, and toured the country to
examine its agricultural progress. He did not return to
Washington until September 10, four days after Secretary
Byrnes had delivered a speech in Stuttgart. The contrast between this speech and the one Wallace gave on September
12 is what caused Byrnes and Senator Vandenberg to tell
Truman that he had to choose between them or Wallace. In
his speech Byrnes attacked the Russians for departing from
the Potsdam agreements about the postwar disposition of
Germany. He also advocated the political and economic
strengthening of Germany. This, coming only a little more
than a year after the defeat of the Nazis, alarmed the Russians, French, and many British. It sounded as if the United
States were seeking to enlist a unified and renascent Germany on its side.

Wallace's appearance on September 12 at Madison Square
Garden, in New York, before an NC/PAC rally had been
scheduled for several months. Baldwin convinced Wallace
to speak on foreign affairs. A friend in the Commerce Department had shown him Wallace's June 23 letter. Before
leaving for New York Wallace met with President Truman
and, according to Wallace's diary, "went over" the forthcoming speech "page by page with him."[84] This language
is important because of the controversy, a political sensation that was soon to be front-page news the world over.
Wallace had taken the speech to the President because
Beanie Baldwin had warned him that the State Department

would never clear it. In that case, Wallace told Baldwin, he would take it to the President.[85]

Curtis Macdougall wrote that he and numerous others heard Wallace speak of that meeting many times. "According to him, it lasted over an hour. He held one copy of the speech while the President patiently read another. There were frequent pauses in the reading for questions and brief discussions."[86] Wallace's diary reports: "Again and again he said, 'That's right; yes, that is what I believe.' He didn't have a single change to suggest. He twice said how deeply he appreciated my courtesy in showing him my speech before I gave it. . . . The President apparently saw no inconsistency between my speech and what Byrnes was doing—if he did he didn't indicate it in any way."

Copies of the speech were widely distributed to the press the day of delivery and that afternoon Truman was asked about it at a press conference by a reporter from Wallace's home state, William Mylander of the *Des Moines Register and Tribune*.

Q.: In the middle of the speech are these words: "When President Truman read these words he said they represented the policy of this Administration."
The President: That is correct.
Q.: My question is, does that apply just for that paragraph or for the whole speech?
The President: I approved the whole speech.
Q. (by Raymond P. Brandt of the *St. Louis Post-Dispatch*): Mr. President, do you regard Wallace's speech as a departure from Byrnes's policy?
The President: I do not. They are exactly in line.[87]

Harry Truman did not mince words, but this was one of many times he may have wished he did. With Secretary Byrnes in Paris at a peace conference, Will Clayton was Acting Secretary of State. About six o'clock an aide brought him a copy of Wallace's speech. He recognized immediately, as Truman apparently had not, that it would be interpreted as signaling a departure in American policy. It was still not too late to get Wallace to change his remarks, although this would have occasioned awkward questions since the speech had been so widely distributed in advance. Clayton called Truman's press secretary, Charles Ross, at the White House. Ross refused to take it up with the President; he's already committed himself to it and it was too late to change.[88]

So Henry Wallace made one of the most explosive speeches in American political history. Today it seems reasonable and moderate—as indeed it was even then—but then it was so contrary to Truman's policy as perceived at home and abroad that it was treated as an astonishing document. Perhaps what it proves most of all is that by late summer 1946, just a year after the end of the war, America's mind set had already been so established that a Pax Americana seemed entirely natural.

Although "The Way to Peace" was the most important speech Henry Wallace ever gave, there is no entirely satisfactory text of it because in a number of places he improvised, adding material here and deleting it there. However, the speech as written and distributed to the press, was in delivery changed in only the most minor way. This version is based on the large-print copy from which Wallace actually read.[89]

. . . During the past year or so, the significance of peace has been increased immeasurably by the atom bomb, guided missiles, and airplanes which soon will travel as fast as sound. Make no mistake about it—another war would hurt the United States many times as much as the last war. We cannot rest in the assurance that we invented the atom bomb—and therefore that this agent of destruction will work best for us. He who trusts in the atom bomb will sooner or later perish by the atom bomb—or something worse.

I say this as one who steadfastly backed preparedness throughout the thirties. We have no use for namby-pamby pacifism. But we must realize that modern inventions have now made peace the most exciting thing in the world—and we should be willing to pay a just price for peace. If modern war can cost us four hundred billion dollars, we should be willing and happy to pay much more for peace. But certainly, the cost of peace is to be measured not in dollars but in the hearts and minds of men.

The price of peace—for us and for every nation in the world—is the price of giving up prejudice, hatred, fear, and ignorance.

Let's get down to cases here at home.

First we have prejudice, hatred, fear, and ignorance of certain races. The recent mass lynching in Georgia was not merely the most unwarranted, brutal act of mob violence in the United States in recent years; it was also an illustration of the kind of prejudice that makes war inevitable.

Hatred breeds hatred. The doctrine of racial superiority produces a desire to get even on the part of its victims. If we are to work for peace in the rest of the world, we here in the United States must eliminate racism from our unions, our business organizations, our educational institutions, and our employment practices. Merit alone must be the measure of men.

Second, in payment for peace, we must give up prejudice, hatred, fear, and ignorance in the economic world. This means working earnestly, day after day, for a larger volume of world trade. It means helping undeveloped areas of the world to industrialize themselves with the help of American technical assistance and loans.

We should welcome the opportunity to help along the most rapid possible industrialization in Latin America, China, India, and the Near East. For as the productivity of these peoples increases, our exports will increase. . . .

I supported the British loan of almost four billion dollars because I knew that without this aid in the rehabilitation of its economy, the British government would have been forced to adopt totalitarian trade methods and economic warfare of a sort which would have closed the markets of much of the world to American exports.

For the welfare of the American people and the world it is even more important to invest four billion dollars in the industrialization of underdeveloped areas in the so-called backward nations, thereby promoting the long-term stability that comes from an ever-increasing standard of living. This would not only be good politics and good morals. It would be good business.

The United States is the world's great creditor nation. And low tariffs by creditor nations are a part of the price of peace. For when a great creditor demands payment, and, at the same time, adopts policies which make it impossible for the debtors to pay in goods—the first result is the intensification of depression over large areas of the world; and the final result is the triumph of demagogues who speak only the language of violence and hate. . . .

The Republican Party is the party of economic nationalism and political isolation—and as such is as anachronistic as the dodo and as certain to disappear. The danger is that before it disappears it may enjoy a brief period of power during which it can do irreparable damage to the United States and the cause of world peace.

Governor Dewey has expressed himself as favoring an alliance of mutual defense with Great Britain as the key to our foreign policy. This may sound attractive because we both speak the same language and many of our customs and traditions have the same historical background. Moreover, to the military men, the British Isles are our advanced air base against Europe.

Certainly we like the British people as individuals. But to make Britain the key to our foreign policy would be, in my opinion, the height of folly. We must not let the reactionary leadership of the Republican Party force us into that position. We must not let British balance-of-power manipulations determine whether and when the United States gets into war.

Make no mistake about it—the British imperialistic policy in the Near East alone, combined with Russian retaliation, would lead the United States straight to war unless we have a clearly defined and realistic policy of our own.

Neither of these two great powers wants war now, but the danger is that whatever their intentions may be, their current policies may eventually lead to war. To prevent war and insure our survival in a stable world, it is essential that we look abroad through our own eyes and not through the eyes of either the British Foreign Office or a pro-British or anti-Russian press.

In this connection, I want one thing clearly understood. I am neither anti-British nor pro-British—neither anti-Russian nor pro-Russian. And just two days ago, when President Truman read these words, he said that they represented the policy of his administration. . . .

To achieve lasting peace, we must study in detail just how the

Russian character was formed—by invasions of Tatars, Mongols, Germans, Poles, Swedes, and French; by the czarist rule based on ignorance, fear, and force; by the intervention of the British, French, and Americans in Russian affairs from 1919 to 1921; by the geography of the huge Russian land mass situated strategically between Europe and Asia; and by the vitality derived from the rich Russian soil and the strenuous Russian climate. Add to all this the tremendous emotional power which Marxism and Leninism gives to the Russian leaders—and then we can realize that we are reckoning with a force which cannot be handled successfully by a "Get tough with Russia" policy. "Getting tough" never bought anything real and lasting—whether for schoolyard bullies or businessmen or world powers. The tougher we get, the tougher the Russians will get.

Throughout the world there are numerous reactionary elements which had hoped for an Axis victory—and now profess great friendship for the United States. Yet, these enemies of yesterday and false friends of today continually try to provoke war between the United States and Russia. They only long for the day when the United States and Russia will destroy each other.

We must not let our Russian policy be guided or influenced by those inside or outside the United States who want war with Russia. This does not mean appeasement.

We most earnestly want peace with Russia—but we want to be met halfway. We want cooperation. And I believe that we can get cooperation once Russia understands that our primary objective is neither saving the British Empire nor purchasing oil in the Near East with the lives of American soldiers. We cannot allow national oil rivalries to force us into war. All of the nations producing oil, whether inside or outside of their own boundaries, must fulfill the provisions of the United Nations Charter and encourage the development of world petroleum reserves so as to make the maximum amount of oil available to all nations of the world on an equitable, peaceful basis—and not on the basis of fighting the next war.

For her part, Russia can retain our respect by cooperating with the United Nations in a spirit of open-minded and flexible give-and-take.

The real peace treaty we now need is between the United States and Russia. On our part, we should recognize that we have no more business in the *political* affairs of Eastern Europe than Russia has in the *political* affairs of Latin America, Western Europe, and the United States. We may not like what Russia does in eastern Europe. Her type of land reform, industrial expropriation, and suppression of basic liberties offends the great majority of the United States.

At this criticism of Russia some of the audience hissed. There were a good many Communists in the audience, since the rally was attended by members not only of the Democratic and Liberal parties but also of the American Labor Party, which had a number of Communist members. Wallace added extemporaneously, "Yes, I'm talking about people outside of New York City when I talk about that, and I think I know about people outside of New York City. Any Gallup Poll will reveal it—we might as well face the facts."

But whether we like it or not the Russians will try to socialize their sphere of influence just as we try to democratize our sphere of influence. This applies also to Germany and Japan. We are striving to democratize Japan and our area of control in Germany, while Russia strives to socialize eastern Germany.

As for Germany, we all must recognize that an equitable settlement, based on a unified German nation, is absolutely essential to any lasting European settlement.

At this point there is some uncertainty as to what Wallace actually said. Professor Blum quotes him as saying: "This means that Russia must be assured that never again can German industry be converted into military might to be used against her—and Britain. Western Europe and the United States must be certain that Russia's German policy will not become a tool of Russian design against Western Europe." However, on the back of the preceding page of the reading copy, Wallace had written these words in his own hand: "This means that the nations of the world and particularly Europe must be assured that never again can German industry be converted into military might to be used against them nor that any single nation will use Germany as a tool in a struggle for balance of power." There is not a great deal of substantial difference in the two versions.

The Russians have no more business stirring up native Communists to political activity in Western Europe, Latin America, and the United States than we have in interfering in the politics of eastern Europe and Russia.

At this point, Wallace added, according to Professor Blum: "Now, when I say that, I realize that the danger of war is much less from communism than it is from imperialism, whether it be of the United States or England—or from fascism, the remnants of fascism, which may be in Spain or Argentina. Let's get this straight, regardless of what Mr. Taft or Mr. Dewey may say, if we can overcome the imperialistic urge in the Western world, I'm convinced there'll be no war." This differs very slightly from what is scrawled on the reading copy in Wallace's hand: "We know what Russia is up to in Eastern Europe, for example, and Russia knows what we are up to." (On the reading copy this sentence is scratched out, but he may have read it anyway.) "But we cannot permit the door to be closed against our trade in Eastern Europe any more than we can in China. I'm Secretary of Commerce, and I'm interested in trade. And I want the biggest market we can get. I want China, I want Eastern Europe, as places where we can trade. But, at the same time, we have to recognize that the Balkans are closer to Russia than to us, and that Russia cannot permit either England or the United States to dominate the politics of that area."

China is a special case and although she holds the longest frontier in the world with Russia, the interests of world peace demand that China remain free from any sphere of influence, either politically or economically.

At this point there again was hissing and Wallace added these sentences: "And I know of my own positive knowledge that that was in Roosevelt's heart and mind, most specifically in the spring of 1944—because I talked it over with him in detail." Hissing. "Mr. Truman read that particular sentence, and he approved it." Hissing.

We insist that the door to trade and economic development opportunities be left wide open in China as in all the world. However, the open door to trade and opportunities for economic development in China are meaningless unless there is a unified and peaceful China—built on the cooperation of the various groups in that country and based on a hands-off policy of the outside powers.

We are still arming to the hilt. Our excessive expenses for military purposes are the chief cause of our unbalanced budget. If taxes are to be lightened we must have the basis of a real peace with Russia—a peace that cannot be broken by extremist propagandists. [Deleted: We do not want our course determined for us by master minds operating out of London, Moscow, or Nanking.]

Russian ideas of social-economic justice are going to govern nearly a third of the world. Our ideas of free-enterprise democracy will govern much of the rest. The two ideas will endeavor to prove which can deliver the most satisfaction to the common man in their respective areas of political dominance. But by mutual agreement, this competition should be put on a friendly basis [Deleted: and the Russians should stop conniving against us in certain areas of the world just as we should stop scheming against them in other parts of the world]. Let the results of the two systems speak for themselves.

[Deleted: Meanwhile, the Russians should stop teaching that their form of communism must, by force if necessary, ultimately triumph over democratic capitalism—while] we should close our ears to those among us who would have us believe that Russian communism and our free enterprise system cannot live, one with another, in a profitable and productive peace.

Under friendly, peaceful competition the Russian world and the American world will gradually become more alike. The Russians

will be forced to grant more and more of the personal freedoms. . . .

At this point more hissing, and Wallace added these sentences: "You don't like the word 'forced'? I say that in the
process of time they will find it profitable enough and op-
portune to grant more and more of the personal freedoms.
Put it any way you want. That's the course of history just
the same."

. . . And we shall become more and more absorbed with the
problems of social-economic justice.

Russia must be convinced that we are not planning for war
against her and we must be certain that Russia is not carrying on
territorial expansion or world domination through native Communists faithfully following every twist and turn in the Moscow party
line. [On Wallace's reading copy, it says ". . .and we must be certain that Russia is not out for territorial expansion and world domination." The rest of the sentence is deleted.] There will always be
an ideological conflict—but that is no reason why diplomats cannot work out a basis for both systems to live safely in the world
side by side. . . .

In the full development of the rights of small nations, the British
and the Russians can learn a lesson from the Good Neighbor policy of Franklin Roosevelt. For under Roosevelt, we in the Western
Hemisphere built a workable system of regional internationalism
that fully protected the sovereign rights of every nation—a system
of multi-lateral action that immeasurably strengthened the whole
of world order.

In the United States an informed public opinion will be all-
powerful. Our people are peace-minded. But they often express
themselves too late—for events today move much faster than public opinion. The people here, as everywhere in the world, must be
convinced that another war is not inevitable. And through mass
meetings such as this, and through persistent pamphleteering, the
people can be organized for peace—even though a large segment
of our press is propagandizing our people for war in the hope of
scaring Russia. And we who look on this war-with-Russia talk as
criminal foolishness must carry our message direct to the people—

even though we may be called Communists because we dare to speak out.

I believe that peace—the kind of a peace I have outlined tonight—is the basic issue, both in the congressional campaign this fall and right on through the presidential election in 1948. How we meet this issue will determine whether we live not in "one world" or "two worlds"—but whether we live at all.

Before discussing the explosive controversy set off by this speech, several observations can be made. In the passages dealing with world trade, Wallace was anything but radical; he sounded like any conventional big businessman, demanding an open door for U.S. trade. But when it came to economic aid and technical assistance to what were then called the "backward" nations, he was years in advance of Harry Truman's justly praised Point Four program. Also, Wallace was acutely aware of the dangers presented by the competition for Middle Eastern oil. Finally, and perhaps most important, he recognized the importance of spheres of influence. Although it caused him some embarrassment— Wilsonian idealists were supposed to make believe there were no such things—he understood that to challenge the sphere of influence of a powerful nation caused insupportable world tensions. Which is exactly what happened when the United States refused to recognize Russia's anxiety about its neighboring states. Indeed, the American challenge to the Russian influence over Eastern Europe may have caused the Soviet Union to have been more repressive than it otherwise might have been, although one cannot be sure.

Within a day, a political and diplomatic storm erupted. It was apparent to everyone else, if not to Harry Truman, that Wallace's speech was calling for a radical departure from current policy. And it is apparent now, although evidently it was not so apparent then, that criticism of Wallace was directed not at a lack of critical judgment on his part toward Russia but at his direct, if implicit, opposition to Truman's foreign policy. (One of the nice ironies is that the Communist Party paper, the *Daily Worker*, was far from pleased with Wallace's speech, just as his harsh words about Russia had triggered the hissing by Communists and Communist sympathizers in the crowd.) What immediately happened to Wallace—and it is familiar to just about everyone who had written critically of U.S. foreign policy—was that his criticism of the United States was automatically assumed to be support of the Soviet Union. To those who make this reflex action, often sophisticated intellectuals and journalists, there is no such thing as being critical of both sides. With them it is either/or, and if evidence to the contrary is presented, they somehow do not see it or believe it is not convincing. This either-you-are-for-us-or-you-are-against-us attitude was to plague Wallace for the next two years.

Some of Wallace's opponents made a big point of the fact that he dropped some of the criticism of Russia that appeared in the advance text. Some years later, in his interview for the Columbia University Oral History project, he explained why he revised his speech:

Some "extremely left people" . . . very eager that I delete from my speech several statements which I had made against the Communists and against Russia. They approached me on this an hour before the speech and I did take out some of them because they put it this way: "If you leave these statements in, you're going to take a lot of steam out of the workers in the Congressional campaign. And what's the use of antagonizing these people when you want to get work out of them?" So I did take out some of these statements. I never put it that way in the press when they asked me why I eliminated some of the statements but that was the actual truth. When I published the speech later on I think I may have said that the time was short and I eliminated them for that reason, or that they were booing, or this that and the other thing, but actually the truth was I carefully eliminated them in advance as a result of the pressure that came from those who said it was bad politics.

Plainly, it was not candid of Wallace to have fuzzed over the reason he made the deletions; but it should have been evident to anyone whose eyes were not closed by preconceptions that much, much more criticism was retained than dropped, and that, furthermore, the criticism he inserted spontaneously was harsher than what he had dropped.

Republicans on Capitol Hill were arguing that the Truman administration had two foreign policies, Byrnes's and Wallace's; diplomats at the Paris Peace Conference were wondering whether Truman was signaling a change in direction; poor Byrnes did not know what to tell his diplomatic colleagues, who were frantically seeking enlightenment; and Acting Secretary William L. Clayton could only tell the press that he did not understand how Truman had cleared the speech.

Thus, the hapless Truman had to try to clear up the mess. So on Saturday, September 14, he called in reporters and read the following statement:

> There has been a natural misunderstanding regarding the answer I made to a question asked at the Press Conference on Thursday, September 12th, with reference to the speech of the Secretary of Commerce delivered in New York later that day. The question was answered extemporaneously and my answer did not convey the thought that I intended it to convey.
>
> It was my intention to express the thought that I approved the right of the Secretary of Commerce to deliver the speech. I did not intend to indicate that I approved the speech as constituting a statement of the foreign policy of this country.
>
> There has been no change in the established foreign policy of our Government. There will be no significant change in that policy without discussion and conference among the President, the Secretary of State and Congressional leaders.[90]

The President then left without permitting questions.

Everyone saw through so transparent a statement and Truman got severe criticism in the press and in political circles for his inept handling of the affair. It must have been painful, for when Truman discussed Wallace's "all-out attack on our foreign policy" in his *Memoirs,* he performed a

masterful act of historical ambiguity: "I had a press conference on the morning of the twelfth, and one of the reporters
asked me if Mr. Wallace's speech that night had my approval. I said yes, it did. Of course I should have said, 'He's
told me he is going to make a speech,' because everyone
promptly took my answer to mean that I had read the
speech and approved every part of its content."[91]

That was probably because he specifically said, "I approved the whole speech."

The affair refused to die. The newspapers were having a
field day and in Paris, while Byrnes refused to say anything, Senator Vandenberg was thundering: "The authority
of American foreign policy is dependent upon the degree of
American unity behind it. Rightly or wrongly, Paris is
doubtful of this unity this morning. . . . We [the Republi-
cans] can only cooperate with one Secretary of State at a
time."[92]

On Monday, the sixteenth, Wallace spoke to Truman on
the telephone, and told him, "I thought he had done the
only thing he could do in his statement on Saturday. He
replied that he appreciated deeply my feeling. He said he
wanted to make a statement that would hurt neither Jimmie
Byrnes nor myself. I told him that the object of my speech
was not to hurt Jimmie Byrnes."[93] But that same day, in
a press conference, Wallace not only said, "I stand on my
New York speech,"[94] but announced he would soon speak
again on foreign policy. Furthermore, that day Wallace
learned from Truman's press secretary, Charles Ross, that
Drew Pearson had obtained a copy of his July 23 letter to
Truman. Wallace checked with Harold Young, his personal
aide, who reported that he had heard that Pearson had gotten the letter from the State Department. Wallace notified
Ross "and Ross said he was not surprised; that the State
Department leaked like a sieve."[95] Margaret Truman Daniel, however, says flatly that Wallace leaked the letter.[96]

Ross decided on the seventeenth that it would be better
to release the letter than permit Pearson alone to quote from

it, but when Truman learned of this he "angrily," according to his daughter, countermanded the order. Ross immediately called Wallace, but it was too late; the letter had already been distributed to the press.

Needless to say, this revived the storm. Byrnes sent a message to Truman: "If it is not possible for you, for any reason, to keep Mr. Wallace, as a member of your Cabinet, from speaking on foreign affairs, it would be a grave mistake from every point of view for me to continue in office, even temporarily."[97]

That same day Wallace was summoned to the White House. Before he went he learned that of 1150 communications about the speech received at the Department of Commerce, 950 had been favorable—almost five to one. He also learned that Truman's aides were advising that he politely but unmistakably tell Wallace to stop talking on foreign affairs or leave. And that's what Truman did.

According to Wallace's diary, Truman "said Jimmie Byrnes had been giving him hell. . . . He said Jimmie Byrnes threatened to leave Paris at once unless I stopped talking on foreign affairs. Jimmie had blamed Truman more than he had me. Truman said he himself was really more to blame than I."

Wallace responded that the public wanted peace, that peace was going to be an issue in the congressional elections. "The people are afraid that the 'get-tough-with-Russia' policy is leading us to war. You, yourself, as Harry Truman really believed in my speech." To which Truman replied, "But Jimmie Byrnes says I am pulling the rug out from under him. I must ask you not to make any more speeches touching on foreign policy. We must present a united front abroad."[98]

The meeting lasted two and a half hours, with about an hour being spent on the statement Wallace would make to the press when he left. Wallace pressed his views throughout, and at one point "went into great detail with regard to the tom-toms being continually beaten by the daily press against Russia," saying that he "had no doubt that a good bit of this material came directly or indirectly from . . . the government." Finally, it was decided that Wallace would not speak on foreign affairs until the Paris Peace Conference ended, with the situation to be reviewed again then. But the handwritten statement Wallace read to the scores of reporters outside was worded to make it appear as if the decision were his: "The President and the Secretary of Commerce had a most detailed and friendly discussion, after which the Secretary reached the conclusion that he could make no public statements or speeches until the Foreign Ministers' Conference in Paris is concluded."

But as Ross, who had sat in on much of the meeting, recognized, this merely postponed a decision. The press noticed this too and assumed that Wallace would speak during the last stages of the congressional campaign. As for Truman, he knew that "Wallace had a following" and that "his appeal had some effect," as he wrote in his *Memoirs*. He wanted to keep him in the Cabinet so he "might be able to put some check on his activities. . . . I have never doubted Henry Wallace's sincerity or honesty of purpose, but after this conversation I was afraid that, knowingly or not, he would lend himself to the more sinister ends of the Reds and those who served them."[99]

That was an exercise in Presidential memoirs blandsmanship. His true feelings were expressed in a memorandum he composed the next day:

Mr. Wallace spent two and one half hours talking to me yesterday. I am not sure he is as fundamentally sound intellectually as I had thought. He advised me that I should be far to the "left" when Congress is not in session and that I should move right when Congress is on hand and in session. He said that FDR did that and that FD[R] never let his "right" hand know what his "left" hand did.

He is a pacifist one hundred percent. He wants us to disband our armed forces, give Russia our atomic secrets and trust a bunch of adventurers in the Kremlin Politburo. I do not understand a "dreamer" like that. The German-American Bund under Fritz Kuhn was not half so dangerous. The Reds, phonies and the "parlor pinks" seem to be banded together and are becoming a national danger.

I am afraid that they are a sabotage front for Uncle Joe Stalin. . . .[100]

Those words were written by the man to whom fate had entrusted the future of the United States and the entire world at one of the crucial moments in history.

But if President Truman did not admire Henry Wallace, thousands of American citizens wrote in to say that they did. Among them were Gilbert Harrison, then vice chairman of the American Veterans Committee and later editor of the *New Republic;* Max Lerner, then a young and outspoken liberal columnist for the New York newspaper *PM;* and Albert Einstein, who wrote: "I cannot refrain from expressing to you my high and unconditional admiration for your letter to the President of July 23rd. There is a deep understanding concerning the factual and psychological situation and a far-reaching perception of the fateful consequences of present American foreign policy. Your courageous intervention deserves the gratitude of all of us who observe the present attitude of our government with grave concern."[101]

By September 20 Truman had decided that Wallace had to go. In his *Memoirs* Truman writes that he called Wallace and asked for his resignation. He does not mention that the telephone call was preceded by a letter. This is how the affair is discussed by Cabell Phillips, an admirer of Truman:

. . . He wrote his decision in longhand and dispatched it to the Secretary of Commerce by messenger. No one in the White House knew of this letter until Wallace, in a mild state of shock, called Charley Ross. The letter was so intemperate and bitter, Wallace said, that he doubted, for the sake of propriety, it should even go into the archives, much less be made public. When it was read to him over the telephone, Ross unhappily concurred. In what seems under the circumstances to have been an act of magnanimity, Wallace returned the offending document to Ross, who destroyed it.[102]

Wallace later described the incident a little differently. He said he called Truman directly when he received the letter, saying "You don't want this thing out." Truman agreed. "I'll send a man over to pick it up." Wallace described the letter as "low level": "I called him at once after I received the letter and he was very happy to take it back. I think it was dated that morning. It was not abusive, but it was on a low level. I don't remember anything about it—it didn't contain profanity—I just remember that it was on a low level."[103]

Returning the letter was indeed an act of magnanimity, for had it come out so soon after the severe criticism Truman had received for his mishandling of Wallace's speech, it would have been a serious embarrassment. As far as can be determined, Wallace never made any use of that letter and whenever asked about it said he could not remember what it said.

Later that day Henry Wallace sent a response to President Truman:

Dear Harry:

As you requested, here is my resignation. I shall continue to fight for peace. I am sure that you approve and will join me in that great endeavor.

Respectfully yours. . . .[104]

And Truman met the press and read a statement:

. . . I have today asked Mr. Wallace to resign from the Cabinet. It had become clear that between his views on foreign policy and those of the administration—the latter being shared, I am confident, by the great body of our citizens—there was a fundamental conflict. We could not permit this conflict to jeopardize our position in relation to other countries. I deeply regret the breaking of a long and pleasant official association, but I am sure that Mr. Wallace will be happier in the exercise of his right to present his views as a private citizen. I am confirmed in this belief by a very friendly conversation that I had with Mr. Wallace on the telephone this morning. [105]

Truman also asserted that there was no change in American foreign policy and that he had "complete confidence" in James Byrnes and the delegation at the Paris Peace Conference. Truman was not only telling the American people that his policy was unchanged but he was also telling Moscow that the "get-tough" policy was continuing.

That night in a radio address Wallace said: "I intend to carry on the fight for peace." Wallace recalled later:

I always had in my mind that if I were going to get out of the Cabinet I should get out on the peace issue. Ever since Morgenthau and Ickes had left, I figured it was only a question of months until I'd be getting out. I did want to get out on a basis which would help bring about an understanding between the United States and Russia and insure peace. I wanted to dramatize peace.

It wasn't my objective to have the September 12 speech do that. Knowing the number of people in the Cabinet and in Congress who felt the importance of having a showdown with Russia instead of any understanding, I felt it was inevitable that sooner or later I would get out on that issue. So if it hadn't been this speech, it would have been another one, I have no doubt. [106]

What a startling contrast between the behavior of Henry Wallace and those in the Kennedy and Johnson administration who never found it necessary to make their opposition to the Vietnam war public. Henry Wallace is one of the few top-ranking officials in American history to leave government on a matter of principle and take his case to the public. He was willing to risk his future in public life, whereas the George Balls, the Robert McNamaras, the Adlai Stevensons, the Roger Hilsmans confined their dissent to Georgetown and Park Avenue cocktail parties. They put loyalty to the team and their personal welfare above the national welfare, and they did not make any enemies in high places. But no one will say of them as they will of Wallace: America should have listened.

3

Wallace Decides to Run

The response—private and public—to the dismissal of Henry Wallace was immediate. Letters began to flood to his Washington apartment, some eight thousand within two weeks, thirteen thousand within a month.[1] Almost all were favorable, urging him to continue his fight for peace. Wallace also had his public defenders, many of them. Perhaps first was the outspoken Democratic senator from Florida, Claude Pepper. On September 17 Pepper had criticized Harry Truman's hard-line foreign policy, calling Wallace "a great American statesman," but Pepper was just warming up for angrier statements three days later. These followed actions by Alabama Congressman John J. Sparkman, who, as director of the speakers bureau of the Democratic National Committee had promptly, and publicly, canceled Wallace's scheduled campaign speeches and then extended the cancelations to Pepper's speeches as well. (Later the Democratic National Committee reversed itself because there was such a demand for Wallace and Pepper.)

This enraged the Floridian, who was well named. He denounced Truman's executive order forbidding members of the executive branch from making statements critical of U.S. foreign policy without White House approval. He said it was "obvious that if any of us in Congress dares to discuss what's being done we'll be subject to the most severe denunciation from certain places." He accused the administration of trying to suppress free speech and asserted that Wallace had "done a great service to the country in sacrificing a place in the Cabinet in an honest effort to make the people realize how important are the decisions being made by a few men in Paris to the peace of the nation and

the world." This was hardly surprising, since Pepper's remarks at the same Madison Square rally had been even
tougher than Wallace's. But they had not provoked as much
political controversy, because Pepper, although a Democrat,
was not a member of the Cabinet.[2]

James Loeb, Jr., of the Union for Democratic Action, was
deeply distressed by what had happened to Wallace, calling
the firing "a great loss to progressive forces in the country.
. . . We cannot align ourselves with the conservative and
reactionary forces which have made such enormous political
capital out of the whole episode."[3]

By coincidence a conference of liberals took place in Chicago for two days beginning September 28. Perhaps the
largest gathering of liberals and progressives ever held in
the United States, it was intended to mark the beginning of
a great progressive movement that would profoundly influence American politics and society. Even though Wallace
himself was not present, Wallace affairs dominated the
meeting. This Conference of Progressives adopted a special
resolution commending his fight for peace and for the program of FDR. It urged Wallace "to visit us at every
crossroads in America" and to "carry on with the confidence that you have the support of the millions upon millions who believe in the program of Franklin Roosevelt." It
pledged a "corps of volunteer citizens who will help carry
the fight for peace to every doorstep in the nation."[4]

The foreign-policy statement adopted by the conference
also seemed favorable to Wallace. It called for "a swift return to the progressive global thinking of Franklin Roosevelt. We must base our foreign policies once more on that
world good-neighborliness which was his legacy to us."
And the first step must be a return to "mutual trust among
the great powers." In other ways the statement appealed to
Wallace and his supporters: it opposed colonialism and imperialism, urged that pressure be brought on Chiang Kai-
shek to build a "democratic coalition" in China, opposed
U.S. bases around the world, rejected "the evolving pattern

of close military alliance with Britain," criticized the U.S. atomic-bomb proposals, and so on.

But the statement, like the conference itself, was more of an illusion than a reality. Both appeared to be going in the same direction as Henry Wallace, for that was the genuine conviction of most of the delegates, but neither statement nor conference came to grips with the real implications of the split between Wallace and Truman. The language seemed closer to Wallace but it was general enough so that Truman, who claimed always to be following Roosevelt's path, could be comfortable with it.

This was inevitable, given the sponsorship of the conference. Although it was called by leaders of the National Citizens Political Action Commitee, the Independent Citizens Committee for the Arts, Sciences and Professions, the National Farmers Union, and the National Association for the Advancement of Colored People, most important was the support of Philip Murray and the CIO. But Baldwin, a friend and once close associate of Murray, could not get Murray to go very far along the path that Baldwin, and Wallace, had chosen. He balked at the first draft of the foreign policy statement, and it was only with some toning down that he approved it at all. And in a speech to the conference, Murray, in a departure from his text, declared that "there is no more damn business for an American Communist meddling in our business than there is for any American meddling in the Russian Trade Union Movement."[5]

Without active CIO support, it would be difficult for any mass liberal movement to develop, since the CIO not only had staff and funds but had the reputation, a carry-over from the early union days, of being the heart of American liberalism. And Murray in 1946 had begun to become publicly an anti-Communist. This could not have been easy for him. On the one hand, he was a devoted trade unionist and recognized the vital work the Communists had done in the founding of the CIO during a time when union work required courage and perseverance. Furthermore, he had close personal relationships with a number of Communist labor leaders. On the other hand, he was a devout Catholic, was often in the company of anti-Communist priests, and was friendly to the Association of Catholic Trade Unionists, a vigorously anti-Communist group. Most writers tread carefully when speaking of the political influence of religious groups. Partly it is self-censorship: the fear, especially when discussing Catholics or Jews, of contributing to bigotry. Another reason is the reluctance—timidity might be a better term—to open yourself to a counterattack by so powerful a force. But it does seem to be true that Murray was influenced, to a considerable degree, by some members of the Catholic clergy.

Whatever the influence, Murray in May had caused the United Steelworkers of America, of which he was president, to adopt unanimously a statement that said, among other things, "This union will not tolerate efforts by outsiders— individuals, organizations or groups—whether they be Communist, Socialist or any other group to infiltrate, dictate or meddle in our affairs." And six months later, in November, Murray got the eighth constitutional convention of the CIO to adopt a resolution that said: "We . . . resent and reject efforts of the Communist party or other political parties and their adherents to interfere in the affairs of the CIO. This convention serves notice that we will not tolerate such interference."[6]

Many liberals in America believed, and wanted to believe, that the Conference of Progressives represented the beginning of the powerful liberal coalition they longed for, perhaps even the realignment of the American political structure. But that was an illusion. The conference was not the beginning, but the end. Murray had supported a united front, including Communists, during the war but he did not like the taste of it at Chicago. Later he artfully avoided Baldwin's efforts to get him to support a second conference and to expand it into a mass organization.

While the results of this political ferment were unclear—

there seemed to be both gains and losses for Wallace and those he represented—there were some clear political developments. Anita McCormick Blaine, his longtime admirer, sent a little note to Wallace and enclosed a check for $10,000, an astonishing political contribution in those days, particularly since Wallace was not a candidate for anything. Wallace was away when it arrived. so his wife, Ilo, promptly wrote to Mrs. Blaine, expressing their "warmest appreciation." And Wallace, on his return, had his aide Harold Young speak to her to set up a system of accounts.[7]

Within a few days of receiving that letter, Wallace got one from a Labour Member of Parliament, Donald Bruce. Bruce (who, incidentally, addressed his letter to "The Rt. Hon. Henry Wallace, Congress, U.S.A., Washington, D.C.") wrote that "for many of us over in this country it has been quite clear that within the United States Administration there has been a rapid move to the right. . . . At the present time we are living in an era in which the United States and Great Britain are pursuing a continuity of foreign policy barely distinguishable from the policy pursued in the pre-war years, and though this has not been assisted by Russian intransigence on numerous questions, nevertheless the task of breaking the vicious circle thus established lies clearly upon the Western Powers." Bruce then suggested "that some regular contact be maintained either between yourself and myself or between other Congressmen known to you and sympathetic to your views who would be prepared to keep themselves in communication with myself and my colleagues on this side of the Atlantic." This community of interest between Wallace and British progressives led to a highly controversial trip to Europe some months later. On October 23 Wallace made a friendly reply and suggested that Bruce keep in touch through Senator Pepper.[8]

Early in October Wallace wrote a rather tart letter to Norman Thomas, the ofttimes Socialist candidate for President. Although Thomas had made many admirable proposals that were later adopted by the Democratic Party and passed into

American life with most people unaware that they had once been considered quite radical, he was also a vehement anti-Soviet. Unquestionably, he was motivated in large part by his genuine concern over the lack of freedoms in Russia and Eastern Europe. But part of it may also have been the sectarianism of the Left that surely rivals the sectarianism of the Protestant Reformation, with this or that leader insisting that he, and he alone, has *the* truth. Anyway, for two years Thomas was to pursue Wallace with persistent criticism.

Wallace wrote:

. . . I read the American press today as it publishes news against Russia, then think of the way in which the American press did its best to stir up prejudice against Russia in 1919, 1920 and 1921. I know from Frederick Schuman's well-documented book that the American press was not telling the truth a considerable part of the time in 1919, 1920 and 1921. As to how many of the current stories of the press are really true I simply don't know. I do know that two Department of Commerce men who returned from a visit to Russia, Poland and Czechoslovakia in early September of this year brought back a totally different story about the situation than one would gather from reading the press. One of these men was brought in to the Department by Secretary [sic] Hoover and the other is a former Brookings employee, and I have every reason to believe that both are objective. Both are singularly fitted to get into the real inwardness of the situation.[9]

This expresses Wallace's conviction that the American press was prejudiced against Russia and against anyone who could be made to appear sympathetic to Russia and/or Communism. This is, I think, beyond dispute. Proud of its skepticism, proud of its practice of asking tough questions, the melancholy fact is that the American press was seldom skeptical of Truman's "get-tough" policy, seldom asked any tough questions, and must bear a major responsibility for the disastrous course of American foreign policy.[10] How this affected Henry Wallace will be discussed in some detail later.

Also in October Wallace wrote a couple of letters in which he gave his prescription for competing with communism. To Gilbert Harrison he said, ". . . I think we can completely disprove the underlying Communistic thesis if we are able to devise a lasting peace, produce to the limit, and eliminate the extreme ups and downs of the business cycle. If we get the full production which is implicit in atomic energy, I am sure that Communism will eventually pass out of the picture as a world-wide force. The way to prove the Communists wrong is to prove them wrong about their fundamental thesis. It is quite a job to do that because so many of the big capitalists are so eager to take action which proves the Communists are right."[11]

And to his friend Dr. Frank Thone, of Science Service, he wrote, "Communism can thrive only on scarcity and inequity. Atomic energy properly applied can mean the disappearance of both."[12]

These are hardly the words of a man sympathetic to communism. Indeed, they are the words of a naïve capitalist, a reformist capitalist, who believes capitalism can do what it has never done: "eliminate the extreme ups and downs of the business cycle." And his words also demonstrate what was common then, a belief that atomic energy could work miracles. Wallace, of course, was not alone in thinking that. So did many distinguished scientists; only experience demonstrated how complex, and how dangerous, was the peaceful use of atomic energy. It is indisputable, however, now as then, that communism does thrive on scarcity and inequality.

In mid-October the *New Republic* announced that Henry Wallace would become its editor. Many liberals welcomed the news that he would continue to have a platform. Olin Downes, music critic for *The New York Times,* put it this way: "It amuses me to see the obvious relief of some of our conservative friends and newspapers that you are going to undertake this editorial work, and that, as they fondly imagine, you are thereby to be retired from the active political field. I fully believe that in accepting this editorship you have taken the strongest weapon at your command, which will make you more influential in future political developments than could otherwise have been the case."[13] This was indeed an effective weapon for, it must be remembered, Wallace had been a skilled magazine editor for years at *Wallace's Farmer* before he entered public life. In fact, the publisher of that pre-eminent farm magazine had tried to get Wallace to return. For the next year Wallace used the *New Republic* to call for what we now term détente, as unpopular with the government and press then as it was popular in the last Nixon years.

(A few days later Wallace wrote a letter to a relative that sheds some interesting light on Hubert Humphrey, then the young mayor of Minneapolis, and makes a striking prophecy five years before the Korean war and fifteen before Vietnam:

. . . he probably did not read either the September 12th or the September 20th statement with any care. The problem of one world today is exactly the same as the problem of getting a Federal Government for the United States in 1787. I recommend in my speech of September 12 a much stronger United Nations than we now have, but raised the question realistically as to just what you might have to give up in order to get rid of the veto on the broadest international issues. I am afraid that Hubert doesn't realize that our present program will result in one impasse after another which will eventually result in war a number of years hence; or it will provoke a war in the relatively near future. If we intend to carry our present policy through and back it up by force, it will require at least five million men in the armed forces—and probably eight million. It will require an annual appropriation of at least fifty billion dollars a year—and more probably eighty billion dollars a year.[14]

During the fall Wallace campaigned for liberals from coast to coast. Usually they were Democrats, but in New York he endorsed Johannes Steel, a candidate of the American Labor

Party (who lost). On the last weekend before the election, Wallace appeared with Claude Pepper at a number of New York rallies sponsored by the ALP, the ICC/ASP, the NC/PAC, and several left-wing labor unions. Warren Moscow, a political writer for *The New York Times*, noted the significance of this sponsorship on November 4:

The Wallace-Pepper engagements presented the possibility of future importance. Both men were brought to the city under the auspices of left-wing groups independently of the Democratic command of the state. The leftist character of the last-minute drive was emphasized particularly in the case of Senator Pepper, whose appearance was announced by Irving Potash, manager of the Furrier Joint Council. Mr. Potash is a member of the National Executive Board of the Communist Party. Such activity appears to threaten the continuation in future elections of the Democratic Party's alliance with the American Labor Party though it should not affect the alliance with the Liberal Party.[15]

Warren Moscow was hardly the only one to notice the ties between some leftists and the Democratic Party. The conservative James Farley, former Postmaster and Democratic national chairman, had declared that "The Democratic Party is now in the throes of trying to rid itself of the Communist and Communist fellow-traveler element which attached itself to the party for its own subversive ends. Leadership which continues to play ball with that un-American element faces rejection by the rank and file of the Democratic Party and make no mistake about it."[16]

Wallace, on the other hand, in his speeches during the congressional campaign warned against electing "Soviet-baiters," called for decreased armaments spending, and declared that the United States should accept the proposal of Soviet Foreign Minister Molotov for a disarmament conference. Throughout the campaign he insisted that Democrats could win only if they were progressive, and at an NC/PAC luncheon the day before the election, when things were looking bad for the Democratic congressional candidates,

Wallace said, "I don't mean that the day after tomorrow we are going to form a third party, but I do say that new currents will be forming. What turn they will take I cannot now say but events will tell."[17]

The 1946 election was a disaster for the Democrats. As usual there were many conflicting analyses. Some simply blamed Truman. There's little doubt that he was at least partly to blame. His administration had alienated labor by his draft-the-strikers legislative request, many liberals felt he was deserting the New Deal principles of FDR, and his firing of Wallace did not help. Also the high cost of living, the President's indecisive actions regarding price controls, and consumer-goods shortages caused millions of Americans to be discontented. But one must be fair to Truman. He had to cope, or try to cope, with enormous problems that followed the end of the greatest war in human history. An immense war machine was being reconverted to peacetime uses, millions of servicemen were home seeking jobs and education, much of the world was in a state of collapse causing extraordinary and unprecedented problems of reconstruction. And, no less important, Truman had succeeded a legend. It was an impossible situation. Truman and his advisers clearly recognized his handicaps. He did not make a single campaign speech, not even on Election Eve. Instead, the party played old Roosevelt records.

Exultant Republicans had another explanation. Not only was Truman, in their view, a complete failure as President but the Democratic Party was, as Thomas Dewey had put it, the "captive of left-wing splinter groups." The Republicans had never been successful in Red-baiting Roosevelt; it just seemed to bounce off his hide, but they saw it as a key to their success that fall. Many worried Democrats agreed and concluded that they must purge their ranks of Communists and fellow travelers, a term that was seldom defined but politically devastating. After a while it came to seem that "fellow traveler" was applied to any political foe to the Left of Genghis Khan. In any case, it seems fair to say that many

Democratic liberals were influenced not only by their own genuine anticommunism but by the fear that if they did not equal Republicans in their Red-baiting, they themselves would be Red-baited with disastrous political results.

But Wallace and many liberals saw it differently. They argued that the Democrats had lost because the Truman administration had not been liberal enough, that millions of Roosevelt supporters had stayed home because they felt that Truman had abandoned them. As Wallace put it over NBC radio on November 10, "the Democratic Party cannot win an election in the United States, unless it is a forthright, clear-cut, liberal party with a forthright, clear-cut, liberal program."[18] And many liberals, anti-Communists as well as those who believed in a Popular Front with the entire Left working together for common goals, began speaking of the need for a third party; for it was almost universally assumed, by Democrats, Republicans, and the press, that Truman was an albatross, that if he were to run in 1948 the result would be catastrophic. So low was Truman's prestige that J. William Fulbright, then a young senator from Arkansas, proposed that Truman confer with Republicans, appoint their choice as secretary of state, and then resign in his favor. This ludicrous idea was discussed seriously and even supported by a number of politicians and newspapers, but *The New York Post* suggested that Truman was so incompetent he could not even do that right.[19]

Although he was hardly an admirer of Truman, Wallace thought the idea was absurd and opposed it publicly. As he wrote on November 13, "Don't worry about Truman appointing Vandenberg as Secretary of State and then resigning. He shouldn't do it and he will not do it. Truman is so much better than Vandenberg that there is no comparison. Truman is too much in the hands of the military, but Vandenberg would be no-end worse."[20] Wallace often argued that American foreign policy was not bipartisan—a great catchword then and for decades after—but actually Republican, with Vandenberg its chief architect. One wonders why the term "bipartisan" has always been treated with such reverence, why such substitutes for thought as "politics stops at water's edge" were accepted so unquestioningly by politicians, the press, and even intellectuals who should have known better. This has led to one disaster after another, disasters that might well have been avoided if foreign policy were unceasingly the subject for tough and detailed debate. In fact, as Wallace was often to say, American foreign policy was not truly bipartisan; when it came to foreign policy there was only one party with two branches that differed only in name.

A couple of weeks after the election Wallace wrote to Anita McCormick Blaine with a proposal for using some of the $10,000 she had contributed in September. First, he told her of the enthusiasm during the campaign with which he had been received by college students who "are deeply concerned with what is going on in the world. They do not want a third world war, and they do not believe that Secretary Byrnes and his aides will assure us of lasting peace." In San Diego, Los Angeles, Tacoma, Minneapolis, Madison, Chicago, Detroit, and New York, he told her: "I spoke to much larger crowds than I have ever had before. . . . I wish you could have seen the students at the University of Minnesota and the University of Wisconsin. Most of them, as you know, had their college careers interrupted by the war. They crowded the auditoriums and, because many could not get in, it was necessary for me to make two speeches at each of these schools. When I spoke to non-college audiences the story was much the same. The Stadium in Chicago, for instance, was full. These crowds turned out because they are interested in peace."

Wallace then went on to suggest the activities which he did, in fact, pursue during the next year. He said he wanted to speak widely at universities and off campuses, since his job at the *New Republic* gave him plenty of time it would help the magazine for him to get around the country. He said he also wanted to mail out copies of his July 23 letter to

Truman. He had a small office at 2500 Que Street, Washington, a list of several thousand people who had written him, and the services of Harold Young. Young, a small paid staff, and weekend volunteers would answer "the mass of mail" he was receiving and distribute literature all over America.

Wallace said he wanted within the next few months "to have a meeting of about one hundred sincere leaders who are anxious to take concerted action for peace," and he expressed the hope Mrs. Blaine would attend. What he wanted was "to encourage men and women in every town in America to organize and work for a lasting peace, and I am anxious to cooperate with others who feel as you and I about the problem." If she agreed with these plans, he would deposit her check and use the money as proposed.[21] She agreed.

Wallace's criticism of Truman's foreign policy received powerful support in the fall of 1946 with the publication of Elliott Roosevelt's book, *As He Saw It*. FDR's son wrote that his father was determined to undermine French, Dutch, and especially British colonialism throughout the world, seeing the great imperialist Winston Churchill as his major antagonist in this endeavor. According to Elliott, Truman had turned away from FDR's postwar plans by supporting imperialism and reaction, by supporting Britain to the detriment of Russia, and by refusing to recognize Russia's legitimate interests and fears. "A small group of willful men in London and Washington are anxious to create and foster an atmosphere of war hatred against the Russians, just as though the Russian people had not borne the brunt of the military force of Nazism, borne it, overthrown it, and thereby demonstrated for all time their importance to the coalition for peace."[22]

Many anti-Communist liberals denounced the book and Wallace supporters praised it, but many others also found it persuasive, for not just Popular Fronters were concerned about Truman's "get-tough" policy. However, according to Joseph Lash, himself a strong anti-Communist, Eleanor

Roosevelt did not support her son's conclusions, although she stated categorically: "I assure you that I can corroborate the actual things which he said in his book, and so can a good many other people because they were told many times. He may have misinterpreted but that is a matter of opinion."[23]

Toward the end of November Wallace received a long letter from Kingsley Martin, editor of *The New Statesman and Nation*, the influential British left-wing weekly which had printed the full text of his July 23 letter to Truman. In the most urgent terms, Martin requested Wallace to visit Britain for "a programme of perhaps three or four really big public meetings." Wallace asked his *New Republic* colleague Bruce Bliven to ask Martin to hold the matter in abeyance for the time being because Wallace was "swamped" with work in his new job.[24]

Meanwhile, the organizational structure that was to become the Progressive Party was beginning to form. This is, I am convinced, one of the crucial periods of postwar American history, for it was marked by the polarization of American liberalism. One the one hand was the new Progressive Citizens of America (PCA), which included Communists among its membership and even its leadership. On the other hand, the Americans for Democratic Action (ADA), an outgrowth of the Union for Democratic Action, was determinedly anti-Communist. For arbitrary reasons of convenience, I will now discuss the development of the PCA in the chronological account of Wallace's quixotic quest for the Presidency. But since I believe the ADA, despite its liberal reputation, bears a major responsibility for the Cold War and for the ugliness of McCarthyism that accompanied it, I will devote to it a separate chapter.

The death of Franklin Roosevelt had left a void, as much psychological as political, and liberals were forever trying to fill it. For a while some of them, like Claude Pepper, Oscar Chapman, and Chester Bowles, tried to start a nationwide pressure group called the Roosevelt Forum, invoking the name as if it were a talisman. But the effort never came to anything. For one thing, the Democratic National Committee was not very keen on the idea. Harry Truman was having enough difficulty stepping out of Roosevelt's shadow without perpetuating the problem by establishing the magic name as a banner under which the luminaries of the New Deal would rally. The last thing Truman needed was a constant reminder that he was no Roosevelt and that Roosevelt's men were no longer in the administration. Furthermore, two intense organizational efforts already were reinvigorating the liberal movement. One, the ADA, got most of the famous New Dealers, although by no means all of them, while the other, the PCA, got Henry Wallace, the heir apparent to Roosevelt's liberal mantle. The ADA would grow out of the Union for Democratic Action about a week after the PCA grew out of a merger of the National Citizens Political Action Committee and the Independent Citizens Committee of the Arts, Sciences and Professions.

The PCA was formed at New York's Hotel Commodore on December 28 and 29, 1946. It made sense because NC/PAC and ICC/ASP had similar goals and sought funds from the same sources. More important, a unified organization would be more effective than two separate ones. About the only opposition to the merger came from Communists within each of the groups who believed that no organization that was mainly middle-class could undertake effective political action. But Communists are hardly the only ones to believe the dogma that the working class, working through trade unions, is the basis of liberalism. The fact is that in the United States it is elements of the middle class that have provided most of the impetus for liberalism, whether in civil rights, economic reform, or antiwar movements, while trade unions have often opposed change.

Jo Davidson, a sculptor who had headed the ICC/ASP, and Frank Kingdon, a radio commentator who had headed the NC/PAC, were elected cochairmen of the PCA. Beanie Baldwin of NC/PAC became executive vice chairman of the new organization after a transition period in which he shared the title with Hannah Dorner of ICC/ASP. In contrast to ADA, which specifically excluded Communists, the PCA's bylaws opened membership "to all persons who support the objects of the organization. . . ." Later, when liberal anti-Communists tried to demonstrate that Wallace's campaign was the culmination of a long and devious Communist plot, they termed the founding of the PCA as a major step along the way. That is nonsense. The merger came about as a result of months of negotiations between the two principal constituent organizations, neither of which was dominated by Communists. There were Communists in both groups, some at leadership levels, but in the separate organizations as in the unified one, there was no conflict between Communists and non-Communists for the simple reason that there was no need for it; they shared common goals. When Red-baiting began, non-Communists who remained loyal to the PCA, and later the Progressive Party, saw it as a device to split the American progressive movement and fought back as a matter of honor, often at great personal cost.

Although Henry Wallace was not formally a member—he thought his editorship of the *New Republic* precluded such membership—he was plainly the PCA's leader and was the principal speaker at the founding meeting. He gave a good, tough progressive speech, against reaction at home and imperialism abroad. While he offered nothing specific about a possible third party, he gave ample warning that the Democratic Party must liberalize itself. ". . . We must continually make it clear to the administration that we, as progressives, would prefer the election of an out-and-out reactionary like [Robert A.] Taft in 1948 to a lukewarm liberal. We want this to be a genuine two-party system, and not a country operated by a fake one-party system under the guise of a bipartisan bloc."

Absolutely nothing in the speech suggested that Wallace was pro-Russian. In unmistakable language he was critical of both the United States *and* Russia, as the following two passages demonstrate:

. . . Those who put hatred of Russia first in all their feelings and actions do not believe in peace. Those who hold up Russian standards as a guide for us in the United States do not believe in freedom. As American progressives we are not interested in any fight between the Russia-haters and the Russophiles. We believe that such fighting is engineered by the enemy. We shall not allow the attacks of the enemy to stampede us into foolish Red-baiting. Nor shall we allow those who owe their primary allegiance to some foreign power to determine our course.

. . . We shall never be against anything simply because Russia is for it. Neither shall we ever be for anything simply because Russia is for it. We shall hold firmly to the American theme of peace, prosperity and freedom, and shall repel all the attacks of the plutocrats and monopolists who will try to brand us as Reds. If it is traitorous to believe in peace—we are traitors. If it is communistic to believe in prosperity for all—we are Communists. If it is Red-baiting to fight for free speech and real freedom of the press—we are Red-baiters. If it is un-American to believe in freedom from monopolistic dictation—we are un-American. . . .

Wallace also included one sentence that was clearly directed at those who were about to form the Americans for Democratic Action. "The fundamental progressive faith is so broad that we should not allow ourselves to be divided on any minor issues."[25] [From this point on, in the interest of clarity, I shall refer to those who more or less accepted the PCA position as progressives and those who more or less supported the ADA as liberals.]

On January 3 an old friend, Jake More, Iowa Democratic state chairman, wrote, hoping that Wallace would "conclude that the majority of the people can gain more through a strong Democratic Party than through a conservative Republican Party, which would be continued in office in the event of a third-party movement." Wallace's reply demonstrated that he was now thinking seriously of a third party.

I still think, as I told the PCA group here in New York on December 29, that the best bet is to try to make the Democratic Party into a truly liberal party. I also said, however, that I did not believe in the one-party system and that a continuation of the present bi-partisan bloc might make it necessary for the liberals to find some other mechanism through which to make themselves felt in national affairs. I wonder if the Democrats realize how great is the danger to our party in the continuation of the present bi-partisan bloc tactics. In other words, I am just as much against a strong conservative Democratic Party as I am against a strong conservative Republican Party. If the Democratic Party is not going to become genuinely progressive, the quicker it dies the better. . . .[26]

And indeed, Wallace made such thoughts public on January 10, when he appeared on *Meet the Press* on the Mutual Broadcasting System radio network. On the program he also discussed the role of Communists in a progressive movement and relations with Russia:

Q. Mr. Wallace, don't you think that the Communists, no matter how small a minority they are of any organization, are a disturbing influence, that they are anti-democratic?

A. Oh, sure; I agree with you on that.

Q. Well, why would you want them in any progressive movement?

A. I am not saying I want them in any progressive movement. Who said I wanted them in any progressive movement?

Q. Well, you spoke a minute ago—

A. If you allow that little thing to dominate your mind, it means that you have become a Red-baiter, a person who wants to sic the F.B.I. onto your neighbor; it interferes with everything you want to do, to do a job in the field of progressive authority here. It is just exactly what the enemy wants to see happen. I refuse to allow that to become a dominating consideration in my mind.

Q. What "enemy," Mr. Wallace? Who is the enemy?

A. The reactionaries.

Q. Mr. Wallace, on May 8, 1942, you said: "This is a fight between a slave world and a free world. Just as the United States in

1862 could not remain half slave and half free, so in 1942 the world must make its decision for complete victory one way or the other." Don't you think that thing still holds true today, and that we are fighting against a slave world?

A. I do not think that.

Q. You think Russia is a free world?

A. I do not think Russia is a free world, but I do not think it is a slave world in the way I meant in 1942 and in the way you mean today. If I agreed with you, I would know that we have to fight now. Fortunately, I don't agree with you. . .[27]

Here we have the Hitler-Stalin analogy again. Even sophisticated newsmen seemed unable to see that crucial difference between Hitler and Stalin. Loathsome as was Stalin's repression of liberty at home and in the bordering nations, he was not a threat to world peace. Even if Russia had the capacity for attempting conquest of the West—which it did not—there was no evidence then and there has been none since that Stalin had any plans for military conquest. The Russian scare had no basis in fact and surely the Truman administration knew it.

A couple of days later Wallace wrote a remarkable letter to General George C. Marshall, who had just been named by Truman to be secretary of state. He began the letter in the most respectful and complimentary terms, for Wallace did indeed admire Marshall for his work during the war. And he wrote that Marshall's failure—he phrased it diplomatically: "That you did not succeed completely . . ."—in China was not his fault but the fault of the policy he was trying so "brilliantly" to carry out. Then Wallace, in these prophetic words gave a splendid analysis of and prescription for American foreign policy:

Our relations with China are only one phase of our relations with the world. But you will find, I believe, that the problem everywhere is the same. The basic problem is to adjust the attitude of our country to a world that is in full flood of change. In almost every nation that has suffered heavily in this war, men and

women are desperately trying to alter the old order of things because the old order has brought upon them poverty, disaster and
war.

In the face of this tide of history our foreign policy has been a
static one; everywhere we have been on the defensive, erecting, as
it were, Maginot Lines of the spirit. We have been in the position
of saying "no" at Trieste, "no" in Poland, "no" in Iran, "no" in
China, "no" on the atom bomb, "no" up and down the borders of
Eastern Europe. As a military man, you know that a static defense
is a confession of defeatism, that Maginot Lines all crumble before
dynamic assault.

What we need is a mobile offensive in our foreign policy, an af-
firmation of the revolutionary tradition out of which this country
was born, a loud and ringing "yes" to the change that the wrecked
societies of Europe and Asia are demanding at once.

We have abandoned, almost by default, the sponsorship of these
changes to Russia. We have permitted the Russians to parade
themselves before all the colonial peoples of the world as the only
enemy of "imperialism." Almost without a battle we have yielded
to the Russians the loyalty of millions of workers and peasants in
Europe because they believe that the Russians and not ourselves
are their only guarantors against hunger and war. We cannot permit this to go on or we shall find our only allies the tired men who
have lost the faith of their own people, the same men whom you
characterized as "corrupt" and "reactionary" in China.

We cannot change our foreign policy by new statements, but
only by new actions. We must act to implement the Atlantic Charter; we must help the colonial peoples in their struggle to free
themselves; we must lead rather than follow in opposition to such
men as Franco. We must seek everywhere to find out what
changes are needed in the devastated areas of the world to fill the
stomachs and make busy the hands of the people; and we must be
the first to sponsor them. Wherever we meet Russia in Europe, it
is not Russia that is the enemy, but the devastation itself. . . .[28]

These are the words of a man that the press would soon
delight in calling "fuzzy-minded," "woolly," "mystic," and
so on. What he said we should not do, we did, and what he
said we should do, we did not.

By the middle of January 1947 Wallace's announcement of his forthcoming trip to England (he had accepted Kingsley Martin's invitation on January 6), and the cooperation between progressives on both sides of the ocean that it represented, had roused to anger the editors of *The New Leader*, a sort of Social Democratic weekly that was fairly liberal on domestic issues but unrelentingly anti-Communist. In a long statement addressed to Britain's Foreign Secretary Ernest Bevin which was signed by a number of "liberals" *The New Leader* took issue, not without some validity, with Wallace's criticism of British "imperialism." But, as the language below will demonstrate, their real concern was his "appeasement" of the Soviet Union:

"You should understand that American support for Wallace's position on foreign policy comes from a small minority of Communists, fellow travelers and what we here call totalitarian liberals. Their line has been repudiated not only by the American Federation of Labor, but by an overwhelming majority of the CIO. . . .

Many, perhaps most, of the adherents of the Wallace . . . axis on both sides of the Atlantic are confused innocents. But those who inspire and manipulate that axis know what they are about. They are less anti-British or anti-American than they are pro-Russian. Though the arguments of the two groups [the American and British progressives] are logically beyond reconciliation, their objective is the same. It is to drive a wedge between our two countries in order to prevent effective common policy or common action in relation to the ambition and unilateral acts of Soviet Russia. What these elements seek is a return to those Anglo-American policies of concessions and retreats which have already placed half of Europe and much of northern Asia under Soviet domination; whereas our real problem is not only to halt the retreat but to widen the area of freedom.

The real purpose of the cry of "imperialism" against Britain and America, at the very moment when British and American imperialism are on the wane, from the Philippines to Burma, can only be to divert attention from Soviet imperialism which, in defiance of solemn treaties, has annexed tens of millions of unwilling subjects, has rubbed out the sovereignty of some nations and made puppets of others, and has extended the rule of the secret police from Manchuria and the Kurile Islands to the suburbs of Trieste. These critics overlook or underestimate the evils of police rule, deportation, forced labor and concentration camps, as well as the barriers to the free flow of trade and information which the Soviet Government has erected across Europe. Their message adds up to just one thing—peace by appeasement, which the world has already tried to its cost. . . .[29]

There was much that could justifiably be said in anger about life behind the Iron Curtain, but the public was inevitably inflamed when those critical of American foreign policy did not have their criticisms discussed but were condemned as "Communists, fellow travelers and what we call here totalitarian liberals." Debate, yes, tough debate, but not in language that, in effect, accuses your opponents of disloyalty. Notice here, for instance, the allusion to Munich in the last sentence of the above passage and the use, which could only be deliberate, of the term "axis," the term by which the alliance of Germany, Japan, and Italy was known.

As to the signatories of the statement being described as "liberals," one can only be amused. Some of them were, of course, such as A. A. Berle, Jr., former assistant secretary of state; Dr. Harry D. Gideonse, president of Brooklyn College; A. Phillips Randolph, president of the Union of Sleeping Car Porters; Morris Ernst, the eminent attorney; Norman Thomas, the Socialist leader; Samuel M. Levitas, executive editor of *The New Leader;* Oswald Garrison Villard, former publisher of *The New York Post* and *The Nation;* Arthur M. Schlesinger, Jr., the Pulitzer Prize-winning historian; and Sidney Hook, professor of philosophy. But some of the other "liberals" were Henry Luce, publisher of *Time* and his wife, Clare Boothe Luce; H. V. Kaltenborn, the conservative radio commentator; George Hamilton Coombs, the arch conservative radio commentator; Malcolm Muir, publisher of *Newsweek;* and the Right Reverend Robert I. Gannon, S.J., president of Fordham University. The

list even extended to Republican Congressman Walter H.
Judd of Minnesota, the conservative stalwart of the China
Lobby (supporters of Chiang Kai-shek) which two years
later would accuse Harry Truman of "losing" China.
Wallace's reply was brief:

The cable addressed to the Rt. Hon. Ernest Bevin, sponsored by
the Socialist *New Leader*, is as curious a misinterpretation of my
views as the collection of signers who refer to themselves as
"American liberals." I am not surprised to find myself beset by
Time's Henry Luce, *Newsweek*'s Malcolm Muir, NBC's H. V. Kaltenborn, *Reader's Digest*'s Stanley High, Herbert Bayard Swope,
Bishop Manning and Father Gannon. I am surprised that such an
attack is advanced in the guise of liberalism and that the sincere
liberals who have joined with them in signing this document
should have allowed their names to be used in this fashion.

I have repeatedly stated that I am against all imperialism, Russia, British or American. I stand for civil liberties everywhere.

Whether we like the Russians or not, we have only two ultimate
courses. One is to make war on them. The other is to find a way to
live in the world with them, while striving to advance the Four
Freedoms everywhere in the world. In common with the great majority of the American people, I am in favor of the latter course. I
shall continue to fight for it.[30]

In February Wallace received an invitation from French
progressives to visit that country after Britain. The invitation, however, was initiated on this side of the Atlantic. In
January Wallace had spent an evening at the home of Alfred
and Martha Stern, who lived in Ridgefield, Connecticut, not
far from his farm in South Salem. In discussing his trip to
Britain, Wallace suggested that he might also like to go to
Paris. A few days later, his hosts wrote to a progressive
French friend, Pierre Cot, mentioning this and asking him
to sound out, confidentially, a few people about inviting
Wallace. Cot promptly wired back that there would be an
invitation forthcoming from a wide range of the French
Left. When they told Wallace this and received his accep-
tance, Mrs. Stern wrote again to Cot:

. . . In view of the fracas that attended the English invitation I would like to suggest that you keep my name and Alfred's out of it. No doubt the French press as well as the American will inquire as to the origin of the invitation. I suggest that you take full credit for it since you knew our friend in Washington and followed the recent issuance of the English invitation. We do not want any shadow cast on our friend—and the press might consider our "pre-mature anti-Fascist" records as an unsavory tie-up for him! Reaction as you well know is much stronger in this country than in France but your name has escaped the witch-hunters over here and certainly over there. I am enclosing a copy of this letter to our friend so that he too will not discuss the origin of the invitation except as indicated above.[31]

This kind of maneuvering is a little tricky and the fact that it is done in politics all the time does not make it any the more savory. However, it is true that the Sterns had cause to be concerned about their "pre-mature anti-Fascist" records. As far as the FBI and the right wing were concerned, it was all right to be anti-Fascist once it became acceptable, but to have been anti-Fascist too soon, say, to have supported the Loyalists against Franco was tantamount to being a Communist and, thus, disloyal.

At about that same time Wallace received a thoughtful letter from his nephew Wallace D. McLay, a student at Michigan State College (now University). McLay was concerned about a political inquisition being carried on at the campus by the state police and the FBI. "It seems extremely unfortunate when a student, particularly in a state institution, is refused the right of education and academic freedom because he does not hold the reactionary political views of the present state administration." To this Wallace made a sobering reply: "You had better make up your mind to it that there is going to be a lot of witch-hunting, and if you continue your present course you will probably—sooner or later—be implicated in some way, will be accused of being a Communist, and may get into real trouble of some kind. Please don't misunderstand. I am not giving you advice in any way, but merely telling you what is going on in these United States so that you may guide yourself accordingly."[32]

On February 14 Wallace received the invitation from a number of French political figures, including Léon Blum, the famous Socialist and former Premier; Léon Jouhaux, an anti-Communist Socialist who later won the Nobel Peace Prize; and Jacques Duclos, the Communist leader. Wallace immediately cabled back his acceptance.[33]

A third party headed by Henry Wallace became all but inevitable when the President delivered his famous Truman Doctrine speech of March 12, 1947, probably the most important speech delivered by an American President since the end of World War II. By this time Truman had pushed aside any doubts—if ever he had any—about the "get-tough" policy. Britain had informed the United States in February that it was no longer able to bear its imperial burdens in the eastern Mediterranean, that the United States must assume them or there would be a power vacuum that would be filled by Russia which for centuries, under czars or under communism, had sought an outlet to the Mediterranean.

Truman, Marshall, Acheson, and their top advisers were willing to assume Britain's burden as a bulwark against communism. So were such Republican "bipartisans" as Senator Vandenberg; but the Congress and the country as a whole, that was another matter. Congress particularly was dominated by Republican budget-cutters who had little sympathy with the British Empire and would not be eager to assume the great financial burdens of bailing out London. Only if Truman could impress upon Congress and the nation the enormity of the situation, the seriousness of the Russian challenge was there any chance he could get the necessary support. This decision was reached at an extraordinary meeting in the White House on February 27 attended by Republican and Democratic leaders of both

houses of Congress. Marshall and Acheson were to explain
the situation and enlist congressional support. Marshall,
who began the discussion, was not fully convincing, and
the legislators thought he was asking that the United States
pull "British chestnuts out of the fire." But then Acheson
intervened and advanced what might be termed the first
"domino theory." If Greece and Turkey fell, then their
neighbors would fall and then Western Europe until the
United States was in mortal peril. It was Rome against
Carthage, and, as Joseph M. Jones puts it in his indispensable account, "the two great powers were divided by an
unbridgeable ideological chasm." If we did not stop the
Communists immediately, it might be too late. Acheson
told his rapt listeners that nothing less than freedom itself
was at stake.

Acheson had abandoned the manner of a judge and for ten or
fifteen minutes had spoken as a fervent advocate. When he fin-
ished a profound silence ensued that lasted perhaps ten seconds. It
was broken by the voice of Senator Vandenberg. Slowly and with
gravity, Vandenberg said that he had been greatly impressed,
even shaken, by what he had heard. It was clear that the country
was faced by an extremely serious situation, of which aid to
Greece and Turkey, although of great importance, was only a part.
He felt that it was absolutely necessary that any request of
Congress for funds and authority to aid Greece and Turkey should
be accompanied by a message to Congress, and an explanation to
the American people, in which the grim facts of the larger situation should be laid publicly on the line as they had been at their
meeting there that day.[34]

That meeting had won Dean Acheson a place in history forever, for he was the prime mover.
    Two weeks later, before a somber Congress that was
shaken by what it was hearing, Harry Truman spoke the
words that have profoundly affected the lives of every
American who has lived from that time to this and the lives
of millions of other peoples the world over. Here was the

domino theory 1947-style, or as Truman put it in his *Memoirs:* "This was America's answer to the surge of expansion of Communist tyranny. It had to be clear and free of hesitation or double talk."[35]

It is necessary only to glance at a map to realize that the survival and integrity of the Greek nation are of grave importance in a much wider situation. If Greece should fall under the control of an armed minority, the effect upon its neighbor, Turkey, would be immediate and serious. Confusion and disorder might well spread throughout the entire Middle East. Moreover, the disappearance of Greece as an independent state would have a profound effect upon those countries in Europe whose peoples are struggling against great difficulties to maintain their freedom and their independence while they repair the damage of war. Collapse of free institutions and loss of independence would be disastrous not only for them but for the world. Discouragement and possibly failure would quickly be the lot of neighboring peoples striving to maintain their independence. Should we fail to aid Greece and Turkey in this fateful hour, the effect will be far reaching to the West as well as to the East. We must take immediate and resolute action.

And in that speech were the words that later were used to justify American intervention not only in Greece and Turkey but in Indonesia, Korea, Iran, Guatemala, Cuba, Laos, Cambodia, Vietnam, and elsewhere:

I believe that it must be the policy of the United States to support free peoples who are resisting attempted subjugation by armed minorities or by outside pressures.[36]

This was the call to counterrevolution, everything that Wallace had warned against in his letter to General Marshall only a few weeks before.

Truman aroused a great deal of opposition to his speech, not only from progressives but from some liberals and generally from the press across the country. Some noted that the Greek royalist government was undemocratic, repres-

sive, corrupt, and incompetent and that Turkey had been a
friend of our foes during World War II. Others noted that
the Truman Doctrine, as the proposal came to be known,
completely bypassed the United Nations and it was noted
that the American commitment to intervene was open-
ended, with no limit in time or place. Not unexpectedly
Henry Wallace was a major participant in the ensuing debate. The day after Truman's speech he spoke nationwide
on NBC radio. His was not a response written by a revisionist historian after Vietnam had proved the disastrous
futility of American foreign policy. His response was made
the day after Truman's speech and even now it merits substantial quotation.

Yesterday March 12, 1947, marked a turning point in American
history. Fellow Americans, it is not a Greek crisis that we face, it is
an American crisis. It is a crisis in the American spirit. That which
I feared when I wrote President Truman last July has come upon
us. Only the American people fully aroused and promptly acting
can prevent disaster.
   Yesterday President Truman, in the name of democracy and hu-
manitarianism, proposed a military lend-lease program. He proposed a loan of $400 million to Greece and Turkey as a down
payment on an unlimited expenditure aimed at opposing communist expansion. He proposed, in effect, that America police Russia's every border. There is no regime too reactionary for us provided it stands in Russia's expansionist path. There is no country
too remote to serve as the scene of a contest which may widen
until it becomes a world war.
   . . . President Truman says that the people of Greece are home-
less, hungry and ravaged by the losses of war. We all know this.
It is not only the Greek people who are suffering from the war. It is
the peoples of all Europe, of Russia, of China and of many lands.
   Americans agree with President Truman that we must aid the
people beside whom we fought. Americans ask: If aid to the people of the world is our objective, why did the President and the
Congress allow the United Nations Relief and Rehabilitation Administration to die? Why are we doing nothing to help the million
displaced persons without homes in Europe? Why are we speaking

of only $400 million when the need is far greater? Why is $150 million of those $400 million to be given to Turkey which was no ally of ours and which is in no urgent need of food and supplies?

All Americans agree with President Truman that freedom is the most cherished of human goals, and should be helped to grow in all countries. These same Americans ask: How does support given to the undemocratic governments of Greece and Turkey aid the cause of freedom?

Turkey is a nation which fought against us in the First World War and which in this war refused to help the United Nations. Turkey fattened herself off the Germans and the Allies by offering her vital supplies of chrome to the highest bidder. Out of these sales she built up a gold reserve of a quarter of a billion dollars. Turkish neutrality lengthened the war by months. Turkey was a haven for Nazi leaders at the war's end. It is utter nonsense to assert today that the Turkish government is representative or democratic. Turkish sources state that the $150 million that President Truman proposes to give Turkey is to be used to maintain her army of a million men—equivalent to 7 million men in terms of the United States.

I strongly recommended economic aid to Greece. As Secretary of Commerce I was for a Greek loan for such purposes when most of the administration was against it. But President Truman has made it clear that very little of the $250 million loan to Greece is for economic reconstruction. It is a military subsidy to the Greek government to continue its efforts to stamp out all opposition. It is utter nonsense to suggest that the present Greek government is a democratic one. Secretary of State Marshall condemned many aspects of that government. He called for a political amnesty, substantial unity and many reforms in the government as the conditions of American aid to Greece. Why did President Truman abandon the conditions set by his own Secretary of State? The President asks only that American civilian and *military* personnel supervise the use made of American supplies. What do the activities of American Army officers in Greece have to do with peaceful reconstruction?

A year ago at Fulton, Missouri, Winston Churchill called for a diplomatic offensive against Soviet Russia. By sanctioning that speech Truman committed us to a policy of combating Russia with British resources. That policy proved to be so bankrupt that Britain can no longer maintain it. Now President Truman proposes we take over Britain's hopeless task. Today Americans are asked to support the governments of Greece and Turkey. Tomorrow we shall be asked to support the governments of China and Argentina.

I say that this policy is utterly futile. No people can be bought. America cannot afford to spend billions and billions of dollars for unproductive purposes. The world is hungry and insecure, and peoples of all lands demand change. American loans for military purposes won't stop them. President Truman cannot stop change in the world any more than he can prevent the tide from coming in or the sun from setting. But once America stands for opposition to change, we are lost. America will become the most hated nation in the world.

Russia may be poor and unprepared for war but she knows very well how to reply to Truman's declaration of economic and financial pressure. All over the world Russia and her ally poverty will increase the pressure against us. Who among us is ready to predict that in this struggle American dollars will outlast the grievances that lead to communism? I certainly don't want to see communism spread. I predict that Truman's policy will spread communism in Europe and Asia. You can't fight something with nothing. When Truman offers unconditional aid to King George of Greece, he is acting as the best salesman communism ever had. In proposing this reckless adventure Truman is betraying the great tradition of America and the leadership of the great American who preceded him.

Coming two days after the opening of the Moscow Conference, President Truman's speech has undermined General Marshall's assignment of cooperating with Great Britain, France and Russia in writing the peace. The United Nations, our great hope for peace, rests on the continued cooperation of these nations and will be gravely weakened if America follows the course that Truman recommends. The United Nations Commission is now in Greece investigating the threat to Greek security. If Greece is in danger let the United Nations tell us the facts and recommend action. America will do what the United Nations recommends. Why should President Truman undercut its action? How can we wage a war of nerves against Russia and expect her to take in good faith our proposals to the United Nations on atomic energy? When President Truman proclaims the world-wide conflict between East and West, he is telling the Soviet leaders that we are preparing for eventual war. They will reply by measures to strengthen their position in the event of war. Then the task of keeping the world at peace will pass beyond the power of the common people everywhere who want peace. Certainly it will not be freedom that will be victorious in this struggle. Psychological and spiritual preparation for war will follow financial preparation; civil liberties will be restricted; standards of living will be forced downward; families will be divided against each other; none of the values that we hold worth fighting for will be secure.

Most Americans fear that the actions proposed by President Truman will lead to disaster. That is why congressional leaders were prepared in advance for the President's message. That is why the program was presented piece by piece, and not as an over-all program that Americans could look at and judge as a whole. No hypocritical appeal to the generosity and decency of the American people should be permitted to draw us in a commitment for which there is no end in sight. Americans are for democracy and economic reconstruction. As one American citizen I say: *No loan to undemocratic and well-fed Turkey: No loan to Greece until a representative Greek government is formed and can assure America that our funds will be used for the welfare of the Greek people.*

. . . This is the time for an all-out worldwide reconstruction program for peace. This is America's opportunity. The peoples of all lands say to America: Send us plows for our fields instead of tanks and guns to be used against us. The United Nations is waiting, ready to do the job. We should start with an economic plan for the Near East financed by the International Bank and backed by the United Nations. The dollars that are spent will be spent for the production of goods and will come back to us in a thousand different ways. Our program will be based on service instead of the outworn ideas of imperialism and power politics. It is a fundamental law of life that a strong idea is merely strengthened by persecution. The way to handle communism is by what William James called "the replacing power of the higher affection." In other words, we must give the common man all over the world something better than communism. I believe we have something better than communism here in America. But President Truman has not spoken for the American ideal. . . .[37]

Wallace's speech touched many Americans, and his office was flooded with letters, many written by hand and deeply felt. Many spoke of Wallace's courage and his emulation of FDR; many spoke of fear upon hearing Truman's speech; many were from veterans who did not want to go to another war; and many complained there had been little or no coverage of Wallace's reply to Truman in their local press. This last is not surprising. For another couple of decades the press on foreign affairs largely served as the information arm of whatever administration was in power. With a few exceptions the press made headline news of whatever the President or secretary of state said and dismissed in a few brief paragraphs or ignored altogether what was said by responsible critics—except when the criticism was from the Right, urging that the government take an even tougher line with Russia.[38]

Among the many letters Wallace received was one from a newspaper publisher who was unique, then and for a couple of decades later, Josiah W. Gitt, publisher of *The York Gazette*, probably the only daily paper in the United States that consistently opposed postwar American foreign policy. If ever American journalism had a hero it was he, but, alas, his brave newspaper was published in a small Pennsylvania city and not Washington or one of the great metropolitan centers. Literally, and sadly, a voice in the wilderness.

. . . While one had every reason to anticipate what the President did, nevertheless it came as a great shock to me. I just cannot believe that we can be led into offering up our human resources as well as our material ones in erecting a Chinese wall around communism. And that of course is what Truman was proposing.

It seems to me that the whole future of humanity is hanging in the balance and that a resort to force by reaction to beat off communism will sooner or later put an end to civilization as we know it.

Lining up with reaction can come to no good. Personally I am so firmly convinced that reaction is attempting to commit suicide and carry us with it, that it seems imperative to me that all of us who do know better must speak out fearlessly and regardless of possible present political results. Somehow or other we have got to head off this ignorant and dangerous international policy.

And may I say that like you I am certainly not a communist or fellow traveler or anything of the kind.[39]

Gitt's interpretation of Truman's speech differs somewhat from the President's own private interpretation. In a letter of March 13 to his daughter Margaret, Truman wrote: "The attempt of Lenin, Trotsky, Stalin, et al., to fool the world and the American Crackpots Association, represented by Jos. Davies, Henry Wallace, Claude Pepper and the actors and artists in immoral Greenwich Village, is just like Hitler's and Mussolini's so-called socialist states.

"Your Pop had to tell the world just that in polite language."[40]

Henry Wallace's prediction that "civil liberties will be restricted" did not take long to come true. On March 23, 1947, Harry Truman issued Executive Order 9358, which established a loyalty program for all federal civil servants. (It was later extended to include defense workers.) There was absolutely no evidence then, nor has any been discovered since, that substantial numbers of disloyal federal employees existed at any level. Those accused did not have the right to face their accusers and they could be found disloyal for belonging to any "foreign or domestic organization, association, movement, group or combination of persons which the Attorney General, after appropriate investigation and determination, designates as totalitarian, Fascist, Communist or subversive. . . ." Truman was not only encouraging a Red Scare; he was making it legitimate, providing the institutional basis for ruining the careers and lives of many decent Americans. Yet he was adding nothing to the government's powers to dismiss and punish disloyal employees. There were already sufficient laws for those purposes. This was a shameful act. Even had there been nothing else to criticize in Truman's nearly eight years as

President, this would have been a terrible historical burden to bear, as friends, neighbors, even relatives were encouraged to inform on one another. It is worth noting that even during wartime FDR had not attempted such drastic curtailments of American liberties (with the single terrible exception of sending Japanese-Americans to concentration camps).

Henry Wallace, on March 31, declared, "the Truman program must turn Americans against each other. It will threaten everything in America that is worth fighting for. Intolerance is aroused. Suspicion is engendered. Men of the highest integrity in public life are besmirched. The President's executive order creates a master index of public servants. From the janitor in the village post office to the Cabinet members, they are to be sifted and tested and watched and appraised. Their past and present, the tattle and prattle of their neighbors, are all to be recorded."[41]

Jo Davidson and Frank Kingdon, cochairmen of the Progressive Citizens of America, had, a day earlier, sent an open letter to the President urging that the order be revoked immediately, arguing that Truman's executive order conflicted with the ancient and sacred principles of Anglo-Saxon law that when a person was presumed innocent until found guilty, that he had a right to know the specific charges against him and the right to meet his accusers in open court and cross-examine them.

In melancholy contrast, the ADA officially approved the idea of excluding "from Government employment people who adhere to foreign governments or totalitarian political philosophies in any case where such adherence may endanger the best interests of the United States." The ADA's behavior in this area was most curious, for many ADA people were bravely outspoken in defense of government employees accused of being security risks. It is rather as if brave firemen claimed medals for their daring but selective rescue attempts while hoping no one noticed—perhaps not even noticing themselves—that they had helped fuel the fire. This was not the only such sharp contrast between the PCA and the ADA, for the PCA had attacked the Truman Doctrine speech which the ADA had approved.[42]

Shortly before leaving for Europe, Wallace received yet another invitation to visit France, this time proffered by an even more impressive list of French political figures. Among those signing the cabled invitation were all four leaders of the political parties that constituted the French government: Edouard Herriot, former Premier and head of the middle-class Radical and Radical Socialist Party; Maurice Schuman, head of the Catholic Mouvement Républicain Populaire; and, once again, Blum and Duclos. And on April 2 Wallace announced that he would also be visiting Sweden and Denmark.

Abroad, Wallace said exactly the same things he had been saying at home and, a couple of months before Secretary of State Marshall made his historic speech outlining the Truman administration's plan for a European recovery program, he advocated a $50-billion ten-year economic-assistance program financed through the World Bank and administered by the United Nations. In Central Hall in London, wild applause greeted this statement: "The world is devastated and hungry; the world is crying out, not for American guns and tanks to spread more hunger, but for American plows and machines to fulfill the promise of peace."[43] And on April 13 over the BBC Wallace was again prophetic. "The immense power and wealth of America is being used for strategic and military purposes rather than to raise the standard of living in countries which could become a great market for American exports. . . . A great national awakening has occurred in Asia and in other parts of the world which we used to think of only as colonies. This new nationalism will turn into communism and look to the Soviet Union as their only ally, if the United States declares that this is the American century of power politics rather than the Century of the Common Man." [44]

If Wallace's criticism of U.S. policy had angered the Establishment while he was at home, such criticism abroad drove it to hysteria and beyond. The response, as *The New York Times* of April 13 put it, was "probably the most vehement congressional reaction in years to the pronouncements of a public figure." There was talk of treason, a sort of rage that reduced some of his detractors to incoherence. Even Eleanor Roosevelt, who had serious doubts about Truman's foreign policy, wrote to Beanie Baldwin: "I have such complete confidence in Mr. Wallace's integrity, I am sure he has taken this course because he felt he had to, but with all my heart I wish for his own sake that he had not done so."[45] Even she accepted that slogan that has done such harm, that "politics stops at water's edge."

Louis E. Starr, Commander of the Veterans of Foreign Wars, wrote to Truman suggesting that Wallace's official passport be revoked. Truman replied that Wallace had the right to say anything he chose: "There is not very much that can be done about Henry's wild statements and if I take notice of them it only gives him more publicity." Max H. Sorenson, commander of the Catholic War Veterans, wired the President that his organization stood "four square behind your policy of assistance to Greece and Turkey to prevent expansion of atheistic communism and repudiate statements made abroad by Mr. Wallace."[46] Truman, like all the Presidents who succeeded him, could always count on veterans' groups whenever the flag was waved.

Wallace had a great deal of support in Great Britain, though he was strongly opposed not only by Winston Churchill and the Tories but by segments of the Labour Party. He left England, however, with a letter signed by members of both Houses of Parliament expressing "sincere thanks and warm appreciation" for his words, which had recaptured something of the "high ideals and purposes" of President Roosevelt.

Wallace was a big hit in Sweden and Norway, but his trip to Denmark was carried on in a low key because of the recent death of King Christian X. By the time he got to

Paris, things had changed. Blum's Radical Socialists (who were neither) and Schuman's Popular Republicans had backed away from their sponsorship of Wallace's visit, partly for internal French political reasons—the Communists were attacking the Truman Doctrine. But it is hardly wild speculation to assume that the United States had made its displeasure known and that the French government, desperately needing American aid, had persuaded its members to withdraw support. Wallace was concerned that his sponsorship now was almost exclusively extreme left wing. "I want to avoid being monopolized by the extreme Left who have been so friendly to me in Paris." In France, as in America, even men who shared Wallace's views were afraid to be identified with him. It was too dangerous.

Almost immediately upon his return to the United States, Wallace set off on a cross-country speaking tour, a joint project of the *New Republic,* which hoped to increase its subscription list, and the Progressive Citizens of America, which also hoped to increase membership. It was an extraordinary tour, as even Wallace's foes admitted with no little astonishment. Wallace said little that was new, generally restating what he had pronounced before at home and more recently abroad. What was astonishing was the size of the crowds that paid—and this shattered conventional political thinking—to hear him. Traditionally, the main problem for politicians is to attract crowds. Charging admission was not only unconventional but crazy. Yet it worked. Thousands turned out to hear Wallace speak. And not only did they pay to get in, they usually contributed again inside. On May 14, twenty-two thousand paid to get into the Chicago Stadium with another five to ten thousand outside listening to loudspeakers. The next day there was a huge crowd in Detroit and on May 19, thirty thousand packed the Gilmore Stadium in Los Angeles (chosen because the Hollywood Bowl had refused to let Wallace rent it).
As usual Wallace criticized Truman's foreign policy, but

this time he also turned to a topic of unequaled importance
to many of his listeners (who included such famous Hollywood figures as Katharine Hepburn, Charlie and Oona
O'Neill Chaplin, John Garfield, Hedy Lamarr, Edward G.
Robinson, Budd Schulberg, and Paul Henreid). The House
Un-American Activities Committee had recently made the
first of a series of visits to Hollywood to "uncover" what it
alleged to be Communist influence on the movies. This was
the beginning of an epoch that was not only an insult to the
American right to freedom of thought and speech but
caused a number of liberal Hollywood figures to fall over
one another in their eagerness to save their own careers by
informing on their friends and colleagues. Of course the information consisted almost entirely of unsubstantiated allegations, but in that shameful period such allegations were
gleefully accepted as facts, causing the careers of decent
men and women to be ruined and Hollywood itself to function under a cloud of shame. There were, of course, those
who refused to succumb to fear and they are among the authentic heroes of the postwar years.[47] Wallace listed such
violations of American principles as the Salem witch trials,
the lynching of blacks, the Sacco-Vanzetti trial, the confine-
ment of Japanese-Americans during the war. And after declaring that "those who fear communism lack faith in democracy," he made a statement that he was to repeat over
and over again for the next year and a half, a statement that
cost him enormously socially and politically: "I am not
afraid of communism. If I fail to cry out that I am anti-Communist, it is not because I am friendly to communism but
because at this time of growing intolerance I refuse to join
even the outer circle of that band of men who stir the
steaming cauldron of hatred and fear."[48]

Two days later, on May 21, in Oakland, Wallace again
turned to communism. "If communism is a menace, then
give the people proof in terms that they understand, instead
of rousing hatred and hysteria. . . . Today, in blind fear of
communism, we are turning aside from progress and aside

from the United Nations. We are approaching a century of fear."[49]

The large, paying crowds Wallace attracted did not escape notice. The *Baltimore Sun*, which in the person of reporter Howard M. Norton, consistently gave the most complete coverage of Henry Wallace through 1947 and 1948, said that Wallace was reuniting the Left of the Democratic Party.[50] This unity, of course, later collapsed because of a variety of factors: the political reality that an incumbent President could not be denied the nomination, the liberals' fear of splitting the Democratic Party, and, hardly least, the Red-baiting that was to increase in intensity.

Just as interesting as Norton's political analysis and in the long run probably more important was his characterization of Wallace. Traveling with Wallace, Norton wrote, is "like traveling with a messiah and his disciples. . . . The groups of Leftist leaders in his more intimate meetings listen in rapt silence when he speaks." Norton compared the tour to a series of revival meetings, with Wallace's points "frequently hammered home to the accompaniment of reverent 'amen's' from the audience." Wallace's frequent quotations from the Bible, his abstinence from tobacco and alcohol, his early rising, his stoicism—often scheduling himself to three or four nights in succession in the ordinary seats of commercial airliners—his frequent disregard of meals, all added up to give the impression of a leader of a religious crusade out on a mission. Plainly, Wallace was no ordinary politician, nor was he the kind who could easily be deflected from what he felt to be his duty. From this time on, whether or not he had reached a conscious decision, it was probably inevitable that he would run against Truman.

Not only the press and politicians took notice of Wallace. On June 6 the Department of State issued an internal document classified Confidential and entitled "THE RECENT FOREIGN POLICY VIEWS OF HENRY A. WALLACE." The document noted that Wallace spoke "to large, enthusiastic crowds who paid as much as $3.60 to hear and see him.

Most newspaper reports agree that Wallace spoke to roughly 100,000 people during his trip. . . ." The document ended with this matter-of-fact appraisal:

The size of the audiences has amazed many commentators. Looking at the attendance records, Doris Fleeson concluded that Wallace is "perhaps the only man in the U.S. with a genuine popular following as well as devoted disciples." And Roscoe Drummond, the *Christian Science Monitor*'s veteran political reporter, describing the Wallace tour as "political barnstorming," said: "I have never seen a pre-convention campaign tour, even those of Wendell L. Willkie and Gov. Thomas E. Dewey, command even non-paying audiences of such size."

The press has given considerable—but not particularly sympathetic—attention to the Wallace tour, and his news coverage in the cities in which he has spoken has been extensive. In addition, the *Baltimore Sun* and the Knight newspapers each assigned a reporter to accompany Wallace on the entire trip.[51]

The State Department always gets nervous when any sizable proportion of the American public dissents from the current foreign policy. Since it is one of the professed pieties of the American political system that public opinion is a major factor in the determination of foreign policy, it is therefore necessary, if at all possible, to make public opinion conform to the policy of the administration of the day. Normally that is not difficult, given the instruments of publicity available to the President, secretary of state, *et al.*, the usually unquestioning cooperation of the press, and the normal desire of the people to rally round their leaders. Certainly that was true until the manifest failure of American policy in Indochina finally caused first the press and then the people to ask the serious questions that had been unasked for a generation.

The State Department was not the only nervous institution in Washington. When the Southern Conference for Human Welfare announced that Henry Wallace would be a speaker at an open-air rally at the Watergate Amphitheatre (the same area where an apartment complex would later be constructed), a number of efforts were made to abort the meeting. First a Republican congressman from Kansas, Herbert A. Meyer, attacked Wallace as "the evil tool of those who would destroy America" and asked, "When will the Attorney General of the United States do his duty and indict this renegade?" Three days later, on June 13, a Wisconsin Republican, Congressman Alvin E. O'Konski, went into U.S. District Court seeking an injunction against the use of the amphitheater by the Southern Conference, arguing that it was "a group sympathetic with those who advocate overthrow of our government by force." He also added some irrelevant reference as to why Truman fired Wallace.

Meanwhile, the Republican chairman of the House Un-American Activities Committee, J. Parnell Thomas of New Jersey, did his best to intimidate civil servants from attending the meeting. First HUAC announced that an investigative report would demonstrate that the Southern Conference had been "manipulated" by Communists. To this Clark Foreman, conference chairman, promptly replied by telegram:

> You have announced to the press that you are going to declare the Southern Conference for Human Welfare and me guilty of un-Americanism at high noon Saturday.
>
> May I again point out that in America it is customary to hold a public hearing and to be faced by your accusers before conviction.
>
> The Southern Conference strives for full democracy gained through the democratic process. We are still ready, even though you have announced your judgment, to appear and be questioned before any public hearing of your committee.

HUAC also announced that it would send "observers" to the Watergate rally, who, Thomas said, would take note of those who appeared on the platform with Wallace and analyze any literature that was distributed. Henry Wallace saw another purpose: "to scare Government workers so that they will not attend the meeting. If the 'police state' has not yet arrived in the United States, the government workers will rebuke these tactics by turning out in force. . . . We're going to have sufficient copies of the *New Republic* on hand to pass out to the entire audience. I would be extremely pleased to have them know exactly what I think. It's all in the open every week in my magazine. We welcome all members of the committee and their staff as regular readers."[52]

Neither the District Court nor the government workers cooperated with the House Un-American Activities Committee, for the Watergate rally was a sellout. But the "observers" were there, not very subtly, taking pictures of the audience as well as the speakers—a practice that was continued by one government agency or another until the 1970s.

Wallace, of course, was not intimidated, nor was Clark Foreman, who opened his remarks with, "Friends, Americans, and observers." But the actions the House of Representatives had taken that same day were not encouraging. Rather they were frightening. Congressman Chet Holifield, a Democratic liberal from California, read Foreman's telegram to the House. But Foreman's statement was not even allowed to exist in the record. On the motion of Congressman John E. Rankin of Mississippi, the House expunged the telegram from the *Congressional Record* by a vote of 146–7.

At Watergate Wallace discussed a third party, something he was increasingly to do for the rest of 1947. At one point he said, "It will be important—if the Democratic Party succumbs to Wall Street domination—to have a new party to let the people of the world know that those who believe in peace and understanding still have some means of expression." Yet he also said he preferred "a genuine two-party system. I would rather congratulate the administration on a reversal of present trends and on assuming some dynamic, positive, liberal leadership. The trend of the past year has been the other way."[53]

A third party was unquestionably very much in his mind, but he seemed still to have as first priority an attempt to influence Harry Truman to modify his "get-tough" policy.

This was Wallace's last major speech until the fall. For the next few months the emphasis was on building an effective progressive movement right down to the ward and precinct level. The Progressive Citizens of America provided the driving force. It was similar in many respects to the peace movement of a generation or so later. Among its leading figures were prominent intellectuals, social critics, scientists, writers, and show-business personalities, people like the literary critic Van Wyck Brooks, the radio playwright Norman Corwin, the writer Lillian Hellman, the actors Gene Kelly and José Ferrer, the singer Paul Robeson, and the astronomer Harlow Shapley. At the top were Frank Kingdon and Robert W. Kenny, former attorney general of California, as co-chairmen. Jo Davidson, the first chairman, now in France, was made honorary chairman. Among the vice chairmen were two men trusted by Wallace who became leading figures in the Progressive Party: Elmer Benson and Wallace's old colleague from the Department of Agriculture, Beanie Baldwin. It was Baldwin, with his warm, gentle manner, his Southern courtesy, his amused view of life, who worked tirelessly to build a progressive movement and to convince Wallace, who needed little convincing, that it was his duty to lead it against the bipartisan coalition dragging the nation deeper and deeper into what came to be called the Cold War.

For a time in 1947 it seemed that the progressives of the PCA would overwhelm in significance the liberals of the ADA. For while the ADA remained a fairly small elite, Ivy League in tone and probably in composition, except for a number of labor leaders, the PCA was making strides toward becoming a mass organization. From seventeen thousand dues-paying members in May 1947 it rose to forty-seven thousand by September, with many state and partial-state organizations. With enthusiastic chapters across the country, the PCA seemed to many of its members to be the wave of the future, a growing movement that would revivify the New Deal. It was intended to be a mass movement, and with its rapidly multiplying membership during that summer of 1947, it seemed well on the way. The ADA, too, wanted to be a mass organization but even though it enlisted many of the big names of the New Deal, it was never able to engender similar enthusiasm. Perhaps it was because the PCA was itself enthusiastic about recruiting all kinds of people, while the ADA tended to be academic and bureaucratic, more comfortable within structured institutions, seeking liberal ends through the exercise of bureaucratic skills. Many of the ADA people seemed to be instinctive elitists, whereas the PCA was less cautious, more adventurous even, trying to enlist all who would listen in a crusade to remake America. The ADA, while it had its enthusiasts, seemed cool and deliberate, whereas the PCA seemed warm and impetuous.

While the PCA appeared similar to the Vietnam peace movement of twenty years later, there was one crucial difference. The PCA turned out to be fighting a brave but futile rear-guard action against the Cold War consensus that would smash it and ruin, temporarily and sometimes permanently, the careers of many of its members. The momentum of the Cold War was irresistible then, for the administration, the Congress, the press, and even many intellectuals supported it. But twenty years later when the Vietnam antiwar movement began, it was an advance guard opposed by a Cold War consensus that grew steadily weaker as the nation gradually recognized the military, political, economic, and moral bankruptcy of a policy that had once seemed both right and successful, except to those comparative few who rallied around Henry Wallace.

During the summer months, while Beanie Baldwin and his colleagues were busy at political organization, Wallace devoted most of his time to the *New Republic*, which, of course, gave him a weekly platform with which to discuss national and international affairs.

During the summer Wallace invited to his farm one of the few reporters he respected, Ed Lahey of the Knight Newspapers. In his reply, Lahey remarked, "I'm hoping to be able to follow you in the fall. For a man who's supposed to be 'dead,' politically, an extraordinarily large crowd turns out for the wake. Every day I am newly amazed by the number of columns, editorials, and cartoons all of which say 'Let's not pay any attention to Wallace.' " This is a reminder that Wallace was not the fringe figure that he might appear to those who judge his political significance solely on the mere million or so votes he was to receive the following year. In 1947 he was perceived as a substantial vote getter who would certainly, if he ran as a third-party candidate, cause Harry Truman's defeat.

In September Wallace returned to his campaigning, although it was not yet certain exactly what he was campaigning for. In a Labor Day editorial in the September 1 issue of the *New Republic,* Wallace appealed to liberals and rank-and-file workers to join him in "a new pattern for political action." This was not quite a call to arms for a third party but it was a recognition of the political realities: that most labor leaders were cautious men. They had done well by sticking to the Democratic Party and, with few exceptions, they were not about to desert, even for an old friend like Henry Wallace. Wallace might be closer to their way of thinking—actually he was much more liberal than they on most issues—but he wasn't President, Harry Truman was. So Wallace wanted to appeal directly to the rank-and-file union men: "No labor official interested in political progress will proclaim support of the present administration at this time. . . . On this Labor Day, 1947, we should not be discussing which is the lesser of evils. We should be planning to avoid the necessity of such a choice by winning control of the Democratic convention. . . ."

This part of the editorial sounds as if he wanted to contest

Truman for the Democratic nomination, but his rousing Labor Day speech in Detroit gave a somewhat different impression. While thousands in Cadillac Square shouted approval, he declared, "If we don't make the Democratic Party into a party of peace and prosperity, we shall build a new party."[54] This sounded as if he were ready to leave the Democratic Party." He simply could not make up his mind. He wanted to and he didn't want to.

In truth this was not an easy decision. There is no reason to doubt Wallace's loyalty to the party. He had campaigned tirelessly for an FDR who had dumped him. Not only his loyalty bound him to the party but his recognition that if he left, he would probably forever forfeit his role as one of its leaders. If he stayed with the party and Truman were defeated, as then seemed likely, there was a good chance that he would revert to his role as FDR's heir and head the party, for at that time there seemed to be no competitor.

In contrast, there was his genuine conviction that Truman was leading the nation on a disastrous course. A man of principle like Wallace would not permit himself to put his political career before the national interest. But even having decided that he must oppose Truman in the most effective way possible and at whatever personal cost, Wallace still faced a dilemma. If Wallace decided to oppose Truman within the party that would delay, probably fatally, efforts to get a third party on the ballot in a good number of states. On the other hand, if Wallace left the party, he would be leaving behind many Democratic liberals who did not want Truman and believed there was a chance to deny him the nomination.

While Wallace was attempting to resolve this dilemma, Beanie Baldwin, by now his chief political agent, temporized by allowing advocates of both courses to go along as they saw fit, even though he recognized that eventually the two courses would be mutually exclusive. So in California an Independent Progressive Party was established. At the same time PCA cochairman Robert Kenny, the recognized leader of California's Democratic liberals, began efforts to get the state's Democratic convention delegation behind Wallace.

On September 11, the eve of the anniversary of his famous speech, Wallace, sponsored by the PCA, again spoke at Madison Square Garden—this time to a total of twenty-five thousand people. It was a good speech. "Have we been delivered so completely into the hands of the warmongers that we can't speak or listen or counsel together—to learn truth and seek peace? Has thought control really come to the United States? Is the police state upon us?"

Wallace recalled some words from his speech a year earlier:

. . . we who look on this war-with-Russia talk as criminal foolishness must carry our message direct to the people—even though we may be called Communists because we dare to speak out.

And last fall some of those who spoke out—and many who didn't—were called "Communist" and the Russia haters won an overwhelming victory in the congressional elections. So decisive was their victory that the Democratic Administration decided it would try to out-Red-bait the Red-baiting Republicans. There has developed an interesting competition based on the bi-partisan principle of breeding hate and war hysteria. . . .

Henry Wallace was not accepting the notion that comforted some liberal Democrats: that only right-wing Republicans were Red-baiters. He recognized then that there were Democratic Red-baiters and that many liberals could be found among them.

Wallace went on to discuss another aspect of Red-baiting:

Of communism, let us note, first of all, that the word is used by reactionaries to cover every liberal idea. Reading the *Congressional Record* or our newspapers today it appears that the advocacy of any Christian or democratic principle is proof of communism. It is reaction's purpose to frighten us into silence for fear of a Red label. The distortion is becoming so pronounced that we are heading into a time when it will be called "American" to practice and preach hatred of races and religions and nations; and un-American to practice and preach brotherhood and Christianity. One need look no further than the Thomas-Rankin committee to see this developing philosophy.

The Red-baiting of reactionaries stems, as I have said before, not from fear of communism, but from fear of democracy.

Wallace, as always, discussed foreign policy:

But we can't dispense with the problem of Red-baiting by calling attention to the distortion of the word "communism," for there is real communism—and throughout the world it has tens of millions of followers.

The Communist way is not my way, but I would make two simple points to my liberal friends, who fear the Communists.

First—we can't suppress ideas with force or legislation. If we try, we automatically express a lack of confidence in the give-and-take of the democratic process. We show that we lack faith in our ability to make *our* system produce abundantly.

Secondly—if we believe it is impossible to live in the world with communism, we are accepting the inevitability of suicidal war.

Those two points seem so sensible, so obvious even, but in 1947 they were considered radical, subversive.

Wallace made another point that should have been obvious: that Communists were not responsible for America's problems, that President Truman and Congress were responsible for scarcities and high prices. Wallace also pointed out who was responsible for American foreign policy under Truman: Secretary of State George Marshall, a career soldier; Under Secretary Robert M. Lovett, a former partner in the Brown Brothers Harriman banking firm; Assistant Secretary Charles E. Saltzman, a former vice president of the New York Stock Exchange; Ambassador to Britain Lewis W. Douglas, chairman of the board of the Mutual Life Insurance Company of New York; Defense Secretary James Forrestal, on leave as head of the Wall Street banking firm of Dillon Read; Secretary of Commerce W. Averell Harriman, chairman of Brown Brothers Harriman; Secretary of the Treasury John W. Snyder, a St. Louis banker. "I don't believe that investment bankers and military men are evil men by reason of their profession; but I must admit that the one discrimination in employment making any sense to me is discrimination against such men in public positions where they can consciously or unconsciously further their particular professions."

Henry Wallace, who frequently called himself a progressive capitalist, did not realize how close he was coming to making a critique of American capitalism. In this speech he attacked monopoly capitalists but did not seem to recognize, or perhaps he did not want to recognize, that American capitalism had a vested interest in the Open Door, in forcing the American economic system on the rest of the world. But his instincts were right, even if he did not pursue his analysis through to the end—although he came pretty close in the following passage, one that is still pertinent today: ". . . The men who direct our foreign policy are attempting to export their own reactionary capitalist ideology. They have their foreign agents, just as the Russian Communists have their ideological counterparts in many countries, but it is sad to note that the foreign agents of American capitalism are by and large the most reactionary element in the world today. In some places they are the feudal lords. In others they are men of industry, some of whom were actual collaborators with fascist governments."

Here Wallace was pointing out a characteristic of American foreign policy from that day to this: support not for progressive forces but for those who would, and did, go to any length to stop progress.

And at a time when most economists say that the vast expenditures for the Vietnam war were a major cause of America's severe economic problems, it is interesting to read what Wallace said nearly thirty years ago. "The war-with-Russia hysteria is a propaganda weapon of reactionary capitalism. We are paying for it at home in high prices and

economic instability. People the world over are paying for it
in an armament race which is criminal in a world that can't
stand another war."[55]

Wallace did not say much about his own political plans,
but his attitude was pretty well summed up in words by
New York Mayor Fiorello H. La Guardia read to the audience (he had been scheduled to introduce Wallace but was
ill and unable to attend—he died ten days later): ". . . A
two-party system with one platform is just about as bad as a
one-party system with no platform. This does not mean that
there must necessarily be a third party. It does mean that a
third party must be ever ready in reserve."[56]

Throughout the autumn Wallace continued to speak all
over the country and, as in the spring, the audiences were
large, enthusiastic, and generous. Obviously he devoted a
great deal of thought to his big decision but the political details he left to his trusted associates. His disinterest in such
details became legendary. It is still a matter of dispute
whether this lack of interest was a political benefit or not.
His audiences could sense that he did not have the ordinary
politician's concern for whatever would give him political
advantage. In that regard his unconcern for politics was a
political asset, for it undermined his critics who tried to
convince the public that he was acting out of ambition or
out of a desire for revenge against Harry Truman. On the
other hand, there were sometimes political decisions that
only he should have made: on the famous Vermont Resolution at the Progressive Party Convention, for instance.
When Robert Kenny, his chief supporter in California,
wrote about Wallace's distaste for politics it is hard to know
whether he wrote more in exasperation or admiration. "In
fact, he places his cause on such a high plane that we who
are dedicated to promoting that cause cannot 'sully' it by
discussing the crass issues of political strategy with him.
When we are able to keep him on the subject a few minutes, he falls asleep."[57]

In October Wallace made a two-week trip to the Mediterranean area, spending most of his time in Palestine, where he spent long hours in kibbutzim studying agricultural problems and offering advice from his own expert knowledge of corn, chickens, and strawberries. He was a big hit in Palestine; and although he was a firm supporter of a national homeland for the Jews, he also advocated good relations between Jews and Arabs, asserting that they could get along in peace if outside interests did not stir them up. He also recommended a Jordan River Valley Authority, patterned after the Tennessee Valley Authority, to help all the people of the area and he said the United States should help establish it.

While he was away, the House Un-American Activities Committee began its famed hearings into "communism" in Hollywood, a series of inquisitions that terrorized the film industry, caused ten of Hollywood's most well-known writers and directors to end up in jail because they would not testify on grounds of principle, caused some of the biggest names in Hollywood to become Red-hunters, and caused others, who had till then opposed such "witch hunts" to cave in. The HUAC hearings were opposed by many elements on the American political scene, including the New York chapter of the ADA and a number of newspapers. But no group was more vigorous in its opposition than the PCA. Its national Arts, Sciences and Professions Council held a Conference on Cultural Freedom and Civil Liberties in New York on October 25–26, with Harlow Shapley as chairman. Wallace sent the conference a message from the Middle East: "From here where Elijah fought the prophets of Baal and close to the mount of Jesus' famous sermons, people without fear ask, 'Has America really gone crazy?' Is the un-American committee evidence that America is traveling the road to fascism? On behalf of millions everywhere you must answer no so loudly the people of the world can hear. You must destroy the un-American committee at the polls and in the courts, or it will destroy many of the foundations of democracy and Christianity."[58]

By the fall of 1947 a pattern was developing that was to continue for some years. Efforts were made, sometimes accompanied by violence or the threat of it, to prevent public programs arranged by progressives or liberals or Communists or anyone who offended anti-Communist vigilantes. Wallace and his supporters were often victims. Times beyond number Wallace was refused permission to speak in public buildings or on college campuses or in hotels. And the press was beginning to identify Wallace with the Communists. The following, which appeared in the *Pittsburgh Sun-Telegraph* on November 12, is typical: "It does not follow that because a man may occasionally agree with a Communist he is a Communist. . . . But when a man, or any group, consistently follows all of the party line, it is reasonable to suspect that there is more in it than mere coincidence."

When Wallace announced that during his forthcoming swing through the South he would not speak before segregated audiences, the southern newspapers went into a frenzy. Some measure of the response of the southern press is given by a column on November 15 by the editor of the *Atlanta Constitution*, Ralph McGill, who had a formidable reputation as a southern liberal. He certainly was speaking the truth when he wrote that Wallace's forthcoming trip had made many people "angry to the point of being violent." But then McGill went on to give his own opinion:

In Atlanta, one of the cities where Mr. Wallace will speak, his sponsors, the Communist-infiltrated Southern Conference for Human Welfare (with its officials apparently getting most of the "welfare"), will be grievously disappointed if someone does not create a disorder so as to give them the publicity they seek. Since there is a great deal of similarity between the mental mechanisms of the Ku Kluxers and the officers of the Southern Conference for Human Welfare, we are likely to see a Klan picket line or some other form of protest. Indeed, if there is one I trust someone will look under the robes to see if they be the hired pickets of the SCHW or the real McCoy of the Klaverns.

Although it is not within the scope of this book, it is important to recognize that Wallace in 1947, and much more extensively in 1948, opened up the South to nonsegregated politics. It was a brave achievement and a great one. He was invariably attacked in the southern press; often mobs gathered to attempt to intimidate him; a number of times he was pelted with fruit and eggs; frequently the police were more antagonists than protectors; not infrequently his supporters were roughed up. Wallace's courage was often matched by that of his black supporters, who, unlike Wallace, were not just passing through. Black clergymen were especially brave, often allowing their churches to be used for integrated political meetings in the face of threats of violence (often carried out). His southern campaign brought honor to Wallace and his supporters and changed southern politics for good. Although he spoke mainly of civil rights on his southern swing, he never forgot foreign policy and the related issue of Red-baiting. Even in Norfolk, Virginia, where Wallace and Clark Foreman on November 23 successfully held an integrated meeting in defiance of the police, he attacked the Truman Doctrine, Truman's plan for Universal Military Training, and the House Un-American Activities Committee. And he said, "I'm not a radical, although my enemies frequently accuse me of that. I'm tired of all the good people being called Communists. Communism doesn't deserve that much credit."[59]

While Wallace was perhaps the main voice speaking out against the anti-Communist hysteria that was beginning to sweep the land, there were others. He was encouraged when on November 7 the House of Bishops of the Protestant Episcopal Church adopted this resolution introduced by the Right Reverend Angus Dun, Bishop of Washington, D.C.

Resolved as bishops in the Church of God we call upon the people of our churches to be on their guard lest an hysterical fear of communism shall lead us to fight that danger with weapons de-

structive of the treasures we seek to guard. The surest way to fight
communism is to work unceasingly at home and abroad for a society in which justice and the dignity of free men of every race and
condition [are guaranteed].

An inquisitorial investigation of men's personal belief is a threat
to freedom of conscience. The casting of public suspicion on fellow
citizens under the protection of congressional immunity can readily become an offense against God's commandment, "thou shall
not bear false witness against thy neighbor."

We have no defense for those who while sharing the privileges
of our imperfectly democratic society seek to undermine its fabric.
But we hold it to be the duty of every Christian citizen to guard for
others the freedom of conscience we treasure for ourselves.[60]

It is sad that so few churchmen, who should be the first
defenders of freedom of conscience, spoke in such courageous and eloquent terms. But it was a sign of the times
that even such intelligent and brave men believed that
American Communists were a threat. So pervasive was the
spirit of anticommunism that hardly anyone, even the intelligent and the courageous, was immune.

By mid-November Wallace was coming to the conclusion
which, in retrospect, was perhaps inevitable. Beanie Baldwin and others had been urging him to split from the Democrats all along, and on November 21, in Chicago, Baldwin
had convened a meeting of state directors of the PCA. He
wanted to learn what the chances were of influencing Democratic state delegations to support Wallace at the Democratic convention and to learn if it were possible to get a
new party on the ballot in various states. (Baldwin did not
notify Frank Kingdon, national cochairman, that this meeting was being held. Kingdon was soon to leave the Wallace
camp. Whether he left because he felt affronted by Baldwin's action or whether Baldwin took the action because he
doubted that Kingdon would stay is open to question.)
Baldwin got the support of most of the PCA state leaders for
an independent Wallace drive for the Presidency. The final
decision was made December 2, 1947, at a small meeting at

the New York home of Jo Davidson. Besides Davidson, Wallace, and Baldwin, there were Lewis Frank, Jr., of the *New Republic,* who became Wallace's chief speech-writer, and Hannah Dorner, former executive director of the old ICC/ASP.

A memo prepared for the meeting by Baldwin proposed a prompt decision so that Wallace's candidacy would be declared by January 1. This was important as time was needed for a third party to be able to get on the ballot in states where this was a time-consuming process. Also Baldwin believed it important that Wallace take the initiative by speaking before Harry Truman delivered his State of the Union message in early January.

Baldwin proposed that "the announcement not be in terms of organizing an immediate third party" so as not to undercut the efforts of those working within the Democratic party in states like California and Oregon. "However," he added, "it should be understood that in most states an independent candidacy or third party is the only logical instrument for bringing about the realignment of political forces."

Baldwin also predicted, accurately, that it would be possible to get a third party on the ballot in all but a few states. The PCA had already initiated a number of Wallace for President or Draft Wallace movements that were just awaiting word to go. The PCA, using its national and field offices, "has spearheaded this move up to the present time and will probably have to continue to bear a large part of the responsibility for the campaign." But it was "extremely important" that a national Wallace for President Committee be quickly formed and the campaign organization be set in motion within sixty days.[61]

Three days later another, larger meeting was held in Davidson's studio which was attended by about twenty of the top people in the PCA. The purpose was to convince Frank Kingdon to go along. Although he had often advocated a third party, Kingdon now had political ambitions of his own and wanted to run for the Senate from New Jersey. This would be difficult, at least a successful race would be difficult, unless he had Democratic organization support. Whether related to his own ambitions or not, on November 3 Kingdon wrote in his *New York Post* column that Truman was beginning to rise from the low point in his popularity. Then on December 4 he wrote, "I should like to see Harry Truman and Henry Wallace sit down together to talk over 1948." He went on to mention favorable changes in Truman policy in recent months and continued: "As responsible leaders Truman and Wallace should face the consequences of their continued feud. They should ask whether the alternative to their cooperation is not too grave for them to contemplate. The next four years are altogether too uncertain in world affairs for any of us lightheartedly to hand this country bag and baggage to the party of reaction. I think it's at least worth talking over."

Now there was nothing wrong in suggesting that a continued Truman-Wallace split would mean turning the government over to the Republicans. Many serious and good progressives had similar concerns, and many admirers of Wallace were to vote for Truman, however reluctantly, for just this reason. But Kingdon was intimately associated with Wallace, and if he should leave him on this don't-split-the-Democratic-Party-vote-and-give-the-election-to-the-Republicans basis it would be a blow, and an encouragement to others to desert on the same grounds. So it was important to try to keep Kingdon.

Thus the second Davidson meeting was devoted almost exclusively to trying to convince Kingdon to stay with Wallace. Kingdon felt that his old associates were ganging up on him, but he began to waver when he was read a long and deeply personal letter which Wallace had dictated over the telephone. The substance of the letter summarized:

I shall be happy to talk to any responsible member of the Democratic high command who thinks he can give assurance that the

Democratic Party will take decisive action in the next two or three weeks on the following points:

1. The Democratic Party will no longer push UMT [Universal Military Training].

2. President Truman will no longer heed the advice of the Big Brass or Wall Street.

3. The loyalty order will be rescinded and State Department star chamber proceedings will be changed.

4. The Report of the President's Civil Liberties Committee will be backed by the Administration so continuously and enthusiastically as to produce definite legislation.

5. Truman and Stalin will get together to discuss a basis for lasting peace.

There are other points to be discussed but I know that if we progressives had assurances on these five points we could handle the other points satisfactorily and the Democratic Party would again be worthy to be known as the party of Jefferson, Jackson, Wilson and Roosevelt.[62]

Wallace had long been convinced that he and Truman were irreconcilable. That was why he was running. There was no longer any room for him in the Democratic Party so long as he and Truman differed so deeply on such fundamental points. It was a matter of conscience, not just politics, and Wallace was trying to convince Kingdon of that.

Kingdon went out to South Salem the next day, along with his wife, Marcella, and they spent six hours trying to convince Wallace not to leave the Democratic party. But the next day Kingdon telephoned from New Jersey that after talking to local PCA leaders he had changed his mind and would support an independent Wallace candidacy. He resumed his appearances at Wallace rallies for a few days but eventually changed his mind again and came out against Wallace.

On Monday, December 15, the PCA Executive Committee met to reach a final decision on the Wallace candidacy. Frank Kingdon cast the only vote against supporting Wallace as an independent candidate; there were two abstentions and eighteen yeas. Elinor Gimbel, a member of the committee, reported that "The seriousness of it [the meeting] was something unbelievable. It was the most mature meeting I ever attended. Everyone spoke, not to persuade but to inform and to consider. There was no demogogy. Actually the vote could have gone either way, there was so much conscience and concern in that room. Those people were terribly real. It was a great experience."[63]

Foremost among the reasons discussed as to why Wallace should not run as an independent were the three Kingdon listed in a memo he had prepared for the meeting: the lack of support from, even the bitter opposition of, labor leaders; the inability to raise sufficient money; and the consequent splitting of progressive ranks.

These were not trivial arguments and no one there so regarded them. One of the participants, James Imbrie, chairman of the New Jersey Independent Citizens League, had written to Wallace a week earlier along similar lines: "Non-labor support, other than unorganized rank and file, insufficient financial support, the unreadiness of the PCA and allied state organizations for the task, and the moot question as to whether the third-party movement would not materially hurt rather than help liberal Democratic Congressional and Senatorial candidates." Imbrie suggested that "a well-rounded and increasingly powerful independent political machine" would develop within the PCA within the next year or two. But Imbrie reached a very different conclusion from Kingdon's: "Inasmuch as we are united behind your leadership, we will accept as for the best whatever decision you make in this matter. If you decide to move, you can count that every last man and woman in our organization will go all out behind your leadership and that we will stick to the end and accept any eventuality which such action may portend."[64]

Imbrie was true to his word and stuck with Wallace the whole difficult way. Kingdon, however, who had no obligation to stay and whose reasons for leaving were legitimate, did not stop at leaving and giving reasons. In his *New York Post* column for December 31 he wrote: "Who asked Henry Wallace to run? The answer is in the record. The Communist Party through William Z. Foster and Eugene Dennis were the first. . . . The record is clear. The call to Wallace came from the Communist Party and the only progressive organization admitting the Communists to membership."

What an extraordinary statement, considering that Frank Kingdon himself had been one of the founders of that organization and its cochairman until just a few weeks before. (The ADA circulated Kingdon's statement widely; there is a curious story about this which will be discussed below, p. 307.)

On December 17 several members of the PCA executive called on Wallace to inform him of the resolution adopted two nights earlier: "Millions of Americans will stay away from the polls if they are confronted with only a choice between two brands of reaction. These millions of Americans must not be disenfranchised. They must have a choice. Only if Mr. Wallace runs as an independent candidate will they have a choice between progress and reaction."[65]

All the members of the subcommittee, other than James Imbrie, who restated his reservation, urged Wallace to run and to announce his candidacy before the end of the year. Some of them evidently did not know that at the meeting of December 2, at Jo Davidson's house, he had already decided to do so. During the talks Wallace raised the question of how many votes he might get. Josiah Gitt, the *York Gazette* publisher, responded: "It makes no difference how many votes you get. You are honor bound to run."[66] That essentially was it. Given his conviction that Truman was putting the nation on a disastrous course Wallace had no choice, regardless of the consequences.

Another PCA leader, Bartley Crum, quickly resigned both as national vice chairman and as a member. A couple of weeks later another PCA leader, J. Raymond Walsh, a radio commentator who was New York state chairman, also resigned. Walsh, who was not able to be at the executive committee meeting that asked Wallace to run on December 15, wrote his friend a thoughtful letter that illustrated the dilemma of many progressives sympathetic to Wallace.

> . . . It has not been easy for me to make up my mind regarding the desirability of an independent political movement in 1948. However I finally reached the conclusion a few weeks ago that an independent political effort would have two main consequences: First, it would increase the chances of a political victory by the Republicans, which I fear more than I fear the Democratic Party under Truman; and second, that it would jeopardize the chances of progressive political action, possibly the ruin of them altogether for a number of years. . . .
>
> I am concerned that you know that my position on this matter detracts in no degree at all from my deep and earnest admiration and respect for you. I believe you are the greatest man in American political life. I wish profoundly that you were in the White House. I have no reservation whatever about the position that you take on domestic and foreign affairs. But I do not believe you can serve the cause to which you have given so much by deciding now to lead an independent political party.
>
> For what it is worth I urge that you make no reply to the PCA invitation at all at the present time. You have, I think, a great opportunity still to influence the selection of candidates and definitions of policies within the Democratic Party. I hope that you will retain your freedom, that you will keep the party leaders guessing, and that you will use your great strength to make the Democratic Party as progressive in 1948 as it still can become. If you were to accede to the PCA invitation now, your strength in this respect would be completely dissipated, and I believe the strength of the progressive cause would not grow but perilously diminish. . . .[67]

This was a serious man raising serious questions and this is as good a time as any to deal with them. Walsh, and Wallace, had to face two age-old political dilemmas: do you fight more effectively from within than from without; is it better to accept the lesser evil or refuse to accept either? As to the first part of the question, many prominent American political figures in recent decades have had to make that choice. All chose to stay, none was effective in changing policy, and they deprived the American people of the healthful public debate that would have resulted had they quit in protest. Dozens of upper-level figures in the Kennedy and Johnson administrations, for example, claimed or let it be understood that they were doing all they could to change policy regarding Vietnam, but none was willing to sacrifice his political future by making a public fight. To put personal future above political conscience is, sad to say, a long American tradition. Unlike these other men, Wallace felt, as Josiah Gitt put it, that he was "honor bound" to force a public debate.

Wallace had tried within the party to cause Truman to modify his "get-tough" policy. There was nothing more he could do by remaining within the party than to become an increasingly ignored scold. As to domestic policy, Truman had already begun to move back toward FDR's policies, whether in response to Wallace or as a pragmatic, bread-and-butter strategy, one cannot be certain, possibly both.

As to the lesser-evil theory, it was a tough question for Wallace sympathizers and was a more difficult philosophical and practical question than the choice between forcing a public debate and keeping quiet. It is an impossible dilemma for a progressive when both parties nominate unacceptable men. If he elects the marginally superior man, he prevents necessary change. If he does not, he gets the worse candidate and still no change. That was the dilemma faced by such progressives as J. Raymond Walsh in 1948. They did not want Truman and they did not want a Republican. But in 1948 party loyalty, with the memory of FDR still fresh, was much stronger among Democrats than it has been in recent years. So these progressives thought wistfully of Wallace, swallowed hard, and supported Truman. These were not unprincipled men and women copping out, but people making the only choice they thought they could make. To them, whose last Republican Presidents were

Hoover and Coolidge, it was simply unthinkable to do anything that might result in a Republican victory.

For Cold War liberals a vote for Truman over Wallace was
just right. He was tough on the Russians and slightly liberal. But for progressives, the vote was a terrible mistake. It
was a vote for the Cold War, whereas a substantial vote for
Wallace might have acted as a brake on the Cold War no
matter who won. So Walsh and other progressives who
voted for Truman would have done better to have followed
their hearts and voted for Wallace for the simple reason that
they believed he was right. But in 1948 progressives had not
yet learned that Republican administrations, as demonstrated by the Eisenhower and even the Nixon-Ford years,
were endurable. Perhaps the major lesson of the postwar
years is that the two-party system, held so sacred in 1948
and since, is a failure. When the nation is forced to choose
between a Truman and a Dewey, the nation is in trouble.
(In postwar years, only with Eisenhower and Stevenson was
there a fairly good candidate on either side; and in 1972,
when the nation had a clear choice, between Richard Nixon
and George McGovern, it chose Nixon despite Watergate
and despite four more years of the Indochina war.)

Walsh and other progressives opposed to Wallace's third-
party candidacy also expressed the fear that it would
destroy a growing progressive movement. Here, they were
entirely wrong, for the momentum of American politics,
assisted by the Truman administration, was toward
repression, and if Wallace and his supporters had not made
their stand when they did there would have been no stand
at all; that last stand would have been more effective if it
had been joined by all the progressives whose hearts were
with Wallace.

But that was not to be. Whether it was a failure of imagination or a failure of nerve, one cannot say, but many of
those who should have rallied to Wallace's banner did not.
Not for the last time in postwar America, the "fuzzy-
minded idealists" were far more practical than those who

prided themselves as being "hard-headed realists." There is a curious parallel here to the situation in Washington during the Vietnam war. To hear it now, everyone in the government was a dove, causing one to wonder who planned and executed the war. In like fashion it seems that everyone you meet now (except Republicans) who was old enough to vote in 1948 says he voted for Wallace, causing one to wonder why only a million or so votes were recorded in the Wallace column. The sad truth seems to be that at two critical moments in American history—the beginning of the Cold War and the early years of the Vietnam war—most liberals, like most other Americans, were wrong, terribly, tragically wrong.

4

The Hopeful Months

The 1948 election campaign began in Chicago on December 29, 1947, when Henry Wallace announced his candidacy. Wallace restated his criticisms of Harry Truman's foreign policy and then addressed himself to what was to be the primary reason for his poor showing the next November: the fear of many who sympathized with him that a vote for Wallace would help elect a Republican.

The lukewarm liberals sitting on two chairs say, "Why throw away your vote?" I say a vote for a new party in 1948 will be the most valuable vote you have ever cast, or ever will cast. The bigger the peace vote in 1948, the more definitely the world will know that the United States is not behind the bipartisan reactionary war policy which is dividing the world into two armed camps and making inevitable the day when American soldiers will be lying in their arctic suits in the Russian snow.

There is no real fight between a Truman and a Republican. Both stand for a policy which opens the door to war in our lifetime and makes war certain for our children.

Stop saying, "I don't like it but I am going to vote for the lesser of two evils."

He then turned to the domestic costs of the "get-tough" policy, discussing, as he had earlier, the influence of the "military-industrial complex":

The American people read of the fantastic appropriations that are being made for military adventures in Greece, Turkey, China—and billions for armaments here at home. Slowly it dawns on us that these newspaper headlines have stepped into our everyday lives at the grocery store when we pay $1 for butter, 95 cents for eggs, and 90 cents for meat.

We suddenly realize that we can't have all the people of the world getting ready for the next war without paying for it in our daily lives with less food, clothing, and housing. War preparations create record profits for big business but only false prosperity for the people—their purchasing power shrinks as prices rise, their needs go unfilled, and they are burdened with new debts. Yet, corporation profits are over three times what they were in 1939, but every family is paying for our war policy at the grocery store.

Wallace then explained why he now opposed the Marshall Plan. It is important to remember that support for the Marshall Plan was the big dividing point between the liberals and the progressives. Many liberals had their doubts about the military emphasis of the Truman Doctrine, but most of them were satisfied by the humanitarian aspects of the Marshall Plan. They could not see or, in some cases, would not see what Wallace meant when he argued that the Marshall Plan was the economic phase of the Truman Doctrine. This was how Wallace put it in his first campaign speech:

I personally was for the humanitarian aspects of the Marshall Plan long before it was announced. Because I saw the post-war need of helping human beings I was accused of wanting a quart of milk for every Hottentot. I pushed for help for Greece against the opposition of the administration eight months before the Truman Doctrine was announced.

But I have fought and shall continue to fight programs which give guns to people when they want plows. I fight the Truman Doctrine and the Marshall Plan as applied because they divide Europe into two warring camps. Those whom we buy politically with our food will soon desert us. They will pay us in the base coin of temporary gratitude and then turn to hate us because our policies are destroying their freedom.

We are restoring Western Europe and Germany through United States agencies rather than United Nations agencies because we want to hem Russia in. We are acting in the same way as France and England after the last war and the end result will be the same—confusion, depression and war.

It just doesn't need to happen. The cost of organizing for peace, prosperity and progress is infinitely less than the cost of organizing for war.

Wallace was continually criticized as an apologist for Russia, and it was said time without number that he seldom criticized the Soviet Union. It is true that most of his criticism was directed at the United States, for after all it was American policy he was trying to influence. He was campaigning against Truman, not Stalin. Nonetheless, Wallace often did discuss Russian foreign policy as it related to American foreign policy, as in this first campaign speech:

One thing I want to make clear to both Russia and the United States—peace requires real understanding between our peoples. Russia has as much to gain from peace as the United States, and just as we here fight against the spreaders of hate and falsehood against Russia, the Russian leaders can make a great contribution by restraining those extremists who try to widen the gap between our two great countries.

I insist that the United States be fully secure until there is real peace between the U.S. and Russia [no unilateral disarmament there; Author] and until there is an international police force stronger than the military establishment of any country including Russia and the United States. I am utterly against any kind of imperialism or expansionism whether sponsored by Britain, Russia or the United States, and I call on Russia as well as the United States to look at all our differences objectively and free from that prejudice which the hatemongers have engendered on both sides. . . .

Wallace also discussed another terrible liability that he knew he would carry, one that ranked with the "wasted-vote" or "vote-for-Dewey" theories that cut so severely into Wallace's total. Speaking of his criticism of the Truman Doctrine, Wallace declared: "We who believe this will be called 'Russian tools' and 'Communists.' We are not for Russia and we are not for Communism, but we recognize

Hitlerite methods when we see them in our own land and we denounce the men who engage in such name-calling as enemies of the human race who would rather have World War III than put forth a genuine effort to bring about a peaceful settlement of differences."[1]

When Wallace announced his candidacy, the predictions of what his vote total would be—by friends, foes, and neutral observers (if there were really any of those)—ranged from a high of 10 million to a low of one. At the time, because of the enthusiasm that had attended his fall speaking tour and the widespread discontent with Harry Truman, the high figure did not seem impossible. But as our story proceeds, we shall see why Wallace did not get much above even the most pessimistic prediction.

As it began, 1948 did not seem a good year for Harry Truman. Many liberals wanted to deny him the nomination, the labor movement was angry with him, and, worst of all, if the polls were to be believed, the electorate was prepared to give him a good trouncing in the fall. But as the year went along, everything began going right for the President. Events in Czechoslovakia and Berlin seemed to justify his "get-tough" policy, the Wallace campaign served as a lightning rod for the anti-Communist hysteria that might otherwise have been concentrated, probably fatally, on the Truman administration, and, most of all, the complacent, overconfident Thomas E. Dewey "snatched defeat out of the jaws of victory." Of course, no little credit goes to Truman himself for waging a tireless, spunky "whistle-stop" campaign, which was based on a brilliant partisan political program originally set forth in a long analysis by Clark Clifford, a young White House counsel. This document, and his effective work in the Truman White House, began to establish him as one of those legendary behind-the-scenes figures who seems to flourish in Washington. (Later he became an important adviser to John F. Kennedy and a key adviser to Lyndon B. Johnson, whose secretary of defense he was in the final months of the administration.) Clifford's analysis was that Truman could win only be regrouping the old Roosevelt New Deal coalition and that could be done only by moving to the Left, by becoming more liberal on domestic issues. This "bread-and-butter liberalism" hit the Republicans where they were most vulnerable. Truman would then remove any foreign-policy vulnerability by solidifying the bipartisan, politics-stops-at-water's-edge consensus, thus pre-empting any substantial criticism from the Republicans.

That, of course, left the matter of what to do about Henry Wallace. Clifford recognized that if Wallace got a substantial vote, it would come almost entirely from those who would otherwise vote for Truman. He concluded that the way to prevent Wallace from thereby putting a few crucial states in the Republican column was by having Wallace attacked by, and only by, Democratic liberals. He wanted to discredit Wallace's appeals to liberals, and that could be most effectively done by identifying him with the Communists.[2]

The Wallace campaign got off to a fast start. Even though his party did not yet have a name—it was called the New Party for a while—and even though its convention was still seven months off, those were mere details that would be settled later. The day after his announcement Wallace appeared in Milwaukee and announced a seven-point program for world peace:

1. The U.S. should lead in establishing within the United Nations a world-wide reconstruction agency.

2 The fund should be administered by a U.N. agency similar to the United Nations Relief and Rehabilitation Administration that had been killed by Truman.

3. The fund should be financed by "contributions appropriated by our Congress and other nations possessed of the means in an amount sufficient to finance an over-all five-year plan."

4. Priority in receiving the funds should go "to those nations which suffered most severely from Axis aggression; allocations to

be based solely on these considerations of merit and need, without regard to the character of the politics and institutions of recipient nations."

5. ". . . no political or economic conditions [should be] attached to loans or grants." Economic assistance should not be "conditional upon conformity by any nation with an over-all economic plan."

6. "No moneys shall be made available to finance the purchase of military supplies, armaments or war preparations."

7. The industrial Ruhr valley in Germany should be administered and controlled by the Big Four (U.S., U.S.S.R., Britain, and France).[3]

The first six points constituted Wallace's response to the Marshall Plan. It would have removed the desperately needed economic aid from the Cold War context and certainly have contributed to better U.S.-Soviet relations. Of course such a program was the furthest thing from Truman's mind and probably could not have passed Congress which clearly, and correctly, saw the Marshall Plan as an anti-Communist program.

Wallace had, not surprisingly, decided to make foreign policy the heart of his campaign. Some of his advisers thought that the focus should be on domestic bread-and-butter issues or, at least, that there should be more emphasis on domestic issues. By the very nature of the New Party, there were no serious difference among its leaders who were, after all, like-minded men and women joined together for a common purpose. But there were differences about strategy and tactics and emphasis. Although there were no rigid ideological lines, those more to the Left favored a heavier emphasis on domestic issues, while those not quite so far to the Left favored an emphasis on foreign policy. In other words, contrary to what the press and liberals thought and said, a number of the Communists favored an emphasis on domestic matters. They, of course, were always thought to be pushing Wallace toward positions that favored the Soviet Union. However, it cannot be overstressed that there was very little ideological division within the upper ranks of the Wallace organization for the simple reason that there was little occasion for it. Communist or non-Communist, they were in substantial agreement with positions Wallace had been taking since before he was fired by Truman in September 1946.

As soon as Wallace announced, a number of New Dealers attempted, with considerable success, to get former associates of Wallace to come out against him. One of those approached was a California progressive and friend of Wallace, James D. LeCron. As he wrote to Milo Perkins, Wallace's top assistant from Department of Agriculture and Board of Economic Warfare days, he had received a telegram as follows:

WILL YOU JOIN WITH SUCH MEN AS PAUL APPLEBY MILO PERKINS PETE HUDGENS JACK FISCHER JACK FLEMING MORRIS ROSENTHAL MONROE OPPENHEIMER THURMAN ARNOLD AND ABE FORTAS ISSUING A STATEMENT ABOUT LIKE THIS "AS FRIENDS AND ADMIRERS AND FORMER ASSOCIATES OF HENRY WALLACE WE DEEPLY REGRET HIS DECISION TO RUN AS A THIRD PARTY CANDIDATE FOR PRESIDENT. WE BELIEVE HIS DECISION TO FOUND A THIRD PARTY AT THIS TIME AND UNDER SUCH AUSPICES IS MOST UNFORTUNATE AND OPPOSED TO THE BEST INTERESTS OF LIBERALISM." WOULD APPRECIATE A PROMPT REPLY COLLECT TO AMERICANS FOR DEMOCRATIC ACTION 1740 K STREET NORTHWEST WASHINGTON DC BEST REGARDS.

NATE ROBERTSON AND JACK FLEMING

This was LeCron's reply: "WHY SHOULD WALLACE'S FRIENDS ADD TO THE CHORUS OF HATE? NO I WILL NOT JOIN IN STICKING ANY KIND OF KNIFE INTO HENRY WALLACE. I DON'T STAB MY FRIENDS." Then LeCron went on to scold Perkins:

It seems to me that Henry's friends who didn't approve of his running as a third party candidate should have told him so *before* he made up his mind rather than sounding off publicly afterward. How many of them did? Did *you*? And what satisfaction can you get out of publicly slapping him?

I was not hot for the idea of his leading a third party for the reason that I would like to have him elected President, and I thought the chance of his nomination by the Democrats in 1952 would be pretty slim if he led a third party. (Maybe however it would be almost as slim as if he stayed in the party and Truman wins in 1948.)

I have no objection per se to the idea of a third party. Certainly I don't approve of the present bi-partisan kind of government and I am inclined to think the defeat of the Democrats in 1948 will be useful in the long run, for it might convince the Democratic leaders that the party can win only with liberal candidates. This bi-partisan idea seems to me to be dangerously like the One Big Party of Stalin or Hitler.

I haven't been for the ADA since its first statement on foreign policy, when it endorsed the Truman Doctrine on Greece and condemned Henry Wallace. It seems to me that subsequent events in Greece have now proved that it was wrong then. I am afraid that the application of the Marshall Plan will be the same story. The ADA seems to share the current hysteria about Russia and to base its foreign policy ideas on that hysteria exclusively. If it had made any determined efforts on the domestic front I haven't heard of them—namely on upholding civil liberties, combating race prejudice and discrimination, effective price control, more housing, fighting universal military training, contributing definite ideas and leadership to prevent the next depression, etc., etc.

It seems in fact to be a side show in the Truman circus rather than a liberal independent organization.

I shall of course vote for Henry Wallace if I get a chance in California, and I imagine you will too. How could any liberal vote for Truman or Taft or Dewey if he has a chance to vote for Wallace?

Henry may or may not be making a mistake. But there certainly is no doubt about his high courage or his belief in the justice of his cause. His friends ought not be publicly reviling him, for they know in their hearts he is advocating the things for which they basically stand. If their chief worry is what the statement quoted above indicates (the stuff about "such auspices") then maybe Henry's real friends ought to rally 'round and add their respectability to his "auspices." They haven't any basic differences with him. They have a lot of basic differences with Mr. Truman and Mr. Taft and Mr. Dewey. It seems sort of shameful to me that any of

Henry's friends who are also liberals should be running with the pack who are biting his flanks—the Carroll Reeces, the Rankins, the McCarrans, the Hoffmans, the Fulton Lewises, and such malodorous jackals.

Liberals get themselves into some funny positions, don't they? And it seems nearly always certain that the conservatives, who always know what *they* want, will succeed in splitting them up. . . .[4]

What an extraordinary letter. What an extraordinary friend.

But unfortunately, for whatever reason, most of Wallace's New Deal friends left him. Maybe they genuinely supported Truman's foreign policy. Maybe it was a matter of party loyalty. Maybe it was less attractive considerations, such as concern about their own political futures or fear of being tarred by associating with Communists, or even distaste at associating with them. But if there were a high proportion of Communists among the Progressive party workers, it was for one reason only: that liberals, to a large extent, left the field to them, for liberals were not only welcome, they were solicited. Why are liberals so frightened of Communists, often basing their actions not on the merits of this or that situation but out of reflex reaction to Communists? If they are for it, it must be bad; if they are against it, it must be good. Whatever, LeCron saw exactly what was going on. What he did not know was that the ADA, possibly without the knowledge of many of its members, was carrying out the role assigned to it by the Truman administration.

When Harry Truman delivered his State of the Union message he moved distinctly back to FDR policies on domestic matters. The press and such Republicans as Senator Robert R. Taft of Ohio, who was hoping for the Republican nomination, saw it as a "straight bid" to attract voters away from Wallace. But it was also a bid to attract voters away from the Republicans.

Harry Truman on the one hand and Henry Wallace on the

other. It was a difficult choice for liberals who were Democratic party loyalists. Among those distressed by the choice was Eleanor Roosevelt. She had always admired Wallace and had tried hard to get her husband to keep him as Vice President. But she was a loyal Democrat and, although never a Red-baiter, she did not like Communists and she saw Communists among the leaders of Wallace's new party. She wrote three columns opposing Wallace's candidacy, ending with this statement: ". . . he has never been a good politician, he has never been able to gauge public opinion, and he has never picked his advisers wisely."[5] But not only did she share some of Wallace's criticisms of Truman; she had absolutely no use for her husband's successor. Soon after Wallace's announcement, she wrote to Truman saying, in effect, that she hoped he really meant what he said in his State of the Union message. ". . . The great trouble is that Mr. Wallace will cut in on us because he can say that we have given lip service to these things by having produced very little in the last few years." This stung Truman and he replied that he had the same problems her husband had had: the coalition of southern Democrats and Republicans opposed to him. Mrs. Roosevelt was dubious of that argument, as she had been when her husband used it, and she wrote back to Truman an even sterner letter. "Because this letter is not too pleasant, I have been putting it off." She said she knew how difficult it was for people around a President to tell him what troubled them and that there were those who told him what he wanted to hear. She said that she was worried that his administration was too conservative: "Believe me, Sir, it is going to be impossible to elect a Democrat if it is done by appealing to the conservatives. The Republicans are better conservatives than we are. If the people are going to vote conservative, it is going to be Taft or Dewey and we might as well make up our minds to it."[6]

This was another strong reason for Truman's moving to the Left.

The press, as mentioned earlier, noted Truman's move

toward the New Deal, the Fair Deal, it was now called, but did not make much of it. For some reason the press takes it as a matter of course for a Presidential candidate to move this way or that as his assessment of political expediency dictates but never makes the issue of it that it should. Why should a Presidential candidate not be expected to have principles and convictions and be expected to let his conscience and his belief as to what is in the nation's best interest guide his campaign and, if he is the incumbent, his administration? But the press, and the public, let candidates get away with such political expedience.

Despite the legal and organizational obstacles that any national third party faced, the New Party got off to a good start. The foremost obstacle was basic: getting on the ballot. No matter how popular Wallace might be, no matter how good a campaign he ran, it would all be for nought if he were not on the ballot. American electoral laws, which vary from state to state, generally favor a two-party system, although in a few states it was easy to get a third party on the ballot. This obviously was the first priority, and it was turned over to John Abt, a talented lawyer for the Amalgamated Clothing Workers, close associate of Sidney Hillman, and influential figure in the CIO. Abt performed what many political observers regarded as a miracle. By Election Day Wallace was on the ballot in forty-four states. (Two of the missing states were negligible in terms of potential votes, Nebraska and Oklahoma. But Wallace was denied a place on the ballot in Illinois, where he had a substantial following. And in Ohio although electors favoring Wallace were on the ballot, they were not identified as pledged to Wallace or supporting the Progressive party. This all cost him tens of thousands of votes.)

Money, perhaps surprisingly, did not constitute a major problem. Wallace continued to astonish politicians by drawing huge crowds that paid to hear him speak. Also he had a number of wealthy supporters, especially Anita McCormick Blaine, who could be counted on to provide cash in a hurry when it was needed.

But organization was necessarily a problem. The two major parties had been building their organizations over decades on a national, state, and local level. The yet-to-be-named Progressive Party had to attempt to do this in a matter of months. The task was manifestly impossible; yet it did surprisingly well. It built on the membership of the Progressive Citizens of America, which claimed 100,000 members in 750 communities in 24 states and individual members in all the others. But this figure, even before the desertions for one reason or another, probably was inflated. There were actually only a handful of states—New York, California, Illinois, Massachusetts, and mainly in the big cities—where there was any real organization. The party's real strength was in its energetic and innovative national headquarters. The Progressive Party, as it sorrowfully learned, did not have many supporters but their quality was high. Beanie Baldwin, experienced upper-level New Dealer and once actual head of the CIO's political apparatus, was the campaign manager. Chairman of the National Wallace for President Committee was Elmer Benson, the experienced politician who had been governor of and senator from Minnesota. The cochairmen were all persons of stature: Jo Davidson; Rexford G. Tugwell, one of the leading thinkers of the New Deal; Angus Cameron, a well-known book editor; Anita McCormick Blaine; and Paul Robeson, the legendary singer, actor, and social activist who was probably the best-known black man in the world. One of the extraordinary men of our time, Robeson worked tirelessly for racial equality and world peace but even his unequaled fame and enormous talents were no protection against the Cold War hysteria. In the 1950s he became unable to work, unable for some years to even travel, for his passport was taken from him by the State Department. The Cold War claimed no end of victims but few more tragically. But the days of disgrace and obscurity were not yet upon him in 1948, and throughout the campaign Robeson rested scarcely more than the candidate. His magnetic physical presence and his magnificent voice were a major attraction at Progressive rallies. Someday, soon one hopes, there will be a resurgence of interest in Robeson, especially among blacks for whom he could be a supreme hero.

Among the members of the National Committee were such famous figures from the arts as Louis Adamic, Larry Adler, Stella Adler, Leonard Bernstein, Marc Blitzstein, Kermit Bloomgarten, George Braziller, Henrietta Buckmaster, John Ciardi, Robert Coates, Aaron Copland, Olin Downes, Richard Dyer-Bennett, Howard Fast, José Ferrer, Lukas Foss, Morton Gould, Uta Hagen, Dashiell Hammett, E. Y. Harburg, Roy Harris, Lillian Hellman, Oscar Homolka, John Huston, Canada Lee, Dimitri Mitropolous, Dorothy Parker, Robert St. John, Ben Shahn, Artie Shaw, Louis Untermeyer, and Mark Van Doren. And there were such intellectual figures as Frank Dobie, W. E. B. DuBois, Thomas Emerson, Melville J. Herskovits, F. O. Matthiessen, Linus Pauling, John Rogge, Frederick L. Schuman, Paul Sweezy, and Gregory Zilboorg. This, remember, was just the membership of the National Committee. There were scores of other well-known figures who supported Wallace in various ways. Among writers, for instance, there were Thomas Mann, Norman Mailer, Muriel Rukeyser, Dalton Trumbo, Shirley Graham, Eve Merriam, Norman Rosten, Willard Motley, Pierre Van Paassen, Nym Wales, Philip Van Doren Stern, Kyle Crichton, Arthur Miller, Ring Lardner, Herbert Aptheker, I. F. Stone, Anna Louise Strong, Leo Huberman, Langston Hughes, and S. J. Perelman.

These names demonstrate something important about the Wallace movement: it has appeared to some that this movement was merely an episode, a vain attempt to stop the forces of globalism unconnected with anything that followed, but with even a quick glance at the above names, you can easily pick out a number of persons active in the antiwar movement in the mid-1960s, and in civil rights and other movements as well. This continuity, submerged for a time by the tidal sweep of history, is further demonstrated by the early allegiance of a couple of then young Dakotans, Quentin N. Burdick, later a senator from North Dakota, and George S. McGovern, the senator from South Dakota who was even more prominent in the struggle against the Vietnam war. Nor can one doubt that there were thousands of others, young opponents then of Truman's "get-tough" policy who became middle-aged stalwarts, even if not well known, of the peace movement of the 1960s.

Clearly, the Progressive Party did not lack talented and articulate supporters. Indeed, so talented and articulate were its supporters that students of political campaigns might well find that the Progressive Party conducted the most imaginative campaign in American history. For music the party could call on men like Paul Robeson and Pete Seeger. Posters were drawn by Ben Shahn. Zero Mostel and Canada Lee and other performers often appeared at rallies. Some of the finest writers of Hollywood films and New York radio, like Dalton Trumbo and Norman Corwin, worked on the campaign. And Studs Terkel was often master of ceremonies at Wallace rallies. Here, too, was a parallel with the future.

Wallace was the unquestioned leader of a high-powered political apparatus, but he steadfastly refused to have anything to do with politics. He made even the issue-oriented candidates of the late 1960s and early 1970s appear positively Machiavellian. Only when absolutely forced into it by Beanie Baldwin and his top lieutenants would he make a political decision. This, as we shall see, was often a mistake, sometimes a serious mistake; during the convention and later, when some of the non-Communist Progressives were concerned about the Communists' growing role, it would have been helpful if he had been more concerned with politics. As the very heart of the party, his political decisions would have been accepted, as they were on the rare occasions he made them, by Communists and non-Communists alike; for both, even when they differed on this or that, were genuinely committed to Wallace and to the success of the campaign.

But all Wallace wanted to do was take his message to the American people. During January and February he carried on as he had in 1947. The crowds continued to turn out in numbers that terrified Democratic politicians, and they continued to pay to get in and contributed again when they were inside.

In the first couple of months in 1948, it looked as if there were a mighty surge for Wallace. No one seriously thought he could win—although he would not have been human if that idea did not dance in his head—but it did seem that he might lead a party large in numbers and significant in influence. In California, his supporters—an enthusiastic mixture of left-wing labor, PCA members, and even some old Townsendites—gathered a staggering 464,000 signatures a full month before the March 18 deadline. (Some 295,000 were certified as valid, 15,000 more than required. These valid signatures were more than 100,000 over the total of votes Wallace got in California in November, indicating that this was the high point of his campaign.)

Politicians, however, did not then know what would happen. All they knew was that Wallace had gotten 464,000 signatures. And then on February 17, in the Bronx, an astonishing thing happened. There was a special election for Congress in the 24th Congressional District, a long-time Democratic stronghold. Eleanor Roosevelt and New York's popular Mayor William O'Dwyer campaigned for the Democrat, Karl Propper. Henry Wallace campaigned for Leo Isaacson, the American Labor candidate. The issue was clear: Truman versus Wallace. When the votes were tallied, Isaacson got more votes than the three other candidates, almost twice as many as the Democrat. It was a political sensation and all across the nation, Wallace was given new respect.

The Truman administration was gracious in defeat. When Congressman Isaacson wanted to go abroad, the State Department refused to give him a passport. They must have been cross because Isaacson declared, "This is a victory for Henry A. Wallace and the third party—the People's party. . . . I think that Red-baiting has been used too often to destroy progressive and liberal positions. In my own election there was Red-baiting of myself which was completely unfounded and which was repudiated by the people."[7]

Perhaps Red-baiting was not effective in that liberal corner of the Bronx, but the Truman administration had not given it up as a national strategy. The night after the election, Rhode Island Senator J. Howard McGrath, the Democratic national chairman, told a radio audience that "the loudest applause for Wallace comes from Communists, Communist fellow travelers and reactionary Republicans." And he expressed the "hope that Henry Wallace will realize that the unscrupulous forces who look to Moscow for inspiration and guidance see in his candidacy a chance to disrupt the activities of our two-party system."[8] That sacred two-party system again, even though the two parties were one on the life-and-death issue of foreign policy.

Another measure of Wallace's popularity early in the year was a turnout of seven thousand who paid to see him during a Minneapolis blizzard. (What a contrast that was to his drawing power some eight months later, in fine fall weather shortly before the election, when, in that same city, only about two thousand turned out.) And when Morris Rubin of the *Progressive* wrote an editorial attacking Wallace, it triggered more mail than he had ever received in opposition to an editorial position. "Much as I hate to admit it, I must say that there are tens of thousands of good American progressives who aren't even faintly fellow travelers who are lined up with Wallace." And another anti-Communist liberal, Richard L. Neuberger, later senator from Oregon, wrote: "When Wallace speaks of Wall Street and the Army in government, when he warns of imposing our will on neighbor nations, when he taps the burning American desire for peace, millions of people at their radios will nod in agreement."[9]

Wallace got more good news in February when Senator Glen H. Taylor of Idaho agreed to be his running mate. Wallace's first choice had been Senator Pepper, but Pepper decided that he could not leave the Democratic Party and made his peace with Truman. So Wallace turned to Taylor, another authentic hero in those dark years that followed World War II. Taylor was not an orthodox politician. He was a guitar-strumming (as the newspapers liked to note derisively) itinerant actor who barely scraped by until he narrowly won election to the Senate in 1944 after two unsuccessful attempts. Not only was this, as he often said, "the best job" he had ever had, it was about the only good one. Idaho was not a nest of radicals, and Taylor recognized full well that running with Wallace would probably finish him politically. But he ran—for the simple reason that he thought Wallace was right, that Truman was leading the nation on a disastrous course.

Taylor announced his decision in a nationwide radio address, declaring that "I am not leaving the Democratic Party. It left me. Wall Street and the military have taken over." And he addressed himself to the Communist issue that he knew would be inescapable: "I am happy to have the support of all those who go along with our program. But just let me say to the Communists so there will be no misunderstanding, my efforts in the future as in the past will be directed toward the goal of making our economy work so well and our way of life so attractive and our people so contented that communism will never interest more than an infinitesimal fraction of our citizens who adhere to it now."[10]

That was precisely Henry Wallace's position too, but even though he and Taylor often restated it, it was drowned out by the anti-Communist rhetoric of the time and usually ignored by the press. Anyway, Glen Taylor cheerfully went off on the crusade that ended his political career. And his wife and children went off with him, strumming their guitars and singing their songs on campaign platforms from coast to coast. Now a successfull businessman on the West Coast, one can only wonder what ran through Glen Taylor's mind years later when he heard that Richard Nixon was going to journey to Moscow and Peking.

Anyone who investigates the Progressive Party campaign hears time and again from participants that "the FBI was everywhere." Even before the disclosures much later about the FBI's ubiquitous presence around, and even in, dissenting political organizations, no one was the least bit surprised to hear such assertions. The full dimensions of the FBI's preoccupation with the Wallace movement will not be known until its files have been thoroughly searched. But at least one piece of evidence exists: a letter from J. Edgar Hoover to Attorney General Tom Clark, dated February 12, 1948, dealing with the activities of the Communist Party supporting the third-party petition drive in California. Hoover's letter was passed on to Democratic Party Chairman McGrath in a note from Clark dated February 18.[11] (In typically inflated fashion Hoover cited a "reliable confidential source" about what happened at a *public* meeting. Why the FBI bothered with this is a puzzle, since the connection between the Progressive Party and the Communist Party was hardly a secret, and, indeed, was what the press never tired of reporting.)

In February things were going Wallace's way, with Leo Isaacson's astonishing victory in the Bronx, the extraordinary number of signatures gathered in California, and Glen Taylor's agreement to run. But more powerful forces were beginning to build up against Wallace. First, Wallace's criticism of the Marshall Plan ran contrary to the carefully cultivated American perception that this was a great humanitarian program in which even the Communist countries could participate if they chose. Since the Soviet Union bitterly opposed it, Wallace's opposition meant, to many Americans, that he was, consciously or unconsciously, in

league with the Communists. As we shall see, many liberals
asserted that Wallace's opposition to the Marshall Plan was
in itself sufficient reason for his disqualification.

The Marshall Plan rapidly came to have, in the American
consciousness, a status comparable to the Declaration of Independence or the Monroe Doctrine, a mythic status
beyond criticism. The words "Marshall Plan" have become
an incantation that proves beyond question the extraordinary generosity of the United States. It has become, in any
discussion of the Cold War, the political equivalent of
Motherhood. But it was apparent to Henry Wallace in 1948,
as it is apparent now, that a good case could be made that
the Marshall Plan was a mistake of gargantuan proportion.
Not a mistake, indeed, a most effective program if the desire was to prosecute the Cold War and isolate the Communist world. But a terrible mistake if a peaceful One World
were the goal.

An entire book, and a fat one at that, would be needed
for a detailed discussion of Henry Wallace's criticism of the
Marshall Plan. But an attempt can be made to compress it
into a few sentences, even at the cost of oversimplification.
Wallace often discussed his criticism of the Marshall Plan
but his most effective statement was in his testimony before
the House Committee on Foreign Affairs on February 24,
1948.[12] In brief, Wallace testified that he believed the Marshall Plan was nothing more or less than the economic
phase of the Truman Doctrine, the battle plan to contain
communism. Wallace pointed out that it would serve to
strengthen the grip of American big business on the European economy. It would also strengthen European capitalists vis-à-vis the workers. It was also intended to establish
Eastern Europe, including the Soviet Union, as the agricultural and commodity-providing hinterland of Western
Europe. It would strengthen western Germany in relation to
the rest of Europe. It would mean American supervision
and a substantial measure of control over the national econ-

omies of the participating nations. It would give the United States authority to approve economic plans, allocate materials, and purchase raw materials. It would undercut the UN at the very moment of its greatest opportunity. All this Wallace foresaw and in all this he was correct.

Defenders of the Marshall Plan like to say that the Soviet Union and its satellite nations were welcome to join and share in the plan's benefits. The Marshall Plan was designed so the Soviet Union could not accept membership and so it, not the United States, could be blamed for dividing Europe. The fact is that the Marshall Plan established the United States as the economic overlord of those who participated. There was no conceivable way that the Soviet Union would accept such limits on the administration of its national economy. Beyond that, if Russia and its subservient neighbors had joined, it is unlikely in the extreme that the Marshall Plan would ever have been passed by Congress, which was then dominated by conservative Republicans who were both vigorously anti-Communist and penny-pinching. Truman had succeeded in getting the political and economic aspects of his doctrine approved only by selling it as an essential defense against a Communist tide that was threatening the Free World. How then could he have asked Congress to appropriate money to help a nation that he had persuaded them was a mortal threat to American security? And participation by the Communist nations would have raised the costs enormously at a time when Congress was forcing the administration to cut back its plans for economic assistance.

Russia thus refused to participate and with it, the East European nations, including Czechoslovakia, which had been tempted. Russia, which had suffered more than any other country from the war, decided she would rebuild without American help, that the cost of American help was too high. And she succeeded, as did her satellites, although the lack of American assistance must have presented terrible difficulties. But Western Europe felt it had no choice but accept whatever terms the United States insisted on. Those terms included enlistment in the American anti-Soviet crusade, resulting in a Europe that is just now beginning to reach across the gulf dividing East from West.

But Congress was in no mood to listen, nor were the liberals, nor the press, nor the public whose perceptions were so influenced by these others. Nor were they disposed to listen to Wallace's sensible proposals to alleviate human suffering and help rebuild the war-torn world through a UN program that would unite rather than divide. What they did see was the similarity between Wallace's criticisms and those of the American Communists. But what was Wallace to do? Remain silent on a matter of the most crucial importance simply because Communists made the same valid criticisms? Wallace and the Communists became all the more linked in the public consciousness.

Wallace was seriously hurt also by the Communist takeover in Czechoslovakia in February. American anti-Communists cited the takeover as proof that Russia was on the march and could be stopped only if the United States continued to take a hard line. The Czech situation, like the Marshall Plan, is complex and it also merits a book to itself. A group of non-Communist ministers, in response to actions of the Communist minister of the interior, resigned in a group, hoping to force the forming of a new government in which the non-Communists would be stronger. At this point the Czech Communists, backed by the Russian army, took over. The Communist Party, although not a majority, was the largest single party. Now the American press, almost without exception, accepted the administration's interpretation of the take-over as a characteristic manifestation of Russian perfidy. Wallace did not help to clarify matters much by his own clumsy handling of the event. His first statement was sound enough: speaking in Minneapolis on February 27, he said the take-over resulted from hostility between the two great powers, causing movement and countermovement by one side, then the other. (Clearly Wallace recognized that by 1948, if not earlier, the Cold War was a two-sided affair, with each accusing the other of having started it.) He went on to say:

> This week we are reading of the difficulties in Czechoslovakia. Representatives of recognized political groups have been forced from the government, but before we accept the situation in Czechoslovakia as evidence that we cannot make peace with the Soviet Union, we would do well to recall that our own government under the present partisan administration worked to drive from the governments of France and Italy representatives of those Leftist political parties which did not meet with our approval.
>
> The Czech crisis is evidence that a "get-tough" policy only provokes a "get-tougher" policy. . . . Let's use our heads—not just the headlines. What is happening in Czechoslovakia is not a tempest in a vacuum. There is a clear pattern of cause and effect—a triangular pattern connecting Moscow, Prague, and Washington. Every act under the Truman Doctrine is clearly labeled—"anti-Russian." The men in Moscow would, *from their viewpoint*, be utter morons if they failed to respond with acts of *pro-Russian* consolidation. The Czechoslovakia story will repeat itself so long as our gun and dollar policies in Greece, in China and elsewhere on Russia's doorstep are continued. Only peace with Russia will stop the march toward war. Only an administration in Washington that the Russians will respect—only a peace party at the helm—can secure the peace.[13]

A few days later he issued a statement in which he said, "Men of vision know that the crisis in Czechoslovakia was practically predetermined by the announcements of the Truman Doctrine on March 12, 1947. . . ."[14] Such assertions were hardly convincing to anti-Communists but they did not cause undue stir because they were consistent with what Wallace had been saying all along. But then, on March 10, Czech Foreign Minister Jan Masaryk, fell to his death from a third-floor window of his apartment in the Foreign Ministry. Masaryk, son of Tomáš Masaryk, the George Washington of Czechoslovakia, was a widely respected liberal and democrat who had many friends in the West. At the same time he had long advocated cooperation with the Soviet Union. Although his death was officially termed a suicide, it was widely believed in the West, particularly the United States, that he had been murdered by the Soviets. The matter is in dispute to this day.

In any case, Masaryk's death focused more attention than ever on Czechoslovakia, with people in and out of the U.S. government asserting loudly that he had been killed because he opposed the Communist take-over. Accounts from the Communist side say that Masaryk committed suicide out of despondency because the situation had become impossible for one such as he who wanted to work with both the Soviet Union and the West. In any event, during the subsequent tense days, with the press preoccupied with Czechoslovakia, Wallace, as he did often, put his foot in his mouth. He was not very good at the give and take of press conferences and most of the reporters, sharing in the consensus that the Russians were responsible for tension between the United States and the Soviet Union, generally regarded him with something between extreme skepticism and outright hostility. During a press conference on March 15 Wallace told a reporter that his foreign editor no doubt knew about the intended rightist coup that had provoked the Communist take-over in Czechoslovakia. The American ambassador, Laurence A. Steinhardt, he added, had helped to precipitate the crisis with a statement he had made on February 20. Then, as he was rushing from the room to catch a train, Wallace responded to a further question: "What about Masaryk?" Pausing at the door, Wallace said; "I live in the house that John G. Winant lived in and I've heard rumors why he committed suicide. One can never tell. Maybe Winant had cancer. Maybe Masaryk had cancer. Maybe Winant was unhappy about the fate of the world. Who knows?" And with that he dashed off.

Wallace seemed insensitive to the tragedy of Masaryk's death and seemed to accept the Russian version of his fall from the window. Wallace's remarks, together with angry denial from Ambassador Steinhardt, again seemed to put him in the Communist camp; Steinhardt, who had been in the United States for surgery, pointed out that he had been on a ship en route back to Europe from February 1 until February 18, arriving in Prague not until February 19, the day after the crisis had begun with the non-Communist members of the coalition government walking out, never to return.

But on March 17 Wallace issued a further comment on the matter:

Mr. Steinhardt denies that he communicated with members of the [Czech] Cabinet "directly or indirectly," yet on February 20, immediately on his return to Prague, he issued a statement expressing the hope that Czechoslovakia would be able to take part in the Marshall Plan. He knew and the Communist leadership knew that our policy of aid had been proclaimed as aid for governments that exclude Communists.

Coming at this crucial moment it was a clearly provocative statement and a contributing factor to the Czech crisis. There can be no doubt that Mr. Steinhardt hoped for the same result in Czechoslovakia as in France and Italy where the pressures of our State Department forced Communists from the government.

Mr. Steinhardt can make the apology. He can apologize for meddling in the internal affairs of one of the few countries in the world in which a broad coaltion government had existed.[15]

It is entirely possible that Wallace was wrong about the cause and effect of Steinhardt's statement to the Czech press, but one does not have to be an admirer of Soviet treatment of its East European neighbors to notice a double standard at work. It was acceptable by American standards for the State Department and the Central Intelligence Agency to use extreme political pressure and spread around vast quantities of dollars to influence the governments of France and Italy, to mention just two, but not all right for the Soviet Union to act in similar fashion on its very doorstep. State Department documents released in 1975 disclosed, even with frequent deletions for "security" reasons, that Truman in 1948 approved a secret recommendation that the United States "make full use of its political, economic, and if necessary, military power" to prevent a Communist take-over in Italy.[16] Knowing what we have learned about the CIA in recent years, it would hardly be surprising if the United States had been clandestinely involved in Czechoslovakia as well. Although one can wish that the Soviet Union had left Czechoslovakia alone in 1948 to work out its own destiny, it is difficult to absolve the United States of some responsibility. The Soviet intervention in 1968 had absolutely no security justification, but in 1948 a case can be made that Russia, whether correctly or not, did have a plausible concern about her own safety.

In this tense atmosphere Harry Truman summoned an emergency session of Congress to deal with his proposals for Universal Military Training, re-enactment of the draft, and the Marshall Plan. His campaign strategy was to run against what he called a "do-nothing" Republican Congress. And on St. Patrick's Day, he made one of his rare attacks on Henry Wallace, departing from his practice of leaving Wallace to the liberals. He spoke in New York before the Friendly Sons of St. Patrick, following Francis Cardinal Spellman, who had given a rousing anti-Communist speech to a receptive audience. Truman departed from his text to declare, "I do not want and I will not accept the political support of Henry Wallace and his Communists. If joining them or permitting them to join me is the price of victory, I recommend defeat. These are days of high prices for everything, but any price for Wallace and his Communists is too much for me to pay. I'm not buying."[17] It may sound ungenerous to point it out but neither Henry Wallace nor the Communists were at all interested in joining Harry Truman.

Truman made another significant attack on Wallace in Los Angeles on March 29, when he said, "Communists are using and guiding the third party . . ." and Wallace "ought to go to the country he loves so well and help them against his own country if that's the way he feels."[18] Such a statement well represented Truman's feelings, and had it not been for the general strategy of not attacking Wallace but leaving him to the liberals, he certainly would have attacked Wallace more often. As Truman wrote elsewhere, "There was, however, a sinister aspect to the Wallace movement. It provided a front for the Communists to infiltrate the political life of the nation and spread confusion. Without the conscious knowledge of many members of the new progressive party, the Reds were working swiftly and skillfully to gain control of the nominating convention and to dominate party committees and the platform."[19]

Attacks like Truman's were not only a disservice in themselves but they legitimatized Red-baiting. The irony is that after making such language part of the political vocabulary of the time, Truman himself was later attacked for giving comfort to Communists. He who sows the wind reaps the whirlwind. And why should accusation substitute for a serious discussion of the issues?

Truman's St. Patrick's Day attack caused Wallace to ask for, and receive, radio time on all three major networks to reply to the President. His speech of March 19 on the Mutual Broadcasting System makes particularly interesting reading today. He ranged widely, anticipating by more than a decade President Eisenhower's famous warning about the military-industrial complex—"We must stop the trend towards militarization of America which is so profitable to a few entrenched interests and so dangerous to the freedom of all"—and referring to the situation in Greece, where there were reports of mass political executions by the government: ". . . The situation there is far worse today than it was a year ago when Mr. Truman went to the rescue of the old royalist crowd."

Then Wallace restated what he was to say again and again, without ever getting a direct response from the administration or its supporters: "In this past year I have challenged Mr. Truman and his bipartisan supporters to show a single American principle or a single American public interest which would have to be sacrificed to make peace with Russia."

But most of his speech was devoted to the anti-Communist hysteria that had spread across the land. No man spoke out against it more boldly and more frequently than Henry Wallace. For that, if for nothing else, he deserves honor.

"I get so many letters—lots of them unsigned—from people who ask *me* to fight back. They say that they don't dare open *their* mouths for peace or they will lose their jobs. Speech isn't free when it costs a man his livelihood."

And Wallace discussed the Communists issue in these words:

Mr. Truman has done what other professional politicians have done before him—he has given the Communists credit for all the decent ideas which are advocated in this land of ours.

I don't like to have the President give them credit for ideas that come from Isaiah and Christ; from Jefferson and Lincoln. We all remember the many times Franklin Roosevelt was charged with "communism." Like those who used this tactic against Roosevelt, he presents no evidence that I have ever advocated a single policy inconsistent with the most fundamental American concepts of freedom. . . .

I get the impression these days that the people who are most dominated by the Kremlin—by Moscow—are those who oppose everything the Russians do, whether it is good or bad or inconsequential. By their actions they have convinced me that they are more responsive to Moscow than the American Communists with all their spiritual and ideological affinity for Communists in Russia. We cannot chart a course for America on either blind hate or blind love for what the Russians do.

This word "communism" is a much greater menace than the Communists. The word has been applied to every idea slightly to the left of slavery. I am sure that I could take long passages from the works of Jefferson and Lincoln and get them banned from the classrooms on the grounds that they are too radical. This is the sort of nonsense which threatens everything we have built here in America.

If we want peace, we must challenge everyone who uses the word "communist." We must demand that he define exactly what he is talking about. We shall find, I am sure, that it is used most often by men who are afraid to discuss an issue on its merits.

And indeed, during the entire course of the campaign there was seldom a discussion of the merits of the Wallace arguments by administration, liberal intellectuals, or the press. They had every right to disagree with Wallace and they had persuasive arguments they could have used against him. But seldom did they discuss the merits of his arguments. They preferred to dismiss them by labeling Wallace as a fellow traveler or an unwitting tool of the Communists. One can understand the Truman administration acting in such fashion, for it was committed to a course and it did everything possible to avoid a substantial discussion of its foreign policy. But the liberal intellectuals and the press presumably were independent of the administration. Both liked to proclaim their independence and trumpet how different America was from the Soviet Union, where the intellectuals and the press were handmaidens of the state. Both liked to assert that not only were they institutionally free but independent of mind as well, seekers after truth who by instinct and training were skeptical of government, any government. Yet the sad fact is that they were uncritical accepters of the basic foreign-policy assumptions of the Truman administration—and of succeeding administrations until the war in Vietnam went bad. Even when a man like Wallace—former Vice President, twice a Cabinet member, the leading figure in the New Deal after Roosevelt himself— even when a man of such substance challenged national policy, his challenge was not met head on but deflected by cries of "Communist fellow traveler!" Why, if Wallace's case were so weak, were they afraid to discuss it? One can only assume that such was the temper of the time that criticism

immediately became equated with something akin to treason. Right-wing Republicans alone cannot be blamed for
establishing that atmosphere. The President in that "bully
pulpit" was a Democrat.

Wallace evidently believed that the American people
could see through the manipulations of their leaders. The
truth seems to be that a succession of Presidents of both
parties have been able to disarm the critical faculties not
only of the public—which is not so surprising, since most
people have other things on their mind—but of intellectuals
and the press. How else explain the long run of that horror
movie called Vietnam?

The cry of "Communist" is used against us because we are attacking entrenched interests, because we believe that it is possible
to make peace with Russia, and because we know that you can't
fight the economic theories of Karl Marx with atom bombs. . . .

Last—and certainly not least—we must look the situation over
carefully, and calmly find out just what major differences we have
with the Russians. Having cleaned up our own delinquencies in
matters of civil liberties and interference in the political affairs of
Greece, Turkey, France, Italy, Latin America, and many other
places, we can talk with the Russians about the ways to expand
freedom everywhere. We shall then have moral authority and the
friendship of people in every part of the globe. If there are economic differences—matters of markets and raw materials—we can
work them out. We must recognize the ideological differences between the Russians and ourselves, and demonstrate our own faith
in democracy and the free flow of ideas.

What both the United States and Russia must realize in these
days when war entails widespread civilian destruction by radiant
gas clouds and bacteria, the only sound military defense is a
world-wide good-neighbor policy. . . .

Wallace addresses here *both* the United States and Russia,
asserting plainly that peace is a responsibility of both sides.
What American President has ever had the imagination and
nerve to approach the Russians candidly and ask: What is

keeping us apart? Not in a spirit of appeasement, not with approval of the ugly aspects of Russians society, but in a genuine attempt to convince Russia that the United States wants peace and genuinely wants disarmament. Such an approach is not an implication that only the United States is to blame for international tension but simply a candid, cards-down-on-the-table approach. By the time of the Wallace campaign the Cold War had indeed become a two-sided affair but the United States was still vastly stronger in military might and the Soviet Union, whether or not she had expansionist ambitions, was necessarily still preoccupied with reconstruction after the devastation of World War II. The major responsibility for peace was ours for the simple reason that we were uniquely equipped to take risks for peace. That was what Wallace was saying and that was misconstrued, or distorted, into a program of appeasement.

Recognizing that his criticism of foreign policy had been so distorted, consciously or not, Wallace closed his speech by asking Harry Truman and any other candidate for the Presidency to join him in this pledge: "I shall not knowingly accept the support of any individual or group advocating the limitation of democratic action for any other individual or group; nor the support of any individual or group which would restrict the civil liberties of others for reasons of race, color or creed; nor the support of any individual or group advocating the violent overthrow of the government of the United States."[20]

Wallace was often asked why there was not more criticism of the Soviet Union in his speeches, not intemperate criticism but the kind of valid criticism that Wallace genuinely felt about this or that aspect of Russian policy at home or abroad. In the first place, he did criticize the Soviet Union, in the same way that any believer in democracy would find fault with an authoritarian state, and this frequently pained his Communist supporters. For instance, in the May 1948 issue of *Political Affairs,* the official monthly organ of the Communist Party, Max Weiss wrote a long review of *Toward World Peace,* a slender book in which Wallace summed up his foreign-policy views and took issue with the Soviet Union for its "lack of political democracy."[21] While the review was favorable about most of the book, Weiss was critical of Wallace's unfavorable comments about Russia.[22] Wallace's liberal opponents may have thought that he was "soft" on communism or a "tool of the Communists" but the Communists themselves never made that mistake. His position was explained fully in a letter he wrote to Frederick M. Morris, rector of Trinity Church in Newton Center, Massachusetts:

I share with you a complete abhorrence of all suppressions of human liberty. If I have not accented criticism of Russia in my speeches and writings, it is because there is nothing to be gained in adding to the hate campaign, when our own government is violating our most fundamental principles in almost every section of the globe. I don't believe that we shall extend civil liberties in Russia either with threats or atom bombs. Quite the contrary.

The preservation of freedom demands of us that we win this battle at home. I have hopes that when we act as we preach we shall do much toward extending freedom throughout the world.[23]

Powerful nations seldom respond favorably to threats. Many Americans had a deep, abiding, entirely justified loathing for the repression of freedom in the Soviet Union. But however loathsome, that repression did not threaten the safety of the United States or even of Western Europe. However emotionally satisfying it was to rail at Russian repression, it did absolutely nothing to reduce it, and by helping to fuel a "hard-line" policy toward Russia almost certainly helped to increase it, for Russia, whether under czar or commisar, responds to external threat by increasing the limitations on domestic dissent. To say this, however, is not to say that tempered, well-reasoned criticism of Russian internal practices, when plainly not in a threatening context, cannot have constructive effects. But that was not the Cold War context.

Wallace would not have been a normal human being if he had not been influenced by the fact that many of his most industrious supporters were Communist. It is entirely possible, even likely, that he might have been somewhat more critical of Russia if it had been otherwise, but he never could have been intemperate or Red-baiting. Even if Wallace had been harsher toward Russia, it probably would not have done him much political good, for his criticism of American foreign policy alone would have put him, in the view of many, in the Russian camp. Given the temper of the times—and the tactics of his opponents—there is no way he could have escaped the Red label without surrendering all he held important. Not to criticize Truman's policies would remove all reason for the Wallace movement.

In recent years Harry Truman has been lionized. This was probably a reaction, quite a normal one, to American's dismay over the policies of John Kennedy, Lyndon Johnson, and, especially, Richard Nixon. Truman's openness of manner seemed attractive in contrast to the deviousness that characterized the administrations of those successors. Two enormously popular books, one by his daughter and the other by Merle Miller, capitalized on and increased this sentimental regard for the plain-speaking Truman, but Wallace more than a quarter of a century ago foresaw what the real nature of Truman's legacy would be in Europe and Asia.[24] On April 4, 1948, at the founding convention of the Massachusetts Progressive Party, Wallace foresaw another legacy: the American policy, long continued, of supporting repressive regimes in Latin America. He pointed out that the Ninth Pan American Conference, then under way at Bogotá, Colombia, was dominated, at the insistence of Secretary of State Marshall, by an American plan to enlist all of Latin America in an anti-Communist crusade. The Latin American nations were preoccupied, as always, with political and economic relations with their giant neighbor to the north. But Secretary Marshall was not terribly interested in that. What he wanted was a political and military alliance directed at the Soviet Union and, as usual with United States–Latin American relations, the United States got what it wanted. The clutch of Latin American dictators ruling most of the continent was not slow to catch on. Be sufficiently anti-Communist and you could get all the economic aid you wanted (most of which went into corrupt hands) and all the military aid, weapons, training, and advisers you wanted (much of which went to repressing any internal opposition to their rules). And there would be few questions asked by Washington about your repressive policies. And if you called your political foes "Communists," Washington would help you get rid of them. With anticommunism the pre-eminent criterion, the United States for three decades helped scores of Latin dictators remain in power, a policy that also obtained in the Middle East and Asia. Somehow repression at the hands of our client dictators never received as much attention as that in Communist lands. Occasionally the press or liberals would sincerely criticize such repression but usually it was reluctantly put aside as a lesser evil, a necessary evil in the overriding struggle against communism. Wallace time and time again pointed out that Truman's policy would result in the support of repressive, reactionary regimes the world over but somehow that seemed important only to his supporters.

Also in April Wallace spoke, as he had a number of times, about the forthcoming election in Italy. On April 10 at a crowded Chicago Stadium Wallace said, "They tell us that millions of Italian citizens will vote Communist and Socialist on April 18, but they don't tell us why. They don't tell us that the Italian people are fighting the shackles of huge monopolies and a feudal system of agriculture. . . . They don't tell us that we have already spent $2 billion to maintain the unsound economic system of Italy; that we have spent that money to enable private American oil firms to gain control of the Italian oil industry and to advance the interests of American electrical, automotive, elevator, and airlines corporations."[25]

It is amusing to consider American intervention—both covert and overt—in the Italian election, especially when recalling the alarm of American statesmen and press at the Soviet intervention in Czechoslovakia. The CIA and the State Department were active, so was the American labor movement, functioning as an arm of the U.S. government. In March Secretary Marshall warned the Italians they would get no aid from the recovery program that bore his name if they elected a Communist government. And, with government encouragement, Italian-American groups urged those with relatives in Italy to send letters and cablegrams to their relatives asking them to vote for the Christian Democrats. At the same time the Vatican was using all its immense influence to convince Italians to reject the Communists. (The Christian Democrats won with 48.7 per cent of the vote and were the dominant party for decades after.)

Just as 1948 brought a number of foreign developments that hurt Wallace, so were there developments that could have embarrassed Truman. Events, however, are perceived according to the context of the national consensus of the moment. Thus, events potentially embarrassing to Wallace became more so and those potentially embarrassing to Truman became less so. Take, for instance, the situation in Greece, where the Truman Doctrine had officially been in effect for a year. By May 1948 American newspaper reports that the government was executing many of its political opponents troubled Truman's political aides. No doubt they were troubled on humanitarian grounds, but their immediate concern was political. The director of the research division of the Democratic National Committee, William L. Batt, Jr., a prominent ADAer (the division, which provided much of the substance for Truman's speeches and statements, was dominated by ADA members), wrote on May 8 to Clark Clifford that:

. . . the timing and number of the present executions strongly suggests a reprisal move of terroristic proportions. The action places the Greek government in a highly unfavorable, not to say totalitarian light, and is sure to provoke bitter criticism among Americans of every party. . . . In view of the American program of aid to Greece and of the intimate linkage of President Truman's name with that program as first announced, I suggest that consideration be given at the highest level to publicly denouncing these executions, if the reports of them prove to be correct.

I suggest it would be politically important for the President to denounce publicly and emphatically the excesses being committed in a country which we are aiding in the name of a common defense of democracy.[26]

This memo illustrates something that concerned Wallace then and has concerned critics of American foreign policy ever since. (It was particularly evident in Vietnam.) Although the United States is presumably the master and the dependent country the puppet, almost without exception the puppet ends up controlling the master. Various right-wing dictators—in Greece at the beginning and all around the world later—were quick to perceive that the United States was supporting them not out of a genuine concern for their people but because they were allies in an anti-Communist crusade that took precedence over all other considerations. It is difficult to think of a single instance where the United States took effective measures to end repressive, undemocratic practices of a regime it claimed to be supporting in the defense of democracy. To be sure, under Truman and each of his successors, the United States would occasionally *say* something, once in a while in strong terms, about such-and-such a repressive practice, but one searches for a single instance in which the United States *did* anything effective. That is why the dominoes fell in Southeast Asia: not because we failed to oppose communism but because we supported the kinds of corrupt, repressive, and incompetent "leaders" who made the triumph of communism all but inevitable. In short, American opposition to communism contributed to its triumph. Wallace saw this from the start. So did his supporters.

Nor did the Truman administration suffer any lasting damage from an astonishing series of events that began on May 4. On that day American Ambassador Walter Bedell Smith visited Foreign Minister V. M. Molotov to tell him, in effect, that the American government was not going to accept the foreign-policy proposals of Henry Wallace. Smith ended his statement with a routine assertion: "As far as the United States is concerned, the door is always open for a full discussion and the composing of our differences."

To the surprise, and dismay, of the Truman administration, Molotov on May 9 made this reply: "The Soviet Government has acquainted itself with the statement made by United States Ambassador Smith on May 4 of this year with reference to the present state of Soviet-American relations. The Soviet government views favorably the desire of the government of the United States to improve these relations as expressed in said statement, and agrees to the proposal to proceed with this end in view, to a discussion and settlement of the differences existing between us."[27]

The Soviet Union had blandly taken Smith's routine words about a "full discussion" as an invitation to a conference and accepted the invitation. On May 11 Radio Moscow broadcast reports of both Smith's statement and Molotov's reply. Hastily, that same day, Truman issued a brief statement that Molotov had not addressed himself to the main points Smith had made. Truman did not sound disposed to talk with the Soviet Union: "The policies of the United States government in international questions have been made amply clear in recent months and weeks. They have the support of the overwhelming majority of the American people. They will continue to be vigorously and firmly prosecuted." But Truman softened this tough talk somewhat. "On the other hand, the government wishes to make it unmistakably clear that the United States has no hostile or aggressive designs whatsoever with respect to the Soviet Union." No seeking of détente there.

By coincidence Henry Wallace had a rally scheduled for

Madison Square Garden that night, his first joint appearance with Glen Taylor. The plan was for both men to
discuss the Mundt-Nixon antisubversive bill then pending
before the House of Representatives. Taylor spoke as
planned, but Wallace delivered a political bombshell: an
open letter to Stalin. Wallace told the crowd in the Garden
and a nationwide radio audience that the "whole world was
heartened this morning by the release of the notes
exchanged" by Smith and Molotov. And he announced that
he had released to the press and would distribute there copies of an open letter to Stalin. "I had prepared this letter
several days ago but have revised it to take into account the
events of yesterday." In his speech, Wallace blamed both
sides, repeating his criticisms that Truman's foreign policy
was jeopardizing freedoms at home and profiting the great
corporations abroad, while asserting he did not accept the
Russian approach to economic and social problems. He was
too generous to the Soviet Union when he said that "since
the war the propaganda here in the United States has denied that the Russians have a goal of extending freedom."
There is little evidence that political liberty has ever been
much of a goal to successive Russian leaders. But Wallace
did point out that "propaganda in the Communist countries
has reverted to the old-style damnation of everything in the
capitalist nations." And he was on sound ground when he
argued, "If we let democracy work we need have no fear of
Communist ideas. Today we only fear fear itself—that
growing fear which is infringing freedom at home and re-
tarding the advancement of freedom in Russia."[28] Then he
gave the audience, in New York and across the nation,
highlights of his open letter.

Wallace proposed "immediate action to end the Cold
War" by means of "definitive, decisive steps" toward these
objectives:

1. General reduction of armaments—outlawing all methods of
mass destruction.

2. Stopping the exportation of weapons by any nation to any other nation.

3. The resumption of unrestricted trade (except for goods related to war) between the two countries.

4. The free movement of citizens, students and newspapermen between and within the two countries.

5. The resumption of free exchange of scientific information and scientific material between the two nations.

6. The re-establishment of a re-invigorated UNRRA or the constitution of some other United Nations agency for the distribution of international relief.

Wallace then declared that neither country should intervene in the internal affairs of other countries, that neither should maintain foreign bases nor "terrorize the citizens of member states of the UN by massing land forces, establishing air bases, or making naval demonstrations. Neither the USA nor the USSR should use financial pressure, economic pressure or the pressure of secret agents to obtain political results in other countries." And he called on both countries and the UN to build "a highly productive, economically unified Europe in which there would be no barriers of trade, communication or culture between Eastern Europe and Western Europe." He asserted that the Allies should conclude a peace treaty with Germany "at the earliest possible moment" and remove their troops within a year of its signing. He said both countries should refrain from intervening in China and Korea and that both should withdraw their troops from those countries. And he called on both countries to reach an agreement on atomic energy. In not the slightest degree did Wallace lean toward the USA or the USSR.[29]

No doubt some elements of Wallace's proposal were visionary, expecting one side or the other to act in a generous manner uncharacteristic of powerful nations. But the proposals were directed to both nations. Both nations were asked to make concessions. And those passages that have not been overtaken by events are still a valid blueprint for détente today.

Wallace's letter to Stalin had been brewing for quite some weeks. Wallace and his top aides attributed the idea to Michael Straight, then publisher of the *New Republic*, who had suggested some sort of an approach to Stalin, possibly even a visit to Moscow. Over a period of time the idea of a visit was discarded as being too complicated and susceptible to being labeled as a political stunt. Wallace and his aides no doubt had political ends in view, but there is no reason not to believe that his first concern was slowing down the impetus of the Cold War. Wallace began working on a letter himself on the weekend before his speech, and when news came of the Smith-Molotov exchange, he decided, against the advice of some of his aides, that this was the time to release it.[30]

The New York Times printed the full text of Wallace's letter, but the press by and large gave it minimal coverage, treating it as just another political gambit—although journalists had seen in the Smith-Molotov exchange an opportunity for productive peace talks that the Truman administration should not miss. However, the day after Wallace's speech Secretary Marshall made it plain that the United States had no intention of holding talks with the Soviet Union since, it believed, nothing was to be gained by them.

The Wallace initiative would have quickly slipped into that limbo of half-remembered events if it were not for the astonishing fact that Stalin replied in less than a week, on May 17, with a text broadcast over Radio Moscow. Wallace's letter did not cover all the differences between the two nations and certain improvements might be required on specific points, he said. But, nonetheless, "As far as the Government of the USSR is concerned, it considers that Mr. Wallace's program could serve as a good and fruitful basis for such an agreement, since the USSR Government considers, that despite the differences in the economic systems and ideologies, the co-existence of these systems and a peaceful settlement of differences between the USSR and the United States are not only possible but also doubtless necessary in the interests of a general peace."

There was no mistaking what Stalin was saying: let's talk and try to reach agreement. It is possible, of course, that nothing could have been achieved by such talks, that Stalin was just scoring propaganda points, but there was no way to find that out without trying. The Truman administration constantly asserted it wanted good relations with Russia but here it turned down a chance to see if they could be achieved. This refusal of Truman to talk with the Russians must be kept in mind when considering the Berlin airlift crisis that would soon erupt and dominate relations between the two countries for a year.

That Truman did not genuinely want good relations with Russia was what Wallace had been saying for more than a year, and the administration's response to Stalin seemed to prove it. In San Francisco on May 18, Wallace said, "This morning Secretary Marshall commented that the Stalin letter, while encouraging, was really meaningless because these issues have been discussed in the UN and they do not constitute reasons for bilateral discussions. . . . But General Marshall's statement is hardly satisfying to people who need and want peace. The objective of Marshall and others should be to seek ways of ending the impasse—not reasons for continuing it."[31]

On May 24 in Portland, Oregon, Wallace made a point that is often overlooked: how much could be accomplished if the money spent prosecuting the Cold War were spent at home. If only a tenth of the hundreds of billions of dollars wasted on the anti-Communist crusade had been spent at home, American society could have been transformed, and this does not take into account the hundreds of thousands of lives that would have been spared.

On May 29 Wallace interrupted his western trip to fly back to Washington to testify against the Mundt-Nixon bill.

The repressive "antisubversive" bill had been passed by the House on May 20 by a vote of 319–58, an indication of how much that body cherished civil liberties. It was now before the Senate Judiciary Committee. The Nixon of the bill was, of course, Richard Nixon, then a freshman congressman from California who had already begun his progress to the White House by establishing himself as a relentless Commie-hunter. In introducing the bill, Nixon had called Wallace a "fellow traveler" and an "unconscious follower of the party line."[32]

This frightening piece of proposed legislation would require that all Communist Party members register and be declared ineligible for federal employment, be denied passports, and be subject to immediate deportation if aliens. It would require that all "Communist Front" organizations—as defined by the attorney general—register and be required to keep contribution and membership files available for official requisition. And it would establish the attorney general as sole finder of facts as to "Communist Front" organizations, his findings of fact not subject to review by the courts. Since an organization could be defined as a "Communist Front" on the basis of the "extent and nature of its . . . expressions of views and policies" or on the extent to which its views and policies were the same as those of the Soviet Union, the attorney general could define as a "Communist Front" any organization critical of American policy, foreign or domestic.

The Wallace statement before the Judiciary Committee was blunt and powerful. He pointed out that the nation already had adequate laws to protect it against those advocating the violent overthrow of the government, against treason, subversion, sabotage, conspiracy, and so forth.

The Mundt bill has been proposed precisely because there is no proof that the organizations against which it is aimed have engaged in any of the activities denounced by those laws. The Attorney General himself advised the Un-American Activities Committee that legal proof was lacking. The fact is that no organization has ever been prosecuted—much less convicted—under this more than adequate legislation. . . .

Never in the history of the United States has any public official been vested with such authority. Even the Alien and Sedition Laws, vicious as they were, do not supply a precedent. The only model for this authority lies in the power given to the Nazi minister of the interior by the first laws passed after Hitler's accession to power.[33]

Wallace declared that his party would refuse to register with the attorney general if the bill were passed.

The Senate did not complete action on the bill in that session, but the bill took substantial effect in late 1950 as part of the McCarran Bill, which was passed over Truman's veto. Despite vetoing the bill, Truman more than anyone else established the atmosphere that made its passage in Congress irresistible.

Although Wallace was not to be nominated formally until July, he had, of course, been campaigning since the beginning of the year and it was long since apparent, as far as the Truman administration, ADA-type liberals, and the press were concerned, that the overriding issue was not Wallace's criticism of American foreign policy but his relationship with American Communists. He often took notice of this and at Albuquerque on June 3 made what can be regarded as a basic statement on the matter. It came out in the course of an interview with Edward R. Murrow over KGGM, a local radio station:

According to the newspapers I'm getting a lot of support from the Communists, and the Communist leaders seem to think they have to endorse me every day or so. There's no question that this sort of thing is a political liability. The Communists oppose my advocacy of progressive capitalism. They support me because I say we can have peace with Russia. I will not repudiate any support which comes to me on the basis of interest in peace. The Communists are interested in peace because they want a successful social-

ist experiment in Russia. I am interested in peace because I want
our American system to demonstrate the enormous vitality of
which it is capable. That vitality which is being wasted in preparation for war. If, during the war, we had accepted the idea that you
can't work with Communists, we might not have succeeded in our
joint efforts to stop Hitler. If you accept the idea that Communists
have no right to express their opinions, then you don't believe in
democracy. And if you accept the notion that it is impossible to
live in a world with sharply differing ideas, then you accept the
inevitability of war. I do believe in democracy.[34]

That seems rather reasonable nowadays, but in 1948 there
was simply no way he could escape the Communist taint,
then politically fatal, without denying his own principles.

5

Downhill All the Way

The early summer of 1948 saw both the peak of the Wallace movement and the beginning of its long, steady slide downhill. By June, though Henry Wallace was still attracting large, enthusiastic crowds, the polls were beginning to show his popularity falling back from a high point of 10 to 13 per cent as compared to other Presidential candidates.

Polls in June and July indicated that most people thought the United States was "too soft" on the Soviet Union, hardly a help to Wallace, who was arguing that the United States was too hard. According to a Gallup Poll, 69 per cent of the public felt that way, while a similar National Opinion Research Center Poll showed a 53-per-cent majority answering the same way.[1] This demonstrates the marvelous circularity of American politics. Harry Truman used the unequaled publicity machinery of the Presidency to establish with the American people the conviction that the Soviet Union was a serious danger to national security. Then he cited this conviction, as reflected in the polls, as requiring him to take a hard line with Russia. The response to such polls also demonstrated Truman's political shrewdness and Thomas Dewey's obtuseness. Truman did everything in his power to avoid the discussion of foreign affairs, where he was clearly vulnerable, and struck a posture as a new Roosevelt, using his newly liberal Fair Deal proposals to reconstitute the old New Deal coalition that had served FDR so well. But while Truman decined Wallace's challenge to discuss foreign policy—and Dewey never issued one—the headlines from Europe after the Berlin airlift crisis developed showed him as a man of resolution and courage in standing up against the Communists. And Dewey never challenged Truman to explain how the various foreign crises developed; he just supported the bipartisan foreign policy, saying only that he would administer it better. Thus, Dewey lost an election he could have won had he waged a vigorous and tough campaign against Truman. Dewey thought he was going to inherit the Presidency; he did not realize it had to be won.

While the climate for Wallace was bad, and getting worse, at the same time Beanie Baldwin and his top-level colleagues seemed to be making a functional political organization out of chaos. Given the difficulty of creating a national organization in just a few months, it is not surprising that most of the talent and whatever coherence exist in a political campaign were concentrated at headquarters in New York. There was enthusiasm and hope and a sense of crusade that obscured, for a time at least, the discouraging reality. This, as Wallace and Baldwin saw it, was genuinely going to be a people's party, with the people participating as in no other. Blacks, minorities, women, young people would all be welcome, foreshadowing by a quarter century the reforms made by the Democratic Party in the early 1970s.

The most constant charge against Wallace and the Progressives was that the Communists dominated the convention and the platform it adopted, citing the platform as the ultimate proof. The charge is nonsense and the platform *is* the ultimate proof. The question of dominating the convention or dictating the platform, by the Communists or anyone else, simply did not exist. There were some differences on the convention floor and in the platform proceedings. That is inevitable whenever men and women of strong conviction discuss complex and controversial issues. But these were not irreconcilable positions, for the Progressive Party by its very nature was composed of like-minded men and women. It was not an umbrella party like the Democratic or, to a lesser extent, the Republican, trying to compromise, for instance, northern black activists and southern segregationists. In his detailed, exhaustingly detailed, accounts of the drafting of the platform and of the convention, Curtis Macdougall has made it as plain as can be that differences were resolved democratically and amicably, although a few feathers did stay ruffled for a while. But no one has to believe Macdougall, who is a Wallace partisan—as is, it is no secret by now, this writer. One has merely to read the platform itself. It was a strong and progressive but sound platform then, and even now, with the political reforms that have taken place since, it is still a strong, progressive, and sound platform. Whether those participating in its preparation were Communists, progressives, liberals, reformers is irrelevant. It is the document itself that matters. It represented the genuine convictions of the Progressive Party *as a whole*.

Preparation of the platform began shortly after April 10, when Rexford Tugwell accepted chairmanship of the platform committee on the condition that Lee Pressman be named secretary. Pressman, after years of service as Philip Murray's right-hand man (perhaps that should be left-hand man), had resigned in February as CIO general counsel to participate in the Wallace movement. Pressman's leftist views were no secret, although it was not until some years later that he made known that he had earlier been a member of the Communist Party.

Pressman supervised an outline for the platform. It was approved by Wallace and Tugwell, and on June 22 sent to all state directors of the party with the request that it "be given the widest possible consideration and discussion."[2] With that as a basis, two draft platforms were prepared, one under the supervision of Tugwell in Chicago, the other under Pressman in New York. Eventually the platform committee also had before it a platform prepared at Wallace's urging by Leo Huberman and Paul Sweezy, the well-known non-Communist Marxists. And a long preamble and a short statement of specific platform proposals by the writer and scholar Scott Buchanan.[3]

While his colleagues were working on the platform, Wallace continued campaigning. In New Hampshire, on June 28, he expressed his reservations about Communist support. As reported by the press, for some reason not until five days later, Wallace said: "I'm never going to say anything in the nature of Red-baiting. But I must say this: if the Communists would run a ticket of their own this year, we might lose a hundred thousand votes but we would gain three million. I know if the Communists really wanted to help us, they would run their own ticket this year and let us get those extra votes." But even if the Communists had run their own candidate, whether genuinely or a a tactic to protect Wallace from Red-baiting, it would almost certainly have been exposed, validly or not, as a conspiratorial stratagem and redounded to Wallace's discredit. Despite the allegedly conspiratorial nature of the Communists, they could not have kept such a tactic secret. Not only would too many people have been in on such a decision but the party was infiltrated by the FBI, which fed information to anti-Communist reporters. So Wallace would still have been tainted, and he would have lost the energy and skill of some of his most effective workers. It was an impossible dilemma, and Wallace knew it. The overwhelming majority of his supporters were non-Communists, but that was not news. What attracted the press was any expression of support by a Communist. But the press was less interested when the Communists were cross with Wallace, as they were over his book and over his New Hampshire statement.

Wallace's colleagues were trying to devise a way out of this dilemma. To this end the Progressive Party prepared a long fact sheet on U.S.–Soviet relations and it dealt with most of the important questions that could be raised. But they realized that a point-by-point rebuttal would not solve the problem. This is how the fact sheet began:

Every time an opponent succeeds in switching the discussions about presidential elections in the U.S. on to problems of Russian internal politics or Soviet behavior in international relations, he scores a tactical victory, no matter how successfully you counter his arguments.

If you are not equipped to shatter his assertion, the attention of the audience is diverted from the problems of this country to real or imagined faults of the Soviet government, while you and the candidate you promote suddenly find yourselves in the position of scapegoats for the government of another country.

Even if you destroy every argument, you inevitably achieve this result only though explaining and justifying the actions of the Soviets. Thus, although a winner in the struggle of facts and ideas, you indirectly (in the minds of the public) concede to the adversaries one very important point—by appearing to be an apologist for another government.

All such attempts by opponents should be countered by a reminder that we are not discussing elections in the Moscow Soviet and therefore Stalin's shortcomings are of no consequence whatsoever. What interests all of us is to improve our own government, and the discussion should bear on this and this only. As to the question of normal relations with Russia, advocated by the Progressive Party, such relations are necessary for the maintenance of peace and of American prosperity.[4]

Anyone sophisticated enough to have written such a perceptive paper must have recognized the hopelessness of the task of Wallace and the Progressives. In times of extreme nationalism, reason is usually a vain argument. And so it proved to be.

At about the time that Wallace was campaigning in New Hampshire and complaining ruefully that Communist support was doing him more harm than good, another, rather more prominent, Communist made a decision that greatly increased world tension and thus came to harm the Wallace campaign. Stalin had decided to impose a blockade on West Berlin. Although it was a monumental blunder by Stalin, the situation was not as black and white as the Truman administration and the American press made it appear. The West and Russia had been wrangling over Germany since the end of the war, with first one side, then the other taking actions that disturbed each other. In the spring of 1948 Britain, France, and the United States announced that the West German economy would be integrated with that of Western Europe and that the three Western zones of Germany would be combined. Needless to say, Stalin did not want to see the stronger half of Germany, Russia's mortal foe just three years before, joining the Western camp that he saw as a threat to the Soviet Union. He tried to stop it by imposing, on June 24, a complete blockade of West Berlin. Berlin, although occupied by all four victorious powers by agreement, was deep within the Russian occupation zone.

One cannot be certain of Stalin's move but it appeared that he was trying to achieve an agreement on all Germany that would be more acceptable to the Soviet Union. His immediate goal seemed to be the kind of wide-ranging talks that he had proposed in response to Wallace's open letter but which the Truman administration had rejected. In any case, Truman decided that he was not going to be forced out of Berlin and decided on the famous airlift of food, supplies, and even coal into the besieged half of the city. The West protested the blockade and said it would talk about Berlin but only after the blockade had been lifted. Russia turned down the Western protests and said she was prepared to talk but that the talks could not be limited to Berlin alone but must consider the entire question of Germany. The Truman administration did not want to talk about Germany. It had already decided to make West Germany a part of the Western alliance and saw no point in discussing it. So the blockade and the airlift dragged on until May 1949, when the two sides finally held inconclusive talks. In the meantime, the blockade established the Russians more firmly as villains and the headlines about the successful airlift that continued all through the campaign gave Truman a heroic look. As far as Wallace was concerned, it further discredited his appeals for détente, and it made it difficult for Dewey and the Republicans to attack Truman as "soft" on communism.

About this time, everything began to go right for Truman—politically, that is, for it would be hard to characterize the Berlin crisis as good news in any other terms. Then, after abortive attempts by liberals to dump him, Truman got the Democratic Presidential nomination, as he had been confident all along he would. At the convention, he executed a political, if somewhat cynical masterstroke, and was the recipient of an enormous bit of good luck, one of those clouds with a silver lining that justifies the cliché. He brought the convention to its feet with a pugnacious speech in which he announced that he was summoning into special session that "do-nothing Congress," so it could do the things it should have been doing. Truman knew, of course, and so did anyone else with sense, that a Republican Congress, expecting a great Republican victory in a few months, was not about to do what it had refused to do for a year and a half. But it gave him an issue.

Then, the liberals, led by the young mayor of Minneapolis, Hubert H. Humphrey, decided that if they could not get a liberal candidate, they would at least get a liberal platform. So they insisted on, and won, a strong civil-rights plank. That caused most of the South to take a walk, giving birth to the Dixiecrat Party. This looked like anything but good news. After losing, as everyone then thought, a good portion of the liberal wing of the party to Wallace, Truman was now losing the Right, segregationist wing to Governor J. Strom Thurmond of South Carolina. But Wallace attracted the Red-baiting attacks that would otherwise have been directed at Truman. And Thurmond rehabilitated Truman with the black voters in the northern big cities, a crucial vote, it turned out. While Truman was fairly liberal on civil rights, Wallace had gone far beyond any politician in American history before or since in supporting the rights of blacks and Mexican-Americans. Had the South stayed with the Democrats, the blacks might well have voted for Henry Wallace in great number. But now Truman actively sought black support, the blacks' loyalty to the Democratic Party was aroused as it had not been since Roosevelt days, the black leadership preferred to deal with the reality of power rather than the vision of a promised land, and anyone Thurmond attacked couldn't be all bad. So Dewey, who might well have picked up some southern states, lost them to Thurmond, and Wallace got far fewer black votes than he would have, causing Truman to carry northern states he would otherwise have lost. A few thousand black votes lost by Truman to Wallace in Illinois, Caifornia, and Ohio would have given the election to Dewey.

Just a few days before the Progressives convened for their extraordinary convention, a Gallup Poll brought bad news: that 51 per cent of the voters believed that the Wallace party was run by Communists; only 21 per cent disagreed, with 28 per cent having no opinion. As George Gallup wrote on July 20, "Perhaps one of the reasons why the Wallace third party has not been able to increase its following is the belief held by many American voters that Communists dominate the party.

"Politicians of both major parties have tried to pin the Communist tag on the followers of Henry A. Wallace since his party was launched six months ago. Apparently their efforts have succeeded. . . ."[5]

Clearly the Truman administration wanted the Wallace movement to be colored Red, and indeed, it took surreptitious steps to achieve that end. It also took steps that were somewhat less than surreptitious. Perhaps by sheer coincidence—although few political observers in or out of the Wallace camp thought so at the time—on July 21, just two days before the Progressive convention, a federal grand jury indicted twelve Communist leaders under the Smith Act. This, of course, put the Communist issue on the front page of just about every newspaper in the country and on just about every radio newscast. If it was a coincidence, it was the second such, because in February, just before the special congressional election in the Bronx that was won by a

Wallace supporter, three prominent left-wing labor supporters of Wallace were picked up and taken to Ellis Island
to await deportation proceedings. One of them had appeared in Harlem with Wallace just a few days before. This
"coincidence" resulted in pictures on the front pages of
New York newspapers the day before the special election.

That very same day Wallace made a strong statement, in
which he anticipated by several years the subsequent court
decisions that eventually threw out virtually all such later
indictments or convictions on constitutional grounds:

> I am confident that the courts will eventually find unconstitu-
> tional the Smith Act under which the indictments are handed
> down, to the extent that it makes unlawful the advocacy of any
> doctrine by peaceful means, unaccompanied by a clear and present
> danger to established government. I think that such an application
> of the Smith Act clearly violates the First Amendment and in-
> fringes the American right of free speech. Meanwhile, the bi-par-
> tisans will play up the indictments and hearings and trials to pro-
> mote fear. The present situation makes it essential for the
> Administration to create fear through a continued series of crises.
> We can expect further Red scares and attacks on other minority
> groups with charges that their views are hostile to the govern-
> ment. . . . I fully expect continued attempts to attack the New
> Party with all manner of false and inflammatory allegations. The
> New Party will continue to carry on the fight in defense of the con-
> stitutional liberties of all the American people.[6]

But his remarks, however valid, did not of course decrease
the public's identification of him with the Communist
party.

Often throughout this book I have made reference to Red-
baiting and harassment of left-wing activities. Those who
are too young to have lived through the 1940s and 1950s
may find it so far outside their experience as to be unimag-
inable, although those who were harassed or jailed for their
opposition to the war in Indochina will have some idea
what it was like. But it was worse then, much worse; for not

only did dissenters face such penalties as loss of job and im-
prisonment but virtually all of society was turned against
them. Even those who were well placed, secure, and finan-
cially independent were afraid to speak out. Anyone who
lived through those grim and shameful days has difficulty
recapturing that fearful atmosphere; possibly because they
do not want to remember. These few pages can hardly hope
to do so; it would take an entire book, better still a play or a
movie, to re-create that fear and hysteria.

But in a few kaleidoscopic paragraphs it may be possible
to give a bare hint of what it was like. These few instances,
it must be remembered, are only a tiny fraction of the incidents that took place all over the country.

In many cities and towns Wallace had the utmost difficulty in finding meeting places, being denied publicly
owned facilities that were normally available for political
rallies. Often hotels refused to rent their meeting rooms,
and time after time universities and colleges, public and
private, refused to let Wallace appear on campus. This was
particularly distressing, for universities, above all, are supposed to be open to the clash of ideas. That was seldom the
case in 1948. A number of professors were fired or suspended for publicly supporting Wallace, and no one knows
how many faculty members were intimidated by college
presidents and deans and by state legislatures from publicly
supporting Wallace; there were instances all across the nation. Not infrequently, especially in the South, Wallace rallies were held in truly frightening circumstances. It was not
just a matter of picketing or heckling, which are entirely
normal in American political campaigns, but of mobs rushing into meeting halls, slugging matches, indifferent police
protection, and countless threats.

Several times newspapers printed the names of those who
signed Wallace petitions. They had every right to do so, of
course, but the purpose was obvious: to embarrass or even
harm those who had signed and to intimidate those who
otherwise might. Sometimes the addresses of Wallace sup-

porters were printed, a clear invitation to harassment. Other times vigilante-like groups ostentatiously wrote down the license-plate numbers of cars parked near Wallace rallies. A number of times local Wallace headquarters were vandalized. In perhaps the most extreme case of harassment, a man distributing Wallace campaign literature in Pontiac, Michigan, was seized by a gang of men, taken outside of town, had his head shaved with a penknife, and was beaten.[7] In Illinois a seventy-five-year-old retired lawyer, gathering signatures on a petition to get the Progressive Party on the ballot, had his sign torn down by American Legionaires who paraded around him with their own sign: "Which Joe: GI or Stalin." (The lawyer had had three sons in the war, one of whom lost his life.) Also in Illinois Curtis Macdougall, the Progressive candidate for the Senate, and his companions were stoned and got no police protection.

Indeed the police were sometimes as much hazard as protection. Police in various parts of the country investigated groups and individuals supporting Wallace. In New York and Chicago police raided political meetings in clubhouses and private homes. In Detroit the police commissioner, Harry S. Toy, had declared in a radio broadcast that Russian agents were entering the United States from Canada disguised as Jewish rabbis. The chairman of the Michigan Progressive Party, Allen Sayler, protested, asserting that this absurd charge was likely to incite anti-Semitism and create an atmosphere of fear. In reply Commissioner Toy wrote of Wallace as an "Un-American leader" carrying on "Un-American activities." And he ended his letter with this passage; "I have no doubt that you object to statements that were made by me, especially when I said that I felt that all those engaged in Un-American activities ought to be either shot, thrown out of the country, or put in jail."[8]

Throughout 1948 prominent Wallace supporters were called before national and state un-American activities committees and before federal grand juries in a number of states. John Abt, Lee Pressman, Charles Kramer, and Victor

Perlo, all prominent Progressives, were called before the House Un-American Activities Committee; they refused to testify, pleading various sections of the First, Fifth, and Sixth Amendments to the Constitution. None was cited for contempt. Needless to say, all this received wide coverage in the press, which made much of the fact that so many Progressives were being called up. So pervasive was the atmosphere of fear and so long did it last that six years later, when Curtis Macdougall was doing interviews for his encyclopedic history of the Progressive Party campaign, many participants refused or were reluctant to talk to him. What an irony! Those who most loudly proclaimed the lack of political liberties in Russia were responsible for their curtailment in the United States.

It is necessary to understand the context of anti-Communist hysteria to understand the dispute that broke out during the Progressive Party convention on its final day, July 25. The dispute seemed, to the delegates, a perfectly normal difference of opinion, one item among many others that was settled democratically by vote. This was one of the most extraordinary conventions in American political history. More than three thousand delegates and alternates descended on Philadelphia. They were not the middle-aged, middle-class party worthies who normally constituted Republican and Democratic conventions. These were all kinds of people: the very young and the very old; blacks and members of all sorts of minorities; farmers and workers and housewives. They came by plane and train and old jalopies, in farm trucks and trailers, with tents and backpacks. They were not free-spending conventioneers as were those who had come to Philadelphia for the Republican and Democratic meetings. Many of them had little money and lived on sandwiches and soft drinks. Indeed, so manifest was their lack of money that Philadelphia merchants near Convention Hall reduced their prices to the normal level from the inflated ones that had prevailed during the earlier two conventions. In short, it was a people's convention of progressives and idealists who had come in response to an idea and a man who personified it. And it was a singing convention, with Pete Seeger and other folk singers leading the delegates in familiar union songs and new songs written for the occasion. It was a sort of political revival meeting dedicated to reforming the nation. Perhaps it was best characterized by the writer Shirley Graham, who asserted exultantly that this was one convention where the pickets weren't outside the hall; they were inside. The closest comparison is the 1972 Democratic convention where George McGovern's reformers and radicals apparently horrified solid Middle America. These 1948 Progressives were even more hopelessly optimistic, hopelessly idealistic, and hopelessly doomed.

As it turned out, it was the greatest moment for Henry Wallace and the Progressive Party, and while it lasted it was a good one. The speeches were short. The convention had the first black keynoter in American political history, an Iowan and former Republican, Charles Howard. In open and vigorous debate it adopted a platform that even now is still forward looking. It anticipated the Supreme Court's one-man one-vote decision by a generation, by adopting party rules that based representation on population, not on the customary system that gave additional representation to states that were carried by the party. The ADA was distressed that the Progressives were giving greater representation to the larger population centers. Exactly. And the convention was climaxed by an extraordinary rally at which Glen Taylor and Henry Wallace gave their acceptance speeches. The speeches, in which the candidates restated what they had been saying all along, were not in Convention Hall but in Shibe Park, the venerable home of Connie Mack's Philadelphia Athletics. More than thirty-two thousand persons paid their way in, with tickets ranging from 65¢ to $2.60. The $30,000 this collected paid for the convention's expenses. Then Bill Gailmor raised another $50,000, a huge sum in those days, by using his own technique of asking first for $1000 donations, working his way down in steps to a single dollar, finally asking the audience to empty their pockets of whatever change they had. An astonished Hal Boyle, a famous Associated Press columnist, wrote, "It will remain a thing of awe to professional politicians that people paid hard cash to see a man baptize his own party. This was something new."[9] Altogether a remarkable event, a coming together of true believers.

The press concentrated on the final day's activity, the adoption of the platform. According to many press accounts, the platform was railroaded through by Communists and fellow travelers. Actually, the platform was the result of weeks of work by the platform committee, several days of open hearings at which anyone could appear, and nearly eight hours of debate on the convention floor. In contrast to this "railroaded" platform, the Democratic convention devoted about an hour to discussion of the platform, much of that time taken by three Dixiecrats who opposed the civil-rights plank. The Republicans dedicated to their platform just enough time to have it read, proposed, seconded, and passed unanimously by voice vote, with nary a word of discussion.

Although the press subsequently made out that the vote on the famous Vermont Resolution was the crucial moment of the convention, the delegates took it to be just one item among others. The leadership thought it was of no particular significance, and Henry Wallace did not even discuss it on the train ride back to New York that night. The matter came up early that Sunday afternoon, July 25, when three delegates from Vermont submitted this amendment to the platform: "Although we are critical of the present foreign policy of the United States, it is not our intention to give blanket endorsement to the foreign policy of any nation." At the time that the Vermonters drew up their amendment, they were not aware of an amendment that had been drafted by Frederick L. Schuman, the well-known Williams College political scientist, at the request of Wallace, who believed, as did others, that there was not enough in the platform about Soviet-American relations. Meeting in Wallace's room that morning, Schuman had proposed language that was substantially adopted—although the following two sentences were dropped: "We condemn the totalitarianism of the Left no less than the totalitarianism of the Right. Both are denials of human dignity and freedom though the latter, in the form of fascism, spells slavery and death, while the former, in the form of Soviet communism, has potentialities of freedom and life." As Schuman noted in his diary, "This he—Henry Wallace, not the agents of Moscow—will not have. He insists that he and the party must not, cannot and will not, engage in any form of Russophobia or Red-baiting. I agree in principle. I have doubts in practice and deem his definition of these terms too broad. However, *we all agree.* [I type out the revised draft in Beanie's room. Then a belated breakfast.]"[10]

The convention quickly adopted the Schuman amendment, without any knowledge that Wallace and Taylor had approved it. Wallace did not want to dictate to the convention, and indeed, after the quick morning meeting with Schuman and others, had gone off to play tennis. The Schuman amendment included this language:

. . . Responsibility for ending the tragic prospect of war is a joint responsibility of the Soviet Union and the United States. We hope for more political liberty and economic democracy throughout the world. We believe that war between East and West will mean fascism and death for all. We insist that peace is the prerequisite of survival.

We believe with Henry Wallace that "there is no misunderstanding between the USA and USSR which can be settled by force or fear and there is no difference which cannot be settled by peaceful, hopeful negotiation. There is no American principle or public interest, and there is no Russian principle or public interest, which would have to be sacrificed to end the cold war and open up the Century of Peace which the Century of the Common Man demands."

We denounce anti-Soviet hysteria as a mask for monopoly, militarism, and reaction. We demand that a new leadership of the
peace-seeking people of our nation—which has vastly greater responsibility for peace than Russia because it has vastly greater
power for war—undertake in good faith and carry to an honorable
conclusion, without appeasement or sabre-rattling on either side,
a determined effort to settle current controversies and enable men
and women everywhere to look forward with confidence to the
common task of building a creative and lasting peace for all the
world.[11]

The drafters of the Vermont Resolution had not been
aware of this rather even-handed section when they prepared their amendment. Their real worry was a quite legitimate concern that the Progressives must reduce their vulnerability to Red-baiting. James Hayford of Vermont put it
this way in the debate:

"May I support that motion [the Vermont Resolution]? It
is our feeling that the great weak point of the platform as it
now stands is that it lays us open to the charge of condemning the American foreign policy practically in toto, while
saying nothing critical of the foreign policy of any other
nation.

"It would save us a lot of time in our arguments that we
shall surely have this summer, if we can plug that loophole
right now. It is not the intention of this resolution to Red-
bait or introduce any red herrings. The wording of it, I
think, amply takes care of any such danger."

Earlier Rex Tugwell had mildly opposed the Vermonters
by saying he thought the Schuman amendment had "adequately covered" the point, and Edwin Smith, another Ver-
monter, took the same position. There were supporters for
the amendment, but the sense of the convention seemed to
be expressed by Carl L. Edding of Indiana: ". . . I want to
say that I think this convention is entirely opposed to this
amendment. It is merely an attempt to appease an element
which would not be appeased even if we tried to do so."[12]

And after some more debate, the Vermont amendment was voted down.

It seemed to be the genuine feeling of a majority that the amendment would have been a bow in the direction of Red-baiting. Actually, it was rather an innocuous insertion that would not have significantly affected the platform one way or the other. Since the platform did not give "blanket endorsement to the foreign policy of any nation," there was no real need to say that it did not. On the other hand, it would have done no harm to have used such language. Wallace was off somewhere else. Baldwin was otherwise occupied. Tugwell and Pressman mildly opposed the amendment, but simply because it seemed superfluous. What seems to have happened was that the rank and file simply did not want to have anything that could be interpreted as Red-baiting or even responding to Red-baiting.

Beanie Baldwin told me he would not have opposed the resolution and Ralph Shikes, Wallace's press director, said that it might have been helpful in a public-relations sense if the Vermont Resolution had been passed, but both thought that if the press and the Cold War liberals had not had that to seize on, they would have found something else.[13] Curtis Macdougall and others think it was a tragic mistake not to have adopted the resolution, but given the way the press and the Cold War liberals treated the Progressives before and after the convention, Edding was probably right when he saw it as "merely an attempt to appease an element which would not be appeased even if we tried to do so." But in the chapter on the press, we will see what capital they made of the Vermont Resolution. As for the convention as a whole, there is no reason to dispute Henry Wallace's assessment: "If the Communists did dominate the convention, it certainly was their strategy to let me have my own way." But the proof, or disproof, of his conviction is right at hand for anyone to see for himself. The party platform was not a routine exercise routinely forgotten by the candidate, but the party's—and the candidate's—credo.

The campaign after the convention was little different from the campaign before, because there had never been any doubt about the candidates. Wallace and Taylor continued to pound away at the same issues; the press, with occasional exceptions, continued to ignore the substance of Wallace's campaign and concentrate on tying him to the Communists; and the Cold War liberals continued to do the same thing. So did the Democrats and the Republicans, to the extent they paid any attention to Wallace. And events at home and abroad continued to work against him. From abroad headlines about the Berlin airlift continued throughout the campaign, and in midyear there were the headlines about Stalin's excommunication of Yugoslavia's Tito. In August there was a sensational story when a Russian teacher of the children of Soviet diplomats in New York defected, was kidnaped, and returned to the Russian consulate, and then escaped in a daring leap from a third-floor window. That same month Whittaker Chambers began his disclosures about Communist cells, disclosures that catapulted Richard Nixon to national fame and eventually resulted in the conviction for perjury of Alger Hiss (a conviction that he has contested ever since). And other Communist-hunters in Congress, mostly but not exclusively Republicans, continued to grab headlines, with much more success than they ever achieved in proving their allegations, but it was not a time when proof seemed important. The accusation was the thing. Such as that made by Senator J. Howard McGrath, chairman of the Democratic National Committee. On August 1, a few days after the Progressive Party convention, he spoke of "the mockery of a third-party convention, which was assembled to ratify the unilateral decisions of the Communist leadership of that Party. . . . Henry Wallace and his Gideonites have sought to create confusion. It is the old Communist tactic carried forward with catchwords, catch phrases, trick tunes and stage-managed effects. Their one objective has been to aid the program of Russia. Where our policy has been in conflict with that of Russia we have seen the Wallacites take the line that we must appease Russia."[14]

And on August 5 an Associated Press dispatch quoted the notorious racist Congressman from Mississippi, John Rankin, as proposing that Wallace be called before investigators of the House Un-American Activities Committee for questioning about the "placing of Communists" in "key positions" in the Department of Commerce. So it went for the rest of the campaign.

Wallace met the issue head on, time and time again, in terms similar to those used in his nationwide radio speech over NBC on August 12 when he accused the House Un-American Activities Committee of using "the technique of political gangsterism and tyranny" in its attempt to gain passage of the Mundt-Nixon bill "as the first step toward a reactionary police state." This seems, at first glance, like rather extreme language, but the committee was guilty of extreme practices and the FBI and the CIA were guilty over a period of years of police-state methods—*agents provocateurs,* anonymous letters, attempts to disgrace those whose politics offended them, manipulation of evidence, intimidation, and so on. Perhaps in years to come it will be possible to learn from still secret documents what steps were taken by various government agencies against the Progressive Party. Behind all this, Wallace asserted, were "the international capitalists and the munitions makers whose profits go up and down precisely with the degree of international crisis which can be whipped up—with the amount of Red scare which can be engendered for the purpose of addling the brains of the American public."[15] Again, the language seems extreme but the huge profits made by the "defense" industry are there for anyone to see. So, too, is the practice of the Pentagon, whenever it is seeking more or newer weapons of war, of warning the nation about a new threat from the Soviet Union. But no matter how many times he declared he was not a Communist, explained how his views differed from American Communists, criticized the Soviet Union—and there were many instances of each— there was no way he could escape the taint of communism. He shared certain valid domestic goals of American Communists, he made certain valid criticisms of American foreign policy that were also made by Communists at home and abroad, and he refused to Red-bait: this at a time when the country was fervent in its support of the jingoistic philosophy of "My country right or wrong."

Toward the end of his campaign, on October 6 in San Francisco, Wallace termed the regime of Chiang Kai-shek a "corrupt and failing dictatorship . . . already repudiated by more than half the Chinese people." And he declared that the vast amounts of American aid to Chiang had gone into a "bottomless pit." Wallace had foreseen ever since his trip to China for FDR that Chiang was destined to fail, that we were, as would be the case in other countries for decades to come, backing the wrong side in an internal struggle. This was the sort of thing he had been saying for years, but he also said something else in that speech that must have occurred to many Americans in the years since: "It sometimes has seemed to me that if Russia had deliberately planned for us our bipartisan foreign policy she could hardly have done better for her ends than we have done for her."[16] Ironies abound in these pages but the greatest irony of all is that a quarter century of foreign policy designed to counter communism has done infinitely more harm to the United States at home and abroad than unopposed communism could ever have done.

And on October 26 at Madison Square Garden, Wallace declared, "our party has already accomplished fantastically more than I ever dreamed was possible" . . . that "above all—we have stopped the cold war in its tracks." That was wishful thinking. It was apparent in those final days that Wallace was going down to a disastrous defeat and, more important, that the ideas for which he had committed political suicide were going down with him.

Nonetheless, there were reasons to vote for a loser. It would be difficult to express them better than did Louis Untermeyer, the poet, editor, and translator, in a column for *The New York Star* of October 28.

. . . I will vote for Wallace, first of all, because he is the leader of the Progressive Party. If ever there was need for a new party, that need is now. These are threatening times, not only abroad but here at home. Emerson warned that "Things are in the saddle, and ride mankind." For "Things" read "Reaction." Both the Republican and Democratic parties have failed to grapple with the powers of reaction—if indeed, they even care to cope with them. Only a Progressive Party can act as a check to challenge the growing ruthlessness of reaction.

I will vote for Wallace because he is the only candidate fighting for freedom of expression and freedom of assembly. . . . The right to criticize and speak up—the very foundation of American rights—is no longer a right, but a rare privilege. Tomorrow it may well be a luxury reserved only for the chosen few.

I will vote for Wallace because I am tired of the smear tactics of the opposition. I am a non-Communist liberal, but I resent Red-baiting and the now popular sport of kicking not only the Communist around but baiting and blacklisting anyone who questions the repressions of labor, inflation, the Marshall Plan, or any attempt to settle difficulties by negotiation rather than by threat and force.

I will vote for Wallace because I believe with him—and (since I look for precedents in our poetry) Walt Whitman—that our country cannot be considered a true Democracy until all men, regardless of color, creed, or race, can live and work together without intimidation or discrimination.

I will vote for Wallace since the Progressive Party is the only one which recognizes culture as a potentially powerful spirit in the life of the people. . . .

I will vote for Wallace because he is the only candidate who is unequivocally fighting for peace, as opposed to the continuance of the cold war backed up by our conscienceless threat of atom bombs; for free labor unions, as opposed to the Taft-Hartley law; for free thought and free communication, as opposed to the [J. Parnell] Thomas [Un-American Activities] Committee; for a fully functioning United Nations, as opposed to an organization used merely as a pawn in the game of power politics.

Finally, I will vote for Wallace because his is the only party which has come out flatly against the ever-present terrors of an annihilating war. His program may not be the final blueprint for a constructive and creative peace; but until a better plan comes along, it should be welcome by everyone who wants a decent world—or wants just to go on living.

Not too many Americans shared Untermeyer's view, for on November 2 Henry Agard Wallace received only 1,157,063 votes, compared to more than 24 million for Harry S. Truman, and nearly 22 million for Thomas E. Dewey. Even Strom Thurmond, the Dixiecrat, received more votes, 1,169,032. As a measure of the degree to which he had fallen back since the early months of the year, Wallace received a little less than 200,000 votes in California, where more than 400,000 had signed petitions in his behalf in January and February.

What went wrong? Immediately after the election the Progressive Party subjected itself to a rigorous self-examination and published the results.[17] It found itself deficient in a good many ways but even if the party had been more expert in political organization, even if it had done better in explaining the issues, there is little reason to believe the result would have been much better. Anyone who was interested knew what Wallace and the Progressives stood for. But the results seem to indicate that even many who agreed with Wallace ended up voting for Truman. One hears reports that even some of the workers in Wallace headquarters voted for the President. Many progressives, including those who had little use for Truman, simply could not bear the idea of a Republican in the White House. Truman and his advisers were aware of that and in the closing weeks of his campaign he specifically appealed to Wallace supporters. "There are, however, some people with true liberal convictions whose worry over the state of the world has caused them to lean toward a third party," Truman said.

"A vote for the third party plays into the hands of the Republican forces of reaction, whose aims are directly opposed to the aims of American liberalism.

"A vote for the third party will not promote the cause of American liberalism, but will injure it.

"I say to those disturbed liberals who have been sitting uncertainly on the outskirts of the third party: Think again. Don't waste your vote."[18]

This was a shrewd appeal. Even those who were not convinced by his "work-for-peace" statements did find Truman preferable to Dewey on domestic issues. To many progressives Truman was clearly a lesser evil.

There were other reasons to vote for him, too. Party loyalty was strong, blacks who preferred Wallace found in Strom Thurmond a good reason to justify voting for Truman and the Democratic Party, and the months of Red-baiting had obviously taken their toll. Some Wallace supporters became convinced that Wallace was a tool of the Communists, and others, more sophisticated, while not thinking Wallace was unknowingly being used, found any association with Communists distasteful. The anti-Communist atmosphere was so intense that it was difficult for even intelligent people of good will not to be influenced by it. Communism was generally regarded as an infection, if not fatal, certainly incapacitating. And, finally, the Cold War headlines both increased the anti-Communist fervor and showed Truman as a valiant warrior against the Russians.

No one can ever know to what degree these and other factors cut into the Wallace total. But the wasted-vote theory is one that can be questioned. Indeed, one can suggest that those votes cast for Truman by Wallace sympathizers were the votes genuinely wasted. Since Wallace received so pitifully few votes, Truman quite naturally, for a man of his simplistic thought, assumed that the peace movement was composed of only a relatively few crackpots—to use the

kind of language he often used in his diaries. If another
million or two had voted for Wallace, whoever was President would have had to recognize that there was a strong
and articulate mass of Americans opposed to the Cold War.
That might have done something to slow it down.

Even though Wallace had lost so terribly, he did not give
up in his effort to convince Truman that government policy
should change. Three days after the election he wrote to the
President:

. . . Now that you have been elected in your own right on the
basis of your own campaign with a good majority in the Senate
and House, it is possible for you to stand firmly and squarely on
your own feet in service to the American people and the world.
You can cut loose from the advice of the military and the reactionaries from the South and from Wall Street. You campaigned
against the "gluttons of special privilege" and for the farmers, con-
sumers, and workers. They believed in you and they voted for
you. It is my most sincere hope that you will not let them down.

Now the time has come to demonstrate with actions. And I
know that when you begin to act you will find, sooner or later,
that it is impossible to measure up to the expectations of the people of the United States without getting rid of the terrific expense
of the Cold War.

. . . You cannot give them what they expect unless you
promptly end the Cold War. Therefore, I refer you not only to my
letter of July 23, 1946, but also to my open letter to Stalin of May,
1948. You are aware that my supreme concern in the recent campaign was peace. I believed that you had fallen victim to the "gluttons of special privilege" whose domestic policies you denounced,
but whose foreign policies you accepted.

You now have a unique opportunity to unite the world on the
basis of putting millions to work producing peacetime goods, who
are now forging the implements of destruction. Peace with honor
is possible. Peace with complete security and without appeasement is possible. Not a single American public interest need
be sacrificed. But to attain this peace, you must stand up against
the "gluttons of special privilege" in the foreign field.[19]

This was hardly the humble letter of a badly defeated candidate. But even if Wallace had made an uncharacteristic attempt to ingratiate himself, Truman was executing the foreign policy that he genuinely believed was in the nation's best interest. And he could count votes.

Thus ends one part of our story. But there is more to the story than that. What part had Communists as individuals and the Communist Party played in the Wallace campaign? More important, what had the response been to Wallace's warnings on the part of three powerful forces in the formulation of foreign policy: the labor movement, the press, and the liberals? What responsibility do they bear for the foreign policy that made catastrophe inevitable? That will be discussed in succeeding chapters.

6

The Progressives and the Communists

H enry Wallace never had a chance to win the 1948 election. Everyone knew that from the first day to the last. But he did have, at the beginning at least, the chance to get a big vote, large enough that it might have acted as a brake on the accelerating Cold War. The reluctance of many Wallace sympathizers to waste a vote on him, thus giving the election to Thomas Dewey, is certainly one factor. Another, and there is no way to know which was greater, was the identification of Wallace with the Communist Party, to the extent that by mid-1948 most voters believed the Progressive Party was dominated by Communists.

That simply was not so. There were many Communists in the Progressive Party, a number at high levels. John Abt was the number-two man after Beanie Baldwin in the campaign organization, and Lee Pressman was secretary of the platform committee. Other Communists and Communist sympathizers could be found at various levels at Progressive national headquarters and in the field. That was no secret. Wallace never attempted to keep it a secret, and he would have been unable to if he had tried. Communists were an important and influential part of the Progressive Party. That was so, and there was no moral or ethical reason why it should not have been so. Communists should have the same rights of political participation as other Americans, and the fact that they did not during that dark age should be a lasting source of shame, especially to those who called themselves liberals yet contributed to their persecution. Why was it not possible for Communists to participate fully in American politics as they did—and do—in France and Italy and Britain, with their arguments succeeding or failing, on their merits and political acceptability? That the participation by Communists did serious political harm to both the Progressive and the Communist parties is another matter.

Stories that the Communist Party was responsible for Wallace's candidacy were circulated eagerly in the early days of the campaign. But only one man could have been responsible for Wallace's running. It is true that there were Communists within the Progressive Citizens of America, the organization out of which the Progressive Party grew, who joined Beanie Baldwin, Josiah Gitt, and other many non-Communists in urging Wallace to run. But Wallace ran for one reason and one reason only: because of his deep conviction that Truman's foreign policy was disastrous. The Communist Party supported Wallace because it, too, was opposed to Truman's policy and wanted to join what it believed was a mass movement to that end. Plainly, it also hoped that membership in a mass movement would not only give it broader influence but might serve to protect it against the anti-Communist inquisition that had already begun.

Despite the stories that the Progressive Party was the culmination of a deep, dark Communist plot directed by Moscow and carried out secretly over a period of years, the fact seems to be that the American Communists had a hard time deciding whether or not to back Wallace's third party. For an organization reputed to be conspiratorial, and no doubt it often was (although neither Republicans nor Democrats are strangers to secret meetings), the Communist Party carried out much of its discussion open to anyone who cared to read its publications. The CPUSA was a most verbal organization.

But whatever its ambitions were, whatever it attempted to do, one wonders why liberals were so frightened of Communists. In the first place, on a number of issues Communists and liberals had similar views: a commitment to civil rights and a belief in the virtue of strong trade unions, for instance. In the second place, there weren't very many Communists—seventy thousand seems to be the accepted figure for that period—many of them were lukewarm, and carried on party rolls even though they did not pay their dues. But Communists were regarded in liberal circles as dedicated, willing to do the hard work of ringing doorbells and addressing envelopes and raising money that many liberals thought beneath them, preferring as they did to write articles and letters to the editor and attend the occasional big rally, preferably with an all-star cast. And liberals knew that the Communists usually did not run for cover the first time the government or the press said a cross word about them. Also, the Communists attracted some first-rate people, like Earl Browder, Eugene Dennis, John Abt, Lee Pressman, and many others. Or maybe they feared them because the CPUSA was supposed to be directed by Moscow. Surely from the point of view of the Kremlin the American Communists did not seem worth bothering with. The truth seems to be that the CPUSA would have liked some direction from Moscow, and was forever twisting and turning, trying to figure out from Russian publications or the actions of Communist governments what their line should be. American Communists seemed to regard themselves as loyal Americans, devoted to the Communist ideal and motivated by a fraternal feeling toward the Kremlin, the Communists' Rome. But they failed to attract much support after the Depression faded—beyond the fact that no Socialist movement seems to find America fertile ground—because it did not recognize what Mao Tse-tung and Ho Chi Minh had grasped, that communism, to have any appeal, must be, first of all, national in character. The American Communists attempted to ape Russian communism, and this simply was not relevant to American conditions. Beyond that, they closed their eyes to the ugly repression within the Soviet Union and were guilty of a dogmatism and mental agility that would have done credit to medieval theologians, as they sought to justify each twist and turn of the Soviet line even when yesterday's truth became today's heresy.

In spite of their serious faults, the American Communists did some good work in helping to establish the labor movement, in seeking civil rights and social justice, and in various New Deal agencies. Certainly Roosevelt took advantage of their talents, although, for political convenience, he ostensibly repudiated their support. It was a routine repudiation that troubled neither FDR nor the Communists. But Wallace, for reasons of principle, refused to repudiate them. This was something a man of honor could not safely do in a time of anti-Communist hysteria. With so many frightened to enlist in his cause, he needed talented and energetic workers who would not be scared away. Yet he was uneasy with Communist support, for he was a religious man and a capitalist. He disliked the lack of freedom in the Soviet Union, although he realized that that was not the fundamental issue in determining Soviet-American relations. Only with peace could either society progress toward a better life for its people.

Wallace recognized, too, the political liability of Communist support, but he was deeply convinced that they had the right to full political participation, and he felt he was honor bound to accept their support if they shared his goals. Also, he felt sorry for them, seeing them as "kind of pathetic, like poor lonesome souls."[1] It was an awkward position, an impossible position, but Wallace saw no way out. He wanted them and he didn't want them. He needed them, and at the same time he knew they were hurting him. What is most important is that he, almost uniquely among important political figures, saw Communists as humans, not devils.

These were Wallace's reasons for accepting Communist support. Why did the Communists decide finally to give it? It was a decision that evolved over many months, with a great deal of backing and filling. In the September 1946 issue of *Political Affairs*, the Communist monthly, Eugene Dennis, the Communist Party general secretary, wrote that

Communists should encourage an anti-monopoly, anti-imperialist third party even though "conditions have not yet matured at this time for crystallizing third parties organizationally on a state or local scale. However, the conditions are ripe for, and the situation demands that, broad *political support for a new people's party can be organized* [italics in original], that the mass sentiment for a new political alignment be channelized and further stimulated." He was advocating a mass movement with a broader base than the Communists could supply alone. But he also urged that those favoring a third party not clash with progressives who opposed a third party and wanted to revitalize the Democratic Party. ". . . These people must be shown that their orientation and activity cannot make serious headway unless the trend toward a progressive regrouping in the Democratic Party *is accompanied by the growth of all independent labor and progressive organizations and activities outside of and quite independent from, either of the existing major parties."* [2]

There is nothing conspiratorial or unreasonable in proposing a third party if neither of the present parties is working toward the goals desired. And it is sound politics to begin constructing an alternative, even if the hope is eventually to influence one of the major parties. Organization politicians will generally make substantial concessions to intraparty factions only in two circumstances: to head off a potentially successful take-over by the out faction, or if that faction threatens seriously to hurt the party by defecting. And defection is a much more credible threat if the defectors have some place to go, rather than just muttering vaguely about staying home at election time. In 1946, and thereafter, there was little chance of the liberal/progressives taking over the Democratic Party. Their only hope was to influence its policies by the threat of defection.

The Communists understood that the possibility of a third party waiting in the wings could strengthen the leverage of the Wallace-Ickes branch within the Democratic

Party, although they seemed to perceive before Wallace did that Truman would make no substantial concessions to the critics of his Cold War policies. Later, after Wallace had been dismissed from the Cabinet but before he decided to run, he, too, tried to use the threat of defection, speaking often of the need for an alternative if Truman would not genuinely seek better relations with Russia. But by the end of 1947 it became clear to Wallace that Truman would make no concessions.

Truman, and such aides as Clark Clifford, had a much better understanding of the political realities than either Wallace or the Communists. Truman never believed that many liberal leaders, for whom he had little use, would defect, for he recognized what they hated to recognize, that most of them were not truly independent men, that they and their ambitions were tied to the Democratic Party. He recognized, too, that the leaders of organized labor were more concerned with power than with abstract notions, such as social justice, and that there would be few defections there. Nonetheless, he did not believe in taking chances. That was why he was determined to destroy any third-party alternative that might emerge, using whatever methods promised to be most effective.

All this, of course, developed later, but Dennis in the summer of 1946 was looking into the future. Part of what he saw was that the Democratic Party could not be transformed into an anti-imperialist party. But he was also guilty of a most unrealistic romanticism, even though Communists pride themselves on their social realism. In the first place, the American Communist Party did not then or ever have the slightest chance of gaining a substantial, never mind mass, membership. Dennis allowed Marxist dogma to cloud his vision when he expressed the belief that the American labor movement would play a leading role in a mighty progressive force. One should not blame Dennis too much for this, since Socialists and liberals have similarly deluded themselves, despite overwhelming evidence to the contrary.

Dennis wrote down these views shortly before Wallace made his famous Madison Square Garden speech. Although supporters of a bipartisan foreign policy were outraged by his speech because they saw in it appeasement of Russia, the American Communists did not much like it either. It was sharply attacked in a *Daily Worker* editorial the next day and even some time later, even after the Communists saw the consternation the speech had caused in Washington, their approval was guarded and James Allen in the October *Political Affairs* wrote of the "Red-baiting that diminished the positive values of his speech."[3]

In December a *Political Affairs* editorial explained why the Communist Party favored a third party:

We Communists are for a third party because we are of the opinion that the Democratic Party cannot be transformed into a people's party. This could not be achieved even during the Roosevelt period, and there is no reason to believe that it can be done now. We must convince all the labor and progressive forces of the need for a new people's party. Further, to those progressive forces who favor the formation of a third party eventually, but who doubt that it can or should be done by 1948, we point out that there are no guarantees that the Democratic Party will nominate a Roosevelt candidate on a Roosevelt platform for 1948, which means running the risk of being confronted with two candidates and two tickets controlled by Big Business.

But it is clear that the third party cannot be called into being by the Communists and their supporters alone. It can come into being only when the forces represented at the Chicago Conference of Progressives, or at least a great majority of those represented there, become convinced of its necessity and are ready to build it. . . .[4]

Notice that the CPUSA saw itself as just one element among several. Remember, too, that in 1946 and 1947 many groups, including some firmly anti-Communist, were speaking of the possibility of a third party, so widespread was the dissatisfaction of liberals of all stripes with the Truman administration.

Also in December Eugene Dennis, speaking at a Communist meeting, said: ". . . at this time, the question must be left open as to whether or not it will be necessary or advisable for this new party to place a third presidential ticket in the field in 1948."[5] He went on to explain why the *Daily Worker* had attacked Wallace's Madison Square Garden speech. He criticized

certain sectarian attitudes toward forces, peoples and movements, in the labor movement, as well as in the broad democratic camp, and toward certain potential allies in the labor-progressive coalition who, for one or another reason, have been slow in publicly breaking with the Truman administration and its reactionary policies.

It was in part because of such tendencies that the first editorial in the *Daily Worker* on the Wallace speech adopted such a completely negative attitude toward Wallace's position. This is why some comrades—and not only those on the *Daily Worker*—could not see the woods for the trees and were disoriented by the unjust and harmful remarks by Wallace on the Soviet Union and the Communists. Because of this, the comrades failed to grasp the fact that Wallace, in his own way and within the limitations of his position, was challenging the main line of the Byrnes-Vandenberg policy and, in the first place, the "get-tough-with-Russia" policy.

Only the most determined believer in the "conspiracy theory" of history can refuse to see, in view of what both Wallace and the Communists said over and over again, that their association was based on the paramountcy of one goal—peaceful relations with the Soviet Union—despite the gravest reservations each had about the other. Wallace was a capitalist, albeit a progressive one; he was a devout Christian steeped in the Bible; and he criticized frequently the lack of liberty in the Soviet Union. The Communists not only had to decide whether Wallace was a suitable ally but whether the time was right for a third party. Debate over these points, particularly the latter, continued within the party for about a year. Of course, the dedicated conspiracy

theorist might argue that the Communists were being du-
plicitous, that this debate was a cover-up for the plot conceived in Moscow to use Wallace to its nefarious purposes:
to destroy the two-party system, to elect a Republican so
that conditions in the United States would get worse, to undermine American defense efforts—whatever. But this simply does not make any sense. The Communist leadership was
not addressing itself to outsiders; it was not trying to de-
ceive its *own* membership and sympathizers at formal meetings and in its journals. To say one thing publicly and another privately would have only sown confusion within
party ranks, for these meetings, these journals were the
leadership's primary means of communication and
persuasion.

In the *Political Affairs* of February 1947, William Z. Foster
said that it "remains to be seen" if a third party would be
strong enough to put up Presidential and congressional candidates.[6] In the March issue Dennis called on all progressives to unite, but noted that some progressives favored a
third party while others thought that reaction could be defeated only by winning control of the Democratic Party.[7]
His mind, and those of the party leadership, was clearly not
yet made up. By midsummer Dennis was still speaking of a
third party as a means to influence the Democratic Party
and as an alternative if the Democrats did not nominate a
progressive candidate. He also discussed the issue raised by
many liberals: that the Communists favored a third party
because it wanted a Republican victory, on the theory that
things would get worse under Republicans and thus play
into Soviet hands. "I think that we Communists want it
clearly understood that we, no less than millions of other
workers and progressives, are fearful of a victory in '48 of
the G.O.P.—the main party of monopoly reaction. At the
same time, however, we cannot be indifferent to what the
consequences would be for the people if Big Business were
to continue its control of the government through the Democratic Party and the Truman administration if it continues,

as it probably will, on the basis of its present reactionary policies."⁸

There is no reason to place much credence in the liberal theory that the CPUSA wanted to elect Republicans for devious reasons. It had had good reasons, from its point of view, to support Roosevelt; but with Truman, those reasons no longer existed. There is every reason to take Communist assertions on this point at face value. Even if one believes the "devil theory" about American Communists—that they were disloyal citizens, evilly intent upon serving their masters in the Kremlin (a theory I do not believe)—American Communist opposition to the Cold War makes sense, for if the Cold War seriously wounded the United States, so, too, did it hurt the Soviet Union. It was in their interest as Communists to oppose the Truman administration's known policy, fully as much as it was in their interest to oppose the presumed policy of any Republican successor. Wallace, acting out of the highest patriotic motives, and the American Communists, whatever their motives, had the same goal and it was a valid one.

By mid-1947 the Communists had pretty much decided, from Wallace's public statements, that they and Wallace were compatible allies. The remaining question was political. Was a third party effective politics? It was a Communist writer, John Gates, national board member and editor of the *Daily Worker*, who perceptively noted what would be required for an effective third party:

. . . Such a party must be broadly based if it is to be effective. The decision to form such a party does not lie only in the will of the Communists, left-wing forces, and all others who favor a third party at this moment. Much broader forces than are now committed to a new party will have to join the movement to make it possible for it to come into existence in 1948. Practically, this means that such unions as the United Auto Workers and the Amalgamated Clothing Workers must favor it. It is not necessary that the entire top leadership of the A.F. of L. and the C.I.O. favor a third party before active steps are taken to form it, but certainly more substantial sections of labor must favor it than do so at present. Further-more, there can be no third party without a significant breakaway from the Democratic Party, and the winning of the support of large sections of farmers.[9]

Wallace and the Communists knew that significant labor support was essential, and widespread defections from the Democratic Party also. Both knew that William Green of the AFL and Philip Murray of the CIO were opposed to a third party, but each believed that there would be some signifi-cant union support, both at the leadership and rank-and-file levels. They were terribly wrong. Indeed, if the CPUSA had followed its own logic it would not have supported Wallace; but neither he nor it knew the great lengths to which CIO leadership would go, and the success it would have, in preventing much significant labor participation in the third party.

In September 1947 Jack Stachel, a national board member, discussed two points often raised by Cold War liberals:

. . . They know that many millions are for the third party and that the Communists are only a small fraction of this movement. They know that the Communists have proved that their entire concern today is to defeat reaction, whether as expressed through Republi-cans or through reactionary Democrats. That is why they try to render their arguments plausible by making an even more ridicu-lous charge, namely, that the Communists want a Republican vic-tory in order to promote chaos and strife and by this means pro-mote their ultimate program of Socialism. . . .

The Communists would like nothing better than see the entire trade union movement . . . come together and take the initiative in calling for the formation of such a party. . . . Obviously in such a party the Communists, who would give it their full support, would be only a small group. Under any conditions, a genuine, broad, mass third party, when formed, would be of such propor-tions that the Communists could not possibly dominate it even if they sought to. And they have no such intentions to begin with. All they ask is that they be given the same rights and responsibilities as all others to serve the cause and the interests of the people.[10]

Speaking in Madison Square Garden on September 18, 1947, Eugene Dennis said: ". . . We never did and do not now favor the launching of premature and unrepresentative third parties or independent tickets. Such moves can only succeed and serve the camp of progressives when they arise out of the collective decision and united action of a broad democratic and anti-war coalition which embraces substantial portions of the trade union and progressive movement."[11]

The Communists did not want to isolate themselves. They wanted the effectiveness—and the protection—of a broad coalition of the Left. But by then they were regarded by most Americans as infected with a deadly and contagious political plague. Very few on the Left, even those who had cooperated with Communists for decades, would have anything to do with them. Only the brave, or perhaps foolhardy would be a better term, would associate with them in the exercise of their legitimate political rights. And those who did caught the political infection and were quarantined from the body politic. Thus, the Communist Party, while trying to avoid isolation, caused the Wallace movement to be isolated, damaging both.

In October 1947 Andrei Zhdanov, one of Stalin's closest associates, at a Cominform meeting called for a vigorous counteroffensive against the West's Cold War policies. This may have further encouraged the CPUSA to support a third party, but by this time it needed little encouragement.

By late November or early December the Communists had apparently decided to support a third party headed by Wallace, reaching their decision about the same time Wallace himself did. No doubt this influenced the leadership of the Progressive Citizens of America to ask Wallace to run, but to say that is hardly to give the Communist Party credit for founding the Progressive Party. Non-Communist progressives had reached the same conclusion, and, most important, so had Wallace. It seems fair to conclude the Communists were a factor, perhaps even an important factor. But the crucial decision was Wallace's, and by December 1947 there was probably no way to stop him from running. He saw it as his duty.

In the January 1948 issue of *Political Affairs*, presumably written about the same time Wallace had committed himself to run but before his decision was made public, the Communists announced their support of him, although they recognized that the hierarchy of organized labor was against it. Perhaps they shared Wallace's romantic notion that the workers would follow even if the leaders would not. Or, more likely, they decided, as he had, that the fight must be made no matter what.

The Communist decision to support what would later be named the Progressive Party raises an interesting point. How does one party function as part of another? It was a curious situation. Even though the CPUSA was backing Wallace, the first seven issues of *Political Affairs* in 1948 had articles attacking the reformist economic views that Wallace held. Also, the CPUSA specifically took issue with Wallace's criticisms of the Soviet Union, and it made plain that it would attempt to recruit from the progressive ranks. But while the CPUSA hoped its precepts would attract progressives, it also feared that progressive views would attract Communists or those sympathetic to the CPUSA. Thus, there was a built-in tension in the relationship, a tension that came from both sides, for there were progressives who, even though not Red-baiters, did not want to see the Communists become too influential.

Shortly after Wallace announced his decision to run, he asked John Abt, an extremely able lawyer who had long been identified with the Communist Party, to be Beanie Baldwin's top assistant in the campaign. Abt warned Wallace that he would be Red-baited if Abt joined the campaign, and Wallace replied, "I will be anyway."[12] He was right, but in Abt he got an aide of extraordinary intelligence and experience. Abt had been counsel for the Political Action Committee of the CIO, under Sidney Hillman, where he had worked closely with Baldwin. He had also been counsel for the Amalgamated Clothing Workers and for the American Labor Party, the ticket on which Wallace ran in New York state. He was, and still is, a firm believer in the Popular Front in which the Communists work with other groups holding similar views on major issues.[13]

While the Communists knew that the Progressive Party was not a Communist front, almost everyone else refused to believe it. At a Communist meeting in February Dennis said—it seems almost plaintive now—"It is . . . a fact that this third-party movement *is neither Communist nor anti-Communist.* It is developing as a mass people's party, including diverse anti-war and anti-monopoly elements and groups around a progressive, though non-Socialist program. Naturally, the monopolists and their labor and Social-Democrat agents insist that the new party is thus, *ipso facto,* a 'Communist front' and is damned and doomed because it is not an anti-Communist movement."

Dennis went on to recall what any liberal knew:

there have been many other mass movements and organizations in the United States which were falsely branded as "Communist inspired" and "Communist dominated"; yet these progressive movements lost nothing and gained much from Communist participation and support. Among these we may cite, and with some pride, the organization of the mass-production workers and the formation of the C.I.O.; the establishment of the A.L.P. [American Labor Party] and of C.I.O./P.A.C. under the leadership of Sidney Hillman; and the major role played by all these groups and forces in the Roosevelt-labor-progressive coalition in 1944.

While we Communists energetically aided and supported these movements, we did not seek, nor could we have succeeded even if we had so desired, to dominate or capture them. Neither do we seek today to capture or dominate the new independent, coalition party of the people.[14]

All during the campaign the press reported that Wallace's speeches and speech materials were prepared by a group in New York that was largely Communist or fellow-traveling. There was some truth to that, but it was also true, to the disgust of the writers at headquarters, that most of their material was not used, since Wallace preferred the writing of Lewis Frank, Jr., his *New Republic* colleague, who traveled with him. And many of his speeches were extemporaneous, building on his oft-repeated basic themes. It was the old story, familiar to anyone experienced in political campaigning: headquarters knocks itself out preparing carefully reasoned speeches, only to have them ignored by the candidate, who is responding to day-by-day situations. That is not to suggest that he was saved from the Communists by the realities of a traveling campaign. His speeches, no matter who prepared them, were entirely consistent with what he had been saying privately since Truman took office in 1945, and publicly since September 1946. And, as he told reporters in a long off-the-record bull session in May 1948, he was further to the Left than most of his advisers. He also said that he made no effort to determine whether those appointed to his staff were Communists or not. Wallace had always been disinterested in political mechanics, and when pressed on this point he said he did not know how to identify Communists, implying that there was nothing improper in their criticisms of U.S. policy. It is entirely possible that he did not know the full extent to which Communists were working in responsible positions in his organization. It is something he should have kept himself informed about, even if he had no objection to their participation. A memorandum of this off-the-record discussion written by James Wechsler of *The New York Post* found its way to the files of the ADA, presumably to help it prepare its campaign against Wallace.[15]

Wallace's slender book *Toward World Peace*, a summation of his views on foreign policy, was reviewed in the May edition of the Communist monthly. Max Weiss seemed distressed that Wallace in his book "accepts completely the stock argument about the 'lack of political democracy' in the Soviet Union." He attempted to refute Wallace's criticism and then ended that section with the astonishing assertion that the "socialist democracy of the Soviet Union today, based on the Stalin Constitution, is the most advanced democracy the world has known, precisely because all exploiting classes have been eliminated."[16] This sounds not so much as cynical distortion but, which may be even worse, as a doctrinaire incapacity to see the plain facts. Whichever, the review, an official expression of the Communist Party's position, demonstrated that concrete and significant issues divided Wallace and the CPUSA, differences that were plain for anyone to see. But perhaps the American press and public, too, suffered from a doctrinaire incapacity to see the plain facts. For instance, in that same May issue of *Political Affairs,* an editorial argued, "The Progressive Party is in no sense a Communist Party. While supporting its program of people's demands, we Communists have many points of difference with it and we do not hesitate to express them. The most important of these points of difference is that while many leaders in the Progressive Party believe that the badly crippled world capitalist system can be saved and transformed into 'progressive capitalism,' we Marxist-Leninists do not. Capitalism historically is on its way off the world stage."[17]

This is no slight difference. It is fundamental, for it goes to the very *raison d'être* of the Communist Party.

The relationship between Wallace and the Communist Party—or, more properly, members of the Communist Party—was a matter of genuine concern to Wallace sympathizers inside his movement and outside. For instance, on March 30, 1948, Jonathan Daniels, a North Carolina newspaper publisher and son of Josephus Daniels, a long-time associate of FDR, wrote to Wallace. Wallace had written him in admiration of one of his editorials about President Truman's message of March 17. Daniels' reply is a thoughtful example of disinterested concern about Wallace's association with Communists:

. . . I was deeply disappointed in this message, as indicated in what I wrote. I find myself increasingly critical of a policy which paramounts military preparations and places, it seems to me, little stress on activity for the building of machinery to preserve peace.

I think it is important that you keep on emphasizing your position on some amicable settlement of the quarrel between the great powers. At the same time I could not accept your very generous words without stating that I am very much disturbed by the obvious activity of many Communists among your most enthusiastic supporters. I am critical of this, not because I am fearful of what the Communists may do in the United States, but because I am sure that their presence close to the direction of your campaign reduces the effectiveness of the things you want to say. I am, of course, aware that your opponents will magnify the Communists' part in the Wallace campaign. I cannot, however, escape the fact, which I know from my personal observation, that there is too high a proportion of Communists in the active support of your campaign for the Presidency.

. . . You know that I am a party man in my father's faith, that in the long run a liberal can be most effective if he serves with the most liberal of our two great parties in times of both the feasts and the famines of liberalism. Also, at this time in the South when President Truman is being attacked by the most reactionary Southerners, it seems to me a Southern liberal would be remiss if he withheld support from the Chief of his party.

I still recognize the great need for a voice for peace. While I have no right to advise you under the circumstances, I believe your mission for peace would be made more effective if, without withholding your criticism of the mistakes our own country is making, you found the occasion to condemn the aggressions also of Russia and made it perfectly clear that you have no patience with Americans whose deepest allegiance is to some other power than their own country.[18]

Plainly this letter is the product of an intelligent and decent man, unswervingly loyal to the Democratic Party but not doctrinaire. It is not the kind of letter that a man like Wallace would dismiss out of hand, and he was to receive advice along similar lines from others he admired—advice expressed privately in an attempt to be helpful, not expressed publicly in an attempt to embarrass. The question of divided loyalty is a difficult one, probably one that can be answered, if at all, only by each individual. There can be no doubt that many Communists had a deep and abiding, often blind loyalty to the Soviet Union. Does this mean that they were disloyal to the United States? I do not know. But is it not possible to believe that the national interests of two nations to whom one feels loyal are not irreconcilable? Communists claimed to be motivated by a belief that they were working in the best interests of the United States. And over the decades, any number of dedicated Communists broke with the party when fundamental differences emerged on this or that point. Thus, I believe it is unfair to see Communists as devils, not men. Even if they were wrong in confusing communism as a political-economic philosophy with its brutal practice in the Soviet Union, what did American Communists as a whole ever do to merit being thrust beyond the pale of society and persecuted with a terrible ferocity that will always be a national shame. Were they not Americans with full rights to political expression?

How could Wallace take such advice as Daniels', however reasonably expressed and well intended? As far as his campaign was concerned, the Communists who supported him—and there were many Communists who were deeply convinced that Communists should never associate themselves with a middle-class movement—shared a position that he believed to be fundamentally important to the national interest.

Wallace recognized that politically he would have been better off without the Communists. But if he had expelled the Communists, it would have been a violation of his principle that they had the same rights as others. Beyond that, his expulsion would have removed their last slight protection, for then it could be said that the "Commies" were too un-American even for Henry Wallace. How could he pour more fuel on a fire that was already raging out of control?

That is why Wallace could not accept the advice of his old allies in the National Farmers Union. In a letter from Lee Fryer, executive assistant to James Patton, head of the NFU, they proposed (just two weeks before the Progressive convention): that it be postponed; that the Wallace campaign organization be totally overhauled, with Beanie Baldwin and the Communists kicked out; that a new national committee be formed; that the headquarters be moved from New York. And they believed that all this could be done without playing into the hands of the Red-baiters. Like so many middle-class liberals, they prized respectability and wanted change to take place in the genteel atmosphere of a tea party—or perhaps a more apt metaphor, in the civilized atmosphere of a Georgetown cocktail party. But change requires political risk, rolling around in the dirt of the pit, and choosing your allies on a basis of shared goals rather than on political respectability. Wallace was prepared to risk his respectability; most liberals were not. That still seems true. The liberal seems to be a herd animal, doing useful work when the way has been prepared. But he is seldom a maverick, although the more clever of them have a rare capacity to sense when the herd is going to change direction and they rush to get in front, as if they were leaders. Wallace was a maverick, and it took such bitter opponents as Clark Clifford and Arthur Schlesinger, Jr., two decades to catch up with him, but they succeeded in appearing like leaders.

The NFU letter went to the writer Louis Adamic, who was fairly close to Wallace. Along with his comments, it was sent to someone in the Progressive Party and presumably reached Wallace himself eventually, for it is included in his correspondence file. Adamic himself believed that some changes were necessary, but he was against expelling the Communists. "They simply need to be put in their place, and given a hint that there is no need for them to wear out their welcome." Still, Adamic had some doubts about the organization and Fryer wrote him: "The personnel in the N.Y. hq. is a ticklish problem. Only Mr. Wallace can deal with it. I don't know Beanie at all; I tried to get acquainted with him and be helpful, but couldn't. I'm not sure, but perhaps his chief trouble is that he created a group around him in the PCA days which remained a closed group as we expanded beyond PCA. I should say that it would be too bad to lose his experience. But we do need more open personalities in the organization—the outgoing kind."[19]

Rex Tugwell, after Wallace himself the most prominent figure in the Progressive Party, had serious reservations about the influence of Communists within the party. In August Tugwell told Howard Norton of the *Baltimore Sun* that he was "an uneasy member of the Progressive Party." He said that he hoped "its organization and program will develop in a way that will permit those of us who are old-fashioned American progressives to go along with it," but "if the wrong people get control," the "old-fashioned progressives" would not feel at home in the Progressive Party. Norton asked him, "By the 'wrong people' do you mean the Communists?"

"Who can say whether they are or not?" Tugwell replied. "I certainly don't know whether they are Communists, but they act as though they are."[20]

After several days of consultation with his top aides, Wallace issued a formal statement in response to Tugwell's interview:

I am not a Communist, have never been one and never expect to be one.

The Progressive Party is not controlled by Communists nor was its convention or program dictated by them.

Communism and Progressive capitalism differ fundamentally,

although we share many social objectives. I welcome the support of those who are working for such understanding with Russia that the United States and Russia will be willing to accept a strong United Nations with a world police force stronger than the armed might of either nation.

We believe that neither the United States nor Russia should ever dominate the world. I will never tolerate those whose purpose is to destroy our government by force.

I solemnly pledge that when I am elected President neither the Communists nor the Fascists nor any other group will control my policies or me.[21]

Before reading the formal statement, Wallace had told reporters:

If there are any Communists who do believe in violent overthrow of the government, I certainly don't want their support.

Or if any group put their allegiance to some foreign capital first, whether it be Moscow or any other place, I would not want their support.

My great worry is that out of the conflict between these two systems [communism and capitalism] you can get what is essentially a religious war that can last until all our civilization is destroyed.

I don't like religious wars. That is what I and the New Party are trying to prevent.

The *Baltimore Sun's* and other newspaper reporters reached Tugwell who would give only this comment: "I am very happy that Mr. Wallace made this statement. I think it ought to clear up a great many misconceptions." Plainly, though, Tugwell was far from entirely satisfied, for his support of Wallace was lukewarm for the rest of the campaign, although he refused Democratic urging to repudiate his old colleague and friend.

While Wallace was trying to figure out a way to minimize the damage caused by Communist participation in his campaign, the Communists themselves were confronted with what became a life-and-death struggle for the survival of their party. On July 20, just a few days before the Progressive convention, the United States indicted the entire national board of the Communist Party, charging the twelve members with advocating the "destruction of the government of the United States by force and violence." Included were: William Z. Foster, national chairman; Eugene Dennis, general secretary; John Gates, editor of the *Daily Worker;* and Gus Hall, who would later become the nation's top Communist. Thus began a campaign of terrible ferocity against the Communists. All across the nation, in state after state, Communists were charged with similar offenses. Over the next few years, scarcely a single Communist at any leadership level was not affected, and as one leader succeeded another, he, too, was indicted. It was nothing less than nationwide political persecution, requiring almost the entire leadership to devote itself to legal defense. The physical, intellectual, emotional, and financial drain was incalculable, as scores of Communist leaders sought to avoid long jail sentences on charges that nowadays would not even be considered, let alone brought. Not only were Communists attacked in the courts but also in labor unions, where they had been devoted unionists for decades. Politicians made anticommunism the leading, perhaps the only issue of the day, and the press never tired of trumpeting the charges. And the FBI infiltrated so many agents into rapidly shrinking Communist Party local chapters that it came to be said, not entirely in jest, that the dues of FBI agents were the main financial support of the party. Wallace was not guilty of overstatement when he said on July 21, "We Americans have far more to fear from those actions which are intended to suppress political freedom than from the teaching of ideas with which we are in disagreement."

Because of his age, sixty-seven, and ill health, Foster was never brought to trial, but the other eleven were found guilty on October 14, 1949. The conviction was appealed and upheld by the Supreme Court on June 4, 1951, with Justices Hugo Black and William O. Douglas entering dissents based on their contention that the prosecution had not demonstrated any overt acts that caused a "clear and present danger" to the government. In the multitude of other trials, there were many convictions and a few acquittals but in the late 1950s and early 1960s, as the Cold War fever subsided, courts increasingly overturned convictions or threw out indictments of Communists on constitutional grounds—to the extent that the Smith Act, under which the original indictments were returned, became a dead letter, as did other existing laws applied to Communists, or newer ones passed with them as targets.

The Communists could hardly have been blamed for thinking that they had made a terrible mistake in supporting Wallace, that this decision was responsible for the remorseless attack on the party by all three branches of government, and for its expulsion, as we shall see, from the labor movement. No doubt that was an important factor, but, given the temper of the time, the attacks on the CPUSA seem inevitable. What could the Communists have done to avoid them? Their very existence was an affront to most Americans, whereas now Communists stand on street corners collecting signatures on election petitions. This routine political act arouses little antagonism, not even much interest—it is occurring in a period when national policy seeks the kind of good relations with the Soviet Union that Henry Wallace once advocated and that horrified most of the nation.

Despite the severe trauma caused by the legal assault on the CPUSA, Communists on many levels and in many places worked hard for the Progressive Party, with the relentless dedication that awed and often frightened liberals who were usually better at ideas and their articulation than at the sheer drudgery so necessary in politics. Two men in a position to know, Beanie Baldwin, the campaign manager, and Ralph Shikes, the public-relations director, believed that on the whole the Communists were effective and, in most states, worked well with non-Communists. Only in a few states, notably Colorado, was this not the case—not because Communist doctrine conflicted with the Progressive platform but because some Communists were, as Baldwin put it, "too big for their boots." In these cases, it was the first time individual Communists had been in positions of authority in a broad-based political movement and they tried to throw their weight around—but this kind of behavior is a constant in all political campaigns.[22]

A number of conclusions seem justified by the available evidence. First, and most important, Wallace was his own man throughout the campaign. Not only did he say time and again that the Communists were supporting his position; he was not supporting theirs, but an examination of his speeches demonstrates beyond question that his position was consistent from his famous Century of the Common Man speech of May 8, 1942, right through Election Day 1948. No matter what the proportion of Communists within the Progressive Party, its platform and Wallace's speeches were essentially sound in 1948 and look like uncanny prophecy now. There is no question that the Communist Party decided in late 1947 to support Wallace's third party and that CPUSA members had influence among the leaders of the Progressive Citizens of America, who urged him to run. But the contention, often made in 1948, that the CPUSA was responsible for his running is nonsense. Harry Truman was responsible for the Wallace campaign, for during the last half of 1947 Wallace often said that if the Democrats remained a war party, as he considered the Republicans already to be, that an alternative would be offered and there was no doubt what that alternative would be: him.

There is no doubt that most of the Communists were effective Progressive Party workers, but there is also no doubt that their participation was an albatross around Wallace's neck. It was one of those times that gives pause to a believer in democracy: when the majority becomes a mob, unwilling to listen to a minority and eager, especially when cheered on by "responsible" citizens, to persecute those few who stood up against them. Perhaps the situation was best summed up by Jennings Perry, a newspaper columnist who supported Wallace. He wrote of ". . . a Communist support Wallace has not invited, could not have prevented, and has had the fortitude not to weep over."[23]

7

Labor Friends Become Enemies

The enduring American myth that the labor movement is a mighty force for liberalism persists primarily because even those who know better want to believe it. Those who grew up horrified by the bloody struggles at America's Harlan Counties, those who sang "Joe Hill" at parties, those who wept and raged with Paul Muni as he fought in the movie so bravely, and so inarticulately, to organize the coal miners for an attempt to achieve the humble but then seemingly unattainable goal of being treated like humans by the mineowners, those who now support Cesar Chavez and La Causa, those people want to believe that the labor movement is the heart and soul of liberalism. But the sad truth is that the labor movement, although it still has an important function in serving the economic needs of the workers, has settled for being a junior partner, often a well-paid one, in American capitalism. As far as civil rights is concerned, save for those unions that have large black or Hispanic constituencies, the unions are often among the most retrograde institutions in the nation. And regarding the Cold War, the American labor movement has often been the silent junior partner of the State Department and the CIA.[1] And not so silently, William Green of the AFL and Philip Murray of the CIO in the old days and George Meany of the AFL-CIO in recent years have been superhawks. So, too, has been much of the rank and file, especially Roman Catholic unionists.

But in 1947 and 1948 Henry Wallace and the Communists believed that workers, even if not their leaders, would flock to the Progressive banner. The Communists' conviction was based on the dogmatic truth that workers are the vanguard of the revolution. The poor Communists have never learned that American workers are very different from the European proletariat; they are more likely to be latent capitalists than socialists. But Henry Wallace had better reason to hope for labor support: he was known as a dedicated and long-proven friend of labor. When the conservative wing of the Democratic Party was trying to get Roosevelt to dump Wallace as Vice-Presidential nominee in 1944, the labor movement was his stanch ally, with Philip Murray exerting all his great influence for Wallace. Later that year, perhaps to demonstrate that the CIO still supported Wallace, Murray, as we saw, awarded him a "distinguished service medal."[2]

And throughout 1945, 1946, and 1947 the labor movement, with occasional exceptions, was unsparingly critical of Harry Truman: for his weak policies on inflation and housing, and especially for seizing the coal mines when they had been struck, and for asking Congress for authority to draft striking workers. Labor saw him as betraying Roosevelt's New Deal.

Not only did this relentless criticism of Truman cause Wallace to think he would get substantial labor support but for a while labor even seemed to share his views on foreign policy. An editorial in the *CIO News* of October 22, 1945, said: "All over the country people are asking, what's happening to the victory we won over fascism and reaction? Where is the outline of the new world we fought and worked to attain? . . .

"[The people see] on the foreign front—deliberately induced disunity, deliberate promotion of suspicion and hatred among yesterday's allies, a campaign of distrust stirred up against the very peoples we and our allies sought to liberate."

That same issue carried a story reporting that during a meeting with V. V. Kuznetsov in Moscow's Hall of Columns, a delegation of leading American trade unionists accepted a proposal to form an American-Soviet Trade Union Committee. CIO Vice President Joseph Curran was quoted as saying, "We will ardently support the idea for establishment of an American-Soviet Trade Union Committee." And the chairman of the delegation, CIO Secretary-Treasurer James B. Carey was even more lyrical: "When I visit your plants, I feel that I am in our own American establishments. When I speak here, I feel as if I am speaking in my own country. All this bespeaks the fact that we and you have one mind, the same aspirations, the same community of interests. Both of our great countries can work together. We shall exert all efforts so that in the period of peaceful development of our countries, the friendship of the Soviet and American working class will grow stronger."

A week later, October 29, the *CIO News* carried a story about the labor delegation's final press conference in the Soviet Union. These lines appeared in a story under the by-line of Len DeCaux, editor of the paper:

"We are deeply moved by the personal warmth and friendship shown us on all sides," Carey said. "The eager desire of the Soviet people for closer ties of understanding and friendship with the people of the U.S. has been evidenced again and again. This has greatly strengthened our determination as CIO representatives to do everything within our power to cement our cordial relations with Soviet trade unions and to establish even closer unity between our two great peoples for lasting peace, growing prosperity and democratic progress."

Carey said the delegation was "horrified by wholesale destruction wrought by the Nazis but was filled with the greatest admiration for the determined and united effort of the people which has already brought about substantial reconstruction and promises great things for future elevation of living standards. We believe America can assist greatly by supplying many machines and other products the Soviet Union so sorely needs and that in so doing we shall be promoting our own prosperity and drawing closer together our two peoples for their common goals."

This was exactly the sort of thing Wallace was advocating within the Truman administration and exactly the sort of thing he said after his break with Truman. Whether or not Wallace saw that particular statement, he was certainly aware that the CIO was taking similar positions to his in those days before, for whatever reason, the signals were changed. In the September 16, 1946, issue the *CIO News* reported that Jack Kroll, director of the CIO Political Action Committee, while warning against the "premature dumping of the two-party system," told the annual convention of the Ohio CIO that "when the time is right, independent political action by labor will be on the agenda of the national CIO and PAC." And the paper also reported a speech by Jacob Potofsky, president of the Amalgamated Clothing Workers: ". . . Native fascists and former isolationists 'have rejected the Roosevelt policy of Big Three unity and are stirring up a campaign of hatred and prejudice against the Soviet Union.

" 'Unless we return to the Roosevelt policy, international rivalry and conflict will lead inevitably to war,' Potofsky declared.

" 'They would have our nation give support to the forces of reaction in Europe and Asia in an effort to put down the rising people's movement which the victory over fascism unloosed throughout the world.' "

Again, a prominent labor leader sounding like Wallace.

But by 1947 organized labor was beginning to fall in line with the hard-line policy of Harry Truman and the CIO had begun a campaign to oust Communists from positions of leadership, even though Communists had been dedicated unionists from the days when that took great personal courage and exceptional perseverance. On April 13 Irving Potash, a vice president of the Fur and Leather Workers Union and member of the Communist Party National Committee (and, as such, indicted in July of the next year), was one of the speakers at an emergency rally of CIO officials on the Taft-Hartley Act. This was his prophetic warning: "Not one of you will buy peace for yourselves by joining a witch hunt. Not one of you will escape the same hounding, the same hunting."[3] He was harshly attacked for that prediction, but the facts proved him right. Even outspoken anti-

Communist liberals were often attacked by the witch hunters, for to them even mild liberalism was proof of being a Communist or fellow traveler.

In June 1947, at its twenty-sixth convention, the International Ladies Garment Workers Union rejected "the pro-Russian appeasement sentiment advocated by Henry A. Wallace and his followers," and it accused the Progressive Citizens of America of having "swallowed in toto the Communist Party 'line' on international affairs."[4] But later that same month, when a message from Wallace was read to a huge CIO anti-Taft–Hartley rally at Madison Square Garden, it set off two minutes of chanting: "We Want Wallace! Wallace in '48!"[5]

On June 20 Henry Wallace lost his last chance for substantial labor support when Harry Truman vetoed the Taft-Hartley Act, declaring that it "would reverse the basic direction of our national labor policy" and "conflict with important principles of our democratic society." And he told a nationwide radio audience that night, "We do not need—and we do not want—legislation which will take fundamental rights away from our working people."[6] With that veto Truman won back most of organized labor, though he could not muster enough Democratic votes in Congress to obtain the one-third plus one necessary to sustain his veto.

Whatever his faults, and labor thought them considerable, Truman was a Democratic President, and, save at election time, labor needs a Democratic President more than he needs them. Henry Wallace was both personally and philosophically more acceptable to labor than Harry Truman, but he was out and certain to remain out. Sections of organized labor had backed Robert M. LaFollette in that earlier Progressive adventure of 1924, but labor was young and romantic then. Middle-aged labor would not be so foolish.

The Taft-Hartley Act hurt Wallace in two ways: directly, as we saw, with Truman's veto, and indirectly when the bill survived the veto and became law. Section 9-H of the act required that labor leaders sign a non-Communist affidavit.

At first all wings of the labor movement refused to do this as a matter of principle, but then the ranks began to break. This put Communists on the spot. If they did not sign, they were not eligible to hold office. If they did, they were guilty of perjury. This posed a dilemma for a Communist office-holder—as did the campaign by Philip Murray and other anti-Communist leaders of the CIO to rout out Communists. One or both factors forced Communist officeholders in the labor movement to choose between their unions or the Communist Party. Over a period of months most of these "influentials," as they were called in Communist circles, chose their unions.[7]

Communists and other Marxists—they came in a bewildering array of sects whose differences were apparent mainly to each other—had done invaluable work in establishing and developing the American labor movement. And the various groups understood that, according each other grudging respect and trying to work toward common goals. So the internal bloodletting that took place in the CIO in the late 1940s could not have been happy, even for some of the victors. Phil Murray, for all his anticommunism, was also a dedicated unionist who, with Lee Pressman as an intimate associate, knew how valuable Communists or Communist-sympathizers could be. But Murray and the other anti-Communists must have decided that the labor movement would go the same way the Wallace movement was to go if it did not purge itself of Communists.

The "influentials" who chose their unions over the Communist Party were not necessarily acting out of fear. They had dedicated their lives to the union movement and they believed that they were doing useful work. They might well have believed it was more useful for them to have stuck with the union. It is also true that revealing themselves as Communists would have meant exposure to severe dislocations in their personal lives, including loss of job, various harassments, even legal action. So probably, as is the case with most human beings, these "influentials" acted through a variety of motives, unknown possibly even to themselves.[8]

Over the years until his death, the liberals' favorite labor leader was Walter Reuther of the United Auto Workers. He was attractive, personable, an articulate advocate of civil rights in the nation and within the labor movement, an effective worker for social justice on several fronts, and a skillful leader of his own union. Although he had been a member of the union's left wing at one time, he became president in 1946 in a campaign in which he pledged to oust Communists from the union payroll. He narrowly defeated R. J. Thomas, who, although not a Communist, believed that Communists had the right to participate in union affairs. Reuther won re-election in 1947. This encouraged the anti-Communist forces within the CIO. They were not the only ones to see the tide of anticommunism that was sweeping the nation. They joined it, whether out of conviction or because it seemed the safe thing to do.

There was, of course, no reason why Reuther should not oppose the Communists within the UAW. There is no reason why he should not have welcomed the support of the Association of Catholic Trade Unionists or such conservative publishers as Henry Luce of Time-Life Inc. But it is one thing to oppose and defeat Communists in a democratic fashion; it is quite something else to proscribe them. Communists shared the sectarian hatreds that often caused the Left to be more concerned with internal disputes than with unified action against their common foes on the Right. Communists also sought by every available tactic to control or manipulate groups in which they had significant influence, and their hatred for Social Democrats, a general category that applied to Reuther-unionists and ADA liberals, was fully as great as that which the Social Democrats directed at them. Perhaps this bitter, and foolish, sectarianism can be compared to that which caused Christianity to splinter into smaller and smaller sects, each convinced that it alone knew The Way. It would have been surprising if the Communists had acted any more charitably if they had had the upper hand.

On December 18, when it was apparent that Wallace would soon announce his candidacy, Reuther said at a National Press Club luncheon that Wallace was being "used" by the Communists, adding that they provided the "greatest political valet service in the world. They write your speeches, do your thinking, arrange your meetings, provide your applause and as often as needed they inflate your ego."[9] And two months later he told an ADA gathering in Los Angeles that Wallace was "Joe Stalin's American agent," who was "separating the forces of liberalism and leading them to Stalin's rustlers."[10]

In January 1948 the CIO Executive Board voted 33–11, with two abstentions and six absentees, to oppose a third party in the fall elections.[11] That was fair enough, for the CIO was under no obligation of any sort to support Wallace—even though they had worked closely together for many years. And with eleven votes it appeared that Wallace had done quite well, despite Phil Murray's outspoken opposition, and that some individual unions and union leaders at national, state, and local levels would join the Wallace campaign. But Murray moved swiftly, and drastically, to put down the upswell of support for Wallace. On February 5 he wrote to 387 industrial union councils, 34 regional directors, and 100 lesser CIO officials to tell them that they "should be governed" by national CIO policy in favor of the Marshall Plan and against Wallace. When Harry Bridges of the International Longshoremen's and Warehousemen's Union, one of the eleven who had opposed Murray the preceding month, refused to stop his work for Wallace in California, he was fired as CIO regional director for northern California. And, it could hardly have been a coincidence, a Department of Justice investigator went to San Francisco to seek information for a fourth attempt to deport Bridges. This was Bridges' response: "Truman and his political henchmen are desperate. Any legal technicality, including mere gossip and suspicion is sufficient for Truman's Attorney General, Tom Clark, to chop away at Henry Wallace's political support. It boils down to this: play ball with Truman and support his re-election, or else."[12] This followed a pattern we have discussed earlier: the use of various federal law-enforcement agencies to harass Wallace supporters, a practice that took place on a massive scale against the antiwar movement in the late 1960s and early 1970s.

It would be interesting to learn the full dimensions of the federal law-enforcement effort against Wallace's labor support in 1948. In February the Greater New York City Industrial Council complained that FBI agents were harassing union locals with officers supporting Wallace, asserting that more than twenty locals of eleven unions were visited by FBI men who wanted to examine records pertaining to the 1946 elections (which had already been studied by the Department of Justice). The New York City group later rejected an order from John Brophy, the CIO's director of councils, who wrote to 397 state and local councils, "The CIO in no way is seeking to dictate the voting choice of its individual members, but the CIO does have the right and the power, under the rules adopted by its convention, to secure compliance with its national policies by its chartered councils. . . . No evasion or compromise on this score is permissible."[13] A number of CIO groups refused to follow what they regarded as dictatorial orders, but, with Murray using all his considerable strength, buttressed by timely interventions from federal law-enforcement agencies, most of the CIO fell in line.

While Wallace did have some significant support within the CIO, he did not have a prayer within the more conservative American Federation of Labor. The AFL Executive Council on February 3, 1948, adopted a resolution whose language could hardly have been surpassed by a Richard Nixon or a Karl Mundt:

The Executive Council is completely and unanimously opposed to the Presidential candidacy of Henry A. Wallace.

We make this formal announcement so that the members of the AFL may not be misled by the false liberalism of Mr. Wallace and his so-called third party organization.

The only organization back of Mr. Wallace is the Communist Party. The Communists have now taken him in lock, stock and barrel. He has become their front, their spokesman and their apologist.

The strategy behind the Wallace campaign is devious but transparent. The Communists, of course, have no hopes of electing him. Their purpose is to confuse the workers of America and split the liberal vote. The object of the strategy is to bring about the election of an archreactionary with isolationist leanings. This would play into the hands of Soviet Russia's expansionist policy. It would also bring about a state of affairs in this country which would promote the revolutionary aims of the Communists. Oppression and depression provide converts to their cause.

The Executive Council is confident that the members of the AFL are too intelligent and too patriotic to be hoodwinked by the Communists. They will not support Mr. Wallace.[14]

Despite the opposition of the hierarchies of the AFL and CIO, Wallace did get some union support, almost entirely from within the CIO. All eleven who voted against Murray in the executive committee, with the exception of Michael Quill of the Transport Workers, remained supporters of Wallace: Albert J. Fitzgerald, Electrical Workers; Julius Emspak, Electrical Workers; Grant M. Oakes, Farm Equipment; Donald Henderson, Food, Tobacco; Ben Gold, Fur Workers; Morris Pizer, Furniture Workers; Harry Bridges, Longshoremen, Warehousemen; Ferdinand Smith, Maritime; James Durkin, Office Workers; Hugh Bryson, Marine Cooks.[15] Also Abram Flaxner of the Public Workers, who had abstained in the vote. But several of these leaders, although personally for Wallace, were not able to get their unions to endorse him, though various state and local unions did.

Union support was in any case not nearly as great as Wallace had hoped—and expected. The CIO announced on August 3 that 93 per cent of the four hundred subordinate councils had followed instructions and were opposing the Progressive Party.

The Communist Party used all its influence within the CIO to get CIO backing for Wallace and failed almost completely. Indeed, those unions that had Communist influence would almost certainly have supported Wallace, even without direction from CPUSA headquarters, and the Communist attempt triggered the CIO purge of Communists, but this would have come anyway. Even "Red Mike" Quill, as he was usually called by the newspapers, earlier a vociferous Wallace supporter in CIO circles, deserted him and became, it was assumed, the source of reports that the CPUSA had started the Progressive Party. Quill, whose brogue always thickened when he appeared on radio or television, was a volatile man who apparently decided that he would be wiser sticking with the CIO. Previously, it had never seemed to bother him much that the press often associated him with the Communist Party.

The most important labor supporter of Henry Wallace was Albert Fitzgerald, president of the United Electrical, Radio and Machine Workers and a vice president of the CIO. Not only did he head the labor division of the Progressive Party but he was influential in other areas as well. He was a gutsy and steadfast supporter. When he was called before a subcommittee of the House Labor Committee, he called its hearings an attempt to "snatch" headlines from the House Un-American Activities Committee and to "blackmail" delegates to an imminent convention of his union. Fitzgerald certainly did not believe in mincing words. "By implying that the leaders and members of the UE have been or are likely to be guilty of spying and treason and espionage, [Republican Charles J.] Kersten of Wisconsin reveals himself as a completely unprincipled publicity seeker, liar and slanderer." Then when Kersten tried to read some writings of Stalin, Fitzgerald interrupted: "I'm afraid, Mr. Chairman, you are trying to indoctrinate me. . . . I'm not a bit familiar with his writings and I don't intend to become familiar with them. I don't know the first thing about Communism. I don't care what Stalin or Lenin said. I know nothing of the policies of the Soviet Union." And when Philip Murray charged that the Communist Party had started the Progressive Party, Fitzgerald responded: "I had a whole lot to do with getting Wallace to run, and I never attended a Communist meeting in my life."[16] Years later, at a memorial meeting for Beanie Baldwin on June 9, 1975, Fitzgerald was one of the speakers. Simply and straightforwardly, he said that if the labor movement had followed Wallace, there might have been no Korea, no Vietnam.[17]

In March the United Auto Workers again struck at Wallace when its executive board declared that the Progressive Party was "a Communist Party maneuver designed to advance the foreign-policy interests of the Soviet Union."[18] And the next month Victor Reuther, Walter's brother and the UAW's education director, declared that Wallace was "a tool of Soviet policy," that the Progressive Party was "phony" and inspired by the Communists for the purpose of "speaking for the Kremlin."[19] Also in April Philip Murray said, "This is no time to mince words. I charge . . . that the Communist Party is directly responsible for the organization of a third party in the United States." And he said it "was inaugurated at a Communist Party meeting in the City of New York in October of 1947."[20] Murray was to make similar statements a number of times in subsequent months. Apparently a meeting of Communist leaders in October had been attended by Mike Quill, who was presumably the source for reports of what happened. But whatever took place and whatever Quill may have reported, the fact is that Henry Wallace was the founder of the Progressive Party and, whoever may have attempted to influence him, it was he and only he who could have founded it. That is not to say that Communists at that October meeting and at other times did not recommend a third party and do all in their power to see that one was started. But it was not in their power to start it.

On July 4 the Association of Catholic Trade Unionists termed the Progressive Party "a new front for American Communists." That was harmful, for Wallace's only hope, given the implacable hostility of most of the leaders of organized labor, was to appeal over their heads to the rank and file. But a high proportion of the rank and file was Catholic. On domestic issues he had great appeal to unionists, for no one in American politics after Roosevelt was more closely identified with labor. But Wallace had deliberately chosen to make foreign policy the heart of his campaign, and once he was identified with Communists, at home and abroad, his labor support, at headquarters and in the shops, melted away. Wallace tried to fight back. In September he was the principal speaker before the annual convention of the United Electrical Workers, Albert Fitzgerald's union: "I ask those labor leaders who Red-bait me to think back a few years. I ask the leaders of the CIO to remember how they were called Soviet agents for organizing the open shop strongholds of America. I ask them to remember how they were smeared with the red brush of the Un-American Activities Committee when they organized to elect Roosevelt in 1944. . . .

"With each passing month new blows are struck at our free institutions behind the smokescreen of spy circuses and anti-Russian crusades. . . ."[21]

Labor, despite what the CIO delegation had said in Moscow in 1945, had enlisted in the Cold War, apparently for the duration. And increasingly, it was difficult to tell the union leadership from the management. Wallace came to recognize this, and in Bridgeport, Connecticut, on August 21, he said:

The workers of Bridgeport, like workers elsewhere, are told that war contracts and Marshall Plan contracts mean prosperity. The myth is spread not only by the NAM [National Association of Manufacturers] and chambers of commerce, but by men who pretend to lead labor. There are men inside labor who are using methods against fellow workers which are more ruthless than the Taft-Hartley Bill itself. There are so-called leaders of labor who say they are against Taft-Hartley but use Taft-Hartley to destroy other workers' organizations.

These misleaders of labor have found Red-baiting and Russia-baiting just as useful as the reactionary politicians have found it useful in covering their own failures. And because they have used their energies, power and talents for such a purpose, they are as responsible as the reactionary politicians for inflation, for the draft—for the cold, cold war.[22]

The fact that so many of the nation's economic, physical, spiritual, and intellectual resources were dedicated to the prosecution of the Cold War while so many domestic problems were left partially or completely unattended is often overlooked. And it was particularly unseemly for labor leaders to cooperate with their enemies against those who had long been their friends. Wallace soon came to understand this about the leaders but not until Election Day did he learn it about the rank and file. His campaign to attract votes from the workers had been an almost complete bust.

8

Liberals Attack Their Former Hero

The liberal Left in America gloried in the success of its attacks on Henry Wallace. In 1950, before a House committee, former Attorney General Francis Biddle, then national chairman of the Americans for Democratic Action, testified, "I think the best job on the Wallace movement was done by ADA. They did a pamphlet, which I have here, and which I am going to submit, if I may, *Henry Wallace, the First Three Months.* Now that shows the Commie tie-up right down the line."[1] Later, we will discuss that rather extraordinary pamphlet. It must be remembered then, and in this entire section, that the ADA regarded itself as the foremost force for liberalism in the nation and the first line of defense against what came to be known as McCarthyism.

What happened in 1947 and 1948 was nothing less than a civil war amongst the liberals of America. An admirer of the ADA put it this way: "In the course of this battle liberals were to attack liberals with more venom than they had ever directed at any economic royalist, the labor movement was to divide and choose sides between the two protagonists, and a political party was to arise and die in a matter of months."[2]

The record is plain that the civil war was initiated and sustained by the ADA and its predecessor organization, the Union for Democratic Action (UDA). This represented a turnabout, for in 1944, when Wallace was fighting to retain the nomination as FDR's Vice President, the UDA was enthusiastically for Wallace. Chairman Reinhold Niebuhr of UDA sent this telegram to the Vice President: "PRESIDENT ROOSEVELT'S ANNOUNCEMENT REGARDING HIS CANDIDACY WITHOUT MENTION OF VICE PRESIDENCY IS BEING VARIOUSLY

INTERPRETED BY THE PRESS. ON THE BASIS OF LIBERAL PRINCIPLES AND ALSO OF POLITICAL EXPEDIENCY WE FEEL YOUR RENOMINATION ABSOLUTELY ESSENTIAL TO VICTORY IN NOVEMBER. IF THIS CAMPAIGN IS TO HAVE MEANING FOR THE FUTURE IT MUST BE FOUGHT ON BEHALF OF ROOSEVELT AND WALLACE."[3]

Niebuhr, an eminent Protestant theologian, was a dominant figure in American postwar liberalism. He was not only the spiritual leader but a powerful intellectual force as well. It is no overstatement to term him one of the most influential figures in the first couple of decades of postwar America. His thought was so wide-ranging that it defies brief summation, but long before World War II he had become a fervent but sophisticated anti-Communist. Another vital figure was James Loeb, Jr., who as executive secretary, was the organizational leader of the UDA and later the ADA, and a bitter foe of Henry Wallace. Thus, it is instructive to read a passage from a letter he sent to Wallace in late 1944. After writing that a number of well-known liberals had met with him to "discuss the whole organizational problem of where the progressive movement goes from here on," Loeb said this: "I am sure you understand that we are all anxious to discuss these problems with you because we are united in feeling that you have made yourself the leader of the American progressive movement and we, therefore, are convinced that no steps should be taken by any of us individually or collectively without seeking your advice."[4]

On January 29, 1945, just a few days after he left office as Vice President, Henry Wallace was the guest of honor at a dinner arranged by the UDA and the *New Republic*. The list of sponsors included an extraordinary range of New Dealers, and the message of the dinner, at which extravagant praise was heaped on Wallace, was unmistakable: you may no longer be Vice President and thus direct heir to FDR but we recognize you as his chief lieutenant and leader of the liberal forces within the Democratic Party. Underlining this message was the presence of Eleanor Roosevelt as chief speaker and chairman of the honorary sponsors. Other honorary sponsors were David Dubinsky, president of the ILGWU; Sidney Hillman of the ACW, FDR's man in the labor movement; Mayor Fiorello H. La Guardia; Herbert H. Lehman, former governor of and later senator from New York; Philip Murray, head of the CIO; James G. Patton, head of the National Farmers Union; Milo Perkins, the legendary New Dealer; A. Phillips Randolph, president of the Union of Sleeping Car Porters; Daniel Tobin, president of the Teamsters Union, the largest union in the AFL; and both New York senators, James M. Mead and Robert F. Wagner.[5]

And in announcing the dinner, the UDA had this to say in its monthly bulletin:

Henry Wallace held tenaciously to the course of domestic liberalism which had provided the major reforms and basic social legislation of the New Deal, even after the economic royalists began to move in on Washington as dollar-a-year men. As the President became increasingly preoccupied with the military conduct of the war and the international politics of the Grand Alliance, Wallace became the chief spokesman of the New Deal, the liberal conscience of the administration, the living symbol of its enduring values. Wallace became more and more the eloquent champion of the people. With simple courage, he stated the revolutionary implications of democracy, formulating its timeliness and wisdom in terms of current economic reality. . . . American progressives look to Henry Wallace for leadership in the days ahead.[6]

When the war ended, a split gradually developed between those who were willing to work with Communists for common goals and those who seemed to believe that the Communist Party was the locus of all evil. The war, of course, had submerged this long-standing difference in the liberal community, for it was not possible to smite the Communists while the Russians were suffering the greatest losses from and causing the greatest losses to the Nazis.

The split emerged publicly in May 1946 with a letter to

the *New Republic* by James Loeb of the UDA. He wrote, in
part:

Liberals must decide whether it is their conviction that the *sole* objective of the progressive movement is economic security, or
whether human freedom, which has historically been a co-equal
dynamic of progressivism, is still a commendable objective. . . .
No united-front organization will long remain united; it will become only a "front." This is sometimes, but not always, due to the
fact the Communists are more active, more consecrated, more zeal-
ous than their liberal associates. More pertinent is the fact that independent liberals, whether we like it or not, simply will not
group themselves into a disciplined, semi-conspiratorial caucus
whose aim is to retain or obtain control of the organization. Thus
they are handicapped in their competition with even a small
number of disciplined Communists who automatically follow their
own leadership and make use of any legitimate differences of
opinion to further their own strategic advantage.[7]

A week later a reply to Loeb came from Stanley M. Isaacs,
a liberal Republican [possible in New York and perhaps in
one or two other places], who was often the only Republican on the New York City Council. His reply was not only
brilliant analysis but accurate prophecy:

I disagree wholly with his thesis that Communists must be excluded from organizations supporting a progressive cause and that
when they succeed in infiltrating such an organization, the liberals
should abandon it—and incidentally the cause it advocates. I grant
the difficulty of dealing with well-organized Communists who
want to dominate. But I am not afraid of Communist infiltration
and certainly will not abandon a just cause because I object to
some who have joined in its support. Nor will I secede and help to
organize a new group with the same objective—a move that invariably ends in the two organizations attacking each other instead
of the common enemy. Witness the AFL and the CIO.
    To do what Mr. Loeb suggests is to fall for the strategy which
Fascists and their precedessors have used since time immemorial
to divide and conquer—to destroy their opponents piecemeal.

They procced to attack an organization as a Communistic front and the liberals who are active in it as fellow travelers, if not Communists. Some liberals thereupon are intimidated into public repudiation. Those who persist are now handicapped because the Fascist critics point to those who are left as evidence that all those who remain *must* be Communists. When they succeed in blackening the reputation of those who have stuck grimly to the anti-Fascist cause, they then turn against those who resigned and label them Communists or "fellow travelers" because at one time they were connected with the organization. The end result is demoralizing— the cause is weakened and leaders courageous and important in the fight for liberty and justice are discredited. This is the actual process that is taking place in ruinous fashion in many a field where weak-kneed or tired liberals succumb to Fascist maneuvers.[8]

The simple process, so clearly described by Isaacs, seemed to be beyond the understanding of the ADA. Or perhaps their hatred of Communists—for whatever reason—was simply so strong that they could not help themselves. In any case, what Isaacs described is exactly what happened to Henry Wallace and the Progressives. And the fact that ADA liberals Red-baited did them little good, for many Cold War liberals also became victims of the anti-Communist hysteria.

It might also be added that ADA-type liberals seemed to be in awe of Communists. In any united-front organization the Communists could be outnumbered many times over; if they succeeded in dominating an organization, it was because the liberals were incompetent or threw in the towel. If Communists were as potent as liberals seemed to think, why was it they did so poorly?

The disastrous congressional elections of November 1946 hastened the split in the progressive-liberal forces, for while some Democrats believed that the enormity of the defeat could be attributed to Harry Truman's desertion of the New Deal, more seemed to believe that the cause was the success of the Republicans in pinning the Communist tag on the

Democratic Party. Many liberals seemed to think the only solution was to root out the Communists. Max Lerner, in a series of editorials for the New York newspaper *PM*, asserted that the Republicans had won "largely on the basis of a Red scare." Although he maintained that the reactionary right was still the main enemy, he wrote that "that enemy can be fought effectively by a liberal-labor coalition which has replaced Communist influence by a militant non-Communist leadership." Even though the Communists were not an immediate threat, their ways were alien. Lerner called for the building of "a trade union and political progressive movement which is clearly non-Communist but does not spend its best energies in Communist-hunting."[9] Although it was theoretically possible to have a non-Communist organization that did not "spend its best energies in Communist-hunting," given the circumstances of the time, it was almost inevitable that such a movement would end up following Stanley Isaacs's prescription for disaster. Which is exactly what happened.

On December 28 and 29, 1946, as we saw earlier, the National Citizens Political Action Committee and the Independent Citizens Committee of the Arts, Sciences and Professions merged to form the Progressive Citizens of America. Although Henry Wallace was not a member, he was plainly their leader. A week later the Union for Democratic Action enlarged itself into the Americans for Democratic Action, with such prominent New Dealers as Leon Henderson, Chester Bowles, John Kenneth Galbraith, Elmer Davis, and, most important, Eleanor Roosevelt. And such powerful labor leaders as Walter Reuther, David Dubinsky, and James Carey. Among the younger founders were FDR, Jr., Hubert Humphrey, Wilson Wyatt, Richardson Dilworth, Joseph Rauh, and Arthur Schlesinger, Jr. A number of influential journalists were there, too: Joseph and Stewart Alsop, Marquis Childs, Kenneth Crawford, James Wechsler, Robert Bendiner, and Barry Bingham.

Both of the new organizations had men and women of

reputation and accomplishment. The ADA had many more prominent New Dealers, although the PCA was far from bereft of them. The PCA, however, seemed much stronger in the arts, with dozens of big names from Hollywood, Broadway, publishing, music, and the graphic arts. The ADA had Eleanor Roosevelt and FDR, Jr., then thought to be following in his father's footsteps, but the PCA had Wallace, then the most charismatic figure in American politics. The issue dividing them was plain. Whereas the PCA welcomed anyone who shared its progressive objectives, the ADA statement of principles said: "We reject any association with Communists or sympathizers with communism in the United States as completely as we reject any association with Fascists or their sympathizers."[10]

The ADA claimed, like the PCA, to be an independent force, but not long after its birth it found itself, however reluctantly, tied to Harry Truman. Even though in early 1948 it worked to deprive him of the nomination, it ended up supporting him. Truman knew that the ADA would never walk out on the Democratic Party and it never did. It grumbled and it expressed reservations and it mumbled about its misgivings, but it always went along with the Cold War as it did, for so long, with the Vietnam war.

In early 1947 it seemed as if the PCA was going to capture the liberal-progressive movement, probably because it and Wallace were so critical of Truman, who was then widely perceived as having deviated, at home and abroad, from Roosevelt's policies. The ADA seemed, however, to equivocate. Also, a good many liberals who had not chosen between the two organizations chided the ADA for its preoccupation with Communists. For a while this damaged the ADA but it was precisely the Communist issue, or, rather, the exploitation of the Communist issue, that permitted the ADA to survive. It quickly, as had labor, enlisted in the Cold War and devoted much of its energy to Communist-hunting. The ADA would not swim against the tide, as did the PCA, but with lesser than greater enthusiasm, swam along.

The famous Truman Doctrine Speech of March 1947 was troublesome for the ADA, for they professed to be as much against fascism as against communism. But Greece was an authoritarian and cruelly repressive royalist government, while Turkey had aided the Nazis in the war. Yet Truman wanted to help them in what was clearly, and then perceived as such, a declaration of political and economic war against the Soviet Union. And there was a plain element of militarism to Truman's policy. Nonetheless, after two days of discussion and over considerable opposition the ADA supported the "broad objectives and methods proposed by President Truman for aiding Greece and Turkey but urged use of 'all United Nations facilities now available and operation through the machinery of the United Nations as soon as the United Nations assumes responsibility.' "[11]

This was rather a disingenuous response, since the United States had quite openly decided to avoid the UN in favor of unilateral action.

The big crowds that Wallace drew in the spring of 1947 alarmed the Democratic National Committee and a memo from Gael Sullivan, the committee's top staff man, was sent to Clark Clifford on June 6. After describing the impact of the Wallace appearances and the views of newspapermen and leading Democratic politicians that Wallace was a genuine threat, Sullivan wrote this:

Don Montgomery, of the UAW, a Reuther anti-Communist who once worked for Wallace, said:
"The guy follows the Commy line. He takes orders. But he presents a strong appeal to the American people. Don't mistake that. Don't underplay his appeal. It's tremendous. The average American can't understand this business of sending military aid to Turkey. They can't understand the military aid to Greece. They

could understand food and seed and machines. Not arms. Wallace speaks to them and makes sense."

All of which adds up to this:

Wallace is a major consideration in 1948!

Something should be done to combat him.

The President should:

1. Go on the air in a series of fireside chats which would explain and implement the Truman policy.

2. The non-military side of the Truman Doctrine should be accented.

3. Wallace's fuzzy thinking should be answered by clear, level-headed replies—ignoring the man but answering the issue.

4. Adequate thought should be given to decide whether Wallace is wanted BACK AND SOMETHING SHOULD BE done about it before he gets himself too far committed to a Third Party.

REMEMBER:

Ed Kelly, Ed Flynn, Mayor Hague, Cy Bevan and other Democratic leaders have shifted. They now feel Wallace is a threat.

Action should be taken either to

1. Appease Wallace

    or

2. Pull the rug on him.[12]

The eventual decision was, of course, to "pull the rug on him" and the assignment was carried out by the ADA.

In July 1947 Wilson W. Wyatt, national chairman of ADA, made an attack on Wallace typical of those often made by ADA spokesmen through election time 1948. He said that when Wallace "fronts for a third party with the private cheering of the reactionaries and the beaverish industry of the Communists, he is fronting for a movement which can only injure—perhaps irretrievably—the very liberalism for which Franklin D. Roosevelt fought."[13] This was a common tactic: to identify Wallace with Communists without discussing the issues he raised—curious behavior for an organization of lawyers and academics who claimed to be issue-oriented.

The proposal of the Marshall Plan of the Truman administration in June 1947 cheered the ADA. Not only that, but the ADA was certain the PCA would be isolated in its opposition to the plan. The ADA did not, however, discuss the Progressives' contention that the Marshall Plan was merely the economic instrument of the Truman Doctrine, nor Wallace's suggestion that economic reconstruction should be carried on through the United Nations.

Throughout the late 1940s and during the McCarthy period later the ADA consistently opposed the congressional and press witch hunts directed at Communists and fellow travelers. There is no reason to doubt the sincerity of ADA members in this important and brave work, but there was also, perhaps unconsciously, a curious quality to some of their criticism of the witch hunts. The ADA seemed to be opposed to them not only because they were wrong but because such witch hunts actually harmed the anti-Communist struggle. One got the feeling the ADA was saying, in effect: We're just as anti-Communist as you and we're not criticizing you because we are any less anti-Communist but because you are actually hurting the cause we both share. This may be uncharitable, but anyone who remembers those days, remembers how often liberal criticism of the witch hunts had this characteristic. As an example, here is a passage from an open letter sent by the ADA on October 15, 1947, to J. Parnell Thomas, chairman of the House Un-American Activities Committee shortly before the committee was to begin hearing on alleged Communist penetration into the movie industry. The passage is from a letter over the signatures of Leon Henderson, chairman of the executive committee, and Melvyn Douglas, the actor and chairman of the California ADA organizing committee:

It is undoubtedly true that some Communists have sought to make their influence felt in Hollywood—as everywhere else. The greatest service we can render to them is to discredit a whole community and a whole area of our creative life because some Communists may have found their way into it.

Reckless attacks on liberals committed by the House Committee on Un-American Activities Affairs in the past have repeatedly strengthened the hand of Communist agents. They have used such attacks to prove that our democracy is a frail and frightened thing and to proclaim that legitimate exposure of their activities must inevitably degenerate into a ruthless heresy hunt. The Communists will undoubtedly attempt to raise the same cry in connection with the hearings which you are conducting this month.[14]

Why did the ADA so often have to go that far with the witch hunters? Why could they not have said: You are wrong, period.

During that same period the most eminent ADAer, Eleanor Roosevelt, became critical of Henry Wallace. She was not eager to criticize Wallace, for she had long admired him; nonetheless in her newspaper column she found it "strange" that progressives and the Cominform "are condemning with one voice the Marshall proposals."[15] As a member of the U.S. delegation to the UN General Assembly, she had come to develop a close relationship with George Marshall, and that ended any possibility that she might have subjected the Marshall Plan to the same kind of critical scrutiny that Wallace did.

By November 1947 it was apparent to the Truman White House that Wallace would be running. And Clark Clifford in his famous memo suggested to the President how his candidacy should be handled.

Henry Wallace will be the candidate of a third party. As of November, 1947, the majority of informed opinion does not favor this particular hypothesis. Nevertheless, the factors which impel Wallace toward a third party clearly outweigh those which do not.

For one thing, the men around Wallace are motivated by the Communist Party line. The First Lord of the Kremlin who determines the Party line is still Karl Marx. The Marxists emphasize that the capitalist economy holds within itself the seeds of its own destruction; that it must inevitably destroy itself by depression and collapse. But within this rigid ideology is the directive that when and where possible the Party must hasten the process. Moscow is sufficiently aware of American politics to perceive that a Republican administration would be rigid and reactionary, and would fail to take those governmental steps necessary to bolster the capitalist economy in time of crisis. It is also convinced that there is no longer any hope that the Truman Administration will submit to the Russian program of world conquest and expansion. From the Communist long-range point of view, there is nothing to lose and much to gain if a Republican becomes the next President. The best way it can help achieve that result, and hasten the disintegration of the American economy, is to split the Independent and labor union vote between President Truman and Wallace—and thus insure the Republican candidate's election. . . .

This is interesting not only in what it says but in the mind set it reveals. It demonstrated that Clifford—and everyone else who wrote or spoke about communism—had the capacity to read the Communists' minds. It was really quite simple. If the Communists said what you expected them to say, it was one of those rare instances when they told the truth. If they said what you did not want to hear, they were lying. Thus, if they opposed Truman, it meant they wanted a Republican victory. It could not possibly mean that they did not see much difference between the two parties.

The best evidence supporting this probability is that the men who surround Wallace today are Party-liners such as C. B. Baldwin, political opportunists such as Harold Young, and gullible idealists like Michael Straight. These men will persuade Wallace it is his duty to his country to run, as they have persuaded him to do everything else they ever wanted him to do. The most recent reports on Wallace's personality by men who know him well are that while his mysticism increases, the humility which was once his dominant characteristic has decreased to the vanishing point; there is something almost Messianic in his belief today that he is the Indispensable Man. . . .

Again the mind set. A man who was an eminent farm journalist, a first-ranking farm economist and plant geneticist, the best secretary of agriculture in American history, and an effective Vice President becomes the tool of his subordinates. And his character is suspect. This seems to bear out the contention of Weisband and Franck in *Resignation in Protest*, that American Presidents invariably attempt, and usually succeed, to destroy effective opponents, as, for instance, Roosevelt attempted to destroy Charles Lindbergh before World War II and Truman attempted to destroy Wallace after it.[16]

The casual comment by the professional politicians on third-party talk is that it is futile since a third party cannot get on enough state ballots. This is dangerously unrealistic. . . . If Wallace can get on the ballots of only a few states and can then draw five or ten percent of the vote, that vote alone taken from the Democrats in a close election is enough to give the Republicans the electoral vote of those states and therefore national victory. And Wallace *can* get on the ballot of New York (American Labor Party) and California and other states.

It is also very dangerous to assume that the only supporters of Wallace are the Communists. True enough, they give him a disciplined hard-working organization and collect the money to run his campaign. But he also has a large following throughout the country, particularly of the young voters who are attracted by the idealism that he—and he alone—is talking and who regard war as the one evil greater than any other. He will also derive support from the pacifists, which means a great number of organized women and from whatever irreconcilable and die-hard isolationists remain. He will attract votes—and money—from the "lunatic fringe." The California Townsendites are already pledged to him.

In a close election, no votes can be ignored. The only safe working hypothesis is to assume *now* that Wallace will run on a third-party ticket. Every effort must be made *now* jointly and at one and the same time—although, of course, by different groups—to dissuade him and also to identify him and isolate him in the public mind with the Communists.

*The foreign policy issues of the 1948 campaign will be our relations
with the USSR and the Administration's handling of foreign reconstruction and relief* [italics in original].

. . . There is considerable political advantage of the Administration in its battle with the Kremlin. The best guess today is that our
poor relations with Russia will intensify. The worse matters get,
up to a fairly certain point—real danger of imminent war—the
more there is a sense of crisis. In times of crisis the American citizen tends to back up his President. And on the issue of policy
toward Russia, President Truman is comparatively invulnerable to
attack because of his brilliant appointment of General Marshall,
who has convinced the public that as Secretary of State he is non-
partisan and above politics.

In a flank attack tied up with foreign policy, the Republicans
have tried to identify the Administration with the domestic Communists. The President adroitly stole their thunder by initiating
his own Government employee loyalty investigation and the more
frank Republicans admit it. But their efforts will intensify as the
election approaches, particularly when the meagre results of the
civil services investigations are made public by the Republican
Congress.

Here we see one of the elements of Truman's astounding
success. He would avoid campaigning on foreign-policy issues, thus attempting to avoid any serious criticism of his
policy. This succeeded because Dewey fell for the tactic and
swallowed the contention that "politics stops at water's
edge," thus committing the Republicans to a "me-too" campaign. Wallace, of course, saw through this, but Truman
avoided any foreign-policy debate with Wallace by discred-
iting—or, more accurately, having him discredited—as a
friend of Russia and the American Communists. Yet while
Truman would not campaign on foreign policy, the growing
crisis between the USA and the USSR would cause many
Americans to rally around him, not as Truman the Democrat but as Truman the President. Christopher Lasch once
wrote: "The modern state, among other things, is an engine
of propaganda, alternately manufacturing crises and claim-

ing to be the only instrument which can effectively deal with them."[17] Thus, the crisis in Czechoslovakia in February 1948 and the Berlin blockade during the last half of the year inevitably helped Truman, and he knew they would.

Notice, too, how Truman handled the Red-baiting that the Republicans wanted to direct at him. He "adroitly stole their thunder" with his own loyalty program and then later had the Red-baiting—which would have been fatal—shifted away from the Democrats to Wallace and the Progressives. Then came the domestic aspect of his campaign.

Insofar as it has control of the situation, the Administration should select the issues upon which there will be conflict with the majority in Congress. It can assume it will get no major part of its own program approved. Its tactics must, therefore, be entirely different than if there were any real point to bargaining and compromise. Its recommendations—in the State of the Union message and elsewhere—must be tailored for the voter, not the Congressman; they must display a label which reads "no compromises." The strategy on the Taft-Hartley Bill—refusal to bargain with the Republicans and to accept any compromises—paid big political dividends. That strategy should be expanded in the next session to include all the *domestic* issues.

A brilliant if cynical strategy. The point was not to attempt to pass necessary legislation but to make impossible demands on Congress, then belabor it as a "do-nothing Congress," and make these demands the kind of New Deal legislation that would simultaneously appeal to voters sympathetic to Henry Wallace. Plainly, from Clifford's words, Truman did not attempt to make Taft-Hartley more acceptable legislation; his tactic was to let it stand as legislation unacceptable to labor and liberals and then veto it for maximum political advantage. And it worked, with the added benefit that it was passed over his veto, giving him the kind of authority over labor he had earlier sought while at the same time establishing him as a hero to labor. Whatever Truman's failings, he was not an inept politician.

The Insulation of Henry Wallace. Wallace should be put under attack whenever the moment is psychologically correct. If it is clear that organization work is being undertaken by his men in the West, either for a third party or for delegates to the Democratic convention—and that work seems to be taking effect—the Administration must persuade prominent liberals and progressives—*and no one else*—to move publicly into the fray. They must point out that the core of the Wallace backing is made up of Communists and fellow-travelers. At the same time, some lines should be kept out so that if the unpredictable Henry finally sees the light and can be talked into supporting the Administration, he will have a handy rope to climb back on the bandwagon—if he is wanted.

But there is only futility in the delusion that Wallace can be insulated merely by yelling at him. As his own lieutenants say, and accurately, in their private conversation, "Henry can be stopped quite easily; all President Truman has to do is move to the left and our ground is cut out from under us; but we are quite sure he won't do it." How the Administration can move "left" belongs in the discussion of the "program" (below).

But along with programs there are the men who execute these programs. And here is the strong weapon of the President's arsenal—his *appointing power*. Politicians, like most other people, think of issues in terms of men, not statistics. When the President moves "left" in his appointments, he is putting political money in his bank.

The September 11th speech by Wallace was his first really adroit one. It was a bid to the discontented liberals wavering behind President Truman. What he said publicly they have been saying privately with increasing bitterness—even those who support the President. Henry Wallace appealed to the atavistic fear of all progressives—the fear of "Wall Street." This fear is not the sole property of the progressives. It belongs traditionally to the Democratic Party. . . . In a very important sense, it is the reason for the Democratic Party—because the only way to explain the lasting alliance between the South and the West is their mutual fear of domination by the industrial East. Today the South can agree on no issue with the West—*except* "Wall Street."

The Wallace plan is simplicity itself. It should be—because it has been used before. He merely borrowed it from Fighting Bob LaFollette who received five million votes in 1924 by attacking Coolidge and John W. Davis as "Tweedledum and Tweedledee, the messenger boys of Wall Street." And the significance of the LaFollette third party was not its total vote but that the Progressives ran ahead of the Democrats in *eleven Western states*. The combined Democratic-Progressive vote was larger than the Republican vote in *thirteen* states, including President Truman's own state of Missouri. Democrats who voted for Davis would have voted for *any* Democrat and the LaFollette Progressives would have voted for any *liberal* Democrat. In effect, then this was a present of 86 electoral votes to the Republicans, not enough to change the 1924 election . . . ; but it is more than enough to raise havoc for a close election. Henry Wallace may be fuzzy-minded on many matters, but his mathematics is all right.

President Truman must carry the West to win. To carry the West, he must be "liberal"; he cannot afford to be shackled with the Wall Street label by any so-called progressive movement. And Wallace recalls only too well that the spiritual father of the New Deal was not John W. Davis but Bob LaFollette, *and* that the New Deal came *only* eight years later. . . .

The man-in-the-street understands little and cares less about the personnel difficulties of public administration. These difficulties have no glamour, they are too complex—and so they just don't get across. The Wallace attack does. In the blunt words of the ILGWU (Dubinsky) Union Convention: "Foreign policy is not the private property of . . . retired financiers. Foreign policy is the burning concern of the great mass of the people."

And that is all the working man will remember of *that* issue.

It is imperative that the President make some top-level appointments from the ranks of the progressives—in foreign as well as in domestic affairs. His fight for [David E.] Lilienthal made him the hero of the independent voter. His refusal to withdraw the name of Francis Biddle as American delegate to the Economic and Social Council until Biddle requested it made him many friends among the liberals. Top-ranking appointments of men like young Bob LaFollette are needed. The pattern must be repeated even if some of them are not confirmed. Under their impact, Wallace will fade away.[18]

Clark Clifford's extraordinary document was entirely a *political* document. What he was concerned with was politics and politics only, not with good government.

Truman had swerved sharply away from Roosevelt's New Deal and now he returned to it plainly for political reasons only. For that he was termed a liberal; a better term would have been opportunist. Wallace understood that. So too should have the liberals.

As soon as Wallace announced his candidacy on December 29, 1947, the liberal drumbeat began. Democratic Senator Robert F. Wagner of New York said:

. . . I am disappointed in Henry Wallace's decision for I always classed him as one who steadfastly adhered to the highest ideals of the Democratic Party.

We all want peace, but not peace at any price. Henry Wallace is asking for that when he asks for peace at the Soviet dictator's price. His is a policy of appeasement, not unlike Chamberlain's, and just as surely will it lead to war but worse, war without victory.

Henry Wallace's silence on the Soviets' aggressions, their vetos, their deliberate falsehoods, their repression of even minimal civil rights is deafening. . . .[19]

The ADA chimed in the next day with a statement over the signatures of Wilson W. Wyatt, Leon Henderson, Franklin D. Roosevelt, Jr., and Hubert H. Humphrey, which said in part:

Irrespective of Mr. Wallace's intentions, the goals of his sponsors are clear. They hope to divide progressives, create national confusion and insure the triumph of reactionary isolationism in 1948. They believe the achievement of these aims will serve the world interests of the international Communist movement.

That danger has been apparent since the third party began. But we believe it can be overcome. The overwhelming evidence that the Communists—rather than any progressive force committed to our national interest—are the machine behind the third party is now indisputable. . . .[20]

A typical ADA statement. An assertion of "overwhelming evidence" when that evidence simply did not exist. And not a word about the substance of Wallace's reasons for making the race.

The research staff of the Democratic National Committee, which worked closely with the White House under Clifford's supervision, was largely staffed by ADAers. Some might consider that surprising, since the ADA early in 1948 was doing its best to get the party to dump Harry Truman. What is more surprising, considering the ADA's purported hostility to Truman, is a series of memos between Gael Sullivan, top aide to national chairman J. Howard McGrath, and McGrath himself. On January 19 Sullivan told McGrath that Paul Porter, a leader of the ADA, wanted to see McGrath on January 29. McGrath agreed to the meeting, suggesting that "this appt. might be better *not* at Headquarters. . . ." Then Sullivan, in a memo to Porter, spelled out the agenda for the meeting for, as he wrote McGrath, "otherwise, [Leon] Henderson will put us all out in left field." This is what Sullivan told Porter:

It seems to me that if we could keep our meeting on the 29th within the following terms of reference, it would advance our mutual cause much further:
1. Financial aid to the ADA.
2. Active use of the organization to aid the Democratic cause.
3. A solid show of interest in the organization by the Administration.
I think that this agenda would serve to keep the discussion within reasonable bounds as to time and would certainly be a definite aid to a quick and favorable decision.[21]

It was not possible to get further information as to the planned meeting. Porter wrote: "I regret that I cannot confirm meeting with Howard McGrath in 1948 to discuss financial aid to ADA. Such a meeting could well have taken place but I have no independent recollection of such a meeting or any notes or records that would be of assistance in refreshing my recollection."[22]

It appears, however, from the memos that it was the ADA that was asking for financial aid from Truman's party. This would seem to be rather curious since the ADA proclaimed its political independence and tried to enlist, with some limited success, liberal independents and Republicans on the basis of its independent liberalism. But whether or not the Truman Democrats approved funds for the ADA, it is plain that some leaders of the ADA were considering having it serve as a paid arm of the Democratic National Committee. And whether or not it was paid, the ADA certainly carried out various functions for the Democratic Party, foremost of which was its unrelenting attack on Wallace.

Although the ADA was usually successful in rallying New Dealers against Wallace, occasionally an eminent man of the Left resisted. One such was the Harvard scholar Albert Sprague Coolidge. In January he wrote to James Loeb of the ADA, ". . . I hope you and I may have a little time to talk. I need some persuading why I should not vote for Wallace now that he is running on a program of principles most of which I strongly approve, which seems to me an entirely different question from whether it was wise for him to run. As you know, I have always felt that the Left would be powerless as long as it did not provide itself with a possible alternative to voting for Democrats. Indeed, it seems to me that I notice several signs, since Wallace entered the field, or a renewed interest on the part of the Democrats in winning liberal votes."[23]

But the ADA did not break stride. When Frank Kingdon deserted the Wallace cause and wrote his column asserting that the Communists were behind his candidacy, the ADA not only carried the column on page one of the *ADA World* but distributed it widely through the mail. That would be fair enough if the ADA were convinced that Kingdon was correct, but Loeb wrote on January 27 to Dr. Harry Girvetz, chairman of the ADA in Santa Barbara, "It just happens that some of us worked with Kingdon for quite some time. I can assure you that he is purchaseable. He has double-crossed so many people that there is almost no one left for him to double cross."[24]

A week or so after Loeb heard from Professor Coolidge, Rexford Tugwell wrote a regretful letter to Leon Henderson, chairman of the ADA executive committee.

. . . So far as ADA is concerned I shall have to be counted out. I have concluded prayerfully that it does not move toward strength and cohesion among liberals. In fact I think it demonstrates precisely the opposite.

I joined the ADA quite innocently, feeling that I ought to belong to any group of American liberals who were bent on expressing the desire of many citizens for an end to domestic exploitation and foreign aggression. I did not realize that the split from the Progressive Citizens of America was caused by dissent from Henry Wallace's revolt from complaisance and supineness. I now believe that what prevents you and others from following his magnificent leadership is a fear of the consequences inherent in his clear and fearless statement of the liberal dilemma. The attitudes of ADA seem to me evasive and unrealistic. The real administration policies are not what Mr. Truman says, but they are how Mr. Snyder [Treasury Secretary] and others of his administration act on domestic issues and how General Marshall and his military and Wall Street colleagues actually conduct our foreign relations. I can agree with most of what Mr. Truman says; I look aghast at what his administration does. So, I think, must any realistic liberal.

Yet the ADA quite generally refuses to face the facts; many old hands, who must certainly see through the glossy surface into the frightening reality of events, talk as though they were on leave from the Treasury or the Department of State and possessed no minds of their own.

In contrast Henry Wallace has spoken with increasing strength and clarity straight out of his mind and heart with cold and fearless logic. His actions and analyses have been those of a man with a conscientious concern for the American tradition of progressive action. Your group is inclined to be critical of him for appeasing communists. He has clearly done no such thing; he has merely refused to be confused by a bogey as old as American politics. I have come to believe that this ADA criticism is being used to conceal the frightened consent of the ADA group to an aggressive and dangerous foreign policy and to its reactionary concomitant in domestic life.

He has persuaded me that he is the genuine embodiment of the tradition I value above all: that American hatred of exploitation and concern for the common man which always has had some champion no matter what the cost to himself. Henry Wallace is against war and a policy which leads to war. To say that this is appeasement of Russia is deliberately to refuse to see the distinction between an invincible friendship for the Russian people in an inclusive world-neighborliness and a cowering before the threat of force. The serene strength of firm democratic purpose is not the policy which is being implemented in Greece and China. That is naked aggression. Why is not ADA setting itself too against the torrent of fear-caused hate which is spreading like a plague in our media of mass communication? An official inch is being stretched into the usual journalistic mile and a situation is being created in which no official explorations will be possible even if they are desired. The only step beyond that is war. Yet, as [University of Chicago] Chancellor [Robert] Hutchins says, we cannot have a war. If we do, the human race is through. In the face of all this I must support the only great voice now being lifted for friendship to all men and against the exploitation of any. I wish I could persuade you to do likewise. . . .[25]

No more than Professor Coolidge's letter did this give the ADA pause. In almost every issue of *ADA World* there were one or more stories or columns attacking Wallace. It was sad because it demonstrated that the ADA, not Wallace, was a prisoner of the Communists. Albert Deutsch, a liberal journalist who opposed the PCA decision to back a third party, put it this way in the newspaper *PM:*

While I disagree with the PCA decision on the Wallace candidacy, I believe it was made by a group of sturdy Americans according to the dictates of their democratic and patriotic consciences. To suggest that their decision was made in Moscow is nothing less than irresponsible balderdash.

I am frankly dismayed by some of my shifty-eyed fellow liberals who seem unable to form a conclusive opinion without first looking over their left shoulders to see what Communists think . . . dutifully reading the *Daily Worker* to find out what they should oppose.

If a cause seems right to [the true liberal], he does not discard it because others may follow the same path for longer or shorter distances for their own reasons.[26]

On February 19, 1948, Arthur M. Schlesinger, Jr., perhaps ADA's most articulate member and, over the years, quite possibly its most influential, wrote, "The impulses which gave birth to ADA, indeed, came from the recognition among New Dealers that militant post-war Communism constituted a basic threat to freedom and democracy throughout the world; and that this threat could be met only by the development of an affirmative program along rigorously democratic lines." This is certainly a plausible statement, making plain that the ADA was to a large extent motivated by anticommunism. But where the ADA failed tragically, and along with it Professor Schlesinger, was that it did not insist that the American opposition to communism be based on "an affirmative program along rigorously democratic lines." The ADA, whatever its misgivings, went along with a foreign policy that made anticommunism the first and, in truth, the only criterion. That was so with the ADA, and Professor Schlesinger, until well into the Vietnam war at which point ADA and Schlesinger bailed out. The tragedy was that the ADA did not live up to its professed principles. If it had been able to overcome its preoccupation with communism, if it had pointed the finger at a succession of American Presidents for supporting right-wing despots abroad, it would have been the invaluable independent organization it professed to be.

Although the opposition on the Left to Wallace was concentrated in the ADA, the ADA was not alone. Norman Thomas, leader of the Socialist Party, consistently attacked

Wallace. Another leftist, although difficult to categorize, who bitterly opposed Wallace was Dwight Macdonald. This may seem surprising in view of Macdonald's prominence in the antiwar movement of the mid-1960s but Macdonald was, like Thomas, a vehement anti-Communist and devoted two issues of his magazine, *Politics,* to what is called in journalism "a hatchet job" on Wallace. Macdonald attacked Wallace on every level, including, most emphatically, the personal. He called him "unprincipled," "totalitarian," "a corn-fed mystic," a "demagogue," and especially belabored him as an "apologist for Stalin," as "more and more a fellow traveler"; he even compared him to Hitler. Wallace was, of course, open to attack. There were things to criticize in his years as secretary of agriculture and as Vice President. Certainly there was a Messianic streak to Wallace, and his rhetoric was sometimes apocalyptic. A leftist could find much to criticize in Wallace's "progressive capitalism" and even his foreign-policy positions were legitimate targets for criticism, but Macdonald's attack was savage and personal to a degree that would seem more appropriately directed at Adolf Hitler or Joseph Stalin.

The magazine articles were combined into a book, *Henry Wallace: The Man and the Myth,* and on February 28, 1948, Macdonald wrote to Loeb asking if the ADA had a book service through which it could be sold to members. Or "If there is no such service, would you consider putting the enclosed leaflet in one of your membership mailings?" Loeb replied that the ADA had no such book service and said, "I think the best way to promote the book is by having a review of it in the next issue of the *ADA World.* I'll suggest that to Bill Dufty."[27]

By early March the ADA was beginning its abortive attempt to deny Harry Truman the nomination as it got reports from across the nation that Truman did not have a chance to win. Loeb wrote to the national officers on March 10 that "This seemingly justified defeatism should be given serious attention by the ADA Executive Committee meeting on March 8 and by the National Board meeting on April 10." And publicly the *ADA World* was saying: "The ADA emphasizes its independence of any political party"— although one wonders how this squares with the approach to the Democratic National Committee two months earlier. Perhaps some ADA members were not aware of what others were doing.[28] The most prominent, Eleanor Roosevelt, shared the general feeling: "I haven't actually endorsed Mr. Truman because he has been such a weak and vacillating person and made such poor apointments in his Cabinet and entourage, such as Snyder and [Harry H.] Vaughan, that unless we are successful in electing a very strong group of liberals in Congress, in spite of my feelings about the Republican Party and Governor Dewey, I can not have much enthusiasm for Mr. Truman. Though there are many people in the government that I would hate to feel would not be allowed to continue their work, I still find it very difficult to give any good reasons for being for Mr. Truman. . . ."[29]

Although most of the ADA leadership opposed Truman's nomination he did have some supporters, Paul Porter, for one: ". . . I was certain that Truman would be renominated and, as I recall, urged his endorsement or that ADA reserve its position.

"I definitely remember calling upon President Truman before the ADA convention and informing him that I would not attend if he construed it as an act of disloyalty. In a typical response, he observed that anybody sitting in his chair who would not get the renomination was (expletive deleted)—'even Hoover could do that.' And besides he continued 'we may need those fellows this fall.' "[30]

When the ADA National Board met on April 11, it did not come out against Truman but did declare for an open convention and said "we feel strongly that this Nation has a right to call upon men like Dwight D. Eisenhower and William O. Douglas if the people so choose."[31] The mention of Douglas is not surprising, for there was no doubt about his liberalism; but one wonders about Eisenhower, the ADA's

first choice. Although his views of most issues were unknown, no one, certainly including himself, ever regarded
him as a liberal.

In the ADA correspondence files there are many letters
indicating support for Eisenhower. A typical one was from
Gertrude W. Scheft, executive secretary of the Massachusetts ADA, to James Loeb: "What we shall attempt to
do immediately is to get top people into a Draft-Eisenhower
movement. The CIO promises a good deal of help in this
job. . . . In the case of Eisenhower, if we get CIO cooperation we should be able to get 50,000 signatures just in plants
and factories through the state. . . ." And in an undated
letter, shortly before the Kansas Democratic State Convention on May 28, Vi McGrath of the ADA political department wrote to someone identified only as Dick: "Will it be
possible for you to go over to the Kansas Democratic State
Convention in Wichita next weekend? We are trying to organize anti-Truman sentiment, demonstrations, etc., in as
many conventions as possible. . . . I have sent 500 Eisenhower pamphlets to [James] Yount [of CIO-PAC] to
use. . . ."[32] Although the choice of Eisenhower seems rather
dubious for a purportedly liberal organization, there does
seem to be little doubt of the intensity of ADA's feeling that
Truman was totally unacceptable. But if the ADA had apparently given up on Truman, the Democrats had not given
up on the ADA. ADAer William L. Batt, Jr., a member of
the research division of the Democratic National Committee, on April 15 wrote a memo to Clark Clifford in which he
reported that "Porter's tactics, which he had concocted with
Gael Sullivan, were to let everybody talk himself out and
then come in with the best solution he thought he could
get. My observation was that he did a fine job. . . ."[33]

While the ADA, or most of it, was doing battle with Truman on the Right, it was not neglecting Wallace on the Left.
In April it began leaking stories of a pamphlet on Wallace
that would deal his campaign a serious blow. A few days
later the pamphlet was released and it did deal Wallace a

serious blow, because it was largely concerned with demonstrating that the Wallace movement was a creation of the Communists. And it made plain that the "ADA has assumed the prime responsibility for challenging him and his spokesmen whenever it has appeared that their utterances threatened the welfare or objectives of democratic peoples here and abroad."

The pamphlet, *The First Three Months of the Wallace Campaign*, was used widely in the press, by labor unions, and by the Democratic Party, to the extent that the first printing of twelve hundred copies was quickly exhausted and a second mimeographed edition was necessary.[34] It was never intended that the pamphlet be distributed widely by the ADA itself, but that it would reach a mass audience through its use by friendly newspapermen, unions, and political organizations.

The pamphlet traced the third-party idea back to a 1945 article by Jacques Duclos, a French Communist leader. It cited statements by American Communists calling for a third party; it did not cite statements in which the Communists said, as they did time and again, that they alone did not have the power to create a third party, that they could not dominate it if it were formed, and that they did not want to dominate it.

It was, in short, an intellectually dishonest marshaling of selective evidence, using material out of context, "doctoring" it to make a point. A pamphlet that Red-baited and made the incredible assertion that Wallace was not a friend of the Negro or of labor was entirely unworthy of the liberal intellectuals who prepared it.[35] These latter assertions are amusing, since Wallace conducted down South the first nonsegregated campaign in American history and since the ADA's own files are crammed with material demonstrating the close ties between Wallace and labor.

While many ADA members praised the pamphlet, one, Philip H. Coombs of Amherst College (later an assistant secretary of state in the Kennedy administration), questioned its "heavy emphasis upon the role play by the American Communist Party" in the Wallace movement.

I found the material very interesting and some of it helpful in connection with debates in this area in which I have been involved recently. I do feel, however, that there is a danger of ADA placing disproportionate emphasis on this particular issue. I don't deny the strong influence which the Communists have had upon Wallace's statements and strategy, but I think ADA will be more persuasive with the kind of people we are shooting for if we center our main attack on the significance of Wallace's foreign policy and the stupidity of his political strategy, without making his association with the Communists the central issue. I hope that ADA can get out presently a second brochure, which will be helpful to those of us in the field, on these points.[36]

But that pamphlet and most of the material that followed did precisely what Coombs warned against: it emphasized the Communist issue and devoted very little attention to the substance of Wallace's foreign-policy statements.

The ADA, to its credit, did oppose the Mundt-Nixon bill to "control" subversives, as did, in even stronger terms, Henry Wallace.[37] But even when it did the right thing, the ADA gave it a curious twist. Arthur Schlesinger wrote that the Communists opposed the Mundt-Nixon bill because they wanted it passed. "Enactment would have given Henry Wallace a new and appealing issue; it would have provided the USSR with a potent weapon in the psychological war. Fortunately, in spite of the irritation of some members of the Judiciary Committee, the Senate was not to be stampeded into the Communist trap."[38] Again, this liberal capacity to read the minds of Communists and the incapacity to believe that the Communists ever meant what they said or acted out of conviction. The Mundt-Nixon bill would have been a disaster for the Communists, entirely apart from its violation of American political principles. Was it not possible that the Communists opposed it, if not out of principle, because they knew the terrible harm it would do them?

And Schlesinger recited the tired old ADA line that the Communist Party was responsible for the Wallace movement, using such confident language as this: "All went according to plan. . . . During 1947 the Communist machine moved steadily toward its proclaimed objective. . . . By December the Wallace candidacy was in the bag."[39] This attributes to the Communists the kind of political talent and power that they wished they had. If the Communists had this ability to manipulate men and events, why did the entire national leadership, with the exception of the old and sick William Z. Foster, end up in jail?

In May the Socialist Party joined the ADA in opposing Wallace, calling him a "communist captive," "an apologist for the slave state of Russia," and a "preacher of peace by blind appeasement."[40] And even so decent a man as Donald Harrington, the New York minister who has over the years devoted himself tirelessly to just about every good cause that presented himself, wrote in *The New Leader*, "It becomes clear that the organizational leaders of the Wallace party are either Communists or people very close to them. . . . There are very few liberal leaders supporting Wallace who do not have a Communist or fellow-traveling coloration, and so far as I know, not one single non-Communist leader of labor. . . . Wallace's party does have the wide support of many different types of liberals. But organizationally it is controlled, staffed, supported and held in the iron grip of the Communists and their fellow-travelers."[41]

In July the Democrats nominated Truman as Henry Wallace, and Harry Truman, had known all along. The ADA, which had done its best to dump Truman, soon proved "its independence of any political party" by endorsing him and even finding rather eloquent rhetoric to demonstrate the necessity of his election. But before the ADA could turn its full attention to the election of Truman, it still had to deal with Wallace. James Loeb appeared before the platform committee of the Progressive convention and denounced Wallace's campaign:

> We know that we speak for the great non-Communist liberal and labor majority when we state our conviction that your movement is a dangerous adventure undertaken by cynical men in whose hands Henry A. Wallace placed his political fortunes. . . .
>
> The presence of Mr. Wallace does not alter the fact that the real authority of your party is vested in the hands of men and women, many of whom followed the dictates of totalitarianism in the period of the Nazi-Soviet pact. Mr. Wallace's candidacy does not obscure the fact that the Communists and their collaborators guide the major policies and word the major pronouncements of this party.
>
> It is our conviction that, were the Communists to withdraw from your party today, your organization would soon join that long list of discarded groups which testify eloquently to the inevitable failure of the so-called "United Front"—which always becomes decreasingly "united" and increasingly "front. . . ."
>
> We anticipate, however, that the new party will once again demonstrate that, as an instrument of Soviet policy, it has sacrificed any claim to the support of independent liberals; that it will continue to betray its stated objectives of raising mass living standards, expanding freedom and promoting peace throughout the world.[42]

This was a choice bit of Red-baiting that could not have been surpassed by Richard Nixon or Karl Mundt or Joseph McCarthy, but it was done not by an archreactionary but by the spokesman of a liberal organization. Since the ADA had earlier released its statement to the afternoon papers, the chairman of the Progressives' platform committee, Rexford Tugwell, had a chance to prepare a response:

> The intemperate attack which the ADA has chosen to make on the New Party is, of course, a matter of taste. Others who have appeared before us have done so in good faith and in the attempt to influence the formal statement of New Party policy which is presently to appear.

The statement of the ADA is not intended for this purpose. It impugns the motives of this platform committee and denounces the whole movement of which it is an organ. It might well be ruled to be inadmissible because immaterial. It is obvious that with a consciousness of this the statement was given to the press well in advance of its submission—many hours before, as a matter of fact. . . .

I did not expect that the ADA, of all other groups, would resort to unscrupulous and demagogic denunciation worthy only of the cheapest of politicians—insincere, hypocritical and immaterial.

The ADA only a week or two ago was sitting on General Eisenhower's doorstep, hat in hand, asking for the favor of his candidacy. It turns now, as its next official act, to the denunciation in most immoderate and unhappy terms of Mr. Wallace and the rest of us in this movement.[43]

By midsummer the Wallace movement had peaked and liberals were deserting it in droves, but Wallace's liberal opponents did not intend to let up. In August Freedom House, an organization of anti-Communist liberals, asserted that Moscow was directing the Progressive Party's program.[44] Also in August the ADA "emphatically" endorsed Truman in ringing language that included a statement that the Wallace party "is controlled by communists and their collaborators."[45]

In September Reinhold Niebuhr suggested that the ADA put out a declaration signed by as many prominent New Dealers as possible. In his draft Niebuhr wrote, "Wallace's candidacy was inspired by Communists and the levers of power in his organization are held by notorious followers of the party line." As finally presented, the declaration said: "The Progressive Party does not repudiate Communism, as Franklin Roosevelt did. It represents, on the contrary, the most serious attempt in the history of our nation by a totalitarian group to capture and destroy American liberalism." The declaration was Cold War in tone and language and, as usual with the ADA, it did not address itself to Wallace's proposals. As released about a month before the election, it was signed by thirty-seven well-known New Dealers.[46]

Shortly before the election the ADA published another long attack on Wallace: *Henry A. Wallace, The Last Seven Months of His Presidential Campaign.* Like the first pamphlet, it concentrated largely on the Communist issue. And when the election was over, the ADA boasted, with justice, that they had done the most to pin the Communist label on Wallace. Harry Truman had followed Clark Clifford's plan. Except for two or three outbursts, possibly extemporaneous, Truman left the Red-baiting of Wallace to liberals and the labor movement. It was not one of American liberalism's shining hours.

Although the ADA opposed witch-hunting, its own Red-baiting helped establish the atmosphere for McCarthyism. And its support for Truman's foreign policy contributed directly to the course that led to a Vietnam war planned and executed by liberals. The ADA of 1948 regarded itself as "the best and the brightest," and one can find little difference between them and "the best and the brightest" of the Kennedy and Johnson years. Indeed, they were often the same: Hubert Humphrey and Arthur Schlesinger, James Loeb and John Roche, Averell Harriman and many others.

The ADA made much of the fact that it had most of the famous New Dealers and that was true, which makes it all the sadder that so many of the legendary figures of that time were willing to attack the greatest figure of the New Deal after FDR himself or willing to allow their colleagues to do so. But history, even after these scant decades, has demonstrated that all the New Deal figures in the world could not justify the ADA's unreasoning anticommunism. The ADA was on the winning side in 1948 but history now gives a different account of who won and who lost. America lost in 1948, not because Henry Wallace lost, for his individual fate was not that important. America lost because it had already closed its mind. Henry Wallace had a powerful idea: that the world could go about its important business only if the United States and the Soviet Union could establish peaceful relations. Harry Truman was a man of limited vision and had a vested interest in the policies of his administration, but the ADA people, and Norman Thomas's Socialists, and even the Dwight Macdonald independent leftists were bright and sophisticated. They should have recognized that getting along with the Soviet Union did not mean condoning repressive practices within Russia; they might even have been expected to recognize, as Wallace did, that the best way to mitigate those ugly practices was not by screaming at the Russians but by helping to establish a peaceful world in which the liberal influences of the West would have easier, however gradual, access to the closed world of the East. As liberal or socialist intellectuals they should have been freer of dogma than the Communists, but they responded to "communism" the way Communists responded to "capitalism," with emotion not reason. In the name of freedom they helped establish a climate that did nothing to foster freedom in the Soviet Union and much to damage it at home.

When the tumult of the election had faded away, a debate was held in the pages of *The Progressive* between Hubert Humphrey, a leading member of the ADA who had just been elected Senator from Minnesota and who was later to sponsor a move to outlaw the Communist Party, and Rexford Tugwell, a leading but uneasy member of the Progressive Party. Humphrey continued to belabor the Wallace movement as "a crude Communist-front enterprise, conceived, nurtured and finally wrecked by the Communists with their morbid capacity for destroying the things they profess to love." Tugwell was not much more admiring of the ADA, writing that it

played as futile a role as is to be found in the recorded political history of the United States. They seemed to be dominated by the urge to guess who among the candidates would succeed and to hitch up to him regardless of principle or consequence; they first deserted Mr. Truman, then, after dallying disgracefully on General

Eisenhower's front steps for no defensible reason, tried to pretend that they had been for Mr. Truman all the time. They developed no program and achieved no independence.

. . . Now let me go back to the time when I joined up with the Wallace Progressives, just to show how everything might have been different if (as I think) my fellow progressives had had the courage which proceeds from genuine conviction.

Suppose that, instead of a mere handful, there had been thousands of us—individuals with some local or national responsibility for leadership, to take the collective captaincy of the seven to ten millions who were then progressives, and who might have gone out and got seven to ten millions more.

Let me just ask: If there had been a flood of progressives—energetic, determined, dedicated—where would the Communists, about whom we hear so much, have been? The question, it seems to me, answers itself. They would have been lost as they were always lost when they tried to claim President Roosevelt, or, if there are those still alive to remember, when they made approaches to old Bob LaFollette. The Communists wound up, in both instances, denouncing as base reactionary the man they could not capture. The reason Communist workers were so prominent in the Wallace campaign was that the progressives were—well, where were they? Sitting it out; wringing their hands; and wailing about the wickedness of the Reds.[47]

9

The Press and Henry Wallace

The American press has for the last couple of years been pretty proud ot itself—proud of its work in uncovering the Watergate story, which led to President Nixon's resignation, and proud of its coverage of the war in Indochina, which greatly influenced the United States' decision to withdraw from combat participation in the war. Indeed, the American press is almost always pretty proud of itself, frequently asserting that it is the best and freest press in the world. That, alas, may well be true.

I have suggested that Vietnam might properly be called the "liberals' war," because the liberals in the 1948 election quickly, despite some misgivings, threw their crucial weight behind a foreign policy that led inevitably to Vietnam. Substitute the word "press" for the word "liberals" here, and the sentence would be no less accurate. The press bears a major responsibility for the Cold War and all the tragedy stemming from it.[1] That is demonstrated, beyond question, I believe, by the press coverage of Wallace's campaign, which above all, offered tough, fundamental criticism of American foreign policy. This press coverage disclosed a number of things about the American press as a whole. Although it prided itself on its independence and skepticism, it seldom asked any basic questions about American foreign policy, but, rather, became part of the national consensus even as it helped form it. Indeed, it was often "more Catholic than the Pope." One can understand that the press, be it the publishers or the reporters, is a product of society, although it claims to have the capacity to stand apart from it and examine it. And if no one else were asking tough questions, it would be understandable if journalists did not. Someone was asking tough questions and he was not a crackpot, but a former Vice President of the United States, former holder of two Cabinet posts, and once, after FDR himself, the leading figure in the Democratic party. Henry Wallace made foreign policy the heart of his campaign; it was the reason he was running. Yet with the rarest exceptions, the press simply ignored the substance of his campaign, usually taking the line that to be critical of the United States meant being a partisan of the Soviet Union, and concentrated almost exclusively on the Communist issue. Here, two tendencies reinforced each other. It is normal for the press, especially during a Presidential election, to focus on campaign politics to the detriment of the issues. The human drama of politics seems to interest newsmen more than the issues, which, although crucial, are often complex or, even worse, "dull." Reinforcing this normal characteristic of American political coverage was, in the specific case of 1948, the fact that publishers, editors, columnists, and reporters were largely just as anti-Communist as Harry Truman or Richard Nixon.

The press also, despite a surface irreverence, had a deep reverence for authority and seldom questioned it. What a President or secretary of state proclaimed was solemnly published on the front page; what a critic said appeared briefly inside. For instance, when Harry Truman made his historic speech of March 1947, it was, quite properly, treated as news of the utmost importance. When Wallace made fundamental criticism of the speech, it appeared, if it appeared at all, in a few lines inside. And Establishment journalists in recent years have shaken their heads sorrowfully over "advocacy journalism," mourning the good old days when newspaper reporters were objective. What, then, is one to make of an "objective" journalist like Howard Rushmore of the *New York Journal-American* who in a story on April 13, 1946, about a gathering of liberals referred to ". . . 2000 New Dealers, Communists, 'One World' advocates and parlor pinks. . . ."[2] And this was hardly unique. As we shall see, "objective" journalists on some of the best-known newspapers in the nation easily outdid Howard Rushmore.

The press certainly had no obligation to support Henry Wallace. He would have been the most surprised man in the land if it had. But it did have an obligation to seek the truth, to be fair, and it, above all others, should have defended the rights of free expression under the First Amendment. The truth seems to be—and it is difficult to see how this can be denied—that the American press, while decrying the lack of a free press in the Soviet Union, treated dissent in the United States much as the Soviet press treated dissent in Russia.

There is no implication here of a press conspiracy against Henry Wallace. It is just that there was then—and is now—great uniformity in the American press, despite sometimes serious differences on this or that issue. The newspapers big and small, the networks generally think pretty much alike because their economic health depends on their being pretty much in tune with the society they serve. The press is usually as much follower as leader, sometimes following the government, sometimes following the people, although occasionally as in Watergate (belatedly) and in Vietnam (much belatedly) it becomes a leader. In 1948 it was dedicated, along with much of American society, to crushing the "Communist conspiracy," to which Henry Wallace seemed a party. Nonetheless, there were often matter-of-fact stories about Wallace appearances, strongly critical but fair editorials, and tough but fair cartoons. But the proportion of slanted stories and unfair editorials and cartoons—all pervaded by Red-baiting—was so high that it is no wonder that most voters dismissed Wallace as a Red or a Communist dupe and simply ignored the substance of his campaign.

Henry Wallace had developed a certain skepticism about the press and his diary for June 13, 1945, introduced his view with a marvelous anecdote about *The New York Times:*

. . . At the staff meeting Mr. [Frank A.] Waring gave a most interesting presentation on his experiences at San Francisco. He told how certain members of the delegation had leaked again and again to Scotty [James B.] Reston of *The New York Times* and how one of the delegates one morning said, "I have been studying our agenda for the day and find it differs in certain particulars from what appeared this morning in *The New York Times*. I should like to inquire which is the official version."

. . . He told about the high quality of the Russian delegation and his picture was totally different from that which would be gathered by reading the newspapers. I am more and more beginning to reach the conclusion that it is a mistake to read the newspapers about any controversial matter because they so often give an absolutely inaccurate picture. Undoubtedly the newspapers should be read so far as possible with the idea that account should be taken for the bias. It is just as important to take account of the bias of newspapers as it is to take account of the direction of the wind when flying an airplane.[3]

After the Truman Doctrine speech and Wallace's detailed reply, Clyde R. Miller, associate professor of education at Columbia University Teachers College, wrote this letter to *The New York Times*, a copy of which he sent to Wallace:

There is much talk about Russia's "iron curtain" and "controlled press." In contrast it is said we do not have a "controlled press" and certainly no "iron curtain." However, occasionally there are disquieting symptoms which suggest press control and just a tincture of iron.

Take Henry Wallace's answer to President Truman's proposal on Greece and Turkey. If I know news—and I have been paid money for the past twenty-five years by several universities for a supposed ability to judge news—Wallace's answer was front-page news deserving a streamer head. I look carefully in *The New York Times* for an account of that speech. I finally found it—about a stickful [a few inches] of type on an inside page. Some of the New York papers, apparently, didn't carry it at all.

Would you call this an understanding among the publishers and the editors not to print one of the great news stories of this year and perhaps of this generation? Would you call it "control"? Would you call it "iron curtain"?

There is something in the Scripture on this point about a beam and a mote.

True, *The New York Times* finally did print this speech in full on March 18—as a paid advertisement.[4]

Professor Miller was no doubt stretching it a bit to suggest that there was an understanding not to give Wallace's speech much coverage. But there did not have to be an understanding. News of this nature—speech news—has weight according to the rank of the person who made it.

On April 28, 1947, shortly after returning from his storm-provoking European trip, Wallace held a press conference in which he complained that "I have always criticized Russia, but that is never news. Apparently it falls [in] the situation . . . between the man and the dog. One is news and the other is not." Earlier he had said that "Russia should have joined the International Bank for Reconstruction, that she should have joined the Food and Agriculture Organization, that she should have displayed a greater confidence toward the United Nations than she has."[5] The press kept insisting that Wallace never criticized the Soviet Union, and failed to note his pleas that he was an American, trying to influence American policies, that *that* was what was needed. But few Americans saw that as a need. There was a nice irony here: one of the criticisms of Russia—a valid one—was that criticism within Russia was dangerous, but for about twenty years substantial criticism of the United States was undertaken with no little risk. You could easily lose your job, be ostracized by your community, be harassed by various government agencies, face court action, be attacked in the press, all in the name of freedom. And this seemed to strike the press, with occasional exceptions, as perfectly normal.

That was because the press, having suspended the skepticism which is vital if it is to be effective, had swallowed whole the bipartisan line that civilization was in peril, that the Hun was at the gates. Take, as a random choice, two widely syndicated columns appearing in *The Washington Post* of June 16, 1947; "Matter of Fact" by Joseph and Stewart Alsop and "Washington Calling" by Marquis Childs. All three were intelligent, sophisticated men, ADA-type liberals who, one assumes, prided themselves on their independence of mind. On this day in mid-1947, both columns were devoted to the possibility that President Truman might call a special session to deal with urgent foreign matters. First, the Alsop brothers, those two splendid Horsemen of the Apocalypse:

> . . . it is necessary to understand the nightmare that has begun to haunt the informed leaders of the Administration. It is, very bluntly, the nightmare of a Europe which has largely succumbed to the Soviet Union's present drive to extend its sphere of control. And this nightmare exercises a decisive influence on all planning, for the very simple reason that it is a nightmare which can come true. If the present process of economic and political deterioration is permitted to continue, and Communist regimes are thus installed in Italy, or France, or both, the nightmare will be hard, stark reality.

Then the Alsops shift into high gear:

> . . . If Europe goes, the United States will be forced to place permanent military establishments at the present temporary and civilian airbases in Iceland, Greenland and the Azores. The Belgian Congo [now the Republic of Zaire], with its essential uranium deposits at Shinkolobwe [a nice touch that, naming the specific area; it somehow heightens the drama], will almost certainly have to be occupied, and serious consideration will have to be given to the occupation of Dakar, with its command of the South Atlantic.

Marquis Childs was seldom quite as dramatic as the Alsops but he, too, was aware of the urgency of the situation: ". . . we must examine without fear or prejudice the nature of the crisis which is coming on with such a rush. We must try to understand the speed with which events are crowding in. . . . We cannot delay those decisions much longer. The hands of the clock are moving on toward midnight of the brief day that is left to us."

The reader could hardly be blamed for feeling that the Russian hordes were poised on the border, like the Nazi Panzer divisions on the Polish frontier, ready to strike. But what was the reality? It was less than two years after the end of a war in which the Soviet Union had suffered some 20 million dead and countless numbers of sick and wounded. The economy had been devastated and the Soviet Union had no alternative but to devote itself to restoring its terribly depleted strength. And the United States was unchallengeably strong. Its economy had been vastly strengthened by the war and it alone had the atomic bomb. Whatever Russia's intention, it was absolutely no threat to the United States. The American military knew it, the State Department knew it, the White House knew it, and the Alsops and Childs should have known it. But a drive was on to enlist Congress and the American people in a mighty crusade against Russian communism, and the press eagerly enlisted, for these two columns were hardly unique; they were the common journalistic currency of the day.

On December 18, 1947, before Wallace announced his decision but at a time when it seemed both likely and imminent, Blair Moody, later a senator from Michigan, wrote in *The Detroit News* that "Extreme leftists, meaning Moscow's American agents and those who follow their lines, are doing their best to split the American liberal movement and elect a reactionary President next November. That . . . would be the surest way to wreck the country and bring a violent overturn via a depression." This was a news story not a column. Again, we see the incapacity of anti-Communists to believe that Communists, or anyone else, could have the genuine conviction that a third party could best serve the nation's interests.

The Alsop brothers seemed to feel a special obligation to paint Wallace Red and a collection of their columns on him and the Progressives would take pages. On December 21, 1947, Stewart Alsop wrote in their column that "The Wallace third-party movement has been indecently exposed for what it is: an instrument of Soviet foreign policy. Since the PCA invited him to head a third party, the whole movement has been stripped bare. The bones revealed are communistic bones."

On December 30, the day after Wallace announced his candidacy, *The New York Sun* ran an "objective" news story under the by-line of George Van Slyke: "Henry A. Wallace and his Communist left-wing following are speeding today their plans for the national convention of the Progressive Citizens of America. . . ." And the second paragraph ended by asserting that the PCA delegates "will form the basis for the third-party movement as the Communist front in the nation." This was not a column but a "factual" news story. This pattern ran through the entire campaign. On December 31 the Cincinnati *Times-Star* ran a news story under this headline: PERSONAL/REVENGE/ THE GREAT/ URGE OF/WALLACE. The *Philadelphia Inquirer* of the same date ran a cartoon showing a buck-toothed Wallace stepping up on a box that said "RUSSIA MUST BE RIGHT BECAUSE AMERICA IS WRONG." And off to one side a wild-haired, bearded worker labeled "U.S. COMMIES" holds a paintbrush and a can of "RED PAINT."

On January 6 Ralph McGill in a syndicated column appearing in the *Jacksonville Journal*, wrote that Wallace "certainly is not a Communist, but he has allowed himself to be badgered into becoming the Soviet Union's mouthpiece and best friend in this country."

Two weeks later, in his syndicated column, Milburn P. Akers wrote: "One need not deny Communists their civil liberties to deny them an effective voice in a third party. Yet Wallace, apparently actuated by that fear, denies a far greater number of Americans an opportunity to support his third party and thereby protest through a wholly American agency the conditions and abuses of which he complains, and in many instances, rightly so."

Akers appeared sincere in offering Wallace what he meant as helpful advice. But he did not explain how Wallace could have expelled the Communists without giving comfort to the Red-baiters. And it seems a curious logic to assert that the presence of Communists "denies a far greater number of Americans an opportunity to support his third party. . . ." If voters thought Wallace was right, they should have voted for him and not been frightened off by the presence of some Communists.

On March 3 there was a curious incident involving the *St. Louis Post-Dispatch*, one of the most respected liberal Republican newspapers in the country. It printed this editorial:

> In a recent editorial, based on an Associated Press dispatch, we quoted William Z. Foster, No. 1 Communist American, as saying: "The Wallace Party is the Communist Party." We erred in not taking note of Mr. Foster's heated denial, also printed in an Associated Press dispatch. Mr. Foster said that the original "story was a deliberate falsehood."
>
> We doubt, however, that any substantial injustice has been done to Messrs. Foster and Wallace. Mr. Wallace habitually talks in words that echo the Communist party line. He is admittedly on close terms with Communists and refuses to renounce their support. When he went to Paris, to cite only one instance, he was met by the big-wig French Communists, like Duclos and Thorez and by practically no other Frenchman of importance. Wallace's follower, Isaacson, was the beneficiary of Communist votes and organization in the recent Bronx election. But the point need hardly be labored.
>
> Nevertheless, in fairness, we should have taken note of Mr. Foster's denial that he made the quoted statement. Of course many followers of Henry Wallace are not Communists.

Now there's a gracious apology.

The press was not always subtle. In Columbus, Ohio, in

1947 a Communist organizer, Frank Hashmall, passed out some Communist literature critical of President Truman's March 17 speech. On one occasion there was some scuffling between those passing out the leaflets and workers at a Columbus plant. Thereupon the Columbus *Citizen* several times printed large pictures of Hashmall's residence. It also printed the address and his phone number, including a warning that any violence would only help the Communists who thrive on martyrdom. Whether they got the idea from the newspaper or would have done it anyway, on March 30, while the Hashmall family was away, a mob of some thirty men broke into the house while four hundred spectators milled around outside. They badly damaged the furnishings and the next day the Hashmall's moved out with what was left.

Earlier, on March 26, after receiving a number of protests about the roughing up of the pamphlet distributors and about earlier, less violent incidents at the Hashmall residence, the *Citizen* wrote: "Evidently when you pinch a Communist a Wallaceite hollers. The Commies and the Wallace crowd seem to have connecting nervous systems, like a two-headed calf."

Two incidents connected with this story give some idea of the atmosphere in which Wallace conducted his campaign. Dr. Richard G. Morgan, curator of archaeology at the Ohio State Museum, was fired because his son-in-law had rented the house to Hashmall. And when the police chief was asked why he had denied Hashmall's request for protection, he said, "Columbus is a peace-loving and churchgoing community and the city administration is not going to tolerate any Communist, Communist front or organization interfering with our way of living if it is humanly possible. There will be no special police for this anti-religious group in this city."[6]

In April 1948 the *Pittsburgh Press* began the serial publication of the names of all those who had signed Progressive Party petitions in western Pennsylvania. On the third day,

April 13, the *Press* ran an editorial in which it said, "Gideon's Army, as Henry Wallace calls his followers, doesn't seem to like daylight.

"We were amazed at the sharp reaction of the Henry Wallace forces against publication of the names. . . ."

And the editorial ended by saying, "The strange thing is that those who yell so loud about the legal right of signing petitions should complain against exercise of the legal right to publish them."[7]

The paper, of course, had the legal right to identify the petitioners but it was plain to everyone why they were doing it. Given the atmosphere of the time, publication of the names caused embarrassment and often harassment of Wallace supporters. Other newspapers did the same thing. Among them the *Nashville Tennessean*, the *Birmingham Post*, the *York* (Pennsylvania) *Dispatch*, the *Xenia* (Ohio) *Gazette*, the *Zanesville* (Ohio) *Signal*, the *Concord* (New Hampshire) *Monitor-Patriot*, and the *Boston Herald*.

On April 18 James Reston of *The New York Times* reviewed Wallace's book *Toward World Peace*. Reston is a fair man and it was a fair review. However, *The Times Book Review* illustrated the Reston piece with a big, three-column picture of a smiling Henry Wallace shaking hands with Marcel Cachin . . . French Communist leader. Was it sheer chance that the review was illustrated with a year-old picture of Wallace shaking hands with a Communist when on his European trip he shook hands with politicians of many kinds? Perhaps.

On May 22 the *Saturday Evening Post*, then an enormously popular magazine, carried a little article by Martin Ebon in which he wrote that "the Wallace party has a 100 percent record of doing what the Communists want it to do." And that same month a reporter for the Chicago *Sun-Times*, after saying that "At times he is the classroom Wallace of the broad, long-range philosophy, the Wallace who sees mankind in terms of generations and centuries," wrote that the "second Henry Wallace is an apologist for Russia's ruthless regime and denial of political liberty to the Slavic masses."[8] That was not so. To criticize the United States was not the same thing as praising Russia, but in those dark days even intelligent people seemed unable to make the distinction.

A cartoon distributed on June 10 by the McNaught Syndicate showed a rather moronic-looking Wallace on his knees peering at a bear [symbol of Russia] in a cave and saying, "Hello, you great big peace dove."

So it went all through the campaign. Wallace did not receive nearly the coverage that Truman and Dewey received because the press is as committed to a two-party system as the two parties, not recognizing that sometimes the third party, no matter how badly defeated, is more significant over the long term than either of the major parties. Much of what he did receive was matter-of-fact reportage of his appearances and statements but much concentrated on his association with Communists. Only in rare instances was there any serious analysis of his arguments. Evidently the press had decided—and when I say the press, I mean the entire press—that his arguments did not merit examination, that they were, by definition, beneath notice. Some will question my saying the entire press, but I say it with some confidence, for there were rare exceptions. Although it is clearly impossible for any one person to examine the entire press—there were about seventeen hundred daily newspapers, many weeklies, hundreds of magazines, hundreds of radio stations, and even a few television stations—the Progressive Party subscribed to the American Press Clipping Service and Beanie Baldwin had retained for all those years scores of envelopes of clippings from all across the country, most of which appeared never to have been opened. I spent hours going through envelopes chosen at random, examining hundreds, perhaps thousands of clippings which provided a fairly good cross-section of Wallace's press coverage. It would be difficult, I am convinced, to argue that the press coverage of Wallace and the Progressives was anything but biased.

Perhaps what has been cited earlier has not sufficed to demonstrate that, but at one point, and one point only, Wallace and the Progressives did receive concentrated coverage. That was at the time of the Progressive convention in July 1948. It is to that we now turn.

On July 21, two days before the convention, a story appeared in the *New York World-Telegram* under this headline: "58 OF 72 WALLACE MEN FIGURED IN RED PROBE." Written by Fred W. Perkins, a Scripps-Howard reporter, it presumably appeared in the chain's other newspapers across the country. Here are the first four paragraphs, which accurately give the tone of the story:

Washington, July 21—Files of the House Committee on Un-American Activities throw some light on the committee that begins work today in Philadelphia on the platform for the Henry A. Wallace party.

The committee's files contain references, of greater or smaller length, to 58 of the platform committee's 72 members. Fifty are identified by the committee as belonging to one or more Communist-front organizations. In some cases these connections run to a dozen or more.

Four appear in the files as actual members of the Communist party—an allegation which the committee says is supported by credible evidence, but which it admits it cannot prove.

The composition of the committee is considered important primarily because the platform it produces is expected to be given great publicity in Russia and satellite countries. The aim will be to show opposition to this country's foreign policies.

The Scripps-Howard chain was one of the largest and most influential in the country and here it was printing a story based on unsubstantiated allegations emanating from a committee that was well known to every Washington

newsman as considering as a Communist front any organization even faintly liberal. It is safe to say that any liberal
of any prominence would have been regarded by HUAC as
a Communist fellow traveler.

The *Philadelphia Inquirer* greeted the delegates to the Progressive convention with an editorial under this headline:
"A Convention with Moscow's Blessing." The first few
paragraphs give the editorial's flavor:

The mongrel party which opens its national convention in Philadelphia today is a made-to-order instrument of Communist policy.

This is the dominating factor that overshadows all others in
viewing the third party and its activities.

From its candidate for President, Henry A. Wallace, to the pro-
Communist line faithfully taken by its platform, the new outfit is a
perfect medium for the devious purposes of the Communist Party
and its masters in Moscow.

Between the third party and the Reds it has been a case of love
at first sight.

The Communists welcome the Wallaceites, and the Wallaceites
welcome the Communists.

The two major parties, faithful to their common American traditions, have rejected the Reds and all their works. The third party
greets the Commies with open arms.

There will be many denunciations of the United States Government, Congress and foreign policy at the Wallace convention. But
it is a safe bet that there will be not one word derogatory to Russia
and Stalin.

Henry Wallace fell all over himself to condemn the indictment
and arrest of a number of Communist leaders in New York—a perfectly legal and proper procedure assuring the defendants a just
trial and opportunity to appeal to the Supreme Court.

But there has been no word from him finding fault with Soviet
aggression or Soviet denial of civic rights.

The Wallace platform regarding Russia can be boiled down to
these simple terms: whatever Stalin wants is all right.

In case the point hadn't been made, the editorial was accompanied by a cartoon showing a disheveled man carrying

a "Henry for President" placard illustrated with a dopey-looking Wallace. The man's left sleeve was rolled up and the arm labeled: "LEFT-WING PROGRAM." The man himself was labeled "TUGWELL PINKS," and he was accompanied by a wild-eyed, wild-haired bearded Bolshevik with a hammer and sickle on each forearm and wearing a tunic marked "REDS."

That same day, July 23, the *Detroit Free Press* ran this editorial:

Today there gathers in Philadelphia a convention that is the greatest testimonial to the integrity of our political faith ever presented to the world.

Avowed enemies of the American form of government will meet there, under police protection, in the safeguarding of the inalienable right to free speech.

It is a convention in which Moscow has more influence than Washington.

Every type of crackpot, every known kind of malcontent, every species of hate-blinded neurotic, every element of anti-Americanism, will be on hand to jeer and sneer at all this Nation has ever stood for in its most exalted moments of service and sacrifice.

They are the glorifiers of Russia and totalitarianism. They preach the New Deal doctrine that the "people are too damned dumb to understand." They are disciples—or pretend to be—of the strange, wild creature who might have been President of the United States—Henry Wallace.

Only in America could they meet because we have a national sense of humor. In Russia they would all be shot before they could meet, not because of their Marxian vagaries but because the Stalin gangsters would look upon them as possible rivals in their racket.

Milburn Akers, in his syndicated column of that day, wrote: "The platform—praiseworthy in some respects—contained the Communist Party line in many areas. It is one on which William Z. Foster, head of the Communist Party in the United States, can stand as well as Henry Wallace." But

Akers did not seem able to make the effort to understand why Foster and Wallace could stand on the same platform. The press as a whole suffered from a failure of imagination; it seemed incapable of understanding that there might possibly be justification for fundamental criticism of American foreign policy. It seemed instinctively to feel that basic criticism was akin to disloyalty: my country right or wrong. How else could Akers have written:

> The Progressive Party, demanding negotiations and discussion with the Soviet Union to find areas of agreement, *apparently* [emphasis added] wants unilateral action by the United States first: a complete reversal in foreign policy, disarmament, destruction of atomic bombs, and the cessation of the draft. It proclaims no need of any pre-conference action by Russia.
>
> Stripped of verbiage, the Progressive Party demands, as does the Communist Party, that the United States, ridding itself of all bargaining power, and shorn of military power, go hat in hand to a conference table with Russia, still possessed of military might, and work out an agreement for world peace. It places its confidence and trust in Russia's supposed good will, an attribute it fails to ascribe to America.

Reading the platform, one wonders where Akers found those things that "apparently" the Progressive Party wanted and demanded.

The Alsop brothers in their column for July 24 began with this paragraph: "The Wallace party convention is, of course, not a convention at all. It is, rather, a dreary and sometimes nauseating spectacle, carefully and quite obviously stage-managed by the American Communist Party in the interest of the foreign policy of the Soviet Union."

The Louisville *Courier-Journal* reported that same day that "The party's platform, to be submitted to the convention tomorrow, yields to Russia on every point of conflict between East and West, proposing in this way peace."

The Associated Press that day, in a dispatch about the Progressive Party platform, led with this sentence: "The

platform drafted for Henry Wallace's Progressive Party de-
clares it will fight 'for the constitutional rights' of Communists to freedom of speech." That was in the platform but so
were many others things. Plainly, the judgment causing the
decision to lead with the Communist matter was based on
the press's preoccupation with the Communist issue, for
five paragraphs later the story says: "The Democratic platform condemns communism and pledges the party to ex-
pose and prosecute treasonable activities. The Republican
platform calls for enactment of such laws as necessary to ex-
pose the 'treasonable' activities of Communists and defeat
their objectives." This appears to make an individous contrast between the Progressives and the two major parties.
Of course, on this issue, as on others, the Progressives were
far sounder, for this is how the entire plank read: "The Progressive Party will fight for the constitutional rights of Communists and all other political groups to express their views
as the first line in the defense of the liberties of a democratic
people."

Which is what the Democratic and Republican parties
should have done, instead of pandering to the anti-Communist hysteria of the day.

To students of this era, perhaps the favorite "objective"
news story was that written by W. H. Lawrence on July 25
for the next day's *New York Times*. It began: "With Communists and fellow travelers in complete control, the Progressive Party approved its 'peace, freedom and abundance'
platform at its final session late today after shouting down
an attempt to deny formally any blanket endorsement of the
Soviet Union's foreign policy." (This latter was a reference
to the rejection by the convention of the famous Vermont
Resolution discussed in some detail earlier.) One barely
knows how to approach such an assertion. In one sense, of
course, it is entirely true: if you define as "fellow travelers"
all those who believed the national interest was best served
by seeking harmonious relations with the Soviet Union,
who believed, say, as Richard Nixon and Gerald Ford be-

lieved in the late 1960s and early 1970s. But that does not seem to be what Lawrence, the *Times'* best-known political reporter, had in mind. His intention was plain: to label the Wallace party as a Communist front. He, like most of the American press, seemed unable to understand that the Communists had joined Wallace—not the other way around—because Wallace believed that Truman's "get-tough" policy would lead to disaster and because he was doing all he could to change it. Whether the Communists were acting primarily out of concern for the Soviet Union or for the United States, or because they believed both nations would best be served by good relations, whatever their reasons, they, as history has demonstrated, were right. So was Henry Wallace. That is why they joined forces. They were working toward a goal that each had decided was vital.

Perhaps even more celebrated than the William Lawrence story was an article written for the New York *Herald Tribune* of July 25 by the British novelist Rebecca West. Although West devoted much of her piece to assertions of how Communist-controlled the convention was, which everyone else was doing too, what was different was her view of the young people at the convention, a view that perhaps told as much about her as them:

At the Wallace convention there were quite a number of young people who were very horrible indeed. There were the ones who were embryo Babbitts, having their fling before they settled down to safe and narrow lives, stupid young people, too stupid to understand how the world is run and that the present system, for all its faults, took a great deal of patient and intelligent effort, and who therefore wrote off the whole of the past with a sneer; and who were so smug that they saw their own sneering as idealism.

There were others who wore on their faces the signs of a more serious maladjustment. I never saw so many girls with the restless look on their faces that comes of profound insecurity, of consciousness that neither their physical or mental resources were adequate and that they must create a personality somehow, by revolt if nothing else turned up. I never saw so many boys with the sullen eyes and the dropped chins which mean a brain just good enough to grasp the complexities of life and to realize that it would never be able to master them.

Another famous woman writer also reported on the convention, Anne O'Hare McCormick, the *New York Times* columnist. Writing for the *Times* of July 26, she had a totally different view of the young people. She wrote:

The enthusiasm for Wallace was spontaneous, much more so than the uproar for the winning candidate in the Democratic and Republican conclaves. There was real ardor in the rally last night and in the outburst following the nominations in the convention hall in the afternoon.

These participants have never been delegates before. Most of them are as fresh as daisies—and as innocent—in the overworked field of politics. That is one reason why they are here. They want to be active and important. They want a leader who flatters them and works up all their half-articulate fears, frustrations and resentments.

In a way the genuine emotion behind it makes the fanfare more disturbing. . . .

McCormick used these observations to buttress her lead paragraph:

Henry Wallace appeared in Shibe Park last night as the climax of three hours of song, oratory and frenzied money-raising. He made a triumphal entry in a spotlighted car and rode slowly around the baseball field acknowledging the shrill cheers from 25,000 voices and followed by a long trail of whirling, waving figures in a kind of ecstatic dance. It was a striking spectacle, but there was something in the atmosphere, in the play of lights, in the dark mass of shouting people, that was too reminiscent for the comfort of observers who had witnessed similar scenes of acclaim for a potential "savior" in Rome in the Twenties and in Berlin in the early Thirties.

A few more examples of the "objective news stories" emanating from the Progressive convention. In the *Cleveland Plain Dealer* of July 24, a story by Walker S. Buel, Washington bureau chief, appeared under the headline "NEW PARTY HANGS WASH ON COMMUNIST 'LINE.' " Not to be outdone, the *Cleveland News* two days later ran this headline: "U.S. Reds Stamp Their Brand on Wallace's Party," with the following lead, by associate editor J. B. Mullaney, reporting: "The new Progressive Party departed the scene of its founding today with the brand of the sickle and hammer smeared all over its peace, freedom and abundance slogan." And Doris Fleeson, the respected liberal journalist, began her July 26 report to the *St. Louis Post-Dispatch* with these five sentences:

> The country can now choose between the bipartisan foreign policy of the Democrats and the Republicans and the bipartisan foreign policy of the Progressives and Communists.
>
> An earnest right wing here fought gallantly for a terse platform stating "it is not our intention to give blanket endorsement to the foreign policy of any nation."
>
> It argued this would meet criticism of the Progressive Party's tenderness toward Russia and said Russia ought to be able to take criticism too.
>
> The party-liners beat back the heretics.
>
> There is one true church and Stalin is its prophet.

As for the newspaper editorials based on the Progressive convention, they will come as no surprise. The *Worcester* (Massachusetts) *Gazette* of July 27, under a headline, "Communists Hold Reins In Third Party," wrote: "Henry Wallace's Progressive Party now goes before the voters with the Communist label in plain sight. . . ." *The Washington Star* of July 26 began its editorial this way: "It would be entirely fitting if the new Progressive Party of Henry Wallace and his Communist followers were to adopt the Trojan horse as its symbol. . . ." *The Washington Post* of the same day wrote of the "Commies and the trustful or bewildered cranks who constitute the bulk of Mr. Wallace's following. . . ." The *St. Louis Post-Dispatch* ended an editorial by saying, "We have praised Henry Wallace for his services as Secretary of Agriculture, Vice President and Secretary of Commerce. But, as leader of a Communist-inspired third party, we take our leave of him." And this is how the *St. Louis Globe-Democrat* ended its editorial of July 28: "There can no longer be a shadow of doubt about Henry Wallace and his splinter 'gideons.' It is misnamed Progressive. It should more honestly be called the Communist Party."

The Portland *Oregonian* of July 24 wrote of "the vicious alliance between the international Communist Party, fuzzy idealists and misdirected peaceafists . . . ," and the *Springfield* (Massachusetts) *Union* on July 27 commented on "Wallace's abject surrender to the minority group of Communists who from first to last ran his convention. . . ." The *Philadelphia Inquirer* of that same date editorialized that if the convention "had been held in Moscow, instead of in the birthplace of American democracy, it would not have been more subservient to the Politburo." The *Hartford Courant* of July 26 ran its editorial under this headline: "BY THE REDS FOR THE REDS." The *Denver Post* of July 27 called Wallace "a Communist stooge" and the *Cleveland Plain Dealer* of the previous day ran its editorial under the words "Voice of the Kremlin." The *Chicago News,* while making the customary references to the Communists, also wrote that if Wallace becomes President, "we shall get in tune with the Infinite, vibrate in the correct plane, outstare the Evil Eye, reform the witches, overcome all malicious spells and ascend the high road to health and happiness."

And so it went through the entire campaign. Big city, small town; Republican and Democrat; North, South, East, West; it made no difference. The press was out to get Wallace—not out of malice, except for that segment of the press still trying to do in FDR and using Wallace as a handy surrogate, but out of the conviction that he was a menace. The main theme was of Wallace as instrument, conscious or unconscious, of the Kremlin. A subtheme often played was that of Wallace the mystic, the woolly-minded, fuzzy thinker, the addled idealist.

One can only assume that the press was not very good at its fundamental job: gathering facts and examining them. Take the coverage of the Progressive convention's action in rejecting the Vermont Resolution. Although it would have been practical public relations to have adopted it, the resolution was clearly redundant. There was nothing in the platform that gave "blanket endorsement to the foreign policy" of the Soviet Union or any other nation. Any reporter worth his pay should have recognized that. And any journalist—reporter at the scene or editor at home—should have recognized that there was a quantum jump, that did not exist, between criticism of the United States and support of the Soviet Union. The platform was explicit in speaking of the "joint" responsibility of the two powers for peace and it explicitly rejected appeasement. The press had an obligation to examine Wallace's criticisms. It seldom did; it was generally content to dismiss them without examination as the product of Communist-inspiration or some other such justification of intellectual laziness or intellectual timidity.

The press professed to be horrified by McCarthyism and, much, much later, by the Vietnam war, but the history of the postwar period seems to prove that the press is more often cheering section than skeptical interrogator. One wonders how long the skepticism induced by Vietnam and Watergate will last and whether the press will return to the easier and more comfortable role of admirer, and friend, of the powerful. The press likes its perquisites: the drinks, the dinners, the confidences of the mighty. It is not content to learn "inside" information; it wants to be inside. It has not learned that it is welcome inside the Establishment only so long as it is useful to the Establishment, and not a moment longer. It prefers a cozy relationship, not the adversary relationship that is its only justification. Unless it is prepared instantly to turn on its friends—and what decent person is—the press should not make friends of those in power. To be polite and courteous and fair, by all means; but to establish a friendship with a politician, is to establish a conflict of interest.

The press in Henry Wallace's day, and for much longer, was a part of the Establishment to which he was posing a basic challenge. The press did not stand aside, subjecting the various arguments to rigorous scrutiny. Instead, it plunged in as defender of the established order.

It must be conceded that Henry Wallace did not do much to help himself with reporters. He plainly dreaded press conferences and hated to prepare for them. Even when his aides insisted that he go over potentially embarrassing questions—his press director, Ralph Shikes, threatened to quit if this weren't done—Wallace never became good at the give-and-take of such encounters.[9] He felt the press was hostile—as often it was—and he sometimes lost his temper and became sarcastic. He shared Truman's talent for putting his foot in his mouth, but since he was in a much more precarious situation, with the press always waiting to pounce on him, he got into more trouble because of it.

This is not to suggest that the press should have been easy on him. It should be tough on every politician but it should concentrate on the issues and not be distracted by less important matters, as the press was then by the Communist question. Nor should the press be influenced by a politician's skill at cultivating the press, a skill Wallace totally lacked, to his detriment. Indeed, the press should be most skeptical of those politicians, like John Kennedy, who are good with the press, for those who cultivate the press almost invariably do so so they can use it.

10

Prophet True or False?

There seems little doubt that Henry Wallace was physically and psychically exhausted by the Presidential campaign, probably more from the magnitude of the defeat than the enormous expenditure of physical and emotional resources. Nor is there much doubt that he was at least somewhat embittered, especially by the lack of support he had received from labor and blacks, two groups he had befriended more than any other major politician. But the truth is that labor had eagerly enlisted in the Cold War, and the blacks, however much they admired him and appreciated his unique campaign, especially in the South, recognized that he could do nothing for them. And, as time went on, Wallace became increasingly bitter against the American Communists, believing that they had used him and that they were largely responsible for his poor showing. They *had* used him, but only in the sense that any group uses a politician who serves its interests and shares it goals. Of course, Communist support had hurt him, but there was no way he could have repudiated it without violating his own principles and without adding to the anti-Communist hysteria, the repression of civil liberties, that he so rightly, and bravely, and futilely fought against.

At first, however, Wallace simply continued his criticism of Harry Truman's foreign policy. During the spring of 1949, he attacked the formation of the North Atlantic Treaty Organization and when he appeared before the Senate Foreign Relations Committee in May, he recalled a bitter prophecy that history would vindicate, asserting that "two years ago when President Truman announced the Truman Doctrine of containing Russia and Communism at every point, I predicted that it would cause us to bleed from every pore."[1]

But increasingly he retreated from public affairs to an earlier love, agriculture, devoting more and more of this time to the breeding of chickens and strawberries at his farm in South Salem. But when the Progressive Party held its second national convention, in Chicago at the end of February 1950, Henry Wallace appeared briefly to give the major address. His concern with the Communist issue was evident in his speech:

The Progressive Party believes as Roosevelt believed—that the keystone of American foreign policy should be based not merely on friendship and understanding with the Western powers, but also with the Russian, the Chinese, the Latin American and the colonial peoples. Enemies of progress have therefore stigmatized us as being apologists for Russia and for Communism. We inadvertently gave these enemies ammunition to shoot at us when the Progressive Party turned down the Vermont Resolution at our Founding Convention. That resolution stated: "Although we are critical of the present foreign policy of the United States, it is not our intention to give blanket endorsement to the foreign policy of any nation."

I know everybody in this hall really believes in this resolution and is willing to see the sense of it adopted in our statement on foreign policy. We must not allow anyone the slightest, legitimate reason for believing that any working member of our Party puts Rome, Moscow or London ahead of the United States. We are neither nationalist, racist, nor chauvinist—we stand before the American people as being Americans first, last and all the time. . . .

But before our greatly disturbed peace-loving fellow Americans join with the Progressive Party they will want the facts—not the wild distortions of a prejudiced press—but the actual facts about the attitude of the Progressive Party toward the Communists.

First, it is inevitable that all peace-loving people in times like these should be attacked as Communist dupes. The character assassin is always active in a free democracy. Jefferson, Jackson, and Lincoln all suffered from the foulest attacks. Roosevelt and all his closest friends have been and still are subjected to such abuse as to cause all but the hardiest souls to refuse to have anything to do with government. It was to be expected, therefore, that everyone who fought the Truman Doctrine and the Arms Pact would be branded as pro-Communist.

Second, the policies of the Progressive Party are its own. They are determined by its own members acting democratically within their local organizations and through our national convention and elected party committees. Our policies are not determined and controlled by anyone who owes his supreme allegiance to any other party and we do not—and will not—permit any organized factions or groups within our party.

Third, our principles are vastly different from those of the Communist Party. We do not believe in the one-party system of government for the United States. Our philosophy is not based upon the principles of Marxism and Leninism. Our program is based upon progressive capitalism, not socialism. Our program is not a communist program, nor a socialist program—it is the only program that can save capitalism from itself.

Fourth, the Progressive Party calls to the support of its programs all those who believe wholeheartedly in it no matter what party they belong to. We will not attempt the purge of any individual because of past or present labels. At the same time, we can't waste our time on endless bickering about fine points of doctrine which have little to do with the present world-wide tragedy. Sectarianism should have no place in the Progressive Party.

Fifth, as we approach the 1950 elections, the Progressive Party must convince the American people that we are fighting for peace, not because any foreign power wants us to fight for peace but because we understand the deep needs of the American people and the world. We must make it clear that there are no concealed strings manipulating us.

Sixth, the Progressive Party stands for civil liberties for all. Civil liberties are indivisible. We believe in civil liberties in Eastern Europe but we recognize that except in the case of Czechoslovakia there has been no democratic tradition on which to build. We know that civil liberties will rapidly disappear in the United States as the Cold War is fanned into white heat by H-bomb planning.

The Communists have their party. We have ours. We agree with the Communists that peace with Russia is possible—but that doesn't make us Communists. We agree with the Democrats and

Republicans that capitalism can be made to work—but that doesn't make us Democrats or Republicans.[2]

Although there was little or nothing here that Wallace had not said in 1948, this was plainly his best statement on the Communist issue. But it is doubtful that if he had made it in 1948, it would have made much difference. A few, a very few, might have had their fears about Communist domination of the party satisfied; to most people, however, only a drumming of the Communist out of the party, strong attacks on the Soviet Union, and greatly reduced criticism of the United States would have sufficed. But that would not have been Henry Wallace or the Progressive Party and there would have been no reason for the campaign. And even then few votes would have been changed.

The irony is that when Wallace was so explicit about the differences between the Progressive and the Communist parties, the Communists were proportionately higher in number than they had been in 1948, for by 1950 the Progressive Party was little more than a hollow shell. The terrible defeat in 1948, the escalating anti-Communist fervor, and the harsher Cold War had driven away most of the membership. Nonetheless, the Communists did not object in 1950, publicly at least, because they were still hoping that the Progressive Party might amount to something and it could do so only if it were evident that it was not a Communist front, something, despite what the ADA and the press said, the Communists never wanted. And they recognized that without Henry Wallace the Progressive Party would be nothing.

Although Wallace did concentrate on the Communist issue in his last major speech as the head of the Progressive Party, he continued his attack on Truman's foreign policy, terming containment a failure, something rather evident with the victory of the Communists in China and the development of the atomic bomb by Russia, despite American efforts to keep the process to itself. He also decried the lack of protection for dissent in the United States.

But most of all, Wallace was preoccupied by the hydrogen bomb, which Truman on January 31 had announced the United States would build. Wallace called for:

"1. A public declaration by the North Atlantic Pact nations that they will not be the first to use atomic weapons. To be followed immediately by:

"2. Initiation of official public diplomatic negotiations between the United States and Russia to continue until an agreement has been reached providing for the renunciation of the use of atomic energy as a destructive weapon. This agreement will include a method of inspection through the UN to insure the carrying out of the agreement."

In this, Wallace anticipated the later efforts of Adlai Stevenson and Nikita Khrushchev and John Kennedy to halt or slow down the atomic arms race.

Wallace was also deeply concerned about the enormous expenditures on weapons of war:

There never has been—and never will be—any constructive answer in force. The only real answer, as I pointed out long ago, is in a genuine, non-political Point Four program applied in a big way through the United Nations to all the countries of the world— including Russia and the New China. Today we spend about $600 on destruction for every dollar we are planning to spend on Point Four. I would reverse this and spend at least $5 on Point Four for every $1 spent on arms.

We in the United States now rely on a Department of National Defense for our security. I say we should be relying on a Department of Peace for our security. Such a Department of Peace should devote all its efforts to bringing higher living standards for all peoples when every man shall live without fear under his own vine and fig tree and all peoples shall flow to the Mountain of the Lord and each shall worship in his own way.

That was the last of Henry Wallace, the Protestant evangelist visionary who wanted to substitute idealism for the Cold War. Shortly after the Korean war broke out on June

24, 1950, the Progressive Party leadership wanted to issue a statement critical of the UN Security Council's call for armed resistance to the North Koreans and opposed to any UN action until Russia returned to the council. (Russia had absented itself in protest against the delegation of Nationalist China's being retained in the UN seat to the exclusion of the Communist government that actually controlled China.) The Progressive executive committee also called for the seating of the Chinese Communist government, which was to be blocked by the United States for more than two decades. The executive committee met with Wallace several times in July to try to compose a statement than would reconcile his views and those of the others. But the effort failed, and on July 15 Wallace released his own statement. His sense of torment is evident in it. Arguing that if the People's Republic of China had been seated in the UN, as he had favored since the Chinese Communist victory in 1949, "the world would be in a much more peaceful state than it is today," he also criticized Russia for boycotting UN agencies because the Chinese Communist government had *not* been seated:

From the time I left Government in 1946 I have done my best to save my country and the world from this day. I denounced the Truman Doctrine and the sending of arms abroad. I denounced using our economic aid for purposes of political pressure. I knew such methods could only end by making us hated by all the peoples of the world. In time of peace I have felt completely free to criticize my own Government, provided such criticism was looking toward peace and world understanding of the need for directing the aspirations of the Common Man into constructive channels. Today the U.S. is at war with North Korea. Congress has not declared war but that is a technicality because the overwhelming majority of the Congress and the Senate are in favor of fighting the North Koreans. . . .

I hold no brief for the past actions of either the U.S. or Russia but when my country is at war and the UN sanctions that war, I am on the side of my country and the UN. . . .

Wallace also accepted the then widely held view that "Undoubtedly the Russians could have prevented the attack by the North Koreans and undoubtedly they could stop the attack at any time they wish. . . ."[3] There has in recent years, however, been increasing skepticism about this, for as the United States learned to its sorrow, presumed puppets often refuse to dance to the master's bidding. Furthermore, the UN sanction of a military response to the North Korean attack was not an entirely satisfactory justification, since the UN was at the time totally dominated by the United States and the United States was using that domination to give an international flavor to a decision in fact made unilaterally. And since both the North Koreans and the South Koreans, each headed by a repressive, authoritarian leader, had for months been engaging in increasingly severe battles along the artificial frontier, the war might well have been considered a civil war in which the UN might be better employed as a mediator and peacemaker.

Wallace, however, was acting on the basis of the facts as he understood them, and if his understanding were faulty or incomplete, in that he was no different from most Americans. From that time on he increasingly adopted Truman's line, although he often offered qualifications that harked back to his earlier positions. The ultimate recantation took place on February 13, 1962, when he appeared at a dinner honoring Truman, and told him, ". . . I'm glad you fired me when you did."[4]

Yet throughout the 1950s and early 1960s, Wallace continued to call for support of the UN and for generous economic aid to the underdeveloped nations. Although he did make public appearances occasionally and once in a while wrote an article, usually explaining how he had been wrong earlier, Wallace faded from public view. Nonetheless, he maintained a lively correspondence, dealing both with politics and his beloved farming. And he remained active physically. In 1964, when he was seventy-six, he felt the first pains of what was to be a fatal disease while he was climbing an ancient pyramid in Guatemala. At first he assumed the pain was caused by the strenuous exertion, but when it persisted, he sought medical treatment. The condition was diagnosed as amyotrophic lateral sclerosis, the rare disease that had caused the death of the great Yankee first baseman Lou Gehrig. Even as he lay dying, Wallace maintained a scientist's interest in the course of his disease, keeping a personal record of its progress in the hope that his medical treatment would contribute to a cure of the disease.

When he died on November 18, 1965, in Danbury (Connecticut) Hospital, he was little known to most of the still few antiwar activists who were beginning to make almost exactly the same criticisms of American foreign policy that he had made a political generation before. One wonders if—one hopes that—the pendulum of his thinking had begun to swing back to his courageous but futile struggle against the Cold War policies of Harry Truman, policies that first got us involved in Asia, got us mired so disastrously in an Indochinese civil war at a horrible cost to the people of Indochina, at a cost of fifty thousand American lives, at the cost of domestic dissension unequaled since our Civil War, and at the cost of the election of Richard M. Nixon.

Even if in his later years Henry Wallace had himself been swept up by the anti-Communist tide, psychically shell-shocked by the fierceness of the anti-Communist assault, he had already by 1945, with his service as secretary of agriculture and as Vice President, established himself as a major figure in American history. With his prophetic fight against the Cold War crusade at home and abroad, he established himself as one of America's authentic heroes. The magnitude of Henry Wallace's defeat cannot obscure the prophetic quality of his campaign. As is so often the case, the visionary, "woolly-minded" idealist was in many ways more realistic than the "hard-nosed realists" who were so proud of their toughness. To insure peace by preparing for war, to use the kind of slogan so dear to Truman and his successors, almost invariably insures war, not peace.

This is not to suggest that the Henry Wallace of the late 1940s was without flaw. His "progressive capitalism" was more a romantic notion than a carefully thought-out program. He was aware—by the standards of businessmen, incredibly aware—of the failings of capitalism American style, but he never really articulated what had to be done to replace it or even reform it. And Wallace should have paid more attention to practical politics, for as squalid as politics often is, it is the means in a democracy by which things are done. If in 1948 he had made the kind of speech about the role of the Communist Party that he made in 1950, it would have helped—a little. If he had paid closer heed to the Progressive Party convention and had caused the Vermont Resolution to be adopted, redundant as it was, it would have helped—a little.

As an evangelist, Wallace was sometimes a bit shrill, extreme, apocalyptic in his language. The Christian ethic of duty before self is noble, but it can be off-putting, especially to those who need convincing not scolding. Wallace was a politician, not a preacher—although one must concede it is often hard in America to tell the difference. What it often comes down to is whether or not the politician is preaching the sermon the electorate wants to hear. In 1948 the electorate did not want to hear what Wallace had to say. Still, Wallace might have been more explicit as to how peace with Russia could have been sought and how it would benefit the American people. But even if Wallace's campaign was not as skillful as it might have been, it is probably true that no campaign, winning or losing, is as good as it should be, for campaigns by their nature are chaotic affairs, much like wars, in which the leaders have little idea of what they should be doing or even of what is actually happening. And if Wallace's campaign had shortcomings, there was never a chance, not even the slightest chance, that he would win—whereas all Thomas E. Dewey had to do was lean out and pluck the brass ring, and he couldn't even bring himself to do that.

After all his years in politics, Wallace should have recognized that the press is crucial and that it likes to be coddled, that even the most sophisticated reporters from the biggest city newspapers or the great broadcast networks like to have private chats with the candidate, and that they leave such chats feeling warm toward the candidate even though he has said little different from what he said every day in public speeches. Most important journalists have very big egos and their care and feeding is an important part of politics.

Related to that was Wallace's lack of personal warmth. It is to his credit that he did not cultivate an artificial warmth as so many politicians do, but this lack is a great handicap in politics. No one could doubt Wallace's genuine idealism, his genuine concern about the lives of people the world over. Indeed, it is probably better as an absolute matter that a politician care more about people in the abstract than as individuals, for then he is more likely to put the welfare of the nation or the world above the welfare of a political pal. Wallace genuinely believed that if you shared his ideals, you should not need any personal rewards, any words of thanks, any comradeship: you do what you do out of conviction and for no other reason; but politicians, as much as anyone else, maybe more, need to feel that there is a personal dimension to what they do. In an ideal world, Wallace would have been right, but he lived in a human not an ideal world, and he seldom recognized that politicians, like journalists, needed a little coddling.

And even though Wallace did not want to contribute to the anti-Communist hysteria, he could have been somewhat more critical of the Soviet Union, not only as good politics but as a matter of fact. No doubt Wallace, like many Progressives, was oversensitive on this matter, but that is hardly surprising given the atmosphere of the time, when dissent in the United States was about as welcome as it was in Russia. Although the United States as much the more

powerful nation had a greater responsibility for good relations, the Soviet Union was not without blame. Indeed,
peace was, as the Progressive platform said, the "joint" responsibility of both nations.

Nonetheless, despite these and, no doubt, other criticisms that can be made of him, Henry Wallace was essentially right and Harry Truman was essentially and tragically
wrong. Henry Wallace said that the United States could not
purchase reliable friends. He said that the United States
would end up supporting corrupt, incompetent, and repressive dictators all over the world. He said that the United
States would not be able to stamp out revolution the world
over. He said that the effort to contain communism would
be costly in American blood and treasure. He said that a
crusade against communism would lead to the repression of
civil liberties at home. He said that American foreign policy
would lead to militarism. He said that the Truman Doctrine,
the Marshall Plan, and NATO would divide the world into
hostile camps. He said that Truman's foreign policy would
cause the colonial peoples of the world to identify Russia
and communism as their friends and the United States as
their enemy. He said, in short, that Harry Truman's foreign
policy would lead to disaster at home and abroad. Henry
Wallace was right.

The 1948 election was the last great debate before American foreign policy settled into the course that brought
death, destruction, and misery to so many millions. The
Truman administration, the labor movement, the Cold War
liberals, the press crucified Henry Wallace, believing they
were serving the national interest. But Henry Wallace and
his supporters had a clearer vision of the future. Harry Truman was a decent and sincere man, a successful politician
but one without vision. Henry Wallace was not much of a
politician but he was a prophet. Politicians win or lose in
the here and now, and if they win they enjoy their satisfac-
tions in the present. Prophets often go to their graves torn

by doubt and misgiving and by that worst of frustrations, not knowing. What a terrible torment, never to know, to die thinking perhaps you were wrong, but hoping that you would be vindicated by history. Henry Wallace has been vindicated by history.

Notes

1: WALLACE AND ROOSEVELT

1. October 29, 1948. Henry Wallace Papers, University of Iowa (henceforth HWP). His papers, correspondence, speeches, and other material are filed chronologically.
2. The term "Red-baiting" may be unfamiliar to some younger readers, but not too long ago the climate of the nation was such that it was possible to discredit an opponent simply by calling him a Communist. The accusation alone was usually a sufficient smear. It was a time when it was difficult to be proud to be an American.
3. In this era of revulsion against the Vietnam war and the Cold War that led to it, everyone you meet who was of age then seems to have voted for Wallace, just as everyone apparently voted for George McGovern in 1972.
4. Curtis D. Macdougall, *Gideon's Army* (henceforth Macdougall). So pervasive was the atmosphere of fear that when Macdougall did his research, in 1954 and 1955, many of those who had bravely participated in the Wallace campaign were afraid to speak with him or did so only with the utmost reluctance.
5. The word "liberal" is a difficult one, for those who use it either proudly or pejoratively. I—quite arbitrarily—term as liberals those members of the Democratic Party who generally supported Harry Truman's policy against the Soviet Union. Those who stood with Wallace I term "progressives." No doubt, some in each camp will be affronted by my choice but it seems the only way through a semantic mine field.
6. Letter from Bruce Catton to Edward L. Schapsmeier, September 23, 1963; in Schapsmeier Collection, HWP.
7. *Wallace's Farmer*, November 14, 1924. Wallace's early views are discussed in Norman D. Markowitz, *The Rise and Fall of the People's Century: Henry A. Wallace and American Liberalism, 1941–1948*, pp. 103–104 ff.; also in Macdougall, pp. 90–91 ff.
8. A good account of the taming of the rebellion appears in Jo-

seph P. Lash, *Eleanor and Franklin*, pp. 800–802 ff.; a good concise discussion appears also in Markowitz, pp. 28–30 ff.

9. Frances Perkins. *The Roosevelt I Knew* (New York: Viking, 1946), p. 130.
10. Samuel I. Rosenman, *Working with Roosevelt* (New York: Harper, 1952), p. 206.
11. Eleanor Roosevelt, *This I Remember* (New York: Harper, 1949), pp. 216–18.
12. Rosenman, p. 217.
13. A fine, concise account of this immensely complicated subject appears in John Morton Blum, ed., *The Price of Vision: The Diary of Henry A. Wallace 1942–1946*, pp. 24–25 ff. The diary (henceforth *Diary*) that Blum so superbly edited and annotated makes fascinating reading for anyone with an interest in the 1940s.
14. *Diary*, p. 27.
15. This Byzantine bureaucratic struggle is discussed in just about every book about the Roosevelt Presidency. Blum gives a good, short account, although his sympathies are clearly with Wallace.
16. *Diary*, pp. 635–36 ff.
17. Ibid., p. 638.
18. Macdougall, p. 91.
19. Ibid., p. 92.
20. *Diary*, p. 351.
21. Ibid., p. 352.
22. Ibid., p. 355.
23. Macdougall, who attended the convention, gives a lively account of the maneuverings and quotes a number of politicians who were told by FDR that Wallace was his choice, pp. 14–15 ff.
24. *Diary*, pp. 360–61 ff.
25. Ibid., p. 360.
26. Ibid.
27. Ibid., p. 367.
28. Macdougall, p. 6.
29. Ibid.
30. Ibid., p. 7.
31. Ibid., p. 8.
32. Lash, p. 912.

33. *Diary,* p. 371.
34. Ibid.
35. Ibid., p. 372.
36. Ibid., p. 380.
37. Ibid., p. 391.
38. Ibid., p. 411.
39. Ibid., p. 382.
40. Ibid., p. 385.
41. Ibid., p. 390.
42. CIO, *Proceedings of the National Convention,* pp. 137–38.
43. Cited in Markowitz, p. 167.
44. *Diary,* p. 406.
45. Ibid., p. 417.
46. Ibid, p. 422.
47. Ibid., p. 401.
48. This is discussed in Macdougall, pp. 11–12 ff. He also provides the FDR-Jones exchange of letters.
49. Cited in Macdougall, p. 11.
50. Ibid., p. 12.
51. Ibid., p. 13.
52. Ibid.
53. Ibid.
54. Cited in Lash, p. 922.
55. Ibid.
56. Macdougall, p. 58.
57. Some of these messages, many of them moving, can be found in HWP, Boxes 33 and 34.
58. HWP.

2: WALLACE SPLITS WITH TRUMAN

1. HWP, April 17, 1945.
2. *Diary,* p. 263.
3. HWP, dated April 24, but mailed April 25, 1945.
4. HWP, mailed April 21, 1945.
5. HWP, mailed February 27, 1946.
6. HWP, mailed June 26, 1946.
7. This might be a good time to note, with some shame, that I was not a Wallace supporter in 1948. Indeed, so disinterested

in politics was I then that I cannot even recall being aware of his tumultuous visit to Providence, Rhode Island, or his addressing the students at Brown University, which I then attended. To the extent I cared, I was vaguely for Thomas E. Dewey. A few years later, in my ADA-liberal years, this seemed like the rankest heresy, but more recently I have wondered if the election of Dewey, the dread of which was the only reason many liberals and progressives voted for Truman, would have been much worse or even, in foreign affairs, perhaps even better.

8. The HWP have been microfilmed, and will be available in many libraries. His edited diaries are available in the fine Blum edition, and the complete diaries were opened in November 1975, ten years after his death.
9. *Diary*, p. 437.
10. Ibid., p. 439.
11. Ibid., p. 440.
12. Macdougall, p. 22.
13. The information in this paragraph is from pp. 58 and 59 of Thomas G. Paterson, *Soviet-American Confrontation.* This is a superb account of the economic aspect—originally perhaps the most important—of the developing United States–Soviet conflict.
14. *Diary,* pp. 446–47.
15. Ibid., p. 443.
16. Ibid., p. 450. Although Truman had angered Stalin by abruptly terminating most Lend-Lease on May 8, 1945, a limited amount destined for the war against Japan was still being shipped to Siberia.
17. Ibid., p. 447.
18. Ibid., p. 448.
19. Ibid., p. 454.
20. HWP, June 13, 1945.
21. HWP, June 27, 1945.
22. HWP, July 30, 1945.
23. *Diary*, p. 458.
24. Ibid., p. 480.
25. Barton J. Bernstein and Allen J. Matusow, *The Truman Administration: A Documentary History* (New York: Harper & Row, 1968), p. 220.

26. Ibid., p. 221.

27. *Diary*, p. 482.

28. Ibid., p. 485.

29. HWP, October 11, 1945, Department of Commerce, Statement by Henry A. Wallace.

30. *Diary*, p. 494.

31. A great deal has been written about this terrible injustice. One good book is Philip M. Stern's *The Oppenheimer Case* (New York: Harper & Row, 1969).

32. *Diary*, p. 496.

33. Ibid., p. 497.

34. Bernstein and Matusow, p. 223.

35. *Diary*, p. 516.

36. William G. Carleton, *The Revolution in American Foreign Policy*, p. 132.

37. *Diary*, p. 490.

38. Ibid., p. 503.

39. The refusal to make this loan is discussed in detail in Paterson.

40. *Diary*, p. 499.

41. Ibid., p. 506.

42. Ibid., p. 520.

43. Ibid., p. 523.

44. Ibid., pp. 524–25.

45. Ibid., p. 506.

46. Ibid., p. 478.

47. Ibid., p. 508.

48. Ibid., pp. 509–10 ff.

49. Ibid., p. 528.

50. Ibid., p. 530.

51. Ibid., p. 528.

52. Harry S. Truman, *Memoirs*, vol. I, p. 606.

53. HWP, December 27, 1945.

54. *Diary*, p. 536.

55. Ibid. As an indication of the kind of dinner guests that Joseph Alsop had regularly, on this occasion there were Supreme Court Justice Hugo Black, FDR's former secretary Grace Tully, Benjamin Cohen; one of the legendary New Dealers then highly placed in the State Department; and Charles "Chip" Bohlen, adviser on Russian affairs to a succession of Presidents.

56. HWP, letterhead of letter from ICC/ASP Executive Director Hannah Dorner.

57. Macdougall, p. 55.

58. *Diary*, p. 547.

59. Ibid., p. 550.

60. Ibid., pp. 556–57.

61. Ibid., pp. 558–59.

62. Ibid., p. 561.

63. HWP, letter dated March 14, 1946, filed March 15, 1946; Truman reply March 20, 1946.

64. *Diary*, p. 563.

65. HWP, March 21, 1946.

66. *Diary*, p. 563; Truman, vol. I, pp. 609–11.

67. I got to know Hoffman in later years when he served, despite advanced years, as the enthusiastic and effective head of the United Nations Special Fund, a sort of Marshall Plan outside the Cold War context. Whatever his private views may have been, he did not hesitate to serve UN interests even when Washington made it plain it disapproved.

68. *Diary*, p. 560.

69. Ibid., p. 562.

70. Ibid., p. 563.

71. Ibid.

72. Ibid., p. 567.

73. Macdougall, p. 56–57.

74. For these paragraphs I have drawn heavily on Macdougall, pp. 55–59.

75. HWP, April 26, 1946.

76. HWP, June 14, 1946.

77. Alonzo L. Hamby, *Beyond the New Deal: Harry S. Truman and American Liberalism*, pp. 76–77.

78. HWP, July 23, 1946; filed under September 17, 1946, the day it was released to the press. The entire text was also included in the Blum edition of the Wallace *Diary*, pp. 589–601.

79. Truman, vol. I, p. 612.

80. *Diary*, p. 602.

81. Ibid., p. 604.

82. Ibid., p. 609.

83. The growing talk of a third party and the growing discontent

with Harry Truman which prompted it, is discussed in Macdougall, pp. 42–43 ff.

84. *Diary*, p. 612.

85. Interview with C. B. Baldwin, July 18, 1974.

86. Macdougall, p. 60.

87. Cabell Phillips, *The Truman Presidency*, p. 130.

88. Phillips, a fine Washington correspondent for *The New York Times*, gives a good, concise account of this entire extraordinary episode, pp. 148–49 ff.

89. HWP, speech file, September 12, 1946. The original handwritten draft is also available. Blum's version is in pp. 661–69.

90. The Harry S. Truman Library, Independence, Missouri, Official File, September 14, 1946.

91. Truman, vol. I, p. 612.

92. Cited in Macdougall, p. 70.

93. *Diary*, p. 614.

94. Macdougall, p. 70.

95. *Diary*, p. 615.

96. Margaret Truman, *Harry S. Truman*, p. 317.

97. Harry S. Truman, vol. I, p. 614.

98. *Diary*, pp. 617–18 ff.

99. Harry S. Truman, vol. I, p. 613.

100. Margaret Truman, p. 317.

101. HWP, September 16, 17, and 20, 1946.

102. Phillips, p. 153.

103. Columbia University Oral History, 5028. Cited in *Diary*, p. 629.

104. HWP, September 20, 1946.

105. Truman Library, Official File, September 20, 1946.

106. *Diary*, p. 631.

3: WALLACE DECIDES TO RUN

1. The number of letters cited by Wallace in letters to Norman Thomas October 2, 1946, and Buford C. Tynes, October 23, 1946; HWP.

2. Macdougall, p. 97.

3. ADA Papers, Wisconsin State Historical Society. "Union for

Democratic Action Statement on Henry Wallace" in "Remarks of Dr. James Loeb, Jr., . . . September 29, 1946."

4. *CIO News,* October 7, 1946, p. 7; Norman D. Markowitz, *The Rise and Fall of the People's Century,* p. 202.
5. Markowitz, p. 203. This pivotal conference is discussed in some detail by Alonzo L. Hamby, *Beyond the New Deal: Harry S. Truman and American Liberalism,* and by Macdougall.
6. Macdougall, p. 106.
7. HWP, September 24, 1946.
8. Ibid., September 24, 1946; October 23, 1946.
9. Ibid., October 2, 1946.
10. See a fine book, *The Press and the Cold War,* by James Aronson (New York: Bobbs-Merrill, 1970).
11. HWP, October 11, 1946.
12. Ibid., October 16, 1946.
13. Ibid.
14. Ibid., October 18, 1946.
15. Cited in Macdougall, p. 99.
16. Ibid.
17. Ibid., p. 101.
18. Ibid.
19. Cited in Hamby, p. 138.
20. HWP, November 13, 1946.
21. Ibid., November 19, 1946.
22. Cited in Hamby, p. 145. This book is also discussed by Joseph P. Lash in *Eleanor: The Years Alone,* pp. 90–91.
23. Letter to Joseph Alsop, December 5, 1946. Cited by Lash, pp. 90–91.
24. HWP, November 28, 1946; December 10, 1946.
25. The entire Wallace speech is printed in Macdougall, beginning on p. 114. He discusses the founding of the PCA in great detail. Hamby and Markowitz also provide good, concise discussions.
26. HWP, January 3, 1947; January 8, 1947.
27. Cited in Dwight Macdonald, *Henry Wallace: The Man and the Myth,* pp. 150–53.
28. HWP, January 13, 1947.
29. Ibid., January 19, 1947.
30. Ibid., January 23, 1947.
31. Ibid., February 3, 1947.

32. Ibid., February 6, 1947; February 8, 1947.

33. Ibid., February 14, 1947.

34. Ibid.; Joseph M. Jones, *The Fifteen Weeks,* pp. 138–39 ff. Jones was the top-level State Department aide picked by Acheson to write the first draft of Truman's historic and history-making speech.

35. Harry S. Truman, *Memoirs,* vol. II, p. 128.

36. Jones, p. 122.

37. HWP, March 13, 1947; speech file.

38. The Wallace correspondence file has a great many of these letters. Not a few of them are still moving.

39. HWP, March 17, 1947.

40. Margaret Truman, *Harry S. Truman,* p. 343. This writer lives in Greenwich Village.

41. The speech was run as an advertisement in *The Washington Post* on April 15, 1947.

42. There is a good discussion of the loyalty program in Macdougall, pp. 128–29 ff.

43. Ibid., p. 135. He has a good discussion of the European trip on pp. 133 ff.

44. Ibid., p. 136.

45. Cited in Lash, p. 94.

46. Truman Library, Official File, April 14, 1947; April 16, 1947; April 23, 1947.

47. This melancholy era is discussed in many books, notably, *A Journal of the Plague Years* by Stefan Kanfer (New York: Atheneum, 1973).

48. Macdougall, p. 158.

49. Ibid., p. 160.

50. *Baltimore Morning Sun,* June 3, 1947.

51. Truman Library, Clark M. Clifford Papers; declassified February 20, 1973.

52. *The Washington Star,* June 13, 1947.

53. Macdougall, p. 169.

54. Ibid., p. 187.

55. A copy of this speech was provided by Beanie Baldwin.

56. Macdougall, p. 200.

57. "Reports of Wallace Democrats in California," p. 5, Truman Library, Papers of J. Howard McGrath, Wallace Folder.

58. Macdougall, p. 212.

59. Ibid., p. 224.
60. HWP, November 12, 1947.
61. Macdougall, p. 225. He quotes the entire Baldwin memo and discusses in extraordinary detail the events of the next few days.
62. Ibid., p. 233. The entire letter is quoted.
63. Ibid., p. 240.
64. Ibid., p. 241.
65. Ibid.
66. Ibid., p. 244.
67. HWP, December 19, 1947.

4: THE HOPEFUL MONTHS

1. In a pamphlet distributed by National Wallace for President Committee.
2. The famous Clifford memo of November 1947 can be found at the Truman Library and should be studied by students of practical politics.
3. Macdougall, p. 327.
4. HWP, December 31, 1947.
5. Joseph P. Lash, *Eleanor: The Years Alone,* p. 143.
6. Ibid., pp. 143–44.
7. Macdougall, p. 325.
8. Ibid.
9. Both cited in Alonzo L. Hamby, *Beyond the New Deal: Harry S. Truman and American Liberalism,* p. 230.
10. Macdougall, p. 311.
11. Truman Library, Papers of J. Howard McGrath.
12. Wallace's testimony was made public in a pamphlet by the National Wallace for President Committee. It makes good, solid reading even now.
13. Macdougall, p. 332.
14. Ibid., p. 333.
15. Progressive Party Papers, University of Iowa. These papers (henceforth PPP) were collected by Curtis Macdougall and donated, when his book was completed, to the Wallace Collection at the university; Box 18, Folder 78.
16. *The New York Times,* February 12, 1975.

17. Ibid., March 18, 1948.
18. Public Papers of the Presidents, 1948, pp. 186–90.
19. Truman, *Memoirs,* vol. II, p. 216.
20. Pamphlet distributed by the National Wallace for President Committee; included in HWP.
21. Henry A. Wallace, *Toward World Peace.*
22. *Political Affairs,* May 1948, pp. 400–411.
23. HWP, April 2, 1948.
24. Margaret Truman, *Harry S. Truman;* Merle Miller, *Plain Speaking: An Oral Biography of Harry S. Truman.*
25. Macdougall, p. 349.
26. Truman Library, Papers of Clark M. Clifford.
27. Macdougall, p. 351.
28. Prepared text distributed by National Wallace for President Committee; available in HWP.
29. Wallace's letter to Stalin and Stalin's reply are available in a number of places in the HWP and PPP.
30. Letter from Lewis Frank to Wallace, April 18, 1948; James Wechsler in *The New York Post,* May 19, 1948; Macdougall, p. 357.
31. Macdougall, p. 356.
32. Ibid., p. 368.
33. HWP, May 29, 1948.
34. Macdougall, p. 423.

5: DOWNHILL ALL THE WAY

1. Mildred Strunk, ed., "The Quarter's Polls," *Public Opinion Quarterly,* 12 (Fall 1948), p. 549; 12 (Winter 1948–1949), p. 762.
2. John J. Abt Memo to All State Directors, June 22, 1948; Statement by Lee Pressman, July 20, 1948. PPP, Box 44, Folder 166.
3. Macdougall's awesomely detailed discussion of the platform and the convention begins on p. 534.
4. PPP, Box 18, Folder 78.
5. *Cleveland Plain Dealer,* July 21, 1948.
6. PPP, Box 18, Folder 78.
7. Macdougall, p. 396. Scattered throughout the three volumes are scores of instances of violence and harassment, with specific details given.

8. Ibid., p. 371.
9. Ibid., p. 529.
10. Ibid., p. 565.
11. The platform was published in pamphlet form and Beanie Baldwin gave me a copy. Copies are also available in the HWP and PPP.
12. Macdougall, p. 576; Macdougall reprints most of the verbatim text of the debate on the Vermont Resolution.
13. Interviews: Baldwin, July 17, 1974; Ralph Shikes, March 13, 1975.
14. Truman Library, Papers of J. Howard McGrath, August 1, 1948.
15. Press release, Progressive Party, August 12, 1948.
16. Macdougall, p. 761.
17. PPP, *Ideas for Action*, vol. 2, no. 5, January–February 1949.
18. Truman Library, Papers of Harry S. Truman, President's Personal File, September 23, 1948.
19. HWP, November 5, 1948.

6: THE PROGRESSIVES AND THE COMMUNISTS

1. Macdougall, p. 304.
2. Eugene Dennis, *Political Affairs*, September 1946, pp. 804–807.
3. James Allen, ibid., October 1946, p. 889.
4. Editorial, ibid., December 1946, pp. 1070–72.
5. Dennis, ibid., January 1947, pp. 12–17.
6. William Z. Foster, ibid., February 1947, p. 109.
7. Dennis, ibid., March 1947, pp. 198–99.
8. ———, "Concluding Remarks at Plenum," June 27–30, 1947; *Political Affairs*, August 1947, p. 695.
9. John Gates, *Political Affairs*, August 1947, pp. 720–29.
10. Jack Stachel, ibid., September 1947, pp. 781, 789.
11. Dennis, *Sunday Worker*, September 18, 1947.
12. Interview with Baldwin, July 17, 1974.
13. At a memorial service for Beanie Baldwin on June 9, 1975, Abt was the most effective speaker and still advocated a Popular Front.
14. Dennis, *Political Affairs*, March 1948, p. 209.

15. Memo from James Wechsler to Charles Van Devander; in ADA Papers, Series 7, Box 107, Folder 6.
16. Max Weiss, *Political Affairs,* May 1948, pp. 410–11.
17. Editorial, ibid., May 1948, pp. 775–76.
18. Jonathan Daniels, HWP, March 30, 1948.
19. Lee Fryer to Louis Adamic, HWP, July 10, 1948.
20. *Baltimore Sun,* August 19, 1948.
21. Ibid., August 24, 1948.
22. Interviews with Baldwin, July 18, 1974; Shikes, March 13, 1975.
23. *The New York Star,* October 12, 1948.

7: LABOR FRIENDS BECOME ENEMIES

1. Ronald Radosh, *American Labor and United States Foreign Policy.*
2. *CIO National Convention Proceedings,* pp. 137–38. November 2, 1944.
3. Macdougall, p. 176.
4. Ibid., p. 177.
5. Ibid.
6. Public Papers of the Presidents, 1947, pp. 288–301.
7. Even where I could identify "influentials" by name, I have chosen not to. Although to me the term "Communist" is descriptive, not pejorative, it can still, even in these comparatively enlightened times, be an embarrassment or a handicap. Thus, I have chosen to identify as Communists only those whose affiliation has become public knowledge.
8. This matter of "influentials," indeed the whole unhappy story of the Communist Party in the postwar years, is told in fascinating detail by Joseph Starobin in his *American Communism in Crisis.* A former Communist, he writes without the sourness and bitterness, the unseemly recantation that often marks the writings of ex-Communists.
9. Willard Shelton, *PM,* December 18, 1947.
10. United Press Dispatch, February 28, 1948; *Berkeley* (California) *Daily Gazette,* February 29, 1948.
11. *CIO News,* January 26, 1948.

12. Macdougall, pp. 318–19.
13. Ibid., pp. 320–21.
14. Ibid., p. 315.
15. *CIO News*, January 26, 1948.
16. Macdougall, pp. 614–16.
17. The author was present.
18. Macdougall, p. 619.
19. *St. Louis Post-Dispatch,* April 5, 1948.
20. *The New York Times,* April 29, 1948; *CIO News,* June 7, 1948.
21. Macdougall, p. 615.
22. Ibid., p. 687.

8: LIBERALS ATTACK THEIR FORMER HERO

1. *Francis Biddle, U.S. Congress, House Select Committee on Lobbying Activities, Lobbying, Direct and Indirect, VI, 81st Congress, Second Session* (Washington: GPO, 1950), p. 12.
2. Clifton Brock, *Americans for Democratic Action*, p. 46.
3. ADA Papers, Series 1, Box 33, Folder 8. These papers are a rich source of material about liberalism in the postwar United States.
4. ADA Papers, ibid. The letter is undated but appears to be in late 1944, probably after the Democratic convention, possibly after the election.
5. Ibid., Folder 9.
6. Macdougall, p. 127.
7. *New Republic*, May 13, 1946.
8. Ibid., May 20, 1946.
9. Cited in Alonzo L. Hamby, *Beyond the New Deal: Harry S. Truman and American Liberalism*, p. 157.
10. Ibid., p. 162.
11. *ADA World*, April 12, 1947.
12. Truman Library, Papers of Clark M. Clifford, June 6, 1947.
13. *ADA World*, July 24, 1947.
14. ADA Papers, Series 2, Box 60, Folder 6.
15. "My Day," October 15, 1947.
16. Edward Weisband and Thomas H. Franck, *Resignation in Protest.*
17. *The Nation*, September 11, 1967.

18. Truman Library, Papers of Clark M. Clifford.

19. Truman Library, Papers of Harry S. Truman, President's Personal File, December 29, 1947.

20. ADA Papers, Series 2, Box 60, Folder 6.

21. Truman Library, Papers of J. Howard McGrath: memos dated January 19 and January 27, 1948; two for each date.

22. Letter to author, February 7, 1975.

23. Undated but received January 21, 1948; ADA Papers, Series 2, Box 94, Folder 5.

24. Ibid.

25. Ibid., Series 7, Box 105, Folder 6; January 29, 1948.

26. Cited in Karl M. Schmidt, *Henry A. Wallace: Quixotic Crusade 1948,* p. 270.

27. ADA Papers, Series 2, Box 94, Folder 5; February 28 and March 9, 1948.

28. Ibid., Box 60, Folder 7, March 10, 1948; *ADA World,* March 2, 1948.

29. Letter to Frances Perkins, cited in Joseph P. Lash, *Eleanor: The Years Alone,* p. 153.

30. Letter to author, February 7, 1975.

31. Letter of June 3, 1948, to delegates to Democratic National Convention over signature of Leon Henderson, new national chairman, ADA.

32. ADA Papers, Series 6, Box 2.

33. Truman Library, Papers of Clark M. Clifford.

34. There are a number of copies of this pamphlet among the ADA Papers; the one I used was in Series 6, Box 1, Folder 7.

35. Ibid., Series 2, Box 94, Folder 5.

36. Coombs to Leon Henderson, April 29, 1948, ibid., Series 7, Box 105, Folder 6.

37. ADA Papers, Series 2, Box 60, Folder 7.

38. Arthur M. Schlesinger, Jr., *The Vital Center,* p. 138.

39. Schlesinger, who much later wrote a book attacking imperialism, *The Imperial Presidency* (Boston: Houghton Mifflin, 1973), in *The Vital Center* wrote a tract for a hard-line, anti-Communist imperialism.

40. Macdougall, p. 479.

41. *The New Leader,* May 6, 1948.

42. Macdougall, p. 549.

43. Ibid., p. 550.

44. *The New York Star,* August 2, 1948.
45. *Bay State Citizen,* September 1948, published by the Massachusetts ADA.
46. ADA Papers, Series 2, Box 94, Folder 5, September 19 and 21, 1948, and undated.
47. *The Progressive,* April 1949.

9: THE PRESS AND HENRY WALLACE

1. A fine broader study of this matter is provided in James Aronson, *The Press and the Cold War* (New York: Bobbs-Merrill, 1970).
2. This news item so amused Beanie Baldwin that he placed it on the first page of one of his scrapbooks.
3. *Diary,* p. 461.
4. HWP, March 19, 1947.
5. Cited in Dwight Macdonald, p. 156.
6. Macdougall, p. 401.
7. Ibid., pp. 444–45.
8. Chicago *Sun-Times,* May 2, 1948.
9. Interview, Ralph Shikes, March 10, 1975.

10: PROPHET TRUE OR FALSE?

1. Testimony, May 5, 1949, PPP, Box 4, Folder 4.
2. February 24, 1950 (a copy of this speech is in the possession of the author).
3. PPP, Box 18, Folder 77.
4. *Danbury* (Connecticut) *News-Times,* November 19, 1965. Cited in Norman D. Markowitz, *The Rise and Fall of the People's Century: Henry A. Wallace and American Liberalism, 1941–1948,* p. 321.

Bibliography

BOOKS

Acheson, Dean. *Present at the Creation: My Years in the State Department.* New York: Norton, 1969.

Anson, Robert Sam. *McGovern: A Political Biography.* New York: Holt, Rinehart & Winston, 1972.

Blum, John Morton, ed. *The Price of Vision: The Diary of Henry A. Wallace 1942–1946.* Boston: Houghton Mifflin, 1973.

Brock, Clifton. *Americans for Democratic Action: Its Role in National Politics.* Washington, D.C.: Public Affairs Press, 1962.

Carleton, William G. *The Revolution in American Foreign Policy.* New York: Random House, 1967.

Hamby, Alonzo L. *Beyond the New Deal: Harry S. Truman and American Liberalism.* New York and London: Columbia University Press, 1973.

Jones, Joseph M. *The Fifteen Weeks.* New York: Viking, 1955.

LaFeber, Walter. *America, Russia and the Cold War: 1945–1966.* New York: Wiley, 1967.

Lash, Joseph P. *Eleanor and Franklin.* New York: Norton, 1971.
——— *Eleanor: The Years Alone.* New York: Norton, 1972.

Lord, Russell. *The Wallaces of Iowa.* Boston: Houghton Mifflin, 1947; New York: DaCapo Press, 1972.

Lubell, Samuel. *The Future of American Politics.* New York: Harper, 1952.

Macdonald, Dwight. *Henry Wallace: The Man and the Myth.* New York: Vanguard, 1948.

Macdougall, Curtis D. *Gideon's Army.* 3 vols. New York: Marzani & Munsell, 1965.

Markowitz, Norman D. *The Rise and Fall of the People's Century: Henry A. Wallace and American Liberalism, 1941–1948.* New York: The Free Press, 1973.

Miller, Merle. *Plain Speaking: An Oral Biography of Harry S. Truman.* New York: Berkley, 1974.

Parenti, Michael. *The Anti-Communist Impulse.* New York: Random House, 1969.

Paterson, Thomas G., ed. *Cold War Critics: Alternatives to American Foreign Policy in the Truman Years.* Chicago: Quadrangle, 1971.

—— *Soviet-American Confrontation: Postwar Reconstruction and the Origins of the Cold War.* Baltimore: Johns Hopkins University Press, 1973.

Peterson, F. Ross. *Prophet without Honor: Glen Taylor and the Fight for American Liberalism.* Lexington: University of Kentucky Press, 1973.

Phillips, Cabell. *The Truman Presidency.* New York: Penguin, 1969.

Radosh, Ronald. *American Labor and United States Foreign Policy.* New York: Random House, 1969.

—— "The Economic and Political Thought of Henry A. Wallace." Master's Thesis. Ames: University of Iowa, 1960.

Ross, Irwin. *The Loneliest Campaign: The Truman Victory of 1948.* New York: New American Library, 1968.

Rubinstein, Annette, ed. *I Vote My Conscience: Debates, Speeches and Writings 1935–1950 of Vito Marcantonio.* New York: The Vito Marcantonio Memorial, 1956.

Schapsmeier, Edward L. and Frederick H. *Prophet in Politics: Henry A. Wallace and the War Years, 1940–1965.* Ames: Iowa State University Press, 1971.

Schlesinger, Arthur M. *The Vital Center: The Politics of Freedom.* Boston: Houghton-Mifflin, 1949.

Schmidt, Karl M. *Henry A. Wallace: Quixotic Crusade 1948.* Syracuse: Syracuse University Press, 1960.

Shannon, David A. *The Decline of American Communism: A History of the Communist Party of the United States since 1945.* New York: Harcourt Brace Jovanovich, 1959.

Starobin, Joseph R. *American Communism in Crisis, 1943–1957.* Cambridge: Harvard University Press, 1972.

Truman, Harry S. *Memoirs:* 2 vols. vol. 1: *Years of Decision;* vol. 2: *Years of Trial and Hope.* Garden City: Doubleday, 1958.

Truman, Margaret. *Harry S. Truman.* New York: Morrow, 1973.

Tugwell, Rexford G. *Off Course: From Truman to Nixon.* New York: Praeger, 1971.

Ulam, Adam B. *Expansion and Coexistence: History of Soviet Foreign Policy, 1917–1967.* New York: Praeger, 1968.

Wallace, Henry A. *The Fight for Peace*. New York: Reynal & Hitchcock, 1946.

——— *Toward World Peace*. New York: Reynal & Hitchcock, 1948.

Wechsler, James A. *The Age of Suspicion*. New York: Random House, 1953.

Weisband, Edward and Franck, Thomas H. *Resignation in Protest: Political and Ethical Choices Between Loyalty to Team and Loyalty to Conscience in American Life*. New York: Grossman, 1975.

Yarnell, Allen. *Democrats and Progressives: The 1948 Presidential Election as a Test of Postwar Liberalism*. Berkeley: University of California Press, 1974.

PERIODICALS

ADA World
CIO News
Daily Worker
The Nation
New Republic
New York Herald-Tribune
The New York Times
Political Affairs
The Progressive

Index